S0-BMT-137

R

CCN

This book should be returned to any branch of the

CPP

- 8 FEB 2011

1 8 MAR 2013

1 1 MAR 2011

0 2 JUL 2013

1 0 MAR 2012

1 4 JUL 2014

0 6 JUN 2012   0 2 JAN 2014

2 7 OCT 2012

3 1 OCT 2014

LL 60

Lancashire County Library
Bowran Street *R*
Preston PR1 2UX   1 2 JAN 2010
1 2 APR 2010

Lancashire
County Council

www.lancashire.gov.uk/libraries

Lancashire County Library

30118096422567   LL1(A)

STIRLING'S MEN

'Stand by your glasses steady

This world is a world full of strife

Here's a toast to the dead already

And here's to the next man to die

Let your voices ring out in laughter

As they did in the days now gone by

Here's a toast to the dead already

And here's to the next man to die'

SUNG BY 'A' SQUADRON, 1SAS, 1944

STIRLING'S MEN

The Inside History of the SAS in World War II

Gavin Mortimer

WEIDENFELD & NICOLSON

Weidenfeld & Nicolson
The Orion Publishing Group Ltd
Orion House, 5 Upper Saint Martin's Lane, London WC2H 9EA

Copyright © Gavin Mortimer 2004
First published 2004

© Maps by Peter Harper

British Library Cataloguing-in-Publication Data
A catalogue record for this book is available from the
British Library

ISBN 0 297 84712 0

Printed in Great Britain by Clays Ltd, St Ives plc

0964225567

Contents

Map List

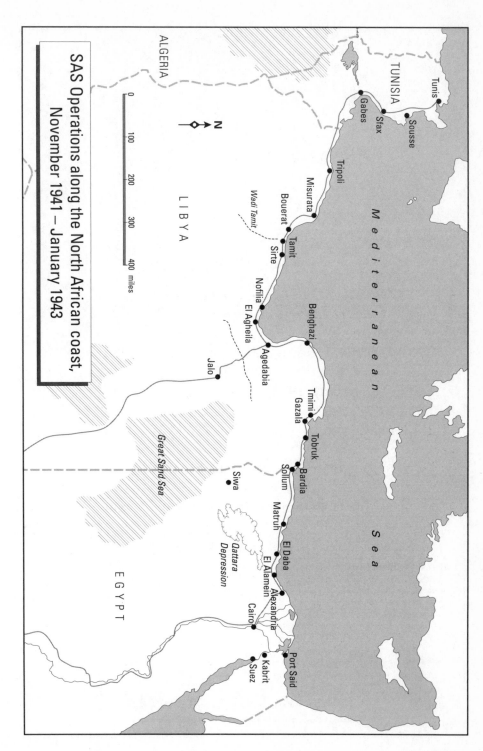

SAS Operations along the North African coast, November 1941 – January 1943

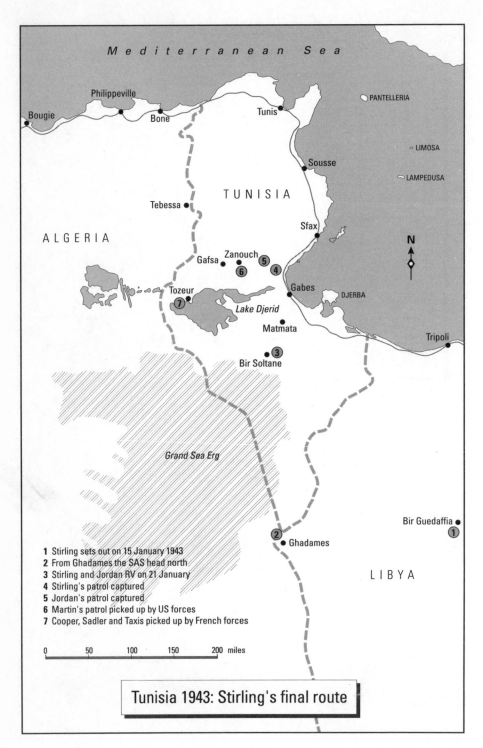

Mediterranean Sea

PANTELLERIA

Bougie
Philippeville
Bone
Tunis

LIMOSA

Sousse

LAMPEDUSA

TUNISIA

Tebessa

ALGERIA

N

Gafsa   Zanouch ⑤
        ⑥   ④
                    Sfax
Tozeur ⑦
        Lake Djerid   Gabes   DJERBA

Matmata

Bir Soltane ③

Tripoli

Grand Sea Erg

Bir Guedaffia ①

1 Stirling sets out on 15 January 1943
2 From Ghadames the SAS head north
3 Stirling and Jordan RV on 21 January
4 Stirling's patrol captured
5 Jordan's patrol captured
6 Martin's patrol picked up by US forces
7 Cooper, Sadler and Taxis picked up by French forces

② Ghadames

LIBYA

0   50   100   150   200 miles

Tunisia 1943: Stirling's final route

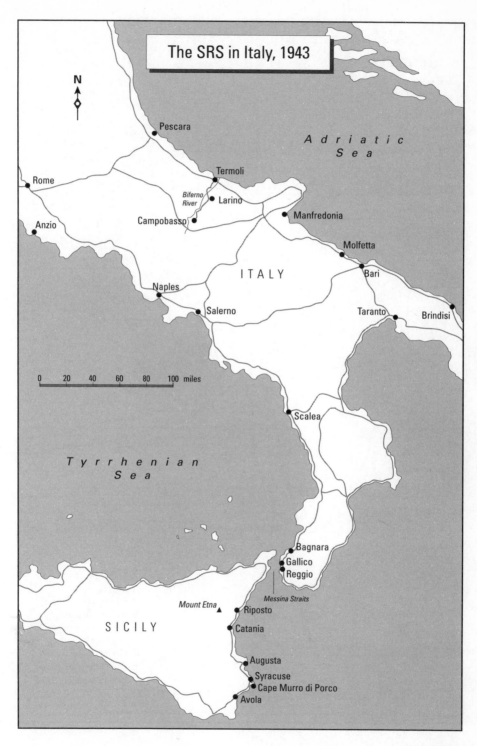

The SRS in Italy, 1943

N

Pescara

Adriatic Sea

Rome

Termoli

Biferno River

Larino

Campobasso

Manfredonia

Anzio

Molfetta

ITALY

Bari

Naples

Salerno

Taranto

Brindisi

0 20 40 60 80 100 miles

Scalea

Tyrrhenian Sea

Bagnara

Gallico

Reggio

Messina Straits

Mount Etna ▲ Riposto

Catania

SICILY

Augusta

Syracuse

Cape Murro di Porco

Avola

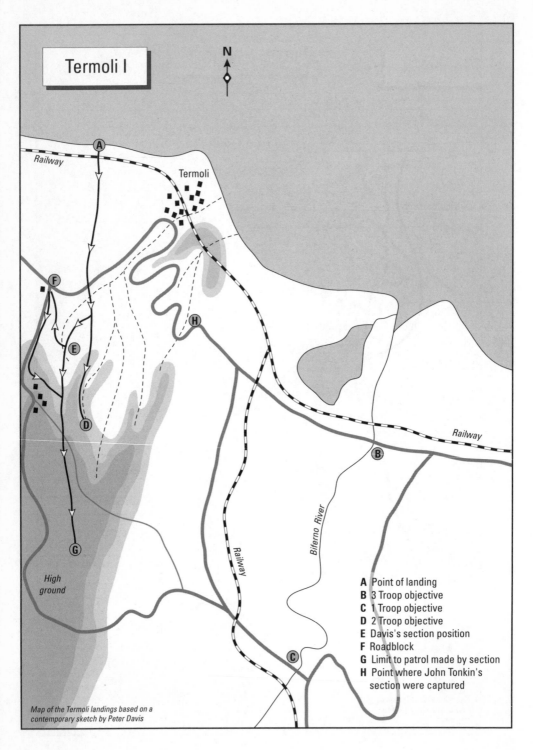

Termoli I

N

Railway

Termoli

Railway

F

H

E

D

B

Biferno River

Railway

G

Railway

High
ground

C

A Point of landing
B 3 Troop objective
C 1 Troop objective
D 2 Troop objective
E Davis's section position
F Roadblock
G Limit to patrol made by section
H Point where John Tonkin's
section were captured

Map of the Termoli landings based on a
contemporary sketch by Peter Davis

x

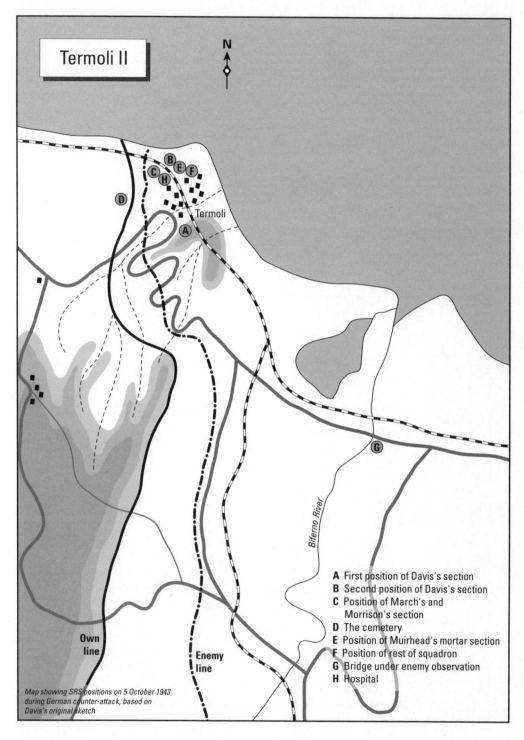

Termoli II

N

Termoli

Biferno River

Own line

Enemy line

A First position of Davis's section
B Second position of Davis's section
C Position of March's and Morrison's section
D The cemetery
E Position of Muirhead's mortar section
F Position of rest of squadron
G Bridge under enemy observation
H Hospital

Map showing SRS positions on 5 October 1943 during German counter-attack, based on Davis's original sketch

xi

SWITZERLAND

AUSTRIA

Brenner Pass

Bolzano

Trento ● ⑤

④

Lake Garda

YUGOSLAVIA

Trieste

Milan ●

Turin ●

ITALY

Verona

Alba

Parma ●

Cuneo ⑦

Genoa ●

Bologna ●

③

①

La Spezia ●

⑥

Florence ●

N

Leghorn ●

Rimini ●

Ancona ●

Adriatic Sea

CORSICA

Pescara ●

Monte Greco ▲ ②

Termoli ●

Rome ●

River Sangro

ITALY

Anzio ●

Tyrrhenian Sea

Naples ●

SARDINIA

1 Greville-Bell's party lands on night of 7 September 1943
2 Greville-Bell's party reaches Allied lines on night of 13 November 1943
3 Walker-Brown's operation Galia – Jan/Feb 1945
4 Littlejohn and Crowley captured on 17 February 1945
5 Operation Cold Comfort incorrectly inserted 30 miles north-east of DZ
6 Ken Harvey leads attack on German HQ at Villa Calvi – 27 March 1945
7 Alba captured during Operation Canuck – April 1945

0 20 40 60 80 100 miles

2SAS Operations in Italy, 1943–5

xii

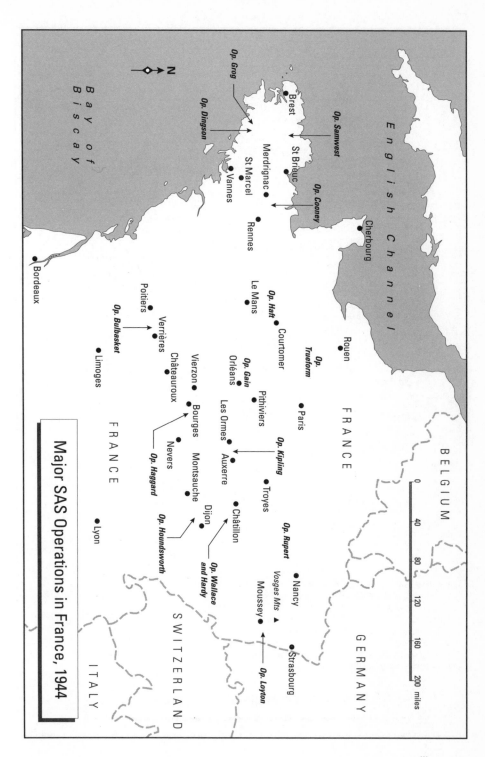

Major SAS Operations in France, 1944

1 Area of 4SAS December/January 1945
2 Area of 3SAS and 4SAS – Operation Amherst, April 1945
3 Belgian Squadron seize Veele Canal
4 SAS cross the Rhine on 25 March on Operation Archway
5 Route taken by 1SAS on Operation Howard, April 1945
6 1SAS ambushed on 8 April: Blakeney, Davies and Ferguson killed
7 SAS discover Belsen and Celle concentration camps
8 SAS cross the River Elbe on 29 April 1945

SAS Operations in Holland and Germany, 1945

Acknowledgements

THERE ARE TWO men who were instrumental in making this book possible. The first is Johnny Cooper, one of the Originals, who approached the SAS Regimental Association on my behalf three years ago. Johnny died in July 2002, a great man sorely missed. The second is the secretary of the Association, whose assistance was invaluable in so many ways.

Then there are the staff at the Liddell Hart Military Archives in King's College, London, the National Newspaper Library, the Imperial War Museum and the Public Records Office.

Mr Arthur Batten, RAF retd and formerly of 190 Squadron, and Sue Mintram-Mason, secretary of the *Stirling Times*, kindly provided me with much important information about Stirling bombers in the Second World War. Similarly, Jim Patch, ex-LRDG, went out of his way to help me in my research. Across the Channel, the debt of gratitude I owe Paul Marquet, secretary of the Belgian SAS Veterans Association, is immense.

Thank you Kari Armstrong for your Norwegian translation skills, John Clifton for tracking down Alf Dignum, Mark Rubenzer for the photo and John Kane and Paul Rea of the Blair Mayne Research Society in Northern Ireland. Various people provided me with free bed and breakfast during my research, notably Tim and Anna Clifton in London, Fred and Latetia Duguet and Stephanie Triau in Paris and Dick Holmes and his wife out in Canada. Not forgetting my brother, Mark, whose offer of a berth aboard his boat in the Atlantic was generous but not really of much use.

My parents spent many hours proof-reading the manuscript and gave me unstinting support and encouragement throughout, as they have from day one.

The generosity of the families of several deceased SAS soldiers in allowing me to quote from their relatives' memoirs was greatly appreciated: Jo and Peter Weaver, daughter and grandson of Peter; the Muirheads, in particular, Colette Baigrie, Alex's eldest daughter; William Oakes (son of Freddie); Joe Patterson's family and that of Malcolm Pleydell for kindly granting me permission to quote from memoirs and diaries held in the IWM; Alasdair Murray (nephew of John Murray) and Peter Davis's family; Richard Druce (Henry's son), Myfanwy Arnold, Mrs Jean MacDonald (husband of the late 'Buck' MacDonald) and Mrs Janet McMillan (husband of the late Neil McMillan) also took time to be of assistance.

And how can I repay the hospitality extended to me by the wives of those veterans I visited? Endless cups of tea, some exceedingly good cakes and, more often than not, an insistence that I stay for lunch or supper. The Harvey family in Harare, Barbara Paley and Ethna Noble in Canada, Betty Long, Betty Robinson, Leonarda Ridler, Morag Storie, Rea Du Vivier, Mrs Wainman, Mrs Holmes, Florence Prochiantz, Marie-Thérèse Bouche-Pillon, Mme Jordan, Mme Le Citol, Mme Papazow, Cecilia Boutinot, Betty Payne, Mrs Redington, Mrs Wiseman, Frances Francis, Mrs Walker-Brown, Juliette Girard, Mrs Rogers and Mrs Burne. Apologies to anyone I've forgotten, it's not a slight on your cakes.

My sincere thanks to my agent, Andrew Lownie, for his guidance and encouragement, and to Ian Drury and Penny Gardiner at Weidenfeld for their belief in the book and their trenchant observations and to Sarah Barlow, for her exemplary proofreading skills.

During the writing of *Stirling's Men* I married my wife, Sandy, in her native France. It was, I think, the first time in two years that we had been to France for a purpose other than the SAS. Darling, your patience, understanding, love and, of course, your interpretation and translation skills, sustained me through thick and thin. It is you who has taught me finally that courage comes in many guises. Thank you.

And finally the men themselves. For hours I have sat here trying to find the right words to adequately describe the privilege it has been for me to write this book. But the words have eluded me, so forgive me for falling back on the Second World War poet, Keith Douglas: How can I live among this gentle obsolescent breed of heroes, and not weep?...

Glossary

3-inch mortar	A range of 2,800 yards and fired 10lb bombs. It weighed 44 lbs plus a base plate of 37 lbs and a mounting of 45 lbs
ATS	Auxiliary Territorial Service
Beretta	Italian-made sub-machine gun with a 9mm calibre
Bofors	A 40mm anti-tank gun favoured by the British Army
Bren gun	Czech-made light machine gun with a range of up to 2,000 yards
DCM	Distinguished Conduct Medal, the equivalent of the DSO – second only to the VC – and awarded to NCOs and officers for exceptional gallantry
Dingo	Wheeled and armoured scout car with a two-man crew
DSO	Distinguished Service Order, during WW2 awarded to junior officers for outstanding gallantry just below that of the VC and to senior officers for outstanding leadership
DZ	Dropping Zone for parachutists and supplies
FFI	Forces Française d'Intérieur – responsible for organizing armed resistance in France
Gestapo	Geheime Staatspolizei, a political police force whose mission was to eradicate political views incompatible with Nazism
LCA	Landing Craft Assault, 12m-long vessel capable of carrying 35 men
LCI	Landing Craft Infantry, 50m-long vessel capable of carrying nearly 200 men

LRDG	Long Range Desert Group
Maquis	The French resistance groups who fought against the German Occupation. Maquis is derived from the French expression 'to take to the maquis', used in pre-war Corsica; a Corsican, having committed a 'crime of honour', would seek asylum in the thick dense vegetation of the island to flee the long arm of the law
MC	Military Cross, awarded to officers of the rank of major and below for gallantry in action
MEHQ	Middle East Headquarters
MGB	Motor Gun Boat
Milice	French fascist organisation working for Germans
MM	Military Medal, awarded to NCOs and soldiers for gallantry in action
MP	Military Police
NCO	Non-Commissioned Officer
Nebelwerfer	A multi-barrelled mortar known to the British as Moaning Minnie because of the ungodly noise made by the rockets
OCTU	Officer Cadet Training Unit
Panzerfaust	The German hand-operated anti-tank weapon; unlike the US bazooka it required only one man to use and its penetrative power was often devastating at close range
PPA	Popski's Private Army
REME	Royal Electrical and Mechanical Engineers
RSM	Regimental Sergeant Major
RTU	Returned to unit, for those men who fail to make the grade in the SAS
RV	Rendezvous
Schmeisser	Standard German issue sub-machine gun with a 9mm calibre and capable of firing 500 rpm; effective at 150 yards
SD	Sicherheitsdienst, the German Security Service, about 3,000 strong
SFHQ	Special Forces Headquarters

SHAEF   Supreme Headquarters Allied Expeditionary Force

SIG   Special Interrogation Group

SOE   Special Operations Executive formed in 1940 to foment clandestine warfare in Occupied Europe

Spandau   The German army machine gun

SS   Schutzstaffeln, Nazi military force whose stated mission was the protection of the Führer and the security of the Reich; soldiers, who were supposed to be racially pure Germans, swore an oath of loyalty to Hitler and wore their SS number as a tattoo

Sten gun   Mass-produced and unreliable 9mm calibre sub-machine gun effective only at close range

Thompson   US-made sub-machine gun with a .45 calibre and a range of 300 yds; capable of firing 725 rounds per minute

Vickers K   Guns taken from Gloster Gladiator fighter planes mounted in the front and back of SAS jeeps, capable of firing 1,200 rounds per minute

WAAF   Women's Auxiliary Air Force

Wadi   The Arabic name for a dried-up river bed or dry ravine

WRNS   Women's Royal Naval Service

Main Players

1SAS (L Det 1941–2 and SRS 1943)*
Roy Close
Johnny Cooper
Doug Cronk
David Danger
Peter Davis
Bill Deakins
Alf Dignum
Jeff Du Vivier
Bob Francis
Bill Fraser
Ronald Grierson
Alex Griffiths
Vic Long
Bob Lowson
Paddy Mayne
James McDiarmid
Bob McDougall
Neil McMillan
John Noble
Sid Payne
Malcolm Pleydell
Harry Poat
John Randall
Reg 'Nobby' Redington
Duncan Ridler

Mike Sadler
Reg Seekings
Billy Stalker
Jimmy Storie
Arthur Thomson
Dennis Wainman
Peter Weaver
Harry Wilkins
Johnny Wiseman
Albert Youngman

2SAS
Granville Burne
George Daniels
Henry Druce
Roy Farran
Tony Greville-Bell
Charlie Hackney
Ken Harvey
Arthur Huntbach
Ross Littlejohn
Freddie Oakes
Jack Paley
Joe Patterson
Cyril Radford
Alex Robertson
Renee Roberts

Bill Robinson
Ray Rogers
Harry Vickers
Bob Walker-Brown
Cyril Wheeler

French 3SAS
Maurice Duno
Marc Mora

French 4SAS
Mike Alexandre
Roger Boutinot
Jean Czarski
Augustin Jordan
Guy Le Citol
André Lemée
Marc Mouflin

Belgian Independent Company
Yvan Brasseur
Jacques Goffinet
Jean-Claude Heilporn
Robert Piron
Jean Switters

* Initially know as 'L' Detachment, it wasn't until September 1942 that Stirling's creation received Regimental status and became known as the Special Air Service Regiment. 2SAS came into existence at the start of 1943, while 1SAS was known as the Special Raiding Squadron in 1943, only reverting to 1SAS on its return to the UK at the start of 1944.

Foreword

THIS IS A TALE OF a group of men who sixty years ago joined a unit commanded by a charismatic and irreverent young officer called David Stirling. They didn't join for glory or medals or King and Country. They joined because they craved adventure. And they found it, in the deserts of North Africa, the mountains and beaches of Italy and the forests of France. They found something else, too: an unbreakable comradeship. They learned to depend on one another, to trust one another, to love one another like brothers. It was a fellowship of a sort few men are privileged to experience.

When the war ended and the men went their separate ways to build careers and raise families, the fellowship remained as iron as ever. But most chose not to talk about their war, wrapping themselves instead in a cloak of silent modesty for over half a century. Now, in the dusk of their lives, they have decided to tell their stories.

This isn't a book that attempts to portray the wartime SAS as a band of indomitable superheroes. The men themselves would snort derisively at such a notion and tell you, 'If it's heroes you're after look in the ranks of the infantry. It's there that epic courage is to be found'.

The wartime SAS were just ordinary men – clerks, builders, business-men, hoteliers – who for a few years did something extraordinary. This book is dedicated to them, and to their comrades who remain in the desert and on the mountainside and in the forest.

CHAPTER ONE

NORTH AFRICA 1941–2

THE SUMMER SEASON was drawing to a close in Felixstowe. Tommy Trinder's *Loads of Nonsense* show had run its course at the Spa Pavilion and the town's entry in the East Coast Beauty Pageant in Lowestoft had failed to impress the judges. As the last of the departing guests tottered imperiously down the steps of the 250-room Felix Hotel, the manager, Mr Humphrey, and his assistant stepped forward to express their hope that everything had been to their satisfaction. Safe journey home and see you again next year. When they were gone, the staff moved quickly back inside; all, that is, except the assistant manager. Jeff Du Vivier stood for a moment warming himself in the September sun, looking forward to his first afternoon off for weeks. He had a jaunty unthreatening face with a slightly receding chin and warm light blue eyes. In the few months he'd been working in the Felix, Du Vivier had endeared himself to the guests. He knew when to talk and when to listen. In short, he was made for the hospitality business.

He turned and bounded up the steps. It was 11.15 a.m. Inside the staff were gathered round a wireless, listening to the flat tones of Neville Chamberlain.

This morning the British Ambassador in Berlin handed the German Government a final note stating that, unless we heard from them by 11 o'clock that they were prepared at once to withdraw their troops from Poland, a state of war would exist between us.

1

Du Vivier stood with them for a minute:

I have to tell you now that no such undertaking has been received, and that consequently this country is at war with Germany.

He then started to organize lunch.

Bob Lowson learned of the declaration of war as he got himself together after a good night's dancing in Liverpool. Even with a thick head the tall 18-year-old had a natural poise to go with his luxuriant mane of brown hair swept spectacularly back. Girls liked Bob Lowson and Bob Lowson liked girls. But he preferred rugby. He liked the way it tested him physically, and he liked the way he stood up to the test. He was also partial to the ribald banter in the bar afterwards, so refreshingly different from the delicate refinement of the dance halls.

Johnny Wiseman heard the news in Sydney where he was on a business trip with his London spectacle-manufacturing company. The 23-year-old, a Cambridge graduate whose face was a symphony of cheerful indefatigability, appeared impervious to the pressures of hard work. It was one of the reasons his company had sent him around the globe, drumming up business in America, New Zealand and Australia: Wiseman could cope with the demands of the trip. Showing admirable initiative Wiseman went down to Sydney Harbour and talked his way on to a flying boat back to England.

France took a few hours longer to come to the aid of Poland. In the late afternoon of 3 September, Prime Minister Edouard Daladier told France she was at war with Germany. In St Malo, on the Brittany coast, 17-year-old Roger Boutinot was unconcerned. War and guns and bombs were too remote to disrupt him, a tubby assistant in a patisserie. And anyway, there was the Maginot Line.

DAVID STIRLING WAS gallivanting across North America in September 1939 when news reached him of war. He was in New Mexico, not too far from the Rio Grande. For the past two years he had pursued dreams the way cowboys pursued buffaloes. He wanted to be the first man to climb Everest.

Mallory and Irvine hadn't reached the summit, he was confident about that. The 24-year-old had climbed peaks in Europe and Canada, honing his skills and feeding his ambition. He would stand on top of the world, looking down on the tutor who had sent him down from Cambridge, and the Parisian art teacher who'd shattered his hope of becoming an artist. Stirling booked himself on the first plane leaving for Britain – first-class, of course.

Stirling arrived back in England and presented himself at the Scots Guards depot in Pirbright. He had joined the supplementary reserve in 1938, just before heading to Canada on another jaunt. Stirling was an execrable soldier. His mind was too creative for the stifling routine of the Guards, and his 6ft 5in body too ungainly for the parade ground. During one weapons inspection his sergeant had peered down his rifle, then recoiled in horror.

'Stirling, it's bloody filthy. There must be a clown on the end of this rifle.'

Stirling nodded. 'Yes, Sergeant, but not at my end.'

His nights were spent at the more racy clubs in London; during the day he caught up on his sleep at the back of army lecture rooms. Stirling's superiors described him as an 'irresponsible and unremarkable soldier'. In January 1940 Stirling's eyes flickered momentarily with excitement; he was posted as a ski instructor to the 5th Battalion, the Scots Guards, 'the Snowballers', and for a while it looked as if they might be sent to aid the Finns in their war against Russia. But this never materialized and Stirling was plunged back into drudgery. Only his trips to White's Club in London broke the boredom.

LOWSON WAS SEEN off to war by his father, a good man cast adrift from his family by his experiences in the Great War. He had raised his children as best he could, but his memories had made him remote. On the morning Lowson left home to join the Liverpool Scottish his father broke with tradition. He sat his teenage son down and talked to him.

'He asked me if I had a watch,' recalls Lowson. 'I didn't, so he gave

3

me his. Then he said, "I'm going to give you some advice: you'll be with men from now on so remember, you don't tell lies and you don't bear grudges."'

In early 1940 Lowson became one of 3,000 territorial soldiers to volunteer for Independent Company (the forerunner of the Commandos), raised by Colonel Gubbins. In April that year his company, No. 4, totalling 300 men, was despatched north, to Norway, to counter the German invasion. Lowson soon realized what Stirling had known right from the start, that the average British staff officer was a dunderhead in comparison to his German counterpart. Everything about the Norway operation, recalls Lowson, was 'stupid ... we'd had no training, all we had done were 12-mile route marches in the morning followed by trench digging in the afternoon'.

No. 4 Independent Company – the first of the ten companies to land in Norway – disembarked at Mo on 4 May and, strengthened by a battalion of Scots and Irish Guards, dug in along the main road from Bodo to Finneid.

'I was a lance corporal in command of a section nearest to the Germans and we could see them over the other side of a bridge,' recalls Lowson. They glared at each other for several days, 'and then we got the order to withdraw and head north for the coast. We walked 40 miles overnight and were picked up by a destroyer'.

That was on 29 May. Nine days later, with Germany overrunning France, the British Army withdrew in its entirety from Norway.

'At times,' says Lowson of his bit part in the doomed mission, 'we didn't know which day of the week it was.'

A FEW DAYS after returning from Norway, the Independent Companies merged with a force of specially trained Royal Marines to form the Commandos. They were officially amalgamated into the British Army on 12 June 1940 with the enthusiastic support of the Prime Minister. In a minute dated 18 June Winston Churchill had expanded on his wish to see the creation of British Special Forces:

'We have always set our faces against this idea, but the Germans

4

certainly gained in the last war by adopting it, and this time it has been a leading cause of their victory. There ought to be at least twenty thousand Storm Troops or 'Leopards' [soon changed to Commandos, a name inspired by the irregular Afrikaner forces who had caused Britain so much trouble in the Boer War at the turn of the century] drawn from existing units.'

Six days later the Commandos mounted their first offensive operation, a reconnaissance raid near Boulogne by 120 men.

Up and down the country notices were pinned in infantry barracks calling for Commando volunteers. Albert Youngman, a lightly built 18-year-old from Norfolk with an artless face, put his name down having spent several months 'patrolling the Norfolk coast sharing one rifle between three of us'. Before enlisting in the Royal Norfolk Territorial Regiment, Youngman had seen little of the outside world beyond his job as a post office clerk. But he liked the army; the salty language of his instructors and the camaraderie and the physical training. He was accepted and posted to No. 7 Commando, an amalgam of infantry regiments.

In the same unit was a Fenman called Reg Seekings, who had previously tried to join Bourne's Naval Commandos and the nascent parachute unit. 'The old RSM [of the Cambridgeshire Regiment] was turning everyone down,' he recalled. 'So what I did was to get all the beds and furniture in the billet, including the NCO's room, and pile them outside ... I refused to let anyone in until I got an interview with the CO.'

The unimaginative Seekings was like a bad-tempered dog, snarling and scowling at anyone who came to close to his kennel. Before the war he had been an amateur heavyweight boxing champion and his fists were the weapon he used to mask his social insecurities. The first pack of Cockney soldiers he had met in the war laughed at his bucolic manner.

'It was because I talked slowly, like Fenmen, but I said to them, "yeah, maybe [but] if there's something we don't understand do you know what we do? We hit it, and we hit it bloody hard, so just watch it".'

Du Vivier had spent the winter of 1939/40 working in the Great Western Hotel in his native London after the Felix had been requisitioned by the army. In April 1940, with the new summer season imminent, he

5

decided 'the best thing I could do was join up and do something to help'. He enlisted in the London Scottish, an affiliated regiment of the Gordon Highlanders, and it was to be Aberdeen where he underwent his training.

'Then one day this fellow came along to say there was a new unit called the Commandos.' Du Vivier volunteered: 'I would have done anything to get away from square-bashing.' He was posted to No. 11 Scottish Commando in Galashiels under the command of Colonel Pedder. 'There were 700 of us there,' remembers Du Vivier, 'but Pedder only wanted 500 so the way he sorted us out was to march from Galashiels to Ayr.'

Marching alongside Du Vivier was Jimmy Storie, a 22-year-old with a cheerful, whistle-while-you-work face. Before the war he'd been a tile fitter in Ayr.

'When we got to Ayr we bedded down in Craigie Woods,' he says, 'in a potato field I had used to dig up with my uncle.'

The day after their arrival, recalls Du Vivier, 'we were given three and sixpence each and told to go and buy some breakfast. Me and a pal, Tom Calderwood, walked down a street and a woman came out of a house and offered to make us breakfast'. The pair accepted the offer. Breakfast was served to them by a winsome young ATS girl called Rea. It was the most enjoyable breakfast of Du Vivier's life.

From Ayr they moved to Arran for more training. One of the officers was Geoffrey Keyes, son of Lord Roger, Director of Combined Operations. He wrote to his father from Lamlash at the end of August, telling him about the training:

'[It] was rather a shocker, as we started off from scratch with eleven miles non stop in three hours, twenty minutes halt for lunch, then another four miles in one hour. No joke.'

Another officer, says Storie, 'was known in Arran to sit on his bed and shoot the glass panes of the window with his revolver'. His name was Blair 'Paddy' Mayne.

SINCE HIS CHAMPIONING of Special Forces in June 1940, Churchill had established a Combined Operations Command and a few months later issued instructions to study the possibility of offensive operations in northern Europe. But a chaotic raid on Guernsey, which had infuriated Churchill – 'Let there be no more silly fiascos like that perpetrated at Guernsey' – convinced him that for the foreseeable future the only theatre of war in which it was practical to blood his Commandos was North Africa.

Thus on 1 February 1941, a troop of No. 3 Commando and the whole of No. 7, No. 8 and No. 11 Scottish sailed for the Middle East under the command of Lieutenant Colonel Laycock. They were known as 'Z' Force (they were soon rechristened 'Layforce') and one of the officers on board was David Stirling, in No. 8 Commando, having heard about them one night in White's. He soon became known to his fellow officers as the 'Giant Sloth', so much time did he spend in his bed.

Layforce's mission was to exploit the success of General O'Connor's offensive, which had culminated in his signal to General Sir Archibald Wavell on 7 February, 'Fox Killed in the Open'. Having advanced into Egypt the previous September the Italians had been all but annihilated and the control of North Africa was within O'Connor's grasp. Initially 'Z' Force was to seize the island of Rhodes as part of a wider strategic goal to control the Aegean and open up a Balkan front. But Germany – as in Norway – were quicker off the mark and invaded Greece before the British landed on Rhodes. The Rhodes operation was now scrubbed, the vessels earmarked for the invasion instead used to evacuate some 45,000 British troops from Greece.

By the end of April 1941, the British High Command seemed befuddled by the incisiveness of the enemy. Germany was in possession of the Balkans and General Erwin Rommel had taken a little over two months to drive the British out of Cyrenaica (except for the besieged coastal town of Tobruk) back on to the Egyptian border.

No one now seemed quite sure how to best employ 'Z' Force. No. 7 Commando launched an assault on Bardia in late April, 'but,' recalls Youngman, 'it was our first raid and as everyone was green it didn't work out'. Seekings was wounded in the leg, while Youngman's section was left behind by the mother ship. 'It wasn't at the RV so after a quick council of war we decided to sail our little dingy to Tobruk, about 90 miles up the coast.'

After acting as garrison troops in Cyprus for a while, No. 11 Scottish Commando was blooded in Syria at the battle of Litani river in June 1941. They established a bridgehead in the face of heavy fire from Vichy French 75mm battery. Colonel Pedder was killed, waving his swagger stick at the enemy, and the Scottish suffered 25 per cent casualties among the banana groves that lined the banks of the river. The most fortunate of them being a young lieutenant called Bill Fraser, who had been shot in the face as he led his section into the hills against a detachment of dismounted French cavalry. The bullet hit the chinstrap of his helmet and he handed over command temporarily to his sergeant, Jock Cheyne, while he gathered himself. A short while later he resumed command, insisting he was suffering just 'slight concussion'.

Stirling and No. 8 Commando, meanwhile, had been deployed in piecemeal fashion; carrying out raids on the Cyrenaica coastline, buttressing the defences of Tobruk and covering the withdrawal from Crete. But with no sign of being able to launch an offensive before late autumn Middle East Headquarters (MEHQ) decided that 'Z' Force should be disbanded and the soldiers dispersed to infantry regiments.

'We weren't a success,' reflects Du Vivier. 'That job we did in Syria [Litani river], well, to this day I still don't know if it was successful. I remember once we heard Lord Haw-Haw describing us on the wireless as "Churchill's Cut-Throats". We looked at each and said "is that us?!"'

Stirling repaired to Cairo, to the flat of his brother, Peter,* who was Third Secretary at the British Embassy, while the future of the Commandos was decided by MEHQ. For the next few weeks he divided his time between the flat and base in a merry-go-round of parties and route marches and parties. Whenever Stirling felt the hedonism might impair his soldiering he would visit the Scottish Hospital, to see a pretty young nurse

* Stirling had three brothers: Peter, Hugh and Bill. Hugh was killed in April 1941 and is commemorated on the Alamein Memorial.

8

he'd befriended, who let him have 'a couple of deep snifters from the pure oxygen bottle ... the hangover vanished in seconds'. Word of his shenanigans reached the ears of his superiors. They were not impressed. More intolerable impertinence. A Board of Officers was commissioned to examine whether Stirling was guilty of malingering.

Stirling was saved from any possible censure by a meeting in the officers' mess with Lieutenant Jock Lewes, a man who was as much a puritan as Stirling was a playboy. Lewes fell short in humour, had no time for frivolity and, as Stirling recalled in his biography, would never be caught having a 'quick drink in Cairo or taking a flutter at the racecourse'. But his ascetic lifestyle had its benefits; while his fellow officers had been living it up in Cairo, Lewes had carried out a raid on an Axis coastal airfield using motorized gunboats. The success of the German paratroopers on Crete convinced him that that was where the future lay for Special Forces units in North Africa. Laycock granted permission to experiment with a batch of fifty parachutes destined for India. On hearing of this, Stirling sought out Lewes and sweet-talked his way on to the scheme as one of the parachute pioneers.

LEWES AND STIRLING, along with four other men, made their jumps in June 1941. They leapt from an obsolescent Vickers Valencia biplane with Lewes and 26-year-old Roy Davies, his batman from the Welsh Guards, going first.

'The instructions were to dive out as though going through into water,' said another of the guinea-pigs, Mick D'Arcy. 'Lieutenant Lewes and Davies dived out. Next time round I dived out, and was surprised to see Lieutenant Stirling pass me in the air.' Stirling's parachute had snagged on the plane's tail section as it ripped away from the static line, tearing the top of the 'chute. He had hit the desert floor hard. For more than an hour he was blind.

As Stirling lay in his hospital bed he digested the news from the desert battlefront and started scribbling down some notes. The arrival of Rommel had knocked the British off balance; Wavell had been sacked after June's

9

'Battleaxe' offensive to relieve Tobruk had failed and his successor, General Auchinleck – an old friend of the Stirling family – had replaced him as commander-in-chief. The 'Auk' was a man who admired swashbucklers. 'Always be bold', he liked to tell his men.

Stirling's notes soon became a lucid appreciation of the situation in the Western Desert: 'Yes, Rommel has the upper hand,' he wrote, but in seizing the initiative he had left himself vulnerable; his lines of communication and airfields, strung out along the coast, invited attack. The reason the Commandos failed, he continued, was because their units were too large and cumbersome. Stirling argued that surprise was the key to success in this sort of guerrilla warfare. Surprise and a small group of men, five at the most. He concluded his analysis in characteristically bullish fashion: that a force of men, handpicked and rigorously trained, could parachute behind enemy lines and attack thirty different targets on the same night. There was a caveat.

'I insisted that the Unit must be responsible for its own training and operational planning,' he recalled after the war, 'and that, therefore, the commander of the unit must come directly under the C-in-C.' Stirling knew Auchinleck was planning an offensive some time in late 1941 and he proposed that a raid be launched to coincide with the attack.

For a man who had a visceral aversion to any form of paperwork Stirling was rather pleased with his military appreciation. He plumped up his pillows and leaned back in satisfaction. Now all he had to do was get the Top Brass to examine it. He rejected the idea of going through official channels; MEHQ's obtuse staff officers, the men Stirling referred to as 'fossilized shits', would pooh-pooh the document before any officer of influence had the chance to examine it. It was time to be impertinent.

A few days later he climbed through a hole in the perimeter fence of MEHQ. There was a shout of 'Halt!' from one of the guards but Stirling had hobbled inside before the man could react.

The first office he barged through contained one of his former lecturers from Pirbright. He remembered Stirling all too well. He tried another door, and found himself addressing General Neil Ritchie, the Deputy

Chief of Staff. When he'd finished leafing through the report Ritchie looked up at Stirling.

'This may be the sort of plan we're looking for,' he said. 'I'll discuss it with the Commander-in-Chief and let you know our decision.'

WHILE STIRLING WAITED to hear if Auchinleck was prescient enough to accede to his Special Forces idea, Johnny Wiseman was fighting nineteenth-century style with the North Somerset Yeomanry.

'We were sent into action at Syria and must have been some of the last people in action on horse,' he says. [The Syrian campaign was indeed the last ever British Cavalry action.]

When his flying boat had touched down in Southampton after an eleven-day flight Wiseman went to enlist in the RAF.

'I'd been in the Volunteer Reserve so I presumed there would be no problem.'

He was told to 'go home and wait until contacted'. A couple of days later he was travelling to work on the London Underground, ever the dapper businessman in his pin-striped suit and newspaper, when he decided he would join the army.

'I got off at Ealing Common and enlisted.' He had the choice of which branch of the army to enter and 'thought the cavalry sounded terrific so I signed on with them and was posted to Shorncliff in Kent as a trooper'.

With his degree in Modern Languages from Cambridge, but more pertinently, his good showing in the regimental rugby team, Wiseman was soon recommended for a commission. But on the eve of his departure to the Officer Cadet Training Unit (OCTU) he heard that a draft was being sent to the Middle East.

'I went to see the CO and told him I was prepared to give up my commission if I could go on the draft. I don't know why I made that decision, I suppose I just wanted to get to where the war was.'

On the night of 7/8 June the North Somerset Yeomanry crossed into Syria as part of a multi-national Allied force. Facing them were over 40,000 Vichy French under the command of General Henri Dentz.

11

Wiseman's regiment was involved in a series of skirmishes for the next six weeks, culminating in an engagement in the Jebel Mazar on 12 July.

'We dismounted in the valley and went in on foot to engage them [French native troops]. It was all fairly innocuous, we killed a few of them and they killed a few of us.' What was notable, however, says Wiseman, was their 'amateur' officers, young well-to-do men probably not unlike David Stirling.

'They didn't show any leadership,' he reflects. 'It was left to the NCOs, the regular soldiers, to do that.'

ON 14 JULY AT Acre, where the British commander Sir Sidney Smith had repulsed Napoleon in 1799, armistice terms in Syria were agreed between Dentz and the Allied generals, Catroux and Wilson. The Vichy Army went up the coast to Tripoli to where most were expected to join the Free French. It soon became clear, however, that Dentz was riddled with perfidy as he enjoined the Vichyistes to return home rather than fight for the Allies. Dentz and several of his associates were arrested, but it was decided to reinforce the Free French forces in Syria in case of a Vichy uprising.

On 21 July the *Cameronian* sailed from the UK for the Middle East. On board were over three thousand troops. Fifty-two of them were French paratroopers under the command of Captain Georges Bergé, one of whom was Roger Boutinot, now 19 years old. When the Maginot Line had failed to frighten off the German Army France had fallen quickly. One day in late June 1940 Boutinot was told to assemble in St Malo's town square.

'They announced that all males over the age of 16 must go to work in Germany.' Boutinot and two other young men decided to flee to England. 'We stole a boat and rowed to Jersey and knocked on the door of the first house we saw.'

The woman who opened the door had some alarming news: the Germans had invaded the previous day, 1 July.

'So we rowed to England,' says Boutinot. 'It took us about five or six days.'

Once in England Boutinot was sent to Olympia in London, the muster station for all young Frenchmen.

'It was there we were addressed by Bergé,' recalls Boutinot. 'He told us de Gaulle was forming an army and he needed volunteers.'

In October 1940 Boutinot stepped forward again, 'when a parachute officer came to visit'. The small band of volunteers became incorporated into the Free French Forces as the *1re Compagnie de l'infanterie de l'air*.

'We were based in Inchmery House, Rothschild's summer residence, opposite the Isle of Wight,' says Boutinot. 'From there we went up to Manchester to do our parachute training.'

In May 1941 they put on a demonstration for Mr and Mrs Winston Churchill. After the jump the Prime Minister congratulated the French.

'Then he turned to an American journalist,' recalled Bergé, 'and said "Come here; this captain will tell you all about the France that fights."'

THREE DAYS AFTER HIS unscripted meeting with Ritchie, Stirling was ordered to return to MEHQ to see Auchinleck, a general that the noted war correspondent Alan Moorhead described as possessing 'a mind of quite exceptional freshness and originality. He would seize on every new idea and explore it at once'. Auchinleck promoted Stirling to captain and gave him the go-ahead to recruit six officers and sixty other ranks. On the orders of Brigadier Dudley Clarke the unit would be called 'L' Detachment, Special Air Service Brigade. Clarke, the man who had come up with 'Commandos', wanted to unsettle Rommel. What better way than to make him think the British had a budding airborne brigade. Stirling queried the 'L'; did it, he wonder mischievously, stand for 'Learner'?

The first man Stirling recruited was Lewes, himself still harbouring ideas of a special forces unit. Stirling convinced him both that the idea had legs and that he wasn't just a feckless 'good time Charlie'. Lewes brought with him some of his most trusted Guardsmen: Roy Davies, Jim Almonds, Pat Riley, a self-assured American whose family had brought him to England when he was a child, Jim Blakeney, a broad-shouldered former trawlerman from Grimsby, and Bob Lilley, a cantankerous

13

tub-thumper. Another Guards Commando to respond to the recruitment drive was 19-year-old Johnny Cooper. 'Young Cooper', as Stirling had called him in the Scots Guards, presented an easy target for Lilley. He had clean good looks, spoke with a hearty middle-class accent and he had an undisguised artistic streak (in one youth production he had played Robin Hood to Dickie Attenborough's Maid Marian). But he was also blessed with a blade of cutting wit, with which he could readily dissect another man's verbal belligerence.

After selecting several men from the Guards Commandos Stirling visited the other Commandos to lure men away from their lazy mediocrity.

'We were just hanging around in the desert getting fed up,' recalls Du Vivier. 'Then along came Stirling asking for volunteers. I was hooked on the idea from the beginning, it meant we were going to see some action.'

Storie remembers that 'he didn't sit down and interview us, he just wanted men'. He was accepted along with his good friend, Jock Cheyne. So was Cornelius McGinn, though the men, with impeccable army logic, soon re-christened him 'Maggie'.

'Cornelius was too much of a mouthful,' says Storie.

Two other Scottish Commandos recruited by Stirling were Ken Warburton and Joe Duffy, a Scottish teetotaller. Warburton was a Mancunian, 'a gifted pianist', remembers Storie.

'One time we were walking through Cairo when we came across a concert hall being prepared for an evening performance. We persuaded Warburton to go and play something on the piano. What he played was just wonderful.'

From No. 7 Commando Stirling recruited, among others, Dougie Arnold and Reg Seekings. Arnold he visited in hospital, where he was recovering from an epic escape that had turned him into something of a local celebrity. Having taken part in the defence of Crete, Arnold became separated from his section during the evacuation. For nearly two weeks he survived in the mountains; then, with ten stragglers, he salvaged a small vessel and navigated her 300 miles south to the North African coast:

14

'I thought this ['L' Detachment] sounded jolly good,' said Arnold, 'but I said I didn't think the matron would let me out ... Stirling went off to see the matron and it didn't surprise me that she turned out to be related to him, had fallen for his charms and said I could go immediately.'

Seekings remembered that he was selected when 'I told Stirling I was an amateur boxing champion and did a lot of cycling and running'.

WITH LEWES ON BOARD Stirling needed five more officers. He recruited two Englishmen, Peter Thomas and Charles Bonnington, and a southern Irishman called Eoin McGonigal. McGonigal recommended to Stirling a fellow Irish officer from No. 11 Scottish Commando, Blair Mayne, who had acquitted himself well at Litani river. Stirling met Mayne and outlined the concept of the SAS; the pair were of similar height but the Irishman filled his frame much better. Mayne was a qualified solicitor and an international rugby lock forward of some repute. He also possessed a vicious temper, at times unnatural in its ferocity. When Stirling met him he was in detention for striking a senior officer, Geoffrey Keyes. Once Stirling had persuaded Mayne to join him, he got the charges dropped.

The last of the six officers recruited by Stirling was Bill Fraser. He was the most experienced of the lot, despite the fact he looked like a boy in a man's uniform with his delicate frame and protruding ears.

'He was a good lad,' recalls Storie, 'but I thought at first that he shouldn't have been in the Commandos because he didn't seem the type.'

Fraser had been at Dunkirk with the Gordon Highlanders, though whether the vertical one-inch scar that ran down between his eyebrows was a result of that no one knew. He had followed his father and grandfather into the Gordons but he was the first of the family to be commissioned. There was an indefinably melancholy quality to Fraser, something 'a bit strange', says Storie. Perhaps it was the weight of his family's expectations on his shoulders, perhaps it was something else.

KABRIT WAS A GODFORSAKEN spot. It was 90 miles east of Cairo, on the edge of the Great Bitter Lake. Cairo had bars and cinemas and women. Kabrit

15

had sand and dust and a wind that blew in from the lake. When the volunteers arrived at 'L' Detachment's base they were greeted by a handful of tents and a swarm of flies. Outside Stirling's tent, the camp HQ, a sign had been stuck with 'L Detachment SAS' scrawled across it. Underneath some wag had written, 'Stirling's Rest Camp'.

Their first job was to augment their camp with tents and supplies, which they did, says Storie, by 'stealing everything' from a nearby camp whose New Zealand occupants were away on exercise.

'We took one truck ... and that night we stole the tents and went into their cookhouse and took their pots and pans.'

Twenty-four hours after arriving at Kabrit 'L' Detachment had several three-man and four-man tents, a trestle table, some easy chairs and an old piano. Provisions were scrounged by a Londoner called Kaufman.

'He asked me if I could get hold of a truck,' recalled Seekings, who could. Then, with a couple of men in the back of the truck, they drove to some of the other camps dotted along the Suez Canal Zone.

'Kaufman would engage the quartermaster of the stores in conversation while we went into the stores and loaded the truck up with stuff.'

It worked every time. Then they would stop at one of the many roadside kiosks near Kabrit.

'They sold sweets, fags, beer, anything you like, really,' said Seekings, 'and Kaufman flogged the army stores to these kiosk blokes in return for cigs and stuff the boys couldn't get easily.' Kaufman's crowning glory, however, was when he visited an RAF camp.

'He excelled himself there,' Seekings recalled. 'He pinched a load of bricks, rounded up some prisoners of war and made them build a brick canteen. So we had this canteen which was better than the officers' marquee.'

The men needed to be well fed in those early autumn months because the physical training was relentless. Jock Lewes oversaw most of it as Stirling was frequently in Cairo fighting the unit's corner for more equipment. Storie describes Stirling as the 'backbone' of 'L' Detachment, while Lewes was the 'brains'.

16

'Jock liked things right,' he continues. 'He was a perfectionist. He thought about things in greater depth than Stirling, who was more carefree. David had the power to get things done but he was always looking further ahead.'

Lewes struck Du Vivier as 'serious-minded, intense and a thinker', the antithesis of his own sanguine personality.

'Jock called us a lot of yellow-bellies,' Seekings remembered, 'and threw out challenges. We met the challenges and then Jock would show us another one and once he'd demonstrated it we had to do it.'

In a little hut in the camp, Lewes invented his eponymous bomb, drawing on his childhood experiences with his brother's chemical set. The beauty of the 'Lewes bomb' was that it was light enough (1 lb) to carry across the desert to their target, but powerful enough to destroy an enemy plane, not just leave it with a damaged wing that could be replaced by industrious fitters. Du Vivier drew an annotated diagram of the bomb in his diary.

> It was plastic explosive and thermite – which is used in incendiary bombs – and we rolled the whole lot together with motor car oil. It was a stodgy lump and then you had a No. 27 detonator, an instantaneous fuse and a time pencil. The time pencil looked a bit like a 'biro' pen. It was a glass tube with a spring-loaded striker held in place by a strip of copper wire. At the top was a glass phial containing acid which you squeezed gently to break. The acid would then eat through the wire and release the striker. Obviously the thicker the wire the longer the delay before the striker was triggered [the pencils were colour coded according to the length of fuse]. It was all put into a small cotton bag and it proved to be crude, but very effective. The thermite caused a flash that ignited the petrol, not just blowing the wing off but sending the whole plane up.

On 15 October Du Vivier had just finished another hard day's training. 'I was about to flop down on my bunk when a head poked through the flap of my tent and said, "You're down for jumping tomorrow." I rushed

17

over to the notice-board and sure enough there was my name, third on the list. My heart began to beat rapidly and I realised that at last the great day had come. Needless to say, I didn't sleep a wink that night.' At breakfast the next morning Du Vivier had 'an empty feeling'. He couldn't touch his food.

'I looked about me at the faces of my colleagues and their expressions told me that they were feeling just as bad as I was.'

The men's trepidation was warranted. For the past few weeks they had practised the rudiments of parachuting on some wooden platforms constructed by Jim Almonds. Lewes had even got them jumping from the tailgate of a moving lorry, an exercise that put Du Vivier, Jimmy Brough and Bill Fraser in hospital with fractures. Now it was the real thing.

The British Army had been experimenting with parachuting for just over a year. Progress had been steady at the training school in Ringway, Manchester, but it still required nerve to clip the thin static line from the parachute to the rail that ran along inside the plane's roof. When the men jumped this caused the static line to yank out the canopy from within their parachute bag. Du Vivier and Storie were in the first 'stick' of ten parachutists who clambered aboard the Bristol Bombay aircraft of 216 Squadron. As the plane taxied across to the main runway, Du Vivier felt 'jittery and I was trembling a little ... nobody spoke; there was only the sickening roar of the engines'. At 900 feet the first man jumped.

'There was a sudden "Swoosh, swoosh",' Du Vivier told his diary, 'as the two men disappeared into space leaving their static lines flapping at the side of the plane. My hair stood on end.'

He attempted to lift his spirits by whistling 'Roll out the barrel' but his mouth and lips were dry. The sergeant called the next two. Du Vivier stepped forward.

Like lambs going to the slaughter we stood up. My knees began to beat a tattoo on one another as I stretched up to adjust my static line. We moved towards the door and I glanced down. Mother Earth looked miles away and I wished I'd never been born ... when the sergeant

18

exclaimed 'Ready' I barely heard him. Down came the hand on my shoulder and I lunged forward. What happened next I can only faintly remember. The earth seemed to be above me and the sky below ... then suddenly a big, white cloud burst over me and I began to recognize it as being my 'chute. Everything steadied itself and I found myself sitting comfortably in my harness. My brain cleared and I felt an overwhelming feeling of exhilaration. I began to sing and shout ... a voice below me shouted 'get your knees up'. Remembering and applying all the rules for a good landing I made contact with the desert. It was a good landing and I felt very satisfied with life in general.

Cooper went after Du Vivier and experienced the same feelings, fear and then a sense that life could never again feel so good. Storie landed without a mishap and joined the rest of the stick on the pick-up truck. Revelling in their *schadenfreude* they watched the second stick jump.

The Bombay climbed into the clear blue sky and on board 21-year-old Ken Warburton prepared to jump first.

'Ready' yelled the RAF sergeant. He put his arm on Warburton's shoulder, and the aspiring pianist threw himself out of the plane. Down on the ground Du Vivier saw the figure exit the aircraft. He waited for the 'chute to open, and waited and waited.

'At first we thought maybe it was just equipment they were throwing out,' he says, 'but it wasn't.'

Next to jump was Joe Duffy, Warburton's best friend. He sensed something wasn't quite right. Where was the static line flapping harmlessly at the side of the plane?

'Ready,' said the sergeant.

Duffy glanced at the static line fitting, hesitated, and looked questioningly at the sergeant. The sergeant saw Duffy's alarm, but not the fitting.

'Come on, get on with it!' For a moment Duffy dithered. But he thought of the humiliation of refusing to jump. Out he went.

'His body,' says Jimmy Storie, 'landed quite close to Warburton's.'

'It was a desperate blow for morale,' says Du Vivier, 'and we felt terrible for the instructor because he took the whole thing on his shoulders as he hadn't tested the thing properly.'

The next morning the men continued parachuting. Stirling jumped first, then Lewes, then the rest. No one jibbed.

'We knew all the time,' says Du Vivier, 'that we were living under the cloud of being RTU'd [returned to unit]. If you didn't do what you were supposed to do you'd be RTU'd. I was determined I wasn't going back to the army business, I would have done anything.'

An investigation subsequently revealed that the deaths had been caused by a simple failure in the static line fitting. As the men jumped into the slipstream the pressure had buckled the clip and disengaged the static line ring from the rail. A similar fate had befallen a paratrooper at Ringway not so long before, but they had neglected to caution Stirling.

THE AIMS OF AUCHINLECK'S November offensive, codenamed 'Crusader', were twofold: to retake Cyrenaica and secure the Libyan airfields then in the hands of the Axis. If these were achieved then supplies to Malta could be increased and eventually air raids could be sent into Sicily and the heart of Italy. Rommel, however, was planning an offensive of his own, one that was also influenced by Malta. Sea and air attacks launched from the island base had been slashing his supply lines. The further east he could push the British the less protection the RAF could offer Malta and the convoys sailing towards it because airfields would be in German hands. That in turn would allow more German convoys to reach North Africa and ultimately enable the Afrika Korps to defeat the Allies. The British assault was to begin on the morning of 18 November, Rommel's a couple of days later. He had been warned by his Italian allies that they suspected the British were on the verge of launching a major offensive. This, according to the Italian official history, was dismissed by the Germans as 'excessive Latin nervousness'.

'L' Detachment's role in the impending battle was small yet significant. On the night of 16 November they would parachute into the desert,

20

march towards the coast and launch five separate raids on airfields between Tmimi and Gazala. Then they would rendezvous three miles south-east of the Gadd-el-Ahmar crossroads on the Trigh-Capuzzo, about 50 miles inland, where they would be met by a patrol of the Long Range Desert Group (LRDG).

THE MEN LEARNED about the operation on 15 November. 'The plans and maps were unsealed, explained and studied,' recalls Du Vivier, 'until each man knew his job by heart. There was a lot of work to be done such as preparing explosives, weapons and rations.'

At dawn on the 16th, Stirling and the fifty-four men he'd selected to take part in the raid took off from Kabrit for their forward landing ground of Bagoush, approximately 300 miles to the west. There was no Fraser; the arm he'd broken jumping from the lorry hadn't fully healed. He was sent overland in a lorry to one of the RV points to wait for any stragglers.

The men arrived at Bagoush after a five-hour flight to find that the RAF had gone to great lengths to make them feel comfortable. Du Vivier recalls that the 'officers' mess was put at our disposal and we kicked off with a first-rate meal after which there were books, games, wireless and a bottle of beer each, all to keep our minds off the coming event'. In the mess the men mingled self-consciously. Storie nursed a beer, chatting to Jock Cheyne and Pat Riley, both of whom stood well over 6 feet. On the flight, recalls Storie, 'neither had been happy with how their parachute felt so they'd swapped'. Cooper and Seekings, who to everyone's surprise had palled up despite their contrasting personalities, relaxed in each other's company.

'Reg was what you would call dour,' says Storie. 'He was a lad from the country, a very good soldier but not too intelligent. Johnny was different, he was very bright and outgoing.'

Du Vivier had no particular friends; the men dipped into his bonhomie when they wanted a chummy natter.

'You could never get to the bottom of Jeff,' says Storie. 'He struck me as quite a private man .'

Du Vivier was a listener, not a talker. If he had something to say he

21

wrote it in his diary, or he sent it in a letter to Rea, the girl he'd met in Ayr during his Commando training. Things had become serious between the two in the intervening twelve months, and shortly before the operation he'd sent her a poem on the back of a portrait photo he'd had taken in Cairo. The final verse ran

> And I, may heaven forgive me, said
> Lay your blonde beloved head
> In the hollow of my arm
> We'll love lightly without harm
> To either's heart; and I'll defy
> Your warmth and loveliness; and I
> Won't love too much.
> Forgive my lie!

At 6.30 p.m. they climbed into a fleet of lorries to make the short distance to their aircraft. Du Vivier and Storie were in Lewes' stick, so were Cooper, Riley and Cheyne. They fitted on their parachutes, and had a final smoke. Du Vivier glanced up at the night sky. The wind was beginning to croon. He was the last man in to his plane and squeezed himself beside the door on the left-hand side of the aircraft. He heard the second plane take off, then theirs began to taxi over the rough ground.

'Then with a terrific roar of engines we sped forward and were on our way.' Du Vivier wondered momentarily if it 'was to be a one-way ticket … I muttered a silent prayer and put myself in God's hands'.

As the plane reached its ceiling of 18,000 feet the men shivered uncontrollably inside the pitch darkness of the fuselage. Du Vivier wrapped himself up in a blanket and tried to sleep. Every few minutes he'd drop off, then wake with a start and curl up further inside the blanket. In the cockpit the poor visibility forced the pilot to descend through the clouds to pick up his bearings. Du Vivier caught a fleeting glimpse of the sea below, then felt the aircraft bank to the south.

'Almost immediately the "fun" began.'

The top speed of the Bristol Bombay was 150mph. Jimmy Storie says the joke among 'L' Detachment was that you could open its door, go outside and have a piss, and then run after it and climb back in. No one was laughing as the plane was buffeted by German flak.

'First came the "flaming onions",' recalls Du Vivier, 'which pointed the way for searchlights – six or more of them. We were blinded by their dazzling beams. I thought to myself, "Now for the fireworks." They didn't keep us waiting.'

Storie, sitting on the opposite side to Du Vivier, tried to take comfort from the fact that he was smaller than Cheyne and Riley, so perhaps less likely to get hit.

'The flak was terrible; we were all leaning back against the side [of the plane] and the flak was coming up through the centre. How the hell no one got wounded I don't know.'

(When Du Vivier returned from the raid he saw their RAF despatcher who was curious to know who had been in the seat next to the rear door on the left. Du Vivier said he had. The despatcher grinned.'We found an unexploded shell embedded under the seat. A couple of inches higher and you'd be talking in a very high voice.')

Du Vivier knew the German gunners were finding their range when he saw a tracer 'enter through the thin fuselage of the wall and make its exit through the roof, narrowly missing the auxiliary petrol tank'. He looked out of the open door, marvelling at a sky 'streaked with yellow, red, green and other coloured tracer bullets as they passed us'. The pilot climbed back into the clouds and away from the flak. Then the signal came through: eight minutes to go.

'That eight minutes seemed like eight hours,' Du Vivier wrote later. 'We waited in suspense for the red light and when it came we stood up all ready for the final plunge. There were a few remarks, a "good luck" or a "see you down there". The green light and out into the inky blackness we went.'

They jumped quickly on each other's shoulders, into a force nine wind. Du Vivier listened to the 'noise of the plane grow fainter and all of a sudden I felt terribly alone … the drop seemed endless'. The first he knew

23

that he was about to land was when he heard a crunching sound from below and saw one of the stick 'sitting in the centre of a large camel thorn bush'. He was one of the lucky ones.

'I had a terrible landing,' explains Storie. 'I was black and blue from the rocks and my back was as stiff as the devil. It was all right when I walked but the moment I stopped it stiffened up.'

Cooper described hitting the desert 'with quite a bump and I was then dragged along by the wind at quite a speed. When I came to rest I staggered rather groggily to my feet, feeling sure I'd broken something but to my astonishment I seemed to have nothing worse than my breath momentarily knocked out of me.'

Du Vivier was hurled by the wind 150 yards over the rocky desert surface, all the time frantically trying to get out of his harness.

'When I finally freed myself,' he told his diary, 'I was bruised and bleeding and there was a sharp pain in my right leg. When I saw the rocky ground I'd travelled over, I thanked my lucky stars that I was alive.'

They'd landed in the middle of the worst storm to hit the region in thirty years.

Within an hour Lewes had rounded up all his men, a remarkable achievement given the strength of the wind. But his worst fear had been realized. Jock Cheyne had broken his back on landing.

'We had been told before the operation,' says Storie, 'that if we broke a leg or something like that, and couldn't go on, we just had to crawl to the nearest roadside and hope. But there weren't many roads in the desert.'

Storie shook Cheyne's hand. Lewes said a few words, then they disappeared into the desert leaving him alone with some water and a pistol.

'That was the last we saw him,' says Storie. 'Whether he was ever picked up and died later, or whether he's still there ... I don't know.'*

Lewes asked Du Vivier to lead them north, towards the airfield. He took a bearing and set off 'just after 12.30 a.m.'. The first three hours were uneventful, then it started to rain. It was only a short shower but it had a

---

* John Cheyne is commemorated on the Alamein Memorial in Egypt for those Allied soldiers who have no known grave.

24

sobering effect on the men who had been marching trance-like across the desert.

'Somehow we all sensed that something had gone wrong as the ground was very unfamiliar and not what we expected from our maps,' says Du Vivier. 'Dawn found us still marching – we had travelled over 15 miles and by this time we were certain that something was wrong.'

Stripped naked by the daylight they laid up under some camel shrub and waited for nightfall. Du Vivier slept for three hours before 'a Jerry spotter plane came overhead very low but he apparently didn't see us and continued on his way'.

Ten minutes before midday it started raining again, not the light rain of the previous night but a torrential downpour. Then came hailstones and thunder.

'The lightning was terrific,' Du Vivier noted admiringly. 'It continued to pour in buckets for about 30 minutes and by the end of this time we were sitting waist deep in a swirling tide of water.'

Lewes ordered them to collect up their kit and make for some higher ground. They huddled together, using their blankets as shelter, and trying to make light of the fact they were wearing only shorts and overalls.

'And at least it meant we didn't have to worry about a water shortage,' Cooper joked later. He was more concerned about the effect the storm was having on their compasses. 'Navigation had been a tricky business before the storm broke, now it was practically impossible.'

The war correspondent Alexander Clifford described the storm that swept the Western Desert that day and night as the 'most spectacular thunderstorm within local memory ... the thunder mumbled and murmured and roared in long growling cadences and burst overhead with a crack like a bomb'. By nightfall the rain was coming down in torrents. Lewes aborted the mission and told the men they would head for the RV. They struck camp and started marching to the Gadd-el-Ahmar crossroads, where they hoped the LRDG were waiting. They made pitifully slow progress, slipping, sliding and stumbling.

'The rains had turned the desert into a river,' says Storie, 'and it was getting deeper and deeper.'

Du Vivier recorded their desperate struggle in simple stark prose.

All that night we marched or rather waded through the water which was sometimes up to our knees. We rested periodically when we could find a piece of high ground which stood out of the water, sometimes we travelled for over an hour and failing to find a dry spot just lay down in the water. Sleep came almost instantaneously but not for long, for a fit of shivering would force us to get moving. I could not explain how cold it actually was, to believe it one would have to experience it. I was not shivering but shaking. All the bones in my body were numbed. I couldn't speak, every time I opened my mouth my teeth just cracked against one another. And so it was with all of us.

Even Lewes succumbed to the battering of the storm. Du Vivier wrote in his diary on his return that he handed over temporary command 'to the senior sergeant whose name I must mention here, Pat Riley, an ex-Guardsman and policeman ... I shall always be indebted to him for what he did. I'm sure he was for the most part responsible for our return'. More than sixty years later Du Vivier's regard for Riley is undimmed.

'He was the one who kept us going because we just wanted to fall out and die. We were demoralized. When you're frozen stiff, soaked to the skin, hungry ... you're not looking forward to a bright future, you just want it all to end.'

Riley kept the men going all through the night. Sometimes he hollered at them, as if he were back on the Guards' parade ground; at other times he nursed them like an anxious mother. They marched for 40 minutes, rested for 20 minutes, marched for 40 minutes, rested for 20.

'I wouldn't call it "resting",' Du Vivier says. 'We just fell asleep. Pat, Jock and I slept huddled together. We placed one blanket on the ground and the other two on top of us. At each resting place we took it in turns to sleep in the middle as it was the warmest position.'

The storm abated the following morning and the sight of a weak sun invigorated the men. Then they had their first good news of the operation when they spotted the Trig el Abd, a rough track that stretched from Cyrenaica to the Egyptian border. They trudged along it throughout the night and into the next day. They were all feeling weak through lack of food. Their rations – dates, raisins, cheese, hard biscuits and a tin each of bully beef – were gone. So was their emergency chocolate ration. Du Vivier gorged with his mind, devouring a 'nice, hot breakfast of eggs, bacon and coffee, things which I had hitherto taken for granted. Never again, I thought, will I be particular about my food'.

In the late afternoon they spotted a metal signpost. It indicated how many miles they were from Bir-el-gubi to the east, and El Mechili to the west. They studied their maps and realized they were tantalizingly close to the RV, three miles south of the Gadd-el-Ahmar crossroads.

'In spite of our weakness we all cheered and danced round the post,' says Du Vivier. 'We even kissed it as though it were something sacred.'

Six hours later, at 2200 hours on 19 November, they were picked up by the LRDG. The first thing they asked for was food.

'We had a meal of bully and biscuits and tea,' wrote Du Vivier, 'which was undoubtedly in my opinion the best meal I have ever had in my life.'

A few hours later Paddy Mayne led his party to the same RV, minus Dougie Arnold and Bill Kendall. Both men had been left on the DZ with serious injuries. Arnold said after the war that the whole operation was a 'fiasco'. The next morning as he and Kendall dragged themselves south towards the RV Arnold saw a figure on the skyline.

'Unfortunately it was an Italian soldier up for an early morning stroll ... he wasn't sure who we were but he knew he had to keep pointing his rifle at us.' The SAS men said they were Royal Engineers who had got lost while building roads. The Italians fell for it, forgetting the fact that the two men were miles behind enemy lines, and treated their prisoners 'kindly and with great amusement'.*

---

* Bill Kendall survived the war but was killed in an accident while serving with the Royal Armoured Corps in 1947.

IN THE EARLY hours of 20 November, David Lloyd-Owen of the LRDG watched two figures tramp across the desert towards the RV. Lloyd-Owen recognized the uniforms and emerged from his shelter.

'My name's Stirling,' said the taller of the pair. 'Have you seen any of my chaps?'

Stirling and the other man, Sergeant Bob Tait, were the only men to have made it back out of their stick. The final list of missing, thirty-four names from the fifty-five who'd jumped, was a roll call of good men: Lieutenants McGonigal, Thomas and Bonnington; Colour Sergeant Major Yates. Sergeants Ralph Lazenby, Ernie Bond, Barney Stone and Jock Cheyne. Jim Blakeney. Roy Davies, who had jumped with Stirling and Lewes all those months ago. All were missing. Even little Dougie Arnold, the great escaper, was unaccounted for.

THE END OF NOVEMBER was a time for men to hold their nerve in the desert. General Cunningham, commander of the Eighth Army, had lost his after early gains in Operation Crusader had been wiped out by a bold Rommel counterthrust that penetrated into Egypt. Auchinleck's nerve remained steady. He was convinced Rommel had stretched his lines of supply to the limit and was trying to bluff the British into retreating. Auchinleck replaced Cunningham with Ritchie, and ordered him to stand firm. The survivors of 'L' Detachment wondered if Stirling's nerve would fray in the face of such bitter disappointment.

'After that first raid we thought it was the end of the unit,' reflects Du Vivier. 'And we'd all go back to our regiments and carry on from there. But Stirling got us together for a chat and was talking about the "next time". I thought to myself "I don't fancy a next time if this is what it's going to be like." But he definitely had no idea of giving up. He told us we weren't going to parachute any more; instead we were going to work with the LRDG because they knew what they were doing. We listened to him and he talked us into it. I think we thought it was the lesser of two evils: to stay put rather than return to our [parent] regiment.'

Stirling had been ruminating on the failures of the mission even as

28

he navigated his way back across the desert to the RV. As he'd waited for any stragglers with Lloyd-Owen they discussed the reasons why the raid had failed. Stirling was muttering about the perils of parachuting when an idea came to Lloyd-Owen. Might it be more practical, and less dangerous, if the LRDG drove them to their next targets? Stirling tried to pick faults with the idea, but Lloyd-Owen batted away each one. The LRDG could get them within a few miles of the target; they could carry the men and their equipment; they would be able to pick them up again within a matter of hours.

When the remnants of 'L' Detachment arrived at Siwa Oasis, base of the LRDG, Stirling asked their CO, Colonel Guy Prendagast, if the plan was acceptable to him. He saw no reason why it wasn't, so long as it didn't interfere with his unit's reconnaissance patrols across the Libyan desert. Stirling felt the colour coming back into the cheeks of 'L' Detachment.

There was still the problem of Cairo and MEHQ. He imagined how the 'fossilized shits' would clap their hands in glee when they heard of the raid's failure. There was no way Stirling was going to Cairo, but he needed to insinuate himself into a fighting unit for reasons of supply. Before he left for Eighth Army HQ, he instructed Lewes to bring up the rest of the equipment and men from Kabrit. He would meet them in a week.

At Eighth Army HQ, Stirling met two commanders in one day. In the morning it was Cunningham, hours before he was sacked. In the afternoon he was called in by Ritchie, his successor. He fed them both the same line: atrocious weather, light casualties, looking forward to having another crack. It was a perfunctory interview. Ritchie had more weighty matters on his mind than a band of saboteurs.

Stirling then had one of those chance encounters that only happen to the bold. He bumped into Brigadier John Marriott, a Scots Guard officer who, with his wife, moved in the same social circles as David's brother, Peter. Stirling engaged him first in dinner party gossip, then steered him towards his pressing problem. Did the brigadier know of a fighting force that might be willing to accommodate his men for a while? Marriott smiled.

29

'Brigadier Denys Reid has just captured Jalo Oasis from the Italians with an armoured squadron. I think that would suit your purposes very well.'

DU VIVIER PEERED between boulders and watched the Germans digging defences. The early morning mist had already been burnt off by the sun and he smiled as he watched them toil. There was about a company of them, 900 yards to the north. He could see more Germans, to his east and west, but they were further away and posed no threat. Du Vivier and the other men well concealed among the rocky high ground – Lieutenant Fraser, Jock Byrne, Arthur Phillips and Bob Tait – were interested in what lay just a few miles beyond the digging Germans, Agedabia aerodrome.

'We took note of where every aircraft was positioned on each side of the runway,' says Du Vivier. 'And we were also able to plan our escape route to reach the LRDG rendezvous.'

The men crouched down among the rocks, and waited for darkness. It was 21 December 1941, the shortest day of the year. There was an air of impatience among them, but also of nervousness. Much was riding on the raid. In the month since 'L' Detachment had been accommodated at Jalo by Reid, they had enjoyed only limited success. Mayne had destroyed twenty-four planes at Tamit in a whirlwind of violence but Stirling and Lewes had failed to emulate his success. Now Reid had asked Stirling to 'lay on a bit of a show' on Agedabia airfield on the night of 21 December. He had orders to move his force up to the Antelat–Agedabia area and link up with Marriott on the 22nd but the last part of the journey was across desert regularly patrolled by the Axis aircraft at Agedabia. Reid knew the carnage there would be if they were caught in the open.

Fraser and his men had left in the back of an LRDG Chevrolet truck on 19 December for the 150-mile journey north-west from Jalo to Agedabia A day later they were dropped 16 miles from their target. Now they were concealed among the rocks.

For Fraser this was the test to see if he was up to the job. He knew some of the men thought he wasn't, that he was a bit 'strange', a bit effeminate. At Kabrit he preferred the company of his dog, Withers, to that of the officers' mess. When he did go in for a drink he was bullied by Mayne.

'Paddy used to give him a hell of a time,' says Storie, 'because he thought he was that way inclined. Paddy could be cruel, especially after a few.'

As a consequence Fraser preferred to have men with him whom he trusted; Du Vivier and Tait had served with Fraser in the Scottish Commandos. Byrne's association went back even further, to Dunkirk and the Gordon Highlanders.

'Fraser was one of the best,' he wrote after the war. 'He did all eight of his parachute [SAS training] jumps in one morning so he could sport his wings on leave in Cairo the next day.' Wings, awarded upon completion of parachute training, were worn on the shoulder. Only when a soldier had completed three successful operations was he allowed to wear them on his left breast.

It was Tait who had designed a cap badge for 'L' Detachment, the flaming sword of Excalibur with the motto 'Who Dares Wins'. The motto was actually Stirling's idea.

'Tait's first suggestion was "Strike and Destroy",' remembers Du Vivier, 'but Stirling said, "A bit too stern."'

'Descend to Ascend' was then mooted, before Stirling stepped in and came up with 'Who Dares Wins'.*

Tait's design was in the hands of 'John Jones' of Cairo, the manufacturer who had been asked to produce the cap badge, along with the operational wings. Lewes had designed these in the shape of the outstretched wings of the scarab beetle. Lewes had asked 'John Jones' to use an embroidery thread of Cambridge and one of Oxford Blue, the former as a mark of respect to Stirling's alma mater, the latter to Lewes's.

---

* The 'Winged Dagger' misnomer was attributed to Roy Farran who, in 1948, published his war memoirs under that title, saying that it was more dynamic than 'Flaming Sword'. However, new evidence points to a SHAEF communiqué in 1944, as the source of the 'Winged Dagger' myth. Both the *Sunday Times* and *Observer* newspapers quoted the communiqué in their 27 August editions and carried the identical explanation: 'Their regimental badge is a winged dagger bearing the legend "Who Dares Wins".'

Phillips, the fifth man in the party, was a chippy Englishman with, says Storie, 'communist leanings'. He was kicked out of the regiment in disgrace in 1943, though not because of his political persuasions.

The five men checked and double-checked their equipment. They were travelling light. Each man carried a revolver and eight primed Lewes bombs. Byrne had the only machine gun, a Thompson, with four spare magazines. Phillips discovered one of his bombs had a damaged time pencil so it was buried among the rocks. Suddenly one of the men hissed a warning; someone was approaching. Over the rocks they saw a goatherd coming towards them with his herd. The goatherd was just a boy, but he had noticed something unusual along his daily route. He climbed right up to where the British soldiers lay hidden.

'He just looked at us,' says Du Vivier, 'and walked on. We told ourselves he wouldn't spill the beans.'

They moved off at 1830 hours, relieved, recalls Du Vivier 'to be able to stand up and stretch our cramped limbs'. On the way towards the airfield they were caught in the beam of a German vehicle's headlights.

'We held our breath, to lie flat or to run would have caused suspicion,' says Du Vivier. 'So we carried on, the vehicle passed on too, and we breathed again.'

At 2115 hours they reached the airfield's perimeter. It took them a further three hours to finesse their way on to the airfield, avoiding sentries and tripwires. Du Vivier described their sabotage in a letter to his mother.

We picked our areas and continued singly placing our bombs on all the planes and making a rendezvous on the runway ... this went on until all but three of our bombs were used up. We found a sand-bagged building with hundreds of aerial bombs and incendiaries inside and put a bomb in the centre of it ... on the way back we counted well over forty explosions and heard the bomb dump go off with a blood-curdling deafening roar. Though we must have been at least half a mile away by this time we felt the concussion press on our lungs. By this time the whole area was in a turmoil and alive with shouting and excited men. You can well imagine that they hadn't the foggiest idea of what was going on ... once out of the camp and danger, we turned around and despite our fatigue, yelled with joy and excitement at the scene in front of us.

AT 0500 HOURS they reached the RV. The Rhodesians were there waiting.

'It was such a fantastic show,' one of them told Byrne, 'that we just had to stay until the end.'

Not long after leaving the RV the LRDG patrol encountered the vanguard of Brigadier Reid's flying column advancing towards Benghazi. As they drove nearer the whole of the combined Brigade Group of armour and motorized infantry emerged through the dust clouds and swallowed them up. Reid wrote in his diary: 'I drove forward to see what was the matter and met Fraser of Stirling's "L" Detachment whom I eagerly asked how he had got on. He said, "Very sorry, sir, I had to leave two aircraft on the ground as I ran out of explosive, but we destroyed thirty-seven." This indeed was a wonderful achievement by one officer and three men [sic]. Incidentally, we heard later that Rommel had been in Agedabia that night. He must have had a bit of a headache.'

As Reid's column continued north the LRDG laid on breakfast for the men they had rescued. The recognition sign (a strip of cloth, the colour of which changed regularly in coordination with the RAF) was laid out to identify the camp for any marauding RAF fighters. Over a mug of tea and some hard-tack porridge Du Vivier told a red-headed LRDG corporal called Laurence Ashby about the raid.

'Then we settled down and got a bit of kip,' recalls Du Vivier. He was woken by the sound of cannon fire. A British Blenheim bomber roared overhead while a second swooped down. Du Vivier 'rolled off my blanket as he began strafing us. The Corporal rolled on to my blanket and was hit'.

One of the Rhodesians jumped to his feet, pointing furiously to the recognition sign. He was blasted off his feet by the plane's guns. The pair were buried later that morning, recalled Byrne who, with the rest of his comrades, was asked to keep away from the graveside.

'We know it was not your fault,' the Rhodesian commander told them, 'but the planes were British and you are British.'

33

Fraser's party reached Jalo Oasis on 23 December. That evening there was a shindig of sorts as Stirling combined the Christmas celebrations with news of the most successful raid to date. Christmas had been brought forward a couple of days, Stirling told Fraser, because he and Mayne were going to have another crack at Sirte and Tamit the next day. Lewes was off to Nofilia airfield; Stirling asked Fraser if he would like to raid Marble Arch, an airfield only 60 miles east of Nofilia. Marble Arch wasn't the real name of the airfield, it was the Arco dei Fileni. But to the British it was Marble Arch; it was easier to say, and it was a small and enjoyable way of poking fun at Mussolini, who had built the towering arch on the Tripolitania border in a fit of monstrous conceit.

Fraser said he was happy to go. Of course, he had no choice; Stirling rarely ordered a soldier to do something, he'd ask with that charming smile of his if 'they would mind'. To decline would have resulted in a rapid RTU, which was what all of 'L' Detachment feared most. Failure to cut the mustard in a particular unit in the Second World War threw up a slew of euphemisms that were humiliating only to those who had experienced the misery of their meaning. The South Africans called it 'Stellenbosched', the French 'Limoges'. The soldier who couldn't hack it in the Afrika Korps was sent 'on his camel'.

To Du Vivier the swift turnaround at Jalo was 'just one of those things'. After seeing off Stirling's and Mayne's force on Christmas Eve, the remaining members of 'L' Detachment set off on Christmas Day with their New Zealand LRDG patrol. On 27 December Fraser – with his same four soldiers – was dropped six miles from Marble Arch aerodrome.

'The plan,' says Du Vivier, 'was that we should be left with water and rations for three days during which time we were to accomplish the job and be picked up again by the same patrol.'

Lewes's party continued west. On the afternoon of 28 December they were dropped by the LRDG 18 miles from Nofilia. The drop-off point was also the pick-up point, arranged for two days hence. Lewes and his four men – Jim Almonds, Jimmy Storie, Bob Lilley and Robert White – marched off across the desert.

34

They arrived back two days later. There was an urgency to their movements as they climbed into the lorries. As the five-vehicle convoy moved off at dusk they told the LRDG about the operation. Initially it had gone as planned. They had penetrated the aerodrome's defences and crept up unseen to the first plane. Lewes planted a bomb on the port wing over the fuel tank. Almonds did the same to the second. They moved forward to the third. It wasn't there. The raiders ran softly across the aerodrome, searching for other planes in the darkness. They must have been moved during the day, they told one another. As the two planes exploded they raced for the RV, fretful as to what would happen at sunrise when the other planes came looking for them.

The Germans found them early on the morning of 31 December. As the lorries bounced across the desert towards Marble Arch a Messerschmitt 110 fighter attacked. Storie remembers that he came in very low, 'at about 30 feet and from behind us with his cannons firing'. Something, a round or a piece of shrapnel, tore open one side of Storie's khaki shorts. Lewes wasn't so lucky. 'He got a burst in his back,' says Storie, 'and the two offside wheels were blown off. I don't know how I got away with it because Jock was alongside me.'

The men flung themselves from the lorry and dashed for the cover of some rocks. The pilot circled for a second attack, diving just as impossibly low and raking the rocks with cannon fire. Only after he'd expended his ammunition on the third pass did he break off the onslaught. When they reached Lewes, says Storie, 'his back was shattered'. They dug a hole and buried him, then 'said a prayer and scratched his name on a helmet, I think, in case someone would go that way again'.

The other four lorries were destroyed not long after by two Stukas. When Storie's party found them the survivors had taken off on foot across the desert. One of the LRDG patrol inspected the wrecks and announced he could get Lewes' lorry up and running with a spot of cannibalization. At sundown on 31 December they started the long drive back to Jalo.

'We saw in the New Year,' says Storie, 'by passing round a tin of condensed milk.'

AT MARBLE ARCH, Fraser, Tait, Du Vivier, Phillips and Byrne were still waiting for the LRDG patrol.

'We waited and we waited,' recalls Du Vivier, 'and we waited. But nothing happened.'

The wait gave them time to discuss the failure of their raid. Having spent the night of 27 December concealed in camel scrub they were overlooking the landing strip by midday the following day.

'What we saw was very discouraging,' according to Du Vivier. 'There was not a plane to be seen ... during the afternoon we saw several aircraft land to refuel, "bomb-up" and take off.' Furthermore German defences had clearly been strengthened recently. 'Between us and the landing strip,' estimates Du Vivier, 'was a long, dug-out defence position, stretching from the escarpment to the sea and manned by at least a division of Germans.'

They expected the LRDG sometime around midday on New Year's Eve. But high up in the sky they heard the wail of Stukas. 'Then we heard muffled explosions and machine-gun fire,' says Du Vivier.

The rest of New Year's Eve was spent under the camel scrub, as was New Year's Day. On the morning of 2 January they finally conceded the LRDG wasn't coming. But what to do? They were low on water and Jalo was 200 miles away. For the second time in quick succession Du Vivier found himself tramping across the desert.

'It was something that had to be done so we did it,' he says, 'but we tried not to think what it was going to be like.'

They set out in a south-easterly direction, each man carrying two days' supply of bully beef and sardines and hard-tack biscuits. A couple of them had some dried fruit and cheese. They had half a pint of water each which, wrote Du Vivier in his diary, 'helped to keep up my morale just to know and to hear the water in the bottle'. Sometimes he took a sip to moisten his mouth, 'but as it got less and less I spat it back again. Then I started to suck a couple of small smooth pebbles to keep the saliva from drying up'.

The next morning, 3 January, brought emotions that would come to torment them, 'a feeling that perhaps today would bring us more luck'.

36

Once or twice they glimpsed the coastal road, and the enemy traffic on it. They 'toyed' with the idea of getting on to it, says Du Vivier, but as they did so they spotted what looked like an inland lake some six miles or so the south-east.

'With renewed hope we hurried our pace,' remembered Du Vivier. When they reached the lake they dropped to their knees and began lapping at the water. 'We found to our dismay that it was salt water.'

They began to distil the water but it was 'back-breaking work and very slow, taking one hour to produce less than a quarter of a pint of fresh water'. They used it to brew up but the tea it produced, said Byrne, 'tasted just like urine, and we all knew what that tasted like, having already tried our own. Bill and Jeff watched all three of us spit out the terrible concoction in disgust, then drank their own without a grimace'.

Bob Tait called for another course of action, recalls Du Vivier.

'He made a suggestion that two of us should carry on with the distilling and the other three should make for the road and raid a truck for water and provisions.'

They drew lots to see who did what. Phillips, Byrne and Tait got the long straw – or the short straw, no one seemed to know which was worse – and set out for the road.

'They returned soon after midnight,' wrote Du Vivier, 'after a highly successful mission bringing with them two jerry-cans filled with crystal clear and cool water. What a feast we had that night. We made a brew of tea – we were carrying dry tea and condensed milk – and feasted on bully stew, cheese and biscuits and dried dates for dessert.'

The next day was a good one. They marched with full water bottles and the only people they met were friendly desert nomads who supplied them with fresh dates and replenished their water. On Tuesday 6 January they encountered some Italian Engineers laying cables in the Wadi-el-Faregh.

'They must have seen us,' says Du Vivier, 'but they probably thought we were also Italian soldiers ... we retired into some tall camel grass about 200 yards away and in doing so were forced to abandon the blankets and ground sheets.'

They remained hidden until nightfall and then moved towards the Engineers' lorry. From inside, said Du Vivier, 'we could distinguish four different voices'. Fraser held a brief and barely audible council of war and then 'at a given signal,' wrote Du Vivier, 'Lieutenant Fraser made for the driver's cabin and, armed with Smith & Wesson revolvers, Byrne and I covered Bob and Phillips while they "downed" the flap and "upped" the canvas. In a matter of seconds we were in the truck, grabbed the "bodies" and pulled them out ... they did not put up a fight but screamed for mercy. We had some trouble in quietening them down but in spite of the din their neighbours did not bother to investigate'.

Du Vivier used his French and 'reassured them that we had no intention of killing them [and] spun them a yarn to the effect that we were a patrol and their position was surrounded by half the British Army.' The Italians begged to be taken prisoner.

'Wait until tomorrow,' laughed Du Vivier, 'and you will all be prisoners.'

Fraser meanwhile was trying to drain the radiator for water. What he extracted was red with rust and undrinkable. In the lorry Tait found some tins of food and a small benzine stove and a full water bottle. He swigged generously from the bottle, then retched violently.

'It was benzine,' says Du Vivier.

They told the Italians to behave and set off northwards, veered east for a mile and then resumed their trek north across a salt marsh. They stopped after a while for a brew, putting the stove in a hole dug out of the marsh. 'We huddled around to keep the light from becoming notice-able,' wrote Du Vivier, 'when suddenly the whole thing blew up in our faces with a loud bang.'

For a few frightening moments they were all temporarily blinded, hands clawing the sand from their eyes. No one had been seriously hurt in the blast but 'we had lost all of our precious water ... a catastrophe'. They sought solace in the tinned food, prising open the unlabelled tins one after the other. The first one 'contained some sort of jam ... then followed in order: spaghetti in some type of fishy sauce, pears and finally more spaghetti'.

38

At daybreak the coastal road was visible a mile to their north. They watched the traffic passing along it from their lying-up position. At nightfall they moved down to the road, keeping just off it until they found a suitable spot for an ambush where the road was joined by a small track that led to an encampment further inside the desert. For 20 minutes they crouched behind a cairn of rocks until 'we saw the headlights of a vehicle coming down the track towards us'. The two signallers inside the wireless car – a Mercedes Benz, remembers Du Vivier – were quickly overpowered.

'There was only seating capacity for three in the car,' he recalls, 'but we were not going to leave the Jerries behind to raise the alarm, and besides, not one of our number could drive the car.' The five British soldiers squeezed themselves in behind the two Germans. 'I sat behind the driver,' says Du Vivier, 'with my revolver alongside his left ear just in case he had any different ideas to mine.'

For an hour they passed a ceaseless stream of enemy traffic. Then they came to the roadside café teeming with Italian soldiers, but no one paid any attention to the little radio car. They carried on along the road for a further six miles, then struck off south across the desert. Fifteen miles later they got bogged down in a salt marsh. When it became clear they were stuck fast, Du Vivier gave the Germans a bearing off the north star and pointed them in the right direction.

'Then we wished them luck. We were glad we weren't in their position, having to return home to your CO and tell him you've lost your vehicle.'

Their own predicament wasn't particularly rosy. They estimated they were about 40 miles from the forward British positions. But between them lay the Axis defences. An hour later they saw fresh tank tracks and footprints. Then the ground dropped away and they saw several enemy gun positions. They made another detour, but found their path barred by a minefield.

'We took a chance and crossed it without mishap,' says Du Vivier. 'But then walked slap into a maze of dug-in positions and almost immediately an Italian sentry sprang up in front of us shouting something. By this time our nerves had got the better of us and in a body we about

39

turned and ran like the devil, the sentry firing at us as we did so, but in the darkness his aim wasn't good.'

With the squawks of twitchy Italians whirling all around them, they dropped to their stomachs and began to crawl. For 400 yards they slithered their way through the bedlam before rising nonchalantly to resume their march.

They were breakfasting on the last of their rations, 'one and a half sardines each and a spoonful of jam,' says Du Vivier, when an RAF patrol of Blenheim bombers attacked the enemy positions. They laid up the whole day within sight of the German positions and at dusk headed off in a south-easterly direction.

'We were too desperate to take any more detours,' wrote Du Vivier, 'so we went right through the enemy's position.'

At some point during the night they encountered a Bedouin encampment. They were given fresh dates and water, then they pushed on. The next day, 10 January, they found the charred skeleton of a German vehicle. Inside were a couple of tins of burnt meat. They wolfed it down. At the end of the day they were hit by a sandstorm.

'Visibility was almost nil,' wrote Du Vivier. 'Each mile seemed like ten and each hour like a lifetime.'

The strength of the storm was so great they didn't see or hear the armoured column until it was almost upon them.

'We stopped to observe,' Du Vivier remembered, 'but still could not determine whether they were ours or not when, suddenly, I heard an unmistakeable Cockney voice and we almost wept with joy and relief.'

They were taken to an officer on the point of a British bayonet. 'No wonder,' wrote Du Vivier a few days later. 'For we must have looked a grim sight. With our long matted hair and beards. Faces and hands caked in dirt and torn, ragged clothes. They must have thought we were a band of savages.' Each man had a 'hearty meal of stew and tinned potatoes washed down with mugfuls of sweet steaming tea'.

Within a week Fraser and his men were back at Kabrit enjoying 'a hell of a booze-up'.

STIRLING LEFT MEHQ feeling rather pleased with himself. The meeting with Auchinleck had gone better than he'd hoped, a result no doubt of the general's satisfaction with the way the initial sluggishness of Operation Crusader had been transformed into a successful offensive. Rommel had been driven out of Libya and the strategically important port of Benghazi would shortly be in his hands. Auchinleck had agreed to Stirling's plan to raid Bouerat, the Axis's new coastal base 350 miles west of Benghazi. Perhaps more significantly, Stirling had been granted permission to recruit a further six officers and up to forty men. He returned to his brother's Cairo flat and began planning the Bouerat raid. He also drafted a recruitment notice to pin in regimental barracks.

In Haifa Albert Youngman learned of the call for volunteers as he recovered from a bout of malaria, contracted in Syria, where he'd spent the end of 1941 patrolling the Turkish border in case the Germans tried to seize the oil wells. He had heard tales about this mysterious outfit where 'blokes jumped off the backs of lorries', so he presented himself at Kabrit. 'It was either that or be thrown back into some infantry regiment. I never had a formal interview as such. They just asked me if I wanted to have a go. I said yes and that was that.'

Similar thoughts galloped through the mind of Reg Redington when he saw a notice pinned up in his Royal Artillery barracks. Brought up in Croydon among twelve brothers and sisters, Redington had always been able to look after himself. He was one of the boys, the one with the impish face. But his quiet modesty won him many friends.

'About twenty-five from my regiment applied,' he says. 'We were called for an interview and he asked me how I'd won my DCM [Distinguished Conduct Medal].'

Redington mumbled something about his part in an engagement with twenty-eight German tanks at Sidi Omar the previous November. Stirling, however, had probably already seen the citation for his immediate DCM that described how, with his gun crew all dead he 'loaded, laid and fired the gun alone until it was hit and put out of action, Redington himself being wounded. In spite of this he at once went to assist at another gun

41

which had casualties ... his very gallant and sustained courage under the heaviest fire was worthy of the highest praise'.

Redington recalls that Stirling 'congratulated me and then asked "what makes you want to join our lot?" I told him that I thought it would be a change, let me see a bit more of life'.

Redington didn't hear anything for a few weeks (probably not until Stirling returned from Bouerat) but then he was called in to see his CO.

'He told me "Nobby, it looks like Stirling wants you. I'm awfully sorry to lose you."'

BY THE END OF 1941 the patience of Roger Boutinot and his comrades was as flabby as their stomachs. The French paratroopers had sailed from England six months earlier, and after brief sojourns in Egypt, Palestine and Beirut, they had been despatched to Damascus. There they practised jumping from an old Blenheim bomber, but all the time they were itching to get at the Germans. Every week Georges Bergé promised his men they would soon get their chance; every week he asked for a little more time.

'One day,' says Boutinot, 'we went to see Bergé and said "If you don't send us somewhere we'll leave, go to the navy, anywhere." We were drunk most of the time in Syria because we were so fed up with nothing to do. "You must wait," said Bergé. "I am in contact with London and de Gaulle."'

In Damascus Bergé recruited a 31-year-old lieutenant called Augustin Jordan. To the untrained eye this intense and self-contained man seemed ill-equipped to survive in a Commando unit. He had a dainty nobility and an austere manner about him; one could have imagined him standing contemptuously unmoved before a baying mob in 1789. He had fled to Britain in 1940 from North Africa where he had been working in the Colonial Service.

'Then I went to Ethiopia with General Le Gentillomme's staff and on to Syria,' he says. 'There I met Bergé and what he told me about his unit seduced me.'

Jordan had the foresight to see its potential even if, when he joined, it

42

continued to languish in Damascus. By the end of December contact had been made with David Stirling. On the last day of 1941, recalls Jordan 'we left for Kabrit in a heavy snowstorm in four lorries we'd requisitioned'. Boutinot says that initially they were openly sceptical.

'At first we didn't believe it, we thought it would be just another camp.'

ON 30 JANUARY, as Stirling and his party returned from a largely innocuous assault on Bouerat, they discovered why the port had been so denuded of shipping and personnel. On the 21st – thirty-six hours before Stirling's raid – Rommel had launched a counter-attack to regain Benghazi. Bouerat had lost its importance for the time being as the Afrika Korps pushed the Allies back across the ground they themselves had ceded to the Eighth Army the previous month. Benghazi was soon in the hands of the Germans, as was most of Cyrenaica, including Jalo Oasis.

At Kabrit, Stirling found Paddy Mayne dripping with truculence, uninterested in how the raid had gone, uninterested in everything. Stirling had planned to appoint Jock Lewes training officer but his death had forced him into a hasty reshuffle in early January. There had been no other suitable candidates so he had asked Mayne to take charge. The Irishman had taken the appointment as an affront, insinuating that it was an appointment motivated by envy (Mayne had destroyed a further twenty-seven planes when he revisited Tamit on 24 December, while Stirling had yet to get off the mark). Instead of training the new recruits Mayne had retired to his tent in a sulk. He emerged when he needed a drink in the sergeants' mess.

'When Paddy walked into that mess and the drinking started you didn't say "I'm off to bed",' recalls Du Vivier. 'You stayed there till he'd finished, till dawn or sometimes later. Rounds would come up one after another and you actually drank yourself sober.'

Stirling realized his error of judgement and promised Mayne he would never again confine him to a non-operational role.

Yet despite Mayne's mulligrubs, Stirling was pleased at the progress made by the recruits. The French were already qualified paratroopers –

43

and they had undergone explosives training in England, too – but they still tackled everything with brio.

'The training was very hard,' recalls Boutinot. 'We did a lot of marching, a lot of jumping from lorries and every morning Sergeant Major Glaze took us for PT. Everybody went, British and French. We played basketball against the English and football and rugby.'

The egalitarian nature of Kabrit surprised Jordan: 'From what I had seen of the British Army a great distinction existed between the officers and men; it didn't in the SAS. At meal times the cook would shout "come and get it" and we would all form one queue.' The food they waited for wasn't spectacular, recounts Jordan, 'soup and corned beef mixed with water and if we were lucky a tin of potatoes'. The British drank tea with their food, the French were given wine.

'They thought all we French ever drank was wine,' says Jordan, 'so even when it was 40°C they insisted on giving us wine. We all wanted tea so eventually we protested and were given tea.'

Some of the British took more readily to the French than others. Storie didn't have much time for them; Du Vivier, fluent in French, chatted happily away. Others, the less shy ones, got by with hand gestures and *Franglais*.

'Johnny Cooper was not a French speaker,' says Boutinot, 'but he was often with us because he was a *bon viveur* who liked a big life. Stirling spoke French with a stutter. "Com ... com ... comment all ... allez vous?" When we first saw him we thought he looked clumsy.'

Mayne was known to the French as '*l'armoire*' [the wardrobe] in tribute to his impressive physique, but to Jordan he was '*le grand tueur*' [the great killer]. Mayne's bloodlust unnerved him. Stirling, in contrast, 'had a productive imagination ... [and] this incredible human warmth that gave you wings!'

THERE WAS LITTLE in the way of entertainment in Kabrit for the men. Just the camp mess. If it was excitement they were after, and they had the time – and the money – Cairo was the place to go.* With the Eighth Army

44

consolidating their defensive positions on the Gazala Line the battlefield was static, and as the next moonless period wasn't until mid-March Stirling told the men to go and enjoy themselves.

While the officers drank John Collinses or Rye Highballs in the elegant surrounds of the Shepheards Hotel, the Turf Club or the sporting club on Gezira Island, the men would seek out one of the many bars where they could get a Stella beer, the local brew that cost two piastres. The more adventurous, or the more naïve, asked for arrack, a Middle Eastern spirit distilled from grain that gave the unsuspecting no mercy.

'Arrack had several names,' recalls Du Vivier. 'Ouzo was one, zibib was another [different regions had different names for it]. It was a colourless liquid that tasted of aniseed. When you added water it went a milky colour and it seemed to take its effect when you came out of the bar into the fresh air. It gave you a feeling of great strength.' Rumours spread through 'L' Detachment that if you had spent the night on arrack and had a glass of water the next morning you were 'just as pissed as you were the night before'.

One of the favourite bars with the British was the Sweet Melodies. Bob McDougall, who was in the Middle East with the Commandos before joining the SAS in 1942 remembers that 'You could go in there at 2.30 or 3 p.m. and you could get a drink and a sandwich and it was very pleasant; go in there at 9.30 in the evening and it was getting a bit noisy; at 10.30 the chairs were flying, the tables were flying'. The resident band moved their stage higher and higher to avoid the fighting before eventually they played behind a wire grille.

For a lot of soldiers the time spent in Cairo's watering holes was an opportunity to build up some Dutch courage before a trip to El Berka, the city's red light district known to the British as the 'street of 1,000 arseholes'.

BILL CUMPER HAD enjoyed his share of wild nights. He had joined the Royal Engineers as a sapper in the 1930s and built a reputation for himself

---

* Cairo had never had it so good as in those early war years. By early 1943 one report said that Allied troops were spending £3,000,000 a month in the city and its note circulation had increased from 20,000,000 before the war to 90,000,000 in 1943.

as a heavy drinker. In peacetime his irreverent Cockney wit had masked a fabulously inventive mind for explosives. When Cumper was seconded to 'L' Detachment in January 1942 he was a captain. The French loved him. He had no airs or graces, no impenetrable English reserve. He taught the French how to make Lewes bombs and how to swear in Cockney rhyming slang. For two weeks he delighted the French, and then he was gone, transferred to another post. Stirling learned of his wizardry on his return from Bouerat. He made some enquiries and discovered that Cumper was now in charge of installing the sanitary fittings of a military hospital in Alexandria. Stirling used his celebrated pull and a week later Bill Cumper rejoined 'L' Detachment.

Albert Youngman came under Cumper's tutelage shortly after he arrived at Kabrit. 'Bill taught us how to make the Lewes bombs, which gave you a bit of a headache because of the ammonal. He'd make us sit there and make them over and over until he was satisfied. He also taught us in the use of gelignite, primer cord, gun cotton, which was used mainly for cutting railway lines.'

Cumper taught the men the difference between a blasting charge and a cutting charge, how to use pressure switches, the formulae for calculating the amount of explosive needed for specific jobs and, perhaps most importantly, his golden rule for all would-be saboteurs: always walk away from a charge. Run and you might trip up, then you're in trouble.

The destructive tentacles of 'L' Detachment reached out into branches of the British armed forces. Seekings spent a morning with an RAF fitter who told them that before they raided an airfield they should agree whether to blow off the left wings or the right wings.

'Because like us,' he told Seekings, 'the Germans will have a certain amount of spare left wings and a certain amount of spare rights. But they won't have enough spare lefts if you blow only left wings off.'

'Similarly,' explained Seekings, 'if you smashed the dashboard of a plane it was out of action.'

Replacements had to be shipped from Italy and that took time, assuming the vessel wasn't sunk on its journey. Storie says that 'sometimes we left the plane alone but put a charge down the hollow tube of the [pilot's] seat and squeezed a 24-hour time pencil in the hope a German would be in the plane when it exploded'.

MARCH TURNED OUT to be a frustrating month for Stirling. Between the 8th and the 13th, a series of raids were carried out against Axis airfields in the Benghazi area. Mayne knocked out fifteen aircraft at Berka, Fraser's party managed one aircraft and eight repair wagons at Barce, Stirling's bad luck continued with a deserted airfield at Benina and Du Vivier's party was unable to penetrate the defences of Slonta airfield.

Stirling then led a daring sortie into Benghazi harbour with the intention of blowing up shipping. The seven-man party entered the town as easily as they had got into Bouerat, but the outcome was even more disappointing than that raid. The folding canoe they had with them lacked a vital component and couldn't be assembled. Stirling cursed his never-ending run of bad luck. Johnny Cooper, who judged a town on the strength of the entertainment on offer, was singularly unimpressed with the place: 'I'm afraid that there's not much nightlife in Benghazi, sir. Completely dead. Can't say it would be my choice of place to live.'

Stirling agreed. But it was the quietness of Benghazi that convinced him another raid would be worthwhile.

Two months later, in late May during a moonless period, Stirling returned to Benghazi with five men, one of whom was the sitting Conservative Member of Parliament for Lancaster, Fitzroy Maclean, and one of whom was Randolph Churchill. The Prime Minister's son was grudgingly accepted by the men of 'L' Detachment, but no more. Since the disbandment of Layforce, Randolph Churchill had had a spell in charge of MEHQ's propaganda branch; it was a role to which he was eminently suited, prone as he was to extruding hot air. Alan Moorhead, the war correspondent, described him at the time as 'aggressive, headstrong, opinionated'. One 'L' Detachment veteran describes him as a 'big, blustering, fat, useless no-good'.

47

When Randolph Churchill turned up at Kabrit in April 1942 he presented Stirling with a problem. He was not 'L' Detachment material; for a start he was overweight and motivated more by wearing the flaming sword cap badge than in going behind enemy lines. But Stirling knew he and his father were close; humour Randolph, Stirling fancied, and the Prime Minister will hear what a good job we're doing. In a letter to his mother dated 14 May, Stirling told her that watching Randolph doing his parachute training is 'tremendously entertaining'. He went on to say that although he had lost $1^1/_2$ stones in training, Randolph was still 'damn fat'. All the pounds he shed during his training he put back on in the evening. He was a Francophile, like his father, and Boutinot remembers him well:

'He used to bring a case of whisky every night and we put it in a big dustbin with some pineapple and mixed it all up. He was drunk all the time and one day I met him outside my tent. He was fast asleep, completely nude, and the sun was beating down on him.'

But Benghazi in May proved to be as fruitless for Stirling as it had been in March. The two inflatable boats they had brought with them had both sprung leaks on the journey across the desert. The noise they had made as they tried desperately to inflate them by the harbour's edge had alerted even the normally docile Italian guards, and only the linguistic skill and icy nerve of Fitzroy Maclean saved them.

'We arrived at the main gate that controlled the entrance to the docks,' said Cooper, 'and Fitzroy called out the guard and tore them off a strip for their appearance and general idleness. They were all Italians, clearly rattled at this tirade, and Fitzroy said we were German officers on a training mission and that, quite frankly, we were appalled at the lax security.' The Italians saluted with a flourish and opened the gate for the British saboteurs.

Cooper had by now become part of Stirling's inner circle. Along with Seekings, he accompanied Stirling on most of his raids and the pair even attended planning meetings, together with Mayne, in the Cairo flat of Stirling's brother. Once Stirling – who loathed administration of any kind – had studied the aerial photographs and the intelligence briefings he decided that, for the next operation, he would leave the minutiae – petrol, ration and ammunition requirements – in the hands of 'young Cooper' and Seekings. They addressed Mayne and Stirling by their Christian names and as Seekings later admitted they became a little 'big-headed'.

'I can imagine why a lot of people didn't like us,' says Seekings, 'particularly Johnny with his tongue ... we owed no allegiance to anyone except the unit and we didn't take any crap from some of these young officers.'

Their task at the end of May 1942 was to tie up the loose ends of a plan Stirling had proposed to Auchinleck for a series of simultaneous raids on coastal airfields. The raids would occur on the night of 13 June, at the same time as Auchinleck launched his own offensive, the objective of which was once again to relieve the pressure on Malta. The Germans had stepped up their blockade and bombardment of the island in the first five months of 1942 and its inhabitants were on the brink of starvation unless Allied convoys could get through. Auchinleck's offensive was to coincide with the departure of two convoys to Malta, one from Alexandria and the other from Gibraltar.

The plan was Stirling's most ambitious yet. He was taking Cooper and Seekings to raid Benina airfield, while Mayne would hit Berka Satellite and a French party (under André Zirnheld, a professor of Philosophy in Tunis before the war), went for Berka Main, all three airfields just a few miles south of Benghazi. Another French section, led by Lieutenant Jacquier, was detailed to attack Barce, 60 miles north-east of Benghazi. Captain Bergé and George Jellicoe, the son of the famous First World War admiral, set sail in a submarine with three men to storm Heraklion airfield on Crete.

The most daring raid was given to Jordan. He would attack airfields in Derna and Martuba with a composite party of fifteen Frenchmen and ten men from the Special Interrogation Group (SIG) under the command of Captain Herbert Buck, an Englishman who had won the Military Cross fighting with the Punjab Regiment.

Most of Buck's men were German Jews who had fled to Palestine in the 1930s. The exceptions were two Germans soldiers called Bruckner and Esser; they were former French Legionnaires who had fought against their own countrymen in 1940 and then switched sides after France's capitulation. After their capture in the desert they vacillated back towards the Allies, declaring themselves fervent anti-Nazis. British Intelligence scrutinized their backgrounds and cleared them.

Buck had obtained four vehicles for the operation, a military Volkswagen, an Opel car and two lorries. All of them had belonged to the Afrika Korps. Jordan and his men would hide in the lorries while the SIG, masquerading as Germans, drove them to three airfields between Martuba and Derna. Jordan wasn't 'warm' to the plan but he was in an invidious position.

'We had been waiting since January for a mission and it was now June. It would have been impossible for me to refuse this adventure.'

They left Siwa Oasis on 8 June, a strange bunch: thirteen Germans and fifteen Frenchmen led by an English officer. The LRDG escorted them over 200 miles to Baltet-ez-Zelagh, still 50 miles south of Derna. On 11 June they parted company. The RV was fixed for a week's time.

The next day, 12 June, they were less than 30 miles from their target. At an Italian roadblock Buck chatted up the two guards. Been fighting the British for a long time. Everyone tired and hungry. What's the password for the month? The two Italians responded without hesitation. The challenge was 'Siesta' and the reply 'Eldorado'. A few miles further on they encountered a roadblock manned by several German military policemen. The driver of the Volkswagen, a Jew called Hass, began talking to the sergeant in charge. He got out of the car and walked round and opened the boot. He handed a crate of beer to the sergeant.

'It's English. Call it the spoils of war'.

The sergeant thanked Hass and stepped aside to let them through.

Jordan and Buck carried out a reconnaissance of the airfields later that afternoon. At Derna West a squadron of Messerschmitt 110s sat obediently on the aerodrome. At Derna East they counted a dozen Stukas. That night they embarked on their mission, leaving Buck at an RV with the

50

Volkswagen; Corporal Jean Tourneret and four men in one lorry left to level Martuba airfield, while Jordan and Pierre de Bourmont, each in command of a stick, shared a lorry to attack the Derna airfields. The driver of their lorry was Bruckner. It took him more than an hour to cover the six miles to the outskirts of the airfield.

'The lorry kept spluttering to a halt,' says Jordan, 'and Bruckner would get out and spend five minutes with his head under the bonnet.'

The Frenchmen's nerves, already rubbed red raw by lack of sleep, became more inflamed with every interruption.

Eventually the lorry arrived at Derna West. Music was audible from one of the nearby hangars. The French could also hear Bruckner and Hass talking in the front of the lorry. Bruckner got out of the lorry and walked towards the hangar.

'It's OK,' Hass told them, 'he's going to ask the Germans for a spanner.'

Jordan admits he was 'at the limit of his nerves', his senses dulled by tiredness. 'I should have done something when Bruckner got out of the lorry,' he reflects. 'I should have got my men out and formed a defensive ring round the lorry. But I didn't, and I still carry the remorse.'

When he heard footsteps outside the lorry Jordan peered out from behind the canvas. 'I was grabbed and pulled out of the lorry.'

His capture triggered a chain of calamitous events. The dozens of Germans surrounding the lorry were clearly agitated, their cries of *'Heraus! Aber Schnell!'* tinged with fear. One by one the Frenchmen jumped down from the lorry, their hands in the air.

'The only one who stayed in the lorry was Hass,' says Jordan. 'He was a Jew, so he knew what would happen to him. He decided to try and save us by sacrificing himself. All our weapons and explosives were in the lorry and he fired at them with his machine gun.'

Hass and the lorry erupted in a ball of fire. Exploding bullets flew in all directions, scattering the Germans. The two men guarding Jordan threw themselves to the floor, 'so I ran off'. Jordan knew from his earlier reconnaissance that the northern edge of the airfield was the way out. He waited there for ten minutes but none of his men followed him.

Jordan slinked towards the RV noiselessly. When he reached it Buck was leaning against the Volkswagen. Jordan told him what had happened. For a moment he was shocked, then the Englishman acted with alacrity. Bruckner must have been the culprit and Bruckner knew the RV. They left immediately, driving towards the meeting point with the LRDG. There they waited cautiously for five days. Jordan insisted that they remained an extra day, until daybreak on the 19th, in case any of his men should appear. None did.*

The betrayal at Derna rebounded on the other raiding parties as airfield defences were put on a heightened state of alert. As Roger Boutinot, in Jacquier's party, neared Barce airfield, 'all the lights came on as we approached ... it was so well guarded it was clear they were waiting for us'. They returned to the LRDG RV, blowing up a petrol dump as they went.

André Zirnheld's party managed to destroy six aircraft on Berka Main airfield but, says Jimmy Storie, 'they went in an hour before their time and we were caught on the damned 'drome putting bombs on various things'. Mayne led Storie, Trooper Arthur Warburton and Bob Lilley off Berka Satellite, a mile from the main airport, as the Germans and Italians opened fire on each other from opposite ends of the landing strip. When they realized their error the Axis troops fanned out in search of the saboteurs. Storie remembers they spent a couple of hours 'lying in a shallow ditch as Germans came up and down beside us'. They split up at sunrise, Storie and Mayne and Warburton with Lilley, their destination the Benghazi escarpment.

'Me and Paddy had been going for a few miles,' recalls Storie, 'when we climbed one escarpment and just over the other side I saw a German armoured car. Fortunately we were on its blind side, so we slid down and

---

* Most were rounded up on the airfield although Guichaoua and Vidal escaped, but were recaptured on 20 June and 13 June respectively. When Tourneret's stick returned to the RV the next morning the Germans were waiting for them. Seven of the French drowned two months later when their prison ship was torpedoed by a British submarine in the Aegean. Guichaoua died of dysentery the same month. De Bourmont, Vidal and Prados later escaped from their POW camp and rejoined the SAS in Europe. From subsequent Intelligence reports it emerged that Bruckner had been awarded the *Deutsch Kreuz in Gold* for his actions, two grades higher than the Iron Class, first class.

52

waited for an hour or so until it moved on.' The pair continued until they reached a Senussi camp. 'We had a meal with them, it was goat meat but we weren't being fussy. While we were there we saw Bob Lilley coming towards us on a bike.' Lilley's tale was one of high adventure. He had lost Arthur Warburton [whose fate has never been determined] so continued on alone, at one point walking through the middle of a German laager. Out on the other side he chanced upon an Italian soldier on his pushbike. Lilley had knocked the man to the ground, throttled him and had been pedalling furiously ever since.

The next day Mayne and his two companions reached the RV. Stirling had already returned. When he heard of Mayne's misfortune he couldn't resist a wee gloat. Finally he had outscored the Irishman. Stirling's raid on the maintenance depot at Benina had been productive. Cooper had accompanied his officer inside the first hangar while Seekings stood guard outside.

'Inside this hangar were an assortment of German aircraft,' recalled Cooper. 'I had just put a bomb on a Me110 when I heard this voice behind me: "Sergeant Cooper, this is my aircraft. Take your bomb off and use it on the JU52 at the other side of the aircraft." I did as I was told.'

They visited two more hangars before withdrawing. On their way, said Cooper, they stopped outside a guard house. They could hear merry chatter inside. Stirling gently pushed open the door with his foot and 'bowled a grenade along the floor and closed the door'. It exploded as they ran into the darkness.

Stirling was so thrilled by his success, he asked Mayne if he fancied seeing for himself the damage. A few hours later the two of them, along with Cooper, Bob Lilley, Seekings, Storie and a Palestinian Jew called Karl Kahane were on their way to Benina on board a truck they had borrowed from the LRDG. Mayne was driving, Stirling sat next to him, and the men were in the back, grinning at their officers' bravado. They hadn't been going long before they saw the roadblock up ahead.

'A German sergeant major came up to the truck,' says Storie, 'and took a good look at it and at us. Kahane spoke German and said we were on a special mission but he could see we were British. But at the same time the German could hear the sound of weapons being cocked, and he was obviously a wise man. He knew that if he made a false move, he would be the first to go. So he turned to the men on the roadblock and told them to open the gates.'

The fraught encounter brought Stirling to his senses. One roadblock had been negotiated but he knew every German in the area would now be on a state of high alert. But as Mayne prepared to swing off into the desert to start the journey home, Stirling spotted a well-lit building a few hundred yards further on.

'It was a roadside café,' says Storie, 'and sitting on the veranda enjoying a drink were a lot of Germans and Italians. We drew up alongside the café and opened fire. They didn't have time to defend themselves, we just blew everything to bits.'

They arrived back safely at Siwa on 21 June. A few hours later the LRDG brought in Buck and Jordan. The rest of the French ran to greet them when they saw the dust from the patrol's vehicles. All they found was Jordan, shrunken and disconsolate.

'He was crying,' says Boutinot, 'it was the only time I ever saw him upset.'

Jordan remembers still the depths of his despair. ' I was very depressed coming back alone, but I was so grateful to Stirling for helping me psychologically. He never doubted my capabilities, never lost faith in me. Instead he gave me the opportunity to create a second French unit.'

A few days later Jellicoe returned from the Heraklion raid with the news that Bergé had been captured during the assault. Jordan was now in charge of the French detachment.

It was not just for Jordan and Boutinot that 21 June 1942 was a mournful day. It was also arguably the date the Allies hit rock bottom in the desert war. In the late afternoon Stirling heard on the wireless that Tobruk had surrendered to Rommel. This news, coupled with the considerable advances already made by the Axis forces since Rommel launched his offensive at the end of May, precipitated a swift evacuation of Siwa by 'L' Detachment and the LRDG. Stirling sent his men back to Kabrit, while he headed to Cairo to drum up support for his next venture.

'IT IS VERY SAD,' wrote Malcolm Pleydell to his girlfriend on hearing of Tobruk's fall. He added that there was an air of depression in Cairo at the news, which was deepened by the pall of smoke that hovered over the city like a baleful vulture as the MEHQ burned their files in anticipation of a German arrival. By the end of June the Germans had been halted at El Alamein, a small railway station whose time would come later.

'The old days of fluid warfare were over,' remembered Heinz Schmidt, Rommel's former aide-de-camp, now a frontline commander. '[We] were condemned to the dreariness and deadliness of static warfare.'

Pleydell, who had recently been appointed 'L' Detachment's first medical officer, preferred to tell his girlfriend about his new life.

'I bathe in the Bitter Lakes at least once a day, though the water seems very salty. One gets pretty tired so that early to bed is the rule ... it's funny to think that I am in this racket [but] I wasn't really happy in the self-satisfied air of stupidity at the canal zone hospital. Few of them knew what fighting was. Doctors, en masse, seem such a dull lot. They forget there is any excitement in life.'

Stirling's flying visit to Cairo was typically frenetic. First, he fulfilled his social obligations by attending the wedding of Bill Cumper. Also present was Bill Deakins, a Canadian-born Royal Engineer corporal who had been recruited by Cumper the previous month. After toasting Cumper and his Greek wife, Stirling embarked on another round of chivvying and chasing. Within a week he'd appropriated fifteen American jeeps – known to the men as Willie Bantams – and a fleet of 3-ton Ford lorries. He also managed to purloin from an Alexandria warehouse a dozen Vickers K machine guns from the obsolete Gloster Gladiator biplanes. The Vickers' rate of fire was 1,200 rounds per minute, and Stirling talked the Royal Electrical and Mechanical Engineers (REME) into mounting the guns fore and aft in the jeeps.

Arthur 'Tommo' Thomson, a newcomer to 'L' Detachment, was one of those responsible for jeep maintenance. He had learnt to drive in south London as a 13-year-old – joy-riding in Morris Cowleys left in the car park of the Olympia Exhibition Centre – and by the age of 16 he was a

55

lorry driver delivering fruit from Covent Garden to country markets up and down the country.

'The jeeps were our saviours,' he says. 'We didn't think much of them at first; thought they were a bloody toy. But they were so strong and versatile; they carried our bedding, ammo, food, water, personal kit, everything.'

In time the jeeps were modified still further by the REME. A water condenser was fitted to the front of the radiator and the suspension was strengthened but even so few jeeps survived more than two operations in the desert.

'Some only did one trip,' says Thomson, 'but most managed two. We gave them such a hiding. Climbing a 150ft sand dune knocks cobblers out of a gear box and engine.'

When the jeeps arrived at Kabrit they drew admiring glances from the men; few, however, had any idea how to handle the vehicle. Stirling told Thomson to put them all through a crash course.

'We'd go off into the desert and I taught them gears, four wheel drive, in and out, changing, clutch, steering, the lot.'

WHILE STIRLING HAD been amassing equipment and transport in Cairo, the Eighth Army under Auchinleck's command (he had dismissed Ritchie after Tobruk's capitulation) had repelled the German advance west of the pyramids and were now dug in between the edge of the Qattara Depression in the south and El Alamein in the north. The Afrika Korps now began to flounder. Rommel, intoxicated by his capture of Tobruk, had stretched his lines of supply to breaking point by pursuing the British so far east. Stirling had caught a whiff of vulnerability.

On 3 July the most experienced members of 'L' Detachment left Kabrit on what was to be a largely self-sufficient operation. On the night of the 7th, as the Eighth Army launched an offensive to regain the coastal region around Mersah Matruh, Stirling's men were asked to destroy the forward German airfields. Stirling established his patrol base at a remote spot called Qaret Tartura on the north-western edge of the Qattara Depression. They then moved 60 miles north, through the German rear positions,

56

until they were within striking distance of the airfields. Here they split into their raiding parties. One section went to attack Sidi Barrani; Zirnheld and Jellicoe were detailed to strafe the coastal road; Fraser and Jordan were to attack two of the Fuka airfields; and Mayne and Stirling headed for Bagoush. Mayne led a small party on to Bagoush, going in on foot initially to plant their bombs. When some of them failed to go off Mayne and Stirling decided to initiate a new method of attack. Johnny Cooper was firing the single Vickers as Stirling drove on to the airfield:

'He kept to a nice steady pace of about 15mph and I opened fire at a line of CR42s that were soon in flames. Unfortunately after three magazines the Vickers had a seizure from overheating ... but the damage done to the gun was more than compensated by the devastation caused to the enemy.'

Subsequent reconnaissance photographs confirmed that thirty-seven planes had been destroyed on Bagoush.

FRASER'S AND JORDAN'S sections drove to within a few miles of the Fuka airfields before covering the home straight on foot. Pleydell and the two drivers remained behind with the vehicles. They were asked to shine a torch at ten-minute intervals between 2 a.m. and 3 a.m., a homing beacon for the raiders. Pleydell watched Fraser, too 'young and boyish for this sort of thing', ginger up his men and 'then away they went, their figures bobbing up and down until they were lost in the darkness'. Five minutes later Jordan's team melted into the night.

Fraser returned to the RV shortly after 2.30 a.m., having found the airfield too well guarded. As they'd crawled away they passed a band of jittery Italian guards, an inviting target, Fraser told Pleydell. He'd withdrawn a grenade from his pack, cradled it in his hand for a few seconds, but he couldn't bring himself to throw it.

Jordan's party showed up a few minutes later, exhausted but elated at having blown up eight planes. They too had found the airfield well guarded and an Italian sentry had challenged them.

'I spoke to him in German and he let us through,' remembers Jordan.

Once they were on the airfield, they followed a well-rehearsed procedure in the shadow of each Messerschmitt 109.

'I prepared the bombs with ten-minute delays,' says Boutinot, 'and Jordan placed them on the planes which were lined up beside each other.'

Sergeant René Martin and Officer Cadet Michel Legrand covered the pair the whole time. Boutinot, as nervous as any 20-year-old would be, derived strength from Jordan's sang-froid. 'He was so calm throughout.'

The Italians realized they had been duped only after the raiders had placed bombs on half a dozen aircraft. They began firing indiscriminately into the darkness. Martin got hit in the hand but Boutinot and Jordan attached bombs to another two planes before withdrawing to the RV.*

The following week Jordan, Legrand, Boutinot and Louis Guégan raided another of the Fuka airfields, No. 16.

'We placed bombs on the first two planes without incident,' says Jordan.

Under each plane was an empty mattress, deserted by the sentry who should have been there. But at the third plane, recalls Jordan, an Italian guard 'challenged us timidly as he sheltered behind the rudder'. Legrand aimed and fired, 'but his gun jammed so he struck him with its butt'. As Boutinot placed the bomb on the plane, Jordan 'felled the Italian with two shots from my Smith & Wesson'. At the same time Legrand collapsed, his right arm haemorrhaging blood. Guégan shouted that they were under fire from the other guards. They ran towards the other three planes they could see, a spoor of blood marking their route, and planted their bombs. Then they slunk off towards the LRDG RV.

Legrand's wound troubled Jordan for a long time, his analytical mind baffled. If Legrand had been shot by an Italian why hadn't he heard more gunfire as they finished their sabotage? He omitted his concerns from the report he wrote on the raid. Now, however, for the first time, he concedes that 'it was me who wounded Legrand ... one of my two bullets

---

* In Pleydell's book, *Born of the Desert*, first published in 1945 under his nom de guerre of Malcolm James, he described the French return to the RV as 'theatrical ... as if they'd just completed a marathon'. Legrand was 'mad' with anger, says Jordan, when he read the condescension. 'We ran only because we thought they might not wait for us at the RV [because of the firing]. He also criticised me for alerting the guards on the airfield ... but this doctor understood nothing about war.'

went through the Italian and hit him'. Jordan failed to report another incident during the raid because 'I was anxious to avoid creating difficulties between the French and the British'. When they were picked up by the LRDG patrol their escape route skirted the airfield's perimeter. They opened fire from their vehicles at the undamaged planes, but the first of the three cars ran into a ditch.

'I was thrown four metres without being hurt,' Jordan says, 'but Guégan suffered multiple contusions and his foot was trapped under the front wheel.' All around them in the darkness 'we could hear discussions between the Italians [guards] who wished to intervene but didn't want to do anything rash'. As they eased Guégan from the wreckage, says Jordan, the leader of the LRDG patrol, 'gripped by panic … ran away towards the aerodrome's exit. I had to run after him and bring him back'.

'WHERE THE HELL IS IT?' Stirling's question was polite but forceful. 'Have we gone wrong?'

Mike Sadler shook his head. 'No. I reckon it's two miles ahead.'

Stirling looked at Jordan, neither of them convinced. Suddenly the desert was bathed in a multitude of shimmering lights. Then 'Whoosh!' a German bomber came in low over their heads and touched down on Sidi Haneish airfield, two miles dead ahead, give or take the odd yard.

'That was when we knew,' says Jordan, 'that Sadler was right again.'

Sadler had navigated the convoy of twenty jeeps across 70 miles in the dead of night to an isolated desert landing strip. It was a masterly accomplishment and, even if Stirling did occasionally take Sadler's brilliance for granted, he knew he would be lost, literally, without him. Sadler had impressed Stirling ever since he had guided his raiding party to Tamit in December 1941.

Sadler didn't strike one at first glance as the unflappable desert adventurer that he was; the 22-year-old Englishman had a gentle and intelligent face with a smile never far from it. His sharp eye for the absurd delighted in some of the more inane foibles of army life. Sadler's penchant for globetrotting had taken him to Rhodesia in 1937 and he spent two

59

years farming before enlisting in the Rhodesian artillery. By the time the regiment was posted to North Africa he had risen to sergeant.

'Unfortunately I fell out with the chap in charge of our battery. We used to lay in bed fully dressed ready to jump out and man the guns in the event of an alarm. I permitted my soldiers to wear sand shoes because you couldn't get out of the sleeping bag in army boots. But this officer was determined we wear boots and so we had an argument, the outcome of which was that I was marched in front of the CO. "This won't do, Sadler," he said. "You must apologise otherwise I might have to reduce you to the ranks." "Oh, that's all right," I said. "I'll reduce myself to the ranks."'

At the end of 1941, over a beer in a Cairo bar, Sadler was invited to join the Rhodesian patrol of the LRDG. Then in June 1942, Stirling managed to prise him out of one specialist unit and into another.

Sadler had done his job in navigating the jeeps to the edge of Sidi Haneish. His crew and another jeep now took up their position on the south-east corner of the airfield to collect any stragglers. Stirling led the other eighteen jeeps on to the landing strip, his vehicle the tip of a double-headed arrow. Jordan was on his left and slightly behind, one of three French jeeps in the raiding party. Normally Jordan liked to drive his own jeep but this evening he was working the guns while Corporal Boven drove.

'I'm afraid to say that because I normally drove the poor man was more scared of me than of the raid.'

As they accelerated on to the airfield Cooper remembered Stirling 'shouting words of encouragement as I began firing the Vickers. He drove up the middle of the runway at around 20mph and either side of us were an assortment of planes. I really couldn't miss'.

Jimmy Storie was the front gunner in the rear jeep of the left-hand column. 'Gun discipline was vital. We had to keep in a strict formation, two abreast, firing outwards the whole time. We reached the end of the runway and swung round, keeping in the same formation and picking off any planes that hadn't been hit.'

The heat from the exploding planes was intense; men's eyebrows were singed and their eyes smarted, but they continued firing.

'It was like a duck shoot,' said Cooper, 'just pouring fire into Junkers and Stukas and watching the bullets tear through the fuselage and then, Bang!, they'd explode.'

Storie remembers the air being full of spent cartridge cases from the Vickers; others talked about the nauseous fumes from the aviation fuel that gushed across the runway. Jordan says the French weren't as profligate with their ammunition as the British [something for which Stirling castigated his own men later].

'We fired only when we had a target clearly in our sights, whereas the British were opening fire all over the place.'

Sadler, meanwhile, over in the south-east corner, had a 'ringside view of the tracer ripping through the aircraft. It was marvellous'.

The airfield's defenders had been dumbfounded by the sudden savagery of the onslaught. It wasn't until the jeeps were making their way back down the airfield that they opened fire. Storie could hear bullets whistling over his head but 'no one much bothered about it'.

'There was quite a bit of return fire from the guards,' recalled Cooper, 'but it wasn't very accurate. The burning planes and all the smoke obscured the guards' view.' Cooper and Stirling were unlucky. Theirs was the only jeep to be hit. 'We got a shell through the cylinder head and hopped on to Sandy Scratchley's.'

Lying dead in the back of Scratchley's jeep was John Robson, a 21-year-old artilleryman who had joined the unit at the same time as Nobby Redington. He had been shot in the head, the only casualty of the operation, but Storie's jeep had run into a problem as they left the scene.

'We drove through the perimeter fence and some wire we'd cut through to get in got wrapped around one of our wheels. With all these bullets flying around I had to jump out with the wire-cutters and free the wheel.'

A mile beyond the perimeter fence Stirling called a halt. They had a little over two hours till dawn. They would split into three parties and make their way south to the RV. Speed was of the essence, he reminded them. Daylight would bring retaliation. Sadler, still in his corner, was taking photos for posterity of the thirty-seven destroyed or damaged

61

aircraft. 'I had taken a camera along with me and I took a lot of photos in the aftermath of the raid. The whole thing had been so impressive. What was also impressive, mind you, was the speed at which the Germans got the airfield working again. Within an hour of the attack there were planes coming into land, even though on either side of the runway there were still burning wrecks.'

From the furious gestures and shouting of the shaken pilots, Sadler could see that the Germans were hell-bent on revenge.

'When you went on an operation in the desert,' says Sadler, 'it wasn't the raid that worried you, it was how the hell you were going to get away afterwards from the Germans.'

Stirling's party hammered their jeeps over the stony desert floor, but at first light they had covered only 40 miles. Sadler was even closer to the airfield. 'I didn't get away until just before dawn,' he says.

He drove through a ground mist, blind beyond 20 yards, when out of the mist loomed the hind vehicles of a German column.

'It was rather a nasty surprise,' recalls Sadler. 'They were all standing round their vehicles and they looked long and hard at us. They weren't very alert, however, so we carried on driving right past the front of the column.'

The same mist shrouded Stirling long enough for him to find a wadi where they concealed the jeeps under some thick camel scrub. They brewed up some tea, then buried Robson. One of the men made a cross out of an old ration box, while the others stood over the grave in silence. The loneliness of the spot touched them all. One, Lieutenant Stephen Hastings, wondered if any living thing, even a gazelle, would ever pass through this desolate spot again.

Similar thoughts went through the minds of François Martin and his men as they buried André Zirnheld. The two officers' jeeps had become separated from Jordan and were assailed by four Stukas as they tried to hide in a wadi. Zirnheld was hit in the shoulder, then the stomach. Martin dragged him to safety but he died a few hours later.

'They buried him at nightfall,' says Jordan, 'and they stuck a wooden cross over his grave with the words "*mort au champ d'honneur*".'

JEFF DU VIVIER WAS pleased to see the old faces return to Kabrit after the Sidi Haneish raid. Of the 'Originals', the fifty-five men who had jumped on 'L' Detachment's first mission, only sixteen now remained. Du Vivier's task as a training instructor was to knock out of the new recruits all the military training they had previously undergone. From now on, they would do things his way.

Du Vivier had been awarded the Military Medal for his exploits in the Agedabia raid. 'I suppose Stirling thought I was capable of training the recruits,' he says. 'Was I happy doing it? Well, I was told to do it so I had no choice. I was doing the job Paddy Mayne hated.'

Du Vivier was involved in the training process from start to finish. 'We used to go round various regiments giving pep talks and getting people interested. We took the names of those who were and then asked them down for an interview. But nine times out of ten it was mighty difficult to get hold of people because officers weren't willing to let their people go. Letting their men volunteer for something else wasn't their idea of running a regiment.'

AMONG THE REGIMENTS visited was the 6th Battalion, Grenadier Guards, in Syria. Doug Wright, Sid Downland and Dick Holmes were among the six Guardsmen who volunteered for the SAS and were accepted.

'I was fed up with normal soldiering,' says Downland, who had joined the Guards in 1937.

Wright had enlisted the following year after packing in his job as a farmhand on a Cheshire farm. 'I spent about a quarter of an hour being interviewed,' he remembers. 'They had all your records so they knew what you'd done. I'd had a few punishments, got a stripe and they had taken it away. But they didn't mind if you'd been in a bit of trouble, as long as you could think for yourself.'

Holmes remembers some of the questions he was asked. 'They wanted to know what we were prepared to do. Parachuting was virtually unheard of and that was one of the questions. And they didn't want a maybe, they wanted a yes.'

Stirling didn't just want fighting soldiers. He was also after more specialist skills. Norman Moran was a bored medical orderly who heard about 'L' Detachment in July 1942. He was a 22-year-old Australian who, at the outbreak of war, had been studying at an American university.

'A notice went up one day in the hospital asking for "Volunteers for special service". Mechanics, wireless operators and near the bottom was medical personnel with at least three years' experience. I put my name down and that was disastrous because for the next three weeks the RSM gave me an absolute dog's life.' Moran was eventually called for an interview. 'They started by asking me why I'd applied. I said because I was fed up with the job I'm doing at the moment. I didn't join the army to be in a base hospital on the banks of the Nile. Then he asked why I wanted to commit suicide. I said I didn't want to commit suicide. "Well," he said "are you a gong hunter?" "No," I said, "nothing like that." "Oh, you just want to fight?" I said "Yes." He smiled. "I think we can accommodate you."'

David Danger was a 19-year-old signaller who volunteered but then went down with a bout of sandfly fever and missed the interview. When he recovered he was told to report to Kabrit.

'Seven of us were lined up by RSM Johnny Rose. He told us we were to learn parachuting and then we would operate behind enemy lines. If we didn't like the sound of that then we could step forward and we would be sent back. Two of us stayed, me and a chap who had worked in Ogden's tobacco factory in Liverpool before the war.'

The first thing the new recruits noticed at Kabrit was the quietness.

'There was no bawling,' confirms Du Vivier. 'None of what is commonly known as bullshit. Drilling, saluting officers every time you passed them, it was all forgotten. It was entirely different to the regular army training. You had to learn to think for yourself. If the sergeant said do this, and you didn't think it was right, then you didn't do it.'

After five years in the Guards, Downland found the transition took time. 'In the Grenadiers you didn't question your NCOs, and you certainly didn't call your officers by their Christian names!'

There were other aspects of the relaxed atmosphere at Kabrit that astonished the uninitiated. 'I went into one of the ablutions one day,' recounts Holmes, 'which was just a bloody trough. I looked to my left and there was a German washing ... then this SAS corporal says "OK, Jerry, finished?" And they walked out chatting away to one another.'

Captured prisoners were a common sight around Kabrit. The Italians, in particular, made excellent servants. Arthur Thomson remembers a couple who were brought back to Kabrit.

'They were as happy as pigs in shit. They swept, cleaned, tidied and waited on us. So we said to them, "Write a letter to your families and next time we attack an airfield we'll deliver them." And that's exactly what we did; we chucked a satchel full of letters on to the airfield.'

But the informality of Kabrit was deceptive. Du Vivier and the other training sergeants were observing all the recruits.

'I suppose I did have a lot of say in who passed and who failed. We watched them very carefully to see how they behaved during training. You sort of knew instinctively who was going to make it and who wasn't. It was a personality thing.'

More than anything it was parachute training that stripped men of their bravado. The unfortunate tale of Duffy and Warburton did the rounds before any recruits made their first jump.

'Anyone who refused to jump,' says Youngman, 'was told to keep the 'chute on his back when he left the plane and walk through camp. That way everyone could see he'd refused.'

Men who shied away the first time were given a second chance to jump, sometimes more. Du Vivier remembers a recruit with several refusals to his name. He gave him a final chance.

'But he couldn't do it, so I told him to unhook [the static line] and go and sit at the front. That was him finished. But when he saw his mates all going out he suddenly changed his mind and jumped. Unfortunately he rushed out without hooking himself up.'

TO STIRLING'S DISGUST 'L' Detachment had been ordered back from the desert at the start of August. It was a bitter blow, particularly after the success of Sidi Haneish. Stirling arrived in Cairo to discover Auchinleck had been sacked by Churchill and replaced with General Alexander. There was also a new commander-in-chief of the Eighth Army, General Montgomery. Neither had had much to do with the planning of 'L' Detachment's next mission. That was the work of men who in Stirling's opinion had no appreciation of the nature of the desert war, let alone the guerrilla warfare in which he specialized.

The Eighth Army was so well entrenched along the Alamein Line that Montgomery was planning a big offensive for the end of October, confident that Rommel could advance no further in the interim. But the concern in MEHQ was that the Axis forces supplies were being bolstered by convoys from Italy landing in the ports of Tobruk and Benghazi. Stirling was told to lead a large-scale assault on Benghazi – he had already tried twice, he was reminded – while a simultaneous raid would be carried out against Tobruk. The logistics of the plan horrified Stirling. Over two hundred men – half of whom came from other units other than the SAS – would be transported over 1,000 miles from Cairo to Benghazi in an eighty-vehicle convoy. They would even have two Honey tanks with them.

'THE TWO TANKS did about ten miles and then went kaput!' recalls Roger Boutinot, who was one of the twenty-five Frenchmen in the raiding force. They had left Kufra Oasis on 4 September under Paddy Mayne; Bill Cumper's convoy set out for the RV in the Jebel mountains the next day and Stirling led the third party on the 6th. Ahead of them lay 800 miles of largely enemy desert. Nobby Redington was Sadler's driver.

'I would drive with the sun compass,' remembers Redington, 'and Mike would look at his map and tell me to keep the shadow on an exact point. And he would always take you to the right spot.'

The lazy smile, the calm instructions, Redington assumed Sadler found navigating easy.

66

'It was as though he was born with a compass in his hand,' says Redington.

But the pressure on Sadler was enormous each time he led a patrol across the desert. The slightest error might have had fatal consequences.

'The essential thing was not to let self-doubt creep into your mind,' he says. 'You had to be confident because it was awfully easy – especially at night – to start to feel you were going wrong and should be a little further to the left, or perhaps the right. I was rigid in sticking to the bearings I'd worked out and not allowing those sort of doubts to creep in.'

All three parties were assembled at the RV in the Jebel mountains on 11 September. Officially this was the moment the men discovered their objective; in reality they had known for weeks.

'In the lead-up to the Benghazi raid,' remembers Sadler, 'rumours had been buzzing around Cairo that something was up.'

Stirling had been concerned for some time that the enemy was expecting them. Waiting at the rendezvous were Fitzroy Maclean and a Belgian called Bob Melot, who was working for the British. They told Stirling that their Arab spy had just returned from Benghazi with a worrying report. There were 5,000 Italian troops in the vicinity, not to mention the German battalion encamped on the north-east side of the city. A message was sent to MEHQ. 'Ignore bazaar gossip' was the terse reply.

The main raiding force would leave at dusk. That gave them a couple of hours to carry out last minute preparations. Cooper, Seekings, Riley and Lilley were among a clutch of 'Originals' present.

Of the 'L' Detachment men on their first job, Chris O'Dowd stood out.

'He was a bloody good soldier,' Seekings remembered. The 22-year-old Irishman was a joyful and untamed spirit. A night out in Cairo with O'Dowd was always uproarious. Bob McDougall, who joined 'L' Detachment at the same time as O'Dowd, remembers drinking with him in a bar when a swaggering Australian threw down a challenge.

'They had a competition to see who could punch the hardest,' he says. 'The prize was a crate of Stella beer. The Aussie went first and hit O'Dowd so hard that his chin practically went round his head. O'Dowd just stood

67

there. The Aussie looked at him, reached into his pocket for his wallet, paid for the crate, then buggered off.'

Now, 'Up the Blue' (in the heart of the desert) with the SAS, O'Dowd had taken on a buccaneering look with two mischievous eyes just visible between a scraggy beard and a mass of black curls.

Anthony Drongin was another who'd been identified as a natural soldier, but his personality couldn't have been more different from O'Dowd's. He was quiet and introspective, a troubled man in the opinion of Bill Deakins.

'Apparently before joining us he'd been an RSM before being stripped [of his rank]. No one could ever find out what he'd done but I think he had a mission with death.'

The column of jeeps and lorries moved off at sundown on 13 September. Their Arab guide turned out to be inept. They got lost on the approach and the RAF diversionary raid on Benghazi had finished before they were anywhere near the harbour. Mike Sadler was with Stirling at the front of the convoy.

'He said, "we're never going to get there driving in the dark; switch on the lights". So we did, and this long column of glow worms approached Benghazi. The whole thing was doomed.'

They were driving along a sunken road shortly before 0430 hours when they saw a cantilever gate in front of them weighted down and secured by a barrel of earth.

'Jim Almonds was sent for,' recalls Sadler, 'because there was thought to be a pill box further up the road that he was going to take, and the rest of us would drive through.' Almonds drove up to the roadblock in his jeep.

Bill Cumper, who was standing by Stirling at the roadblock, lifted the barrier. 'Let battle commence!' he roared.

Almonds' jeep accelerated down the road and in instant machine guns opened up from either side of the road.

'Almonds' jeep went up,' says Sadler, who being at the front of the column now had what he calls the 'laborious process of trying to turn round'.

68

Redington remembers the ambush as a 'disaster ... it was every man for himself. Stirling gave orders to retire and we had to make for the escarpment as quick as possible'. Heavy Vickers fire from Almonds' jeep had momentarily cowed the Italians and allowed the raiders a precious few seconds to extricate themselves from the precarious position. Now it was a frantic race to reach the shelter of the escarpment before first light.

'The convoy didn't stay together,' says Redington, 'it was just straight across the sands as quick as you could.'

Sadler describes it as a 'rather hairy journey back across open country watching for any planes ... but Nobby was an excellent driver and we got back to the entrance [of the escarpment] as it got light. We could actually see the planes taking off to come and chase us'.

One of them caught Boutinot.

'We were about 20km from Benghazi when we were attacked. We jumped from our jeep just before it was blown up.' They threw themselves down in the sand as the fighter came in again. 'We had no cover at all,' he says. 'It was all down to luck. You just laid there and hoped you wouldn't be hit.' Boutinot managed to scramble aboard one of the few lorries that wasn't destroyed. 'There were about forty men clinging to that lorry when we reached safety.'

It was 25 miles from the escarpment to the rendezvous in the Jebel. Over the next day or two men reached the RV either on foot or hanging off the back of a laden-down jeep or lorry. Twelve vehicles had been destroyed by the aircraft but fatalities had been mercifully light. Stirling, with Cooper and Seekings, was still out looking for stragglers. The main priority was to bring back the fit, the men who could fight again. They brought in about 'sixteen or seventeen', according to Seekings. But those too badly wounded were left behind.

'I didn't like telling them they'd had it,' said Seekings. 'It was one of the hardest things I ever had to do.'

One of the wounded they found was Drongin, shot while standing in the back of his jeep firing his Vickers at a strafing Italian fighter.

'I'm sorry to have given you so much trouble, sir,' he told Malcolm Pleydell as his wounds were examined.

In a letter to his girlfriend two weeks after the Benghazi raid, Pleydell described the surgery he performed on Drongin: 'As a last case I had a retention of urine due to the perineal urethra being shot away. I had to do a supra pubic cystotomy eventually, being unable to find the proximal end of the urethra. It was the devil.'

Later that day Stirling came to Pleydell and told him they would be moving off in two hours' time. The seriously wounded would have to be left behind. Pleydell decided that a couple, including Bob Melot, were fit to travel. But four weren't. Drongin was one, although as Pleydell recalled he was 'too ill to care what happened'. Another was Arthur Sque, a fitter sergeant from the REME whose job it had been to look after the transport.

'He was brilliant at his job,' Seekings remembered. 'He had actually taken leave to come with us because he wanted to learn on a raid. But we had to leave him.'*

Life was looking up for Stirling. The Benghazi debacle (the Tobruk raid was even more of a fiasco with all but six of the raiding force killed or captured) had been his first major setback but that had been offset by the decision on 28 September to expand 'L' Detachment to a full regiment. As he wallowed in the bath of his brother's flat, he reflected on what he had achieved in little over a year: he was now in command of a regiment comprising four combat squadrons and an HQ squadron. Regimental strength had been set at twenty-nine officers and 572 ranks. Finding the men shouldn't be too hard either he thought, as he heard the doorbell ring, he had already selected several officers and men from the recently disbanded Special Service Regiment.

His thoughts were interrupted by a commotion in the passageway and the next moment he found himself looking up into the face of a short, stocky cavalry officer.

'Sir, may I join your regiment?'

* The four wounded men all died in captivity. They have no known grave and are commemorated on the Alamein Memorial in Egypt.

70

'He looked me up and down,' recalls Johnny Wiseman, who had just been commissioned and was looking for some adventure. '"There's a draft going out tomorrow," he said. "If you are on one of the trucks, yes. If you're not, no." I found out where they were going from and was on a truck that took me to Kabrit. There I had an interview which lasted just a few minutes. He didn't really want to know anything about me, I think he thought I'd shown initiative in finding him.'

Since arriving in the Middle East in early 1941 Bob Lowson had been at the whim of MEHQ. His Commando unit had been officially designated the First Special Service Regiment, though others persisted in calling them the Middle East Commando.

'In June 1942 we were sent up south of Benghazi to do some SAS-style stuff,' he remembers. 'All we did was end up losing our vehicles. Then we were ordered to move up to attack a place called Fort Mararau, a big station post. I was the one supposed to strangle the sentry. Instead we ended up running for our lives in the general stampede [the Gazala Gallop].'

At the Alamein Line Lowson's unit was ordered into defensive positions already dug by some Polish troops.

'We were there for a few days until we saw the Australian 9th Division coming marching over the hills.' A couple of days later Lowson was wounded by a strafing Italian Macchi fighter. 'I also picked up dysentery at the same time so they sent me to a hospital in Palestine.' From there he had been packed off to a convalescent camp in Nathanya, 'where there were two types of canteen, a dry one and a wet one, thank God I was in the one that served beer. I spent most of my time trying to get my weight from 8 stone back up to 13'.

He rejoined his unit at Beirut, delighted to be reunited with his two pals from the Liverpool Scottish, Billy Stalker and Charlie Backhouse. A short time later the three of them were posted to Kabrit.

'When we arrived we were told we were now part of the SAS. Choice didn't come into it.'

71

STIRLING POSTED Wiseman to 'A' Squadron, under the command of Paddy Mayne with Fraser his second in command. The squadron was preparing to head up into the desert to harass German forces between Tobruk and Matruh. Wiseman had found Stirling a 'delightful fellow' with an 'incredible personality'. Mayne was different.

'Paddy was a wonderful soldier and in action you couldn't have a better man. He was an exceptional man ... and I admired him enormously. You don't meet many Paddys ... the kind of chap that gets thrown up in wars.'

Malcolm Pleydell went on a weekend's leave with Mayne in early October. When he returned he wrote to his girlfriend: 'He is now my squadron commander and I'm damned glad I'm with him. You can rely on him 100 per cent to get you out of anywhere if things look a bit sticky.'

It was when he was in his cups, however, says Wiseman, that Mayne 'was a menace'.

'When he drank you felt your life wasn't safe ... I didn't provoke him purposely but I must have. I always talked too much. Once I said something that upset him so he threw me on the ground – at this stage we all had beards because we weren't allowed to shave – and he put his knees on my arms and called for a razor. Without water and soap he shaved off half my beard, and he was as drunk as a lord. That was the most dangerous moment of the war for me!'

It was the Military Police, says Youngman, who often bore the brunt of Mayne's drunken excesses. One time 'he'd smashed the window of a furniture shop and went inside to sit on a settee. The Redcaps arrived and stood outside interrogating him. He came outside and asked them why they didn't stand to attention when they addressed a major of the British Army. So they did and he thumped them both. Then he got in their jeep and drove merrily away'.

Another time he laid out the Provost Marshal and six Redcaps in front of a startled audience of drinkers on the balcony of the Shepheards Hotel. He was finally bundled into a van and thrown in a cell but the next morning – much to the consternation of the Military Police – MEHQ ordered his unmuzzling:

'Release this officer. He is more use as an officer than as any other rank.'

Mayne found most young English officers on first acquaintance only slightly less disagreeable; to him they were pompous oafs with mincing accents. Lieutenant Harry Wall Poat possessed neither of these traits, but he was, in Mike Sadler's opinion, a 'professional Englishman'. Before the war the 27-year-old had been a tomato grower on Guernsey. He spoke with a cut-glass accent, sported a Ronald Colman moustache and even in the desert he was immaculately attired.

'You could have taken Harry Poat,' says McDougall, 'pulled him through a smoking chimney and he would have still appeared as if he'd just come out for dinner.'

Arthur Thomson, raised in the poverty of London in the 1930s, had met few Poats but he remembers him as 'wonderful ... polite, quiet, but underneath a man of steel'. Just before 'A' Squadron left for the desert Poat had asked Thomson if he could get him to Cairo as he had some urgent business.

'I didn't have a jeep but I did have a 3-tonner, so I drove him at about 100mph and he looked terrified. When we got back to Kabrit he thanked me and politely informed me that would be the last time he'd ask for a lift.'

Most of the men and NCOs in 'A' Squadron – Storie, 'Chalky' White, Cooper and Lilley – were 'L' Detachment veterans. An exception was James McDiarmid, a Commando whose military career had begun as a drummer boy in the Black Watch. McDiarmid had a sinister glamour. His looks were smouldering, he had a touch of the Errol Flynn about him, and men admired his fearlessness. But his cold-blooded streak startled them; it was as if he enjoyed savage violence.

'He could be the nicest bloke you've ever met,' says Bob McDougall, a robust Liverpudlian who joined the SAS at the same time, 'but he could also be the last person you ever wanted to see.'

In October the squadron operated out of a base in the Great Sand Sea, cutting the railway line between Tobruk and El Daba in one place or another for thirteen of the twenty days leading up to the start of the El Alamein offensive. Once the Germans began to retreat, says Wiseman, 'we operated against the coast road, going out and shooting up Germans. We mined roads ... blew up quite a lot of trucks and then retreated into the desert for three days before returning'. Wiseman found life at their remote desert base 'clean and agreeable'. He discovered he had a mutual interest with Mayne in rugby and they discussed organizing a regimental team.

'It was all a great adventure,' Wiseman says. 'I was young and glad to see some action ... and the desert was a jolly good place to have some action because of its size.'

In his letters home Pleydell marvelled at the 'vast Wagnerian sunsets, which reminded one of Turner, and which mesmerised the senses' or he described with adolescent enthusiasm how 'I once woke to find a Neolithic or Palaeolithic arrow head within arm's length of my resting place. Perhaps someone of my own age had discarded it 15 or 20,000 years previously!'

STORIE, BY NOW a corporal, was on patrol with another of the new officers, a fair-skinned Irishman called McDermott.

'There were three jeeps in the patrol,' says Storie, who was in the second vehicle. 'Next to me was a new lad who'd only just arrived. I couldn't even tell you his name.'

The patrol was heading back to base after mining the coastal road when they strayed too close to a German 88mm battery. The first Storie knew about it was when an armour-piercing shell tore through the front of his jeep.

'It took the engine right out,' he says. 'Another yard and it would have taken me too. We were sitting there with no engine.' As more shells landed about them the other two jeeps accelerated out of range. Storie and his crew scrambled behind some cover and waited to be rescued. 'The other jeeps were full of new lads and what they should have done is come right round and picked us up, but they didn't.'

After walking for a day and a half without seeing any SAS patrols, Storie decided they would have to get on to the coastal road and ambush a vehicle. 'A German Luftwaffe truck came up behind us with three lads in it.' The truck drove past and one of the men waved and shouted something in Italian. Storie waved back. Then the truck stopped and reversed.

'They realized we were British,' says Storie, 'but being in that part of the world they presumed we were shot-down RAF men. Obviously when we were in the desert we didn't wear any insignia because of who we were so we played along with it. We were treated like gentlemen.'

THE GERMANS WHO'D captured Storie were heading west towards their defensive positions at El Agheila near the Cyrenaica/Tripolitania border. But Rommel's forces knew the Desert War was approaching a denouement that would end in a crushing defeat for them. The Americans had landed at Algeria on 8 November and their First Army was advancing east to link with the Eighth Army driving west.

'A' Squadron left their hideout in the Great Sand Sea in mid November and established a new base at Bir Zelten further west. They were joined by Stirling and 'B' Squadron on 29 November. Pleydell was concerned about Stirling's health, as he was suffering from two of the most common desert conditions, solar conjunctivitis and sores. The former, as Pleydell told his girlfriend in a letter, was caused by 'the dust whipping in behind your glasses or goggles, with the glare of the sun on the white sand'. Stirling had arrived at Bir Zelten wearing dark glasses.

Desert sores were a plague on all who fought in North Africa. An innocuous scratch might quickly grow into a festering sore, an erupting volcano of pus that soaked through dirty bandages.

'I had two desert sores on the two fingers on which I wore rings,' recollects Bill Deakins, 'and they went right down to the bone. I also got one on my forehead which put me hospital for a week. There they wrapped them up, to take away all the pus, and left it to dry out in the atmosphere.'

If you were out on operations, however, with no recourse to a clean hospital bed, there was little that could be done.

'You would never get rid of it,' says Albert Youngman. 'Some of them would just ulcerate right down to the bone.'

If the pain became too much severe measures might be taken.

'I had very bad desert sores on my legs,' says David Danger, 'and they used to try and get these off by putting a heated bottle a couple of inches over the top of the sore to draw out the poison and pus.'

Du Vivier says the most effective remedy 'was a scrubbing brush. It was agony but you had to do it to get rid of the poison'.

Stirling's poor condition had been exacerbated by the workload he had taken on during the weeks Mayne had been in the desert. As well as overseeing the training of 'B' Squadron at Kabrit, he had successfully lobbied, with brother Bill, for a second SAS regiment to be raised (in Algeria). In addition, he'd been informed that the Special Boat Squadron of the regiment was soon to be placed under his command and there was an influx of French recruits to deal with. Stirling had also found time to rifle through the ranks of the old Middle East Commando and bring the regiment up to full strength.

At Bir Zelten he told Mayne of the latest developments, then briefed him on the operations for the next month. 'A' Squadron was to shoot up enemy transport between Sirte and El Agheila, while 'B' Squadron would proceed 200 miles west and lay waste to targets around Tripoli. But first Stirling threw a regimental party around a campfire.

'That was a good night,' says Deakins. 'There was quite a lot of beer flowing and it developed into a good old singsong.'

The first melody was 'Lili Marlene', the regimental song of the Afrika Korps that had been seized by the SAS. Then John Hodgkinson, a rugby league player before the war, led the men in a succession of bawdy tunes. Chris O'Dowd and one or two of the southern Irish were good-humouredly shouted down when they suggested singing an Irish rebel song. The longer the night went on the more maudlin the songs became: 'My Melancholy Baby', 'I'll Never Smile Again' and 'Dancing With Tears in My Eyes'.

Mike Sadler remembers that Redington was 'frightfully plastered ...

76

he went round everyone saying, "Repeat after me, Mike Sadler is the best navigator in the SAS." It was all absolute nonsense but I think that's where my reputation came from!'

FIVE WEEKS LATER Stirling hosted another party, this one in Bir Guedaffia, a sort of belated Hogmanay party. But many of the men from 'B' Squadron who had sung with such gusto at Bir Zelten were now dead or POWs. The month spent raiding between Tripoli and Misurata had been costly. 'A' Squadron losses had been minimal and they were now on their way back to Kabrit.

Stirling, however, had just returned from Eighth Army Headquarters where Montgomery had congratulated the regiment on all they had achieved from before the start of the Alamein offensive to the beginning of January 1943, with the British on the verge of taking Tripoli. 'Quite, quite mad,' was Montgomery's description of Stirling, and that was before he'd heard his plan to head north-west, carry out reconnaissance patrols in north Tunisia, ravage the enemy's lines of communications and then continue to link up with the First Army advancing east, the first fighting unit from the Eighth Army to do so.

As Stirling waited for Jordan and his French detachment to arrive at Bir Guedaffia, he fretted about the amount of petrol he would need to get him across Tunisia. Seekings was one of the men missing from the December raids [he eluded capture and returned safely], but the faithful Cooper was with him. Stirling asked him to hunt down some more petrol. Cooper sent a message back to the oasis El Djofra, where the regiment's base was, and asked for some petrol to be brought up. Bob Lowson was in one of the lorries that set off north across the sand dunes.

'The petrol was carried not in jerry-cans but in four-gallon drums and the petrol just poured out of them when you went over rough terrain; there was little you could do about it.'

Stirling had been expecting more petrol. He told a smirking Cooper to pass on a message to the drivers.

'Colonel Stirling says if he had time he would come and shoot you.'

77

Cooper also said one of the drivers was needed on the operation. Bob Lowson and Charlie Backhouse looked at each other and shrugged.

'I'll go,' said Backhouse.

The French arrived on 14 January: Jordan, three officers and eighteen soldiers. One of the men, Alain Papazow, was just 17. For him, the implacable and courageous Jordan was a surrogate father, a replacement for the real one, a Bulgarian businessman, who had been murdered by communist agents in Iran in the 1930s. Papazow had been brought up by his French grandparents, weaned on self-sufficiency and stoicism. If Jordan was a father figure to Papazow, Stirling was the daredevil uncle who made an ebullient appearance on special occasions.

'He was a man with whom you immediately had a good feeling,' says Papazow, 'and he always made a point of reminding the French that he was Scottish, not English. He would always affirm to us, loudly and clearly, that he was Scottish before anything else. He was a great man, liked by all of us.'

Harry Poat was the first to leave Bir Guedaffia, taking a patrol to make a show of strength on the west side of Tripoli at the express wish of Montgomery. They shot up any Axis vehicle they encountered, occasionally with unhappy results.

'Italian high-ranking officers travelled in very lavish caravans,' recalls one of the men with Poat. 'One day we saw three of these caravans. "Christ, it's got to be some bigwig," we thought. They didn't have an escort so we got down on to the road – there were three jeeps – and while one waited at the back the other two drove up along either side. These caravans had windows at the top and because it was so hot the doors were open; we just drove along, raked them with machine-gun fire and chucked grenades through the doors.'

The SAS dismounted, eager to count their bag, but to their dismay they discovered that 'it wasn't officers we'd killed, it was Italian prostitutes. We'd wiped out three travelling brothels'.

At sunrise on 15 January Stirling led a column of eight jeeps west towards Ghadames. Three of the vehicles were French, under the command of François Martin and including Papazow. The remaining French detachment left Bir Guedaffia 24 hours after Stirling. Jordan described the first day's travelling in his operational report:

'Sand soft, sand dunes one to two metres, with tufts of vegetation at the top. Difficult with the jeeps and progression slow ... we found traces of Colonel Stirling's passage.'

Stirling's column had found the going equally arduous, but it deteriorated when they swung north at Ghadames towards Bir Soltane. The eastern edge of the Grand Sea Erg lapped over their route. The terrain was appalling, like a choppy ocean suddenly frozen.

'The surface was terrible,' says Sadler, 'all covered in rocks that cut the tyres. I remember David [Stirling] saying "that's the last of the Mohawks". These were the tyres we were using and they just weren't up to that sort of terrain. Once or twice we had to cannibalize vehicles to keep them going.'

Sadler was again navigating them towards their destination. His earlier immaculate displays had induced Stirling to commission him in the field.

'"I want you to be an officer," he told me, "go and buy some pips." So I went down one of the Cairo bazaars and bought a couple.'

Redington recalls that at night Sadler 'showed me how to navigate using the stars'. During the day, however, words were used sparingly.

'We didn't talk an awful lot when we were driving,' says Sadler, 'because the air was full of dust and your eyes were full of dust and on the whole we were just concentrating on what we were doing.'

On 21 January the two patrols rendezvoused a few miles south of Bir Soltane where Stirling told Jordan they had been overtaken by events. HQ had signalled him with the news that Gafsa and Tripoli had fallen to the Allies. Rommel was punch-drunk. The SAS must attack the Axis lines of communication between Sfax and Gabes with the utmost urgency, before the Eighth Army came out of its corner for what might be the deciding round of the conflict. It had always been Jordan's mission to operate in this area, just not so soon. Taking Martin's patrol with him, he departed at 1600 hours for the Gabes Gap, 80 miles north. Stirling

79

followed 12 hours later, aiming to thread his way through the Gap and wreck coastal installations further north of Jordan.

Before Jordan left Stirling he had calculated that to reach his operating sector before daybreak he would have to average 7mph. They ran into problems almost straight away, says Jordan, 'when the sun compass broke'. Navigation became easier at nightfall with the stars, but the darkness reduced their speed to 2mph.

'It was impossible to judge the slope of the dunes.'

Papazow says the dunes were so towering they were 'reduced to pedestrian speed ... and some times we would walk in front of the jeeps to make sure we were going the right way'. The biggest dunes could only be surmounted by 'hooking sand channels to the front of the jeeps and dragging them down one by one. It was an absolute nightmare'.

Jordan tried to radio a message to Stirling, warning him what lay ahead. But there was no signal.

'The radio in that country was unbelievable,' recalls Jordan. 'Sometimes we could pick it up from hundreds of miles away; other times we couldn't make contact from 40 kilometres.'

By dusk on the 22nd Jordan's nine-jeep patrol was nestled in the vast dunes to the north of Bir Soltane. In the 24 hours since they'd left Stirling they had covered less than 30 miles. They stopped for some soup. Jordan moved among the men, geeing them up for another night's hard slog. What they encountered was infinitely worse than the night before. Then, suddenly, at 0245 hours on 23 January, as they manhandled the vehicles down another dune, one of them spotted a telegraph pole. Fifteen minutes later they were driving north on the road that led through the Gabes Gap.

'I took that road pretty fast,' remembers Jordan, who was driving the lead jeep. For nearly an hour they touched speeds of 40mph. 'Then ahead a vehicle coming towards us flashed its headlights. I tried to do the same but mine weren't working.' Jordan moved over to the right, as the first armoured car drew level, the German markings clearly visible. It rumbled past, followed by several lorries and another armoured car. As Jordan began manoeuvring past the column a third armoured car appeared in the middle of the road.

'I swerved to avoid it and got bogged down in the sand on the side of the road.'

The German vehicle stopped a few metres from the jeep. A man emerged from the turret. His stare was met by Jordan's, who 'will always remember the look of amazement on his face ... then I changed gears and accelerated down the road'.

Six jeeps roared forward, following their officer past the last of the three armoured cars before its driver had time to react. When he did he swung the car into the middle of the road, and fired a burst of cannon fire at the seventh jeep.

'Martin's and my jeep were the last two in the column,' says Papazow, 'and when the firing started we raced off into the desert.'

Jordan was told what had happened by Legrand, driving the sixth jeep. 'I had no worry about Martin because I knew he could look after himself.'

Papazow remembers that no one in their two jeeps was flustered by the sudden turn of events. 'We knew what our mission was and where it was.'

An hour later Jordan's column ran into three German lorries and 'this time we opened fire'. In the firefight that followed one of their vehicles, a British-manned radio car, became separated and Legrand's jeep fell into a ditch. Now down to four jeeps they continued north and passed through the Gabes Gap on 24 January. The next night they began laying mines on the routes from Gabes to Sfax. The following evening a skirmish with an armoured car fractured the patrol in two. Jordan decided to turn west and ransack the roads leading to Gafsa. Towards sundown on 28 January they saw a shepherd with his herd. Jordan stopped to ask if he had seen any soldiers in the area. There was fear in the shepherd's eyes.

'I looked up behind the old man and saw a whole section of Italians come into view on a ridge,' he recalls. 'They had two heavy machine guns pointing right at us.'

As the French surrender was accepted by the Italians, Jordan bearded the officer in charge. 'He was a young lieutenant and I told him that his country was heading into chaos. "Yes, I agree," he laughed. "Why don't you give me your name and address so when the moment happens you can testify that I treated you decently!"'

MARTIN'S PATROL HAD also managed to squeeze through the Gap without being apprehended. On the night of 25/26 January they laid explosives on a stretch of railway between Gabes and Gafsa.

'We also mined the road that ran parallel to the track,' says Papazow. They withdrew 900 yards into the desert and 'had the opportunity to see a train blown up at the same time that a staff car, with a motorcycle escort, drove over a mine. The two exploded within about 50 metres of each other.'

The following evening, while lying up in a wadi, their position was betrayed by some local Arabs.

'We saw the German vehicles coming towards us but had time to blow up the jeeps before running away,' remembers Papazow.* For the next three days they walked towards Gafsa, subsisting on 'a big packet of dates and some chocolate'. Each of their emergency packs also contained two litres of water.

On 30 January they were picked up by an American unit at a deserted railway station called Zanouch. They were taken at gunpoint to Gafsa where their identities were verified with MEHQ. A few hours later they were paraded in front of the American press as the vanguard of the Eighth Army.

'They described us in an American magazine as wild, bearded and burnt brown,' says Papazow, 'like five Robinson Crusoes.' A photographer stepped up to take their photo. He pointed at Papazow and said something in English. 'The rest of the boys all had these big beards but I was too young to grow one. So the photographer told me to step aside as I didn't look "wild" enough for his picture.'

* Each jeep carried a Lewes bomb with a short fuse in a haversack behind the gear lever and between the front gunner and driver. The SAS had instructions to blow the jeep to prevent it falling into German hands.

82

AFTER FOLLOWING IN the tyre tracks of Jordan it didn't take Stirling long to realize that their original schedule was unfeasible. The convoy of five jeeps and fourteen men, recalls Redington, 'took a hell of a battering going up and down the dunes; it was exhausting work'. They were all dog-tired, enduring the same tiredness that had debilitated Jordan during the Derna raid.

'That had made me realize,' says the Frenchman, 'that even though I had a strong constitution there are limits to everything.'

Stirling knew no limits. He wanted to get through the Gap as quickly as possible. In the twilight hours of 23 January, as they neared the Gap, they were spotted by a Storch reconnaissance plane. None the less they crossed safely and as dawn broke the next morning they were on the road west to Gafsa. Sadler and Redington were the first to see the German armoured column parked up on either side of the road. Sadler, an old hand at bluffing it out, 'just drove through looking straight ahead'. Cooper was more bullish.

'A lot of them were sitting on their tanks having a coffee and warming themselves in the sun. The more alert among them looked at us with a quizzical expression but we just looked back at them, nodded, and kept on going.'

A few miles further on, with the road becoming busier with enemy traffic, Stirling told Sadler to strike off north, cross country for a few miles, where they could find a place to lie up, sleep and wait for the road to quieten down.

'It was a lovely morning,' recalls Sadler. 'We were driving in bright sunshine across farmers' dust fields until we got up into more hilly terrain [the Jebel Tebaga]. There were some wadis running through the hills and we got into one of these wadis.'

Once they'd dusted off the tracks and camouflaged, the first thing Redington did was light up a cigarette.

'I had a big box of "Cape de Cairos" with me,' he remembers, 'and, of course, you couldn't smoke when you were driving because it was so bumpy you needed both hands on the wheel the whole time. Once I'd

83

had a fag, I took my boots off, put them with my Smith & Wesson revolver next to my head, and went to sleep.'

Stirling and McDermott were a few feet from Redington, resting in the shade of an overhanging rock. Sadler and Cooper scrambled to the top of the wadi for a quick scout of their position. They could see the road in the distance, still with a lot of traffic moving along it.

'Then we turned in to our sleeping bags and fell asleep in front of the jeep,' says Sadler. No sentries were posted.

Sadler woke to the crunch of boot on desert. He opened his eyes and got a 'nasty start looking up at two Afrika Korps fellows'. Cooper remembers 'someone kicking at my feet. I opened my eyes to find a German standing there pointing his Schmeisser at me'. To the surprise of the British pair, one of the Germans motioned for them to remain where they were. Then the two continued over the lip of the wadi.

'We didn't do as we were told,' said Cooper. 'We ran like madmen up and out of the wadi.' Their French interpreter, Freddie Taxis, had been asleep close by and he too joined the escape bid.

'It was a hard run up a hillside,' says Sadler, 'but luckily we managed to get into a little narrow gully among some camel scrub. By now we were absolutely knackered and we just lay there.'

Redington was woken by a scream of *'Raus! Raus!'* He opened his eyes and saw dozens of Germans running through the wadi.

'I reached for my revolver but it was gone,' he remembers, 'and so were my boots. They'd even pinched my fags.'

The eleven men, including Stirling and McDermott and Backhouse, were bundled into the back of some lorries.

Sadler, Cooper and Taxis were sure it was only a matter of time before they were caught.

Sadler suddenly began searching through his pockets. 'I remembered that I had some signals with me.' Gingerly, he burrowed into the desert floor and buried them. They soon heard the sound of movement coming up through the gully. 'We lay doggo,' says Sadler.

Cooper peeped through the camel scrub and saw a dozen mangy

goats. In a couple of minutes their hidey-hole was surrounded by the animals. There was a shepherd with them, who watched as German soldiers searched the hillside and looked down into the gully. Then they moved on.

'We didn't make ourselves known to the shepherd,' says Sadler, 'so I've no idea whether he was deliberately protecting us or whether it was by chance he came into the gully.'

The three of them listened to the sounds of vehicles leaving the wadi but it wasn't until dark that they emerged from under the camel scrub.

Redington's journey in the back of a German lorry ended after two hours. Along with three others, he was marched towards a hut.

'I thought we were going to be bumped off,' he recalls. 'As we were bundled into this building I said to one of the lads, "If it looks like they're going to shoot us, let's rush them because we've got nothing to lose."' The hut was bare inside, though Redington remembers that the walls looked as if they had already been 'peppered with bullet holes'. They were threatened with execution and when that didn't produce a reaction they were beaten. 'They started hitting us with their rifle butts, stuff like that,' says Redington.

Sadler's predicament was only marginally more favourable than Redington's. Cooper had a map, but they were deep in enemy territory with no weapons, no food and no water. They decided to head west towards the French whom they knew to be at Tozeur on the north banks of the Djerid, a large salt lake. They marched through the night and early the next morning Taxis, who spoke fluent Arabic, approached a camp and was given some dates and a jug of water. In late afternoon they ran into a tribe of Berbers.

'This lot weren't so friendly,' says Sadler. 'They demanded our clothes so Johnny threw them his leather jerkin.' This only seemed to antagonize the tribesmen still further and their leader yelled something at Taxis.

'What's he saying?' Cooper asked the Frenchman.

'He's saying, "Give us everything because you know we are going to kill you whatever."'

'It was at that point,' recalls Sadler, 'that we decided to move on.' The three men fled but one of the Arabs hurled a rock at Cooper. It ripped open the left side of his forehead and the spewing blood temporarily blinded him. 'Taxis and I grabbed Johnny by the arms and we just sprinted down this hill.'

They continued marching through the night and into the next day, receiving another lesson in the vagaries of human kindness when they encountered an elderly Arab who gave them water and a foul-smelling goatskin bag full of dates. The sustenance kept them going until the next day, but Taxis was now 'getting a bit demoralized'. Their thirst was torturing them and all their boots had worn through.

'Taxis had six toes and so his feet were in very poor shape,' remembers Sadler. 'At one stage he started doing a Captain Oates and saying "Leave me here."'

The three men staggered on, the strain increasing as they began to hallucinate. When Cooper saw some buildings he wasn't sure if they were real or his mind playing tricks. Only the supporting hands of some French soldiers convinced him they had made it to Tozeur.

'We had a great night with the French,' remembers Sadler, 'and then the Americans arrived.'

The French had wired the American First Army at Tebessa, 120 miles north, that three members of the Eighth Army had come up from Tripolitania. The Americans arrived, suspicious and heavy-handed.

'At first they were very hostile,' says Sadler. 'We were loaded into an ambulance for the trip north but we had a jeepload of armed guards following us in case we made a break for it. When we arrived at their HQ, the officer said, "Have these men covered, Sergeant", and they all surrounded us with their Tommy Guns. We were in pretty poor shape but they had clearly decided we were shady characters.'

When their identification had been authenticated by Cairo the trio were pounced on by a scrum of American newsmen. Sadler's parents read about their son a few weeks later in the *Stroud Journal & Cirencester Gazette*. Their journey, he told the journalist, had been 'very interesting ... some of

86

it was a lot of fun'. Cooper was then asked if he needed some leave to recover.

'His reply was adequate for the admiring American troops who stood around,' commented the paper. '"Oh," he said. "I've only been going at this for two months. Some of the chaps have been out since August."'

REDINGTON WAS FLOWN first to Sicily, then on to Rome and a special interrogation centre in a cavalry barracks. He was taken into a room where an interrogator was waiting for him at a table. 'I could have you shot for what you are.'

Redington shrugged innocently. 'I'm just a soldier, an ordinary chap.'

The German asked Redington about the desert, its vastness, its beauty. What did he like about it?

'Corporal Reginald Redington, 893567.'

The German leaned forward and 'told me something along the lines of we have "ways and means". I thought, "Uh-oh, I'm in for a bloody good hiding here."'

Stirling was also in the cavalry barracks. Between 15 and 20 February he was interrogated by a German staff officer, then an Italian. It was all perfectly routine. Then he was taken back to his cell. In the adjoining cell was another British officer awaiting interrogation, a Captain John Richards of the Royal Army Service Corps. He came and sat next to Stirling at supper, chatting to him about their rotten luck and the poor quality of the food. At the next meal, too, Richards was his usual chatty self. He was a Londoner. Stirling told him a little bit about himself. He also mentioned that he was CO of the Special Air Service.

Richards, whose real name was Theodore Schurch, was indeed a Londoner. It was there that he'd joined Oswald Mosley's Blackshirts in the 1930s. He had subsequently been recruited by the Italian Secret Service and had been planted to worm out information from captured British prisoners.

How much information Schurch tweezered out of Stirling has never

87

been conclusively established. But on 18 February the British codebreakers intercepted a message sent from Rome that read:

'Lt Col Stirling, commander of the Long Range Desert Group [sic], who was captured in Tunis, has explained that all groups of the LRDG (28 patrols altogether) are operating at present in night actions in the Gabes-Sfax sector, with a strength of six to eight men each.'*

REDINGTON'S 'GOOD HIDING' never happened. Instead, he was well fed on his first night, and he was also struck by the friendliness of some of his fellow inmates. As he was about to leave the dining area a British officer brushed past him.

'Be careful what you say in here because we know for a fact that there are the enemy among us. Keep your lip buttoned up.'

For three days Redington kept himself to himself. On the fourth morning his cell door was opened.

'"Come on," this German said to me. "You're going somewhere far worse than this place."'

---

* In a statement made at the trial of Schurch in 1945 Stirling, who had spent the rest of the war in Colditz, admitted he had told Richards he was the CO of the SAS but that he couldn't remember discussing the name of his successor. He vehemently denied he had disclosed sensitive information to 'Captain Richards'. In a written statement he said: 'At no time did I tell Richards any accurate secret information or discuss the true workings of the SAS. Such information as I passed to him was untrue and designed to deceive him.' Schurch was executed.

88

CHAPTER TWO

SICILY AND ITALY 1943

IT WAS ANOTHER agreeable evening in the officers' club of 2SAS, encamped a few miles east of the coastal town of Philippeville in Algeria, 40 miles north of Constantine. The club was in fact a large tent, with a bar at one end and a log fire at the other, around which the officers sat sipping gins and spinning yarns.

The officers selected by David Stirling's brother, Bill, were a disparate bunch. Some, like Lieutenant David Leigh and Captain Sandy Scratchley, had served with David Stirling in 'L' Detachment before being transferred to 2SAS in early 1943. Leigh was a handsome Scot who had only recently been commissioned and Scratchley was a 37-year-old former jockey. Towering over the diminutive Scratchley was Grant Hibbert, a tall, bespectacled English officer who had come from the Pay Corps. One of his contemporaries remembers him as 'having the air of a schoolmaster'. He was ten years younger than Scratchley and new to the SAS.

Captain Philip Pinckney was another newcomer. The 28-year-old was something of a rum cove, believing, amongst other things, that a soldier could live off the land eating just plants. He once sat down in the officers' mess wearing nothing but a tie, his excuse being that daily orders had stated quite clearly that 'officers will be properly dressed for dinner wearing a tie'.

Pinckney's views on survival were of interest to Lieutenant Jim Mackie, a fair-haired former medical student from Edinburgh. Mackie had postponed his studies – to the chagrin of his father, a prominent professor – to join the Cameronians on the declaration of war. Mackie was unassuming and quiet, docile even, but he was popular with the men. So was Captain Pat Dudgeon, though the 23-year-old from Hampshire had a more rumbustious character than Mackie. His father, a lieutenant colonel, had won the DSO in the First War and Dudgeon had grown up conscious of his courage. He was 6 feet tall and, like Mackie, blond-haired and well-built. Dudgeon's men nicknamed him 'Toomai', after the elephant in Rudyard Kipling's Samu story.

To the hoi polloi, Lieutenant Anthony Greville-Bell was all la-di-da accent and foppish affectations. In the officers' club, however, the rakishly handsome 22-year-old was as popular with his fellow officers as he was with the nurses of the general hospital a few miles up the road. Greville-Bell's peers looked forward to hearing about his latest amorous escapade.

'The nurses were charming girls,' he remembers. 'Very friendly.'

Greville-Bell had arrived in the Middle East with the Hussars, a tank commander in a venerable regiment where the courage of the troopers was no match for the tanks and 88mm anti-tank guns of the Afrika Korps. Greville-Bell ended up in hospital having been shot through the leg as he baled out of his burning tank.

'The tank business was becoming extremely unpleasant,' he recalls, 'and I didn't want to be any more at the mercy of World War One field officers who said "when in doubt, charge!". Next to me in hospital was an SAS officer who had broken his leg in a parachute accident. He told me about the regiment and it seemed the right thing for me.'

Greville-Bell transferred from 'D' Squadron 1SAS to 2SAS when the latter was encamped at Philippeville. The camp lay on a long sandy bay overlooked by hills. It appeared to have everything, the ideal location for a regiment: sun, sea, sand and at close hand a plentiful supply of eager young women. But Philippeville was the wrong place to build a camp. It

90

was in the middle of a malarial belt and while the men trained, frolicked and flirted, large swathes were being ravaged by toxic mosquitoes.

The training at Philippeville was 'absolute hell' remembers Greville-Bell, particularly as the 'officers' club took a pounding most nights'. Most feared was the 'Jebel Run', an endurance test that had to be completed within a certain time. Charlie Hackney was an 'Old Sweat', a regular soldier before the war who had served with the Lancers on the North-West Frontier, yet even he found the 'Jebel Run' a new experience in pain.

'We started in the camp and had to run up this rocky hill, through a cork forest, to a checkpoint at the top and back down again. It was about 700 feet and we had to run with a full pack on.'

'It was up and down in less than 60 minutes,' recalls George 'Bebe' Daniels, one of the training instructors at Philippeville. 'It was their [the new recruits] first test and if they couldn't do it they were out.' Daniels ran the Jebel once a week, 'in around 56 minutes', so the recruits knew he practised what he preached.

Daniels was a roll-your-sleeves-up sort of man, all hard graft and no grumbling. As a young boy in Derby he had earned extra pocket money by delivering the sports edition of his local paper to neighbouring villages every Saturday. In the course of an evening he covered over 10 miles. The Jebel Run caused him few problems.

Daniels had been one of four men transferred to 2SAS at the end of 1942 to help train the new recruits. Selection was left mainly in the hands of Major Barlow and Lieutenant David Leigh, while Daniels and Dave Kershaw, one of the Originals, imbued the new recruits with the SAS ethos.

'The recruits were quick learners,' says Daniels. 'But a lot of that was down to Barlow's selection. He had a fixed idea of the people he wanted in the regiment; he wanted people who could look after themselves and thus the operation as a whole. Cunning was far more important to him than macho toughness.'

Barlow winkled out most of the unsuitable candidates; those that managed to sneak through the preliminary interviews were usually found out during the training until Bill Stirling was left with a residue of highly trained and competent soldiers. Like the officers, they couldn't be pigeon-holed. Charlie Hackney and Sergeant Bill Robinson were pre-war regulars. The latter was a shrewd former artilleryman from Peckham in south London with a worldly nature. With a wife and young child back in England, Robinson didn't go out 'hunting' in town with the single men. But he did enjoy listening to their exaggerated tales of conquest the morning after.

Bernie Brunt and Cyril Wheeler were two short men, burnished with the characteristics of their native region. Brunt was 5 feet 5 inches and from Rotherham; he could be cussed and dogmatic, but that was his Yorkshire prerogative. Wheeler, 28, spoke with a Portsmouth burr and had the adventurous spirit of a man born by the sea. He was a Barnardo's boy and had spent much of his childhood moving from one educational establishment to another; he hadn't had much of a formal education but he was well schooled in the wily ways of the world.

Wheeler was a former Royal Engineer who had survived Dunkirk. 'I was in a transit camp in Algiers when the SAS came along and started talking to us. No one knew what it was but I was bored and thought it looked a good chance to get out of the camp.'

Another man who didn't know what he was volunteering for was Keith Kilby. He was idling away his time at the Royal Army Medical Corps in early 1943 when he offered his services to a 'special unit' based in Kabrit.

'When I found out what the SAS did I thought "well, they won't want me",' he says. Kilby looked round at the menacing collection of bearded, tawny soldiers and their jeeps festooned with a bewildering array of weaponry. It was all very intimidating for a conscientious objector. He was called in to see Paddy Mayne.

'I'd heard a bit about him,' says Kilby. 'I went in and he said, "How do you do? You're under my command now." I asked him if he knew I was a conscientious objector. '"Yes," he said, "I accept that. But can you tell me why? Is it religion?" I told him it was nothing to do with religion; it

92

was a story I had heard when I was a schoolboy about a pudding that took 1,000 hands to make. The pudding basin had come from Czechoslovakia, the raisins from Australia, the flour from Canada, and so on. It left a deep impression on me that the world was one. Paddy listened and said, "fine".'

The training intensified as the campaign in North Africa reached its climax. 2SAS carried out a few jeep raids in front of the First Army's advance through Algeria and Tunisia, but Bill Stirling was planning bigger, more strategically important operations.

Despite the failure of his brother's first parachute operation in November 1941, Bill Stirling saw this means of insertion as crucial to his regiment. Parachute jumping was carried out at Mascarah in Algeria, but not before the recruits had endured the same sort of drills as their 1SAS comrades.

'There was a stretch of railway that ran down this little hill and up the other side,' says Wheeler. 'We had to push this railway bogie to the top, sit on the sides, and as we came down the hill we jumped off and learnt how to roll. There were a lot of serious injuries doing that.'

Weapons training was done down by the seaside.

'There were no red flags like you get on a proper range,' says Daniels. 'You knew someone was shooting when you heard the shots. We fired a variety of weapons, we didn't have anything thrust upon us. I tried the Tommy Gun, a Colt 45, a Sten and a German Schmeisser. But I chose the American carbine because it was light and fairly accurate. You could use it at close quarters or at a reasonable distance.'

There were lessons in explosives, unarmed combat and navigation. The men's initiative was also put under scrutiny.

'We were taken a few miles outside the camp one night,' says Robinson, 'and told we had to get back in past the guards who were patrolling the perimeter. There were some big pipes at one end of the camp that had been put in place in readiness for the construction of a sewage farm on the outskirts of Philippeville. The farm had been postponed so me and another chap crawled right along these pipes which came out just behind the Quartermaster Stores. We were the only two to get past the guards.'

Stirling took only a passing interest in the men's progress. Much of his time was spent at the HQ of 15th Army Group, but he was also less of a 'hands-on' commanding officer than his younger brother.

'David was more charismatic and more physical than Bill,' says Greville-Bell, 'and he was outwardly very good at dealing with the higher ups. But I actually think Bill was better at dealing with authority. He was quieter, cleverer and more intellectual than David.'

Bill, however, possessed the same common touch as his brother.

'He could handle himself in any company,' says Daniels. 'He certainly did with the men. They admired him enormously.'

Stirling was just as tough as his sibling, never shrinking from upbraiding fellow officers if they stepped out of line.

'My tent was right next to the fence,' says Greville-Bell, 'and I had some sappers dig a little tunnel from my tent under the fence and beyond, so I could get my girlfriend in. Unfortunately, one night I was caught.'

Stirling punished Greville-Bell by despatching him on a temporary attachment to another special forces unit based in Philippeville, Popski's Private Army [PPA]. Formed and commanded by a Russian major called Vladimir Peniakoff, the PPA was a small and cosmopolitan desert raiding force.

'What an appalling experience that was,' says Greville-Bell. 'Popski as an operator was pretty good … [but] he got all the chuck-outs that no one else wanted.' There was another reason why Greville-Bell's secondment wasn't a success. 'Popski was very left wing and the one thing he loathed above all else were young English army officers, from public school, who had served in a cavalry regiment. He really hated me. We did a couple of stupid little raids but I was sending pleading messages back to the SAS saying "I'll be good, I'll be good!"'

Greville-Bell was recalled to 2SAS in time to prepare for a raid on Lampedusa, an Italian-held island 75 miles east of Tunisia. Their objective was to destroy a radar station perched on top of a cliff. In the weeks leading up to the raid, Greville-Bell and his party, among them George Daniels, practised cliff-scaling and canoeing in two-man folboats. At the end of May they boarded three motor torpedo boats (MTBs) and set off for Lampedusa.

'It didn't occur to the planners,' says Greville-Bell, 'that the radar station would pick us up as we approached.'

The men transferred into the canoes about half a mile from shore and started paddling towards the target. 'That was about the nastiest situation I've ever been in,' reflects Greville-Bell, 'because when we got to within 300 yards of the beach we could see it was impossible to get up the cliff. Then a green flare burst over our heads.'

Trooper Burns, who was sitting behind Greville-Bell in the canoe, said simply, 'Fuck'.

The order was given to withdraw just as the canoes were trapped in the malevolent glare of a cliff-top searchlight. They could barely hear the sound of small-arms fire as they paddled manically towards the MTBs; only the soft 'pop' of bullets close to their heads told them they were being fired upon. Then the canoeists heard the roar of artillery shells and around them the sea began to erupt. One canoe was hit. The others ploughed through the lumpy sea, the men bent impossibly low over the hulls in a pathetic attempt to protect themselves.

'I don't know how we survived that,' says Greville-Bell. 'These bloody shells were coming over and we were just paddling back to the boats down this beam. That's where I started my love affair with the navy because without a thought they came right in and picked us up. Dave Kershaw was on board and he got the searchlight with a burst from the twin Vickers. But it was a very nasty situation because we couldn't hit back.'

BY THE TIME THE war in North Africa was officially declared over by the Allies on 12 May 1943, the sandy bay outside Philippeville was congested with special forces units preparing for the invasion of Sicily. As well as 2SAS and PPA, there was also a detachment of the Special Boat Squadron [SBS], under the command of Lord Jellicoe. The loss of David Stirling,

95

and the winding up of the desert war, had led to a reorganization of 1SAS. In March 1943 the regiment was split into two squadrons each with an approximate strength of 300. Jellicoe was in command of the SBS and Paddy Mayne the Special Raiding Squadron [SRS]. 1SAS had temporarily ceased to exist.

The bulk of the SBS was training in Palestine, but Jellicoe had brought a force to Philippeville. Among the men were Keith Kilby, Doug Wright and Sid Downland.

'We had no choice about going in the SBS,' remembers Downland. 'But we were all quite chuffed. We reckoned Jellicoe had picked the best recruits.'

The SBS were to carry out a series of diversionary raids on Sardinia to coincide with the invasion of Sicily on 10 July. Bill Stirling, meanwhile, was still trying to bring round the Special Operations Branch of 15th Army Group to his way of thinking. He wanted 2SAS to be deployed strategically, not tactically in support of a larger army operation. Shortly before the Sicily invasion he wrote a memo to HQ 15th Army Group, reminding them that months of rigorous training meant his troops could 'gain access by any means available … should requirements appear for the disruption of Italian communications'. In his opinion, Stirling continued, the most efficacious deployment of 2SAS would be if 'a force of 300 men could work over hundreds of miles in up to 140 parties … so far rough landings by parachute have not been accepted. Second SAS Regiment is prepared to accept rough, unreconnoitred landings which can easily be undertaken with imperceptible increases in dropping casualties and advantages too obvious to mention'.

Stirling eventually accepted a compromise: 2SAS were instructed to carry out two operations during the initial landings on Sicily. Operation Narcissus, commanded by Sandy Scratchley, would involve fifty men making a beach assault on a lighthouse on the southern coast of the island in which intelligence reports indicated the enemy had installed some guns that could disrupt the main beach landings. Operation Chestnut was more to Stirling's liking, albeit on a smaller scale to that which he had envisaged in his memo. Captains Pinckney and Bridgeman-Evans would parachute into northern Sicily, each with ten men, and carry out a series of sabotage operations against rail, road and enemy communications.

In the event neither operation added much lustre to the reputation of 2SAS. Chestnut was depressingly similar to the first parachute operation carried out by David Stirling's men in November 1941. The men were dispersed over a large area; most of the rations were lost on landing; the radios were damaged so they couldn't send back any information. Bridgeman-Evans got himself captured. Pinckney went off to cut communications on the Gangi–Palermo road but ended up on the wrong road. It was, like the raids on the radar station, a 'bloody balls-up'. The trick was, says Greville-Bell, 'not to seethe against anyone; it's funny. You just have to laugh. You got so used to it in the British Army, or in any army. The thing about war is that you plan and plan but the ones that win are the ones who are most able to overcome the disasters'.

Operation Narcissus was a resounding success, of sorts. The lighthouse was secured, and without a single casualty. But there were no concealed guns. All that was found were three petrified Italians, whimpering and trembling. It was just as well the intelligence information was duff; the original raiding force of fifty men had been decimated by the disease that lay beneath Philippeville's superficial beauty. By the time of the Sicily invasion in July malaria was rife among the soldiers. Sandy Scratchley had been obliged to hand over command of 'Narcissus' to Roy Farran, who in turn rose from his sick bed to lead the thirteen fit men ashore.*

Nonchalance helped fill the hospital beds of Philippeville.

'I was giving Mepachrine to everyone and telling them to take it,' says

*Malaria was the major contributory factor to the failure of the SBS raid on Sardinia. Two men died from its effects during the operation and the others were so weakened by the disease they were easily captured. Doug Wright missed the operation through illness (he served with the SBS for the rest of the war, winning an MM), while Downland and Kilby were taken prisoner. In his report on the operation, Downland wrote of Kilby: 'He did his duty extremely well, attending to us at all times ... we are all indebted to him.'

Keith Kilby, 'but I don't know if many did. Some of the men were a bit complacent about taking it.'

Bill Stirling now had some idea how his brother must have felt after the first disastrous raid of 'L' Detachment eighteen months previously. But resilience was a family trait. He concluded the official report into Operation Chestnut by saying: 'It provided valuable experience for future operations and pointed out the pitfalls which are inevitable in any operation which is the first of its kind.'

Greville-Bell, Pinckney, Dudgeon, Farran and the others returned to the temporary sanctuary of the officers' club in Philippeville and carried on as before.

'The whole defence against the horrors of war,' says Greville-Bell, 'was to make a joke of it. People might have sometimes thought we were heartless but that was how we coped.'

CHAOS HAD REIGNED at Kabrit in the weeks following David Stirling's capture in January 1943. His dislike of paperwork and administration now jeopardized the very existence of his regiment. Operational procedures and other regimental minutiae existed only in Stirling's head. Pat Riley tried manfully to bring order to the chaos. On the day Paddy Mayne brought 'A' Squadron back to Kabrit, General Alexander decided to inspect the camp. Peter Davis, a debonair young officer who had joined the regiment shortly before Christmas, remembered that 'these dirty, bearded men began to trickle in through the main gates at the crucial moment of the general's visit. Poor Pat Riley was tearing his hair trying to hide them all, and his patience was put to the highest test when Johnny Wiseman, a very small and amusing officer, chose to enter the gates sporting a magnificent beard, when the general was less than 50 yards away.' Riley, failing to recognize Wiseman as an officer, told him in soldier's parlance to 'clear off'.

While Mayne struggled to make sense of a pile of unintelligible messages and signals sent by and for Stirling, or signed for another unexpected delivery of equipment ordered the previous month, the men wondered what the future held for them and the regiment. Davis recalled the 'buzz of speculation about the future of the unit'. He, and other new recruits, thought 'the regiment would now be disbanded since it no longer had Stirling's powerful personality to hold it together'. Such pessimism wasn't prevalent among the men who knew Paddy Mayne.

'There wasn't a doubt among us that we would be disbanded,' says Youngman. 'We just waited for the next job. Paddy never gave us a pep talk, we just carried on as normal.'

Malcolm Pleydell, however, shortly to be transferred from the SAS to Malta, told his girlfriend of his worry that 'there is no one with his [Stirling's] flair and gift for projecting schemes ... so now the ship is without a rudder'.

Davis met Mayne shortly after his return from the desert when he went into his tent to discuss a training detail. When he emerged he no longer feared for the regiment's future.

'My first impression of Paddy was amazement at the very massiveness of him ... his wrists were twice the size of those of a normal man, while his fist seemed to be as large as a polo ball. Although he must have weighed at least 17 stone there was not an ounce of surplus flesh on his body.' Mayne was shaving off an 'enormous reddish beard' when Davis entered his tent. He heard the cut-glass accent and turned to scrutinize his visitor. 'Under great jutting eyebrows, his piercing blue eyes looked discomfortingly at me, betraying his remarkable talent of being able to sum up a person within a minute of meeting him.'

Mayne listened to what Davis had to say, then asked him a few questions about himself. Davis was struck by the incongruity of his Olympian frame and the melodious voice. It was 'low and halting, possessing a musical sing-song quality, and the faintest tinge of an Irish brogue'.

As Davis got to know Mayne better he saw another contradiction in his personality. He was 'amazingly shy when he had to speak in public to his men'. Yet Mike Sadler says Mayne 'felt his true vocation in war; he was well suited to it, and he enjoyed it. Yet he wasn't totally fearless ... he was well aware of the risks around and I don't think he fancied

99

the idea of being shot more than anyone else. But he had a very good control of himself.'

There were undoubtedly moves afoot in the fusty corridors of power to bring Mayne under tighter control. When 1SAS was reorganized into the Special Raiding Squadron (SRS) and the Special Boat Squadron (SBS) in March 1943, Mayne was given command of the SRS. But both squadrons were placed under the overall command of HQ Raiding Forces.

AT THE END OF March Mayne addressed his new squadron. 'Paddy, in his shy, halting and barely audible speech to the men informed us that we were about to start a period of very intensive training,' said Davis. Mayne then elaborated on the restructuring of the squadron. There were to be three troops: One Troop was under the command of Bill Fraser. He and Mayne were the only surviving officers from the original seven who had joined in the summer of 1941. Fraser had enjoyed a good Desert War. Now a major with an MC, he had come through the campaign unscathed, save for two black bruises that had circled his sad eyes for several weeks after a Christmas drink in Cairo ended in a scuffle.

Major Harry Poat was appointed OC of Two Troop and Captain David Barnby was in charge of Three Troop (although he was later replaced by Captain Ted Lepine).

Each troop was divided into three sections, with each section consisting of one officer and around twenty men. Within each section there were more divisions; two sub-sections under a corporal or lance sergeant.

The rivalry between the three troops had taken root long before they arrived in their new training camp overlooking the coastal village of Nahariyya in northern Palestine. One Troop, remembers Bob Lowson, 'considered themselves elite and looked down on the rest'. A lot of the men in the troop had come from 'L' Detachment, such as Reg Seekings, 'Chalky' White, Chris O'Dowd and Pat Riley, recently returned from OCTU where he had been commissioned as a lieutenant. Jeff Du Vivier had also been offered a commission.

'I never fancied it,' he says. 'You're a commissioned officer so what

100

happens? You go into the officers' mess as a lieutenant [the rank of second lieutenant didn't exist in the SAS] and you're the tea-maker. I far preferred being one of the blokes in the sergeants' mess ... Jim Almonds, after he was commissioned, called me a chancer and I said, "Well, that's why I joined this lot."'

There were less experienced soldiers too; Thomas 'Ginger' Jones, a 27-year-old former miner from Lancashire; Alex Skinner, a good-looking blond from Essex, who, with his desert beard, had been nicknamed 'Jesus'; 20-year-old Syd 'Titch' Davison, who had already lost two brothers in the war, was a Bren gunner in Seekings' section; John Noble had a similar role in One Troop.

Noble was a craggy-faced former cavalryman from Edinburgh, who'd lied about his age and enlisted in the Scots Greys in 1938 as a 16-year-old. Pawky and self-sufficient, Noble was perpetually bemused by the officer class. He respected them all, admired most of them, but understood none of them. Noble had joined the SAS from the Commandos in November 1942. Within a matter of weeks he was on the brink of being RTU'd.

'There was a problem with a truck I was driving and I didn't know what it was,' he recalls. 'This officer was going nuts and wanted to get rid of me. But Sergeant Major Rose said, "No, he's staying with the regiment."'

During weapons training in Palestine Sergeant Chalky White, one of the Originals, had given Noble a Bren gun. '"Right," he said to me, "from now on I'm going to call you Nobby and you're going to be my Bren gunner." So I was.'

Two Troop and Three Troop were an amalgam of newer recruits, survivors from 'B' Squadron, the most recent arrivals from 'C' and 'D' Squadron, and a handful of 'L' Detachment veterans. One of the section officers in Three Troop was John Tonkin, a 22-year-old who'd joined from the Royal Northumberland Fusiliers in the tail end of 1942. Youngman, who was another of the more experienced members of Three Troop, had been raiding with Tonkin in the desert.

'He was a damned nice fellow,' he says. 'Nothing would faze him. You could see he was well educated in the way he carried himself.' He showed the men how to play bridge. 'We played it all the way up the desert,' says Youngman. 'I think he introduced us to it because he didn't want us playing pontoon and brag. We'd all thought bridge was an officers' game but we liked it because you had to use your noddle a bit more.' Some of Three Troop still preferred pontoon. 'Buttercup' Joe Goldsmith, so called because he spoke with a strong West Country accent, was an inveterate gambler.

'He was always short of money,' says Youngman. 'He would borrow some from the boys, lose it, then have to repay it when we got paid. So he was soon broke again.'

Three Troop had three of the best sportsmen in the squadron in Tim Ransome, Sam Smith and Dougie Eccles. Ransome was unbeatable over 100 yards, while Smith and Eccles were excellent footballers. Being good at sport was a boon in the eyes of Mayne, but some of Three Troop got the distinct impression he didn't hold them in particularly high regard.

'Paddy didn't like us,' says Alex Griffiths who, like Bob Lowson, had been in Norway with the Independent Company and also fought with the Commandos in the Middle East. 'Partly because we were all fairly new. So any dirty jobs we got. But there were a lot of Commandos [in the Troop] so perhaps we did think we knew everything.'

Two Troop was a fusion of comedians and sportsmen and eccentrics and intellectuals. The three section commanders under Harry Poat were Davis, Tony Marsh and Derrick Harrison. At first the trappings of their public school upbringing worked against them; their view of the war as one great jolly whizz of an adventure jarred with men who were in their fourth year of fighting.

'My first memory of Davis,' says Lowson, 'was his telling us before the Sicily operation that it was the most important event that had happened in the war and he was quite prepared to be killed to make it a success. I just thought, "I hope you're not including me in that!"'

Davis described Marsh as never seeming to 'care about a thing except having a good time and yet, in actual fact, none could be more conscientious ... there was little he did not know on the subject of training and handling men'. Davis might have been describing himself, so similar were their personalities.

Harrison was different. He was uptight and punctilious, in marked contrast to the outward insouciance of Davis and Marsh. Davis said he was 'one of those thin nervous types ... he paid the strictest attention to detail and would dwell on small points which we others thought not worthy of attention'.

Harrison had in his troop one of the most notorious characters in the entire squadron, James McDiarmid, recently stripped of his rank and sentenced to 156 days imprisonment for beating a native half to death in Cairo.

'He'd been in there two or three days,' recalls Sid Payne, 'when Paddy Mayne went down and got him released.' Payne was a sardonic 22-year-old, an uncomplicated Brummie who didn't dwell on the vagaries of war. He was closer to McDiarmid than most others in the squadron, but even he never really knew the workings of the Scot's mind.

Other soldiers in Harrison's troop included Bob McDougall and the Ridler brothers, Duncan and Freddie. Both were exceptionally intelligent, though prone to insubordination when they ran up against military pedantry. Duncan, at 23 the elder by two years, had been disciplined three times before he joined the SAS. Freddie had once dared to question Bob Lilley's authority.

'Freddie Ridler was a bit clever,' says Lowson, 'a bit well-educated, and he tried it on with Lilley one time. He took Freddie round the back of the tent and wiped the floor with him.' Lilley was Davis's staff sergeant but, though aware of Lilley's abrasiveness, Davis didn't care.

'As a sergeant in charge he was excellent ... a fine example of loyalty to his officers,' said Davis. 'The fact that he was disliked by his men was principally because he would stand no nonsense.'

Lance Sergeant Bill McNinch was liked by everyone. In peacetime he had managed a Glasgow bank; in the SRS he led one of Davis's sub-sections. In both roles he had a finger-tip feel for getting the best out of his subordinates.

'He was worshipped by the men,' said Davis. 'He was the humorist of the section ... with a gift for leadership.'

McNinch entertained his men, remembers Lowson, 'with a series of risqué poems and monologues. He was a scream of a comic, a one-man stage act'.

Lowson's best pals in Two Troop were Billy Stalker, Charlie Tobin and Sandy Davidson, English, Irish and Scottish respectively. All four had served in the Commandos together where they had been at the heart of a card school.

'Charlie was a keen bridge player,' says Lowson, 'but a hopeless one, too.'

There were some notable absentees. Johnny Cooper was being transformed into an officer at OCTU; Mike Sadler was in hospital being treated for stomach ulcers brought on by the stress of navigation; Jeff Du Vivier was still in charge of training at Kabrit and feeling increasingly 'abandoned'.

THE GIMLET-EYED Mayne enjoyed watching the growing and largely good-natured rivalry between the three troops, as he enjoyed observing everything that went on around him. All the time he looked, he learned. Davis remembers him 'silently watching with those sharp, penetrating eyes of his ... making a mental picture for future reference of the individual, inner character of everyone he observed'.

After a month of what Davis remembered as 'abnormally hard work', Mayne pitted the three troops against one another in an endurance march. Each troop would be dropped off on the banks of Lake Tiberias and march back to their coastal camp in under 24 hours.

'The distance was about 45 miles over rough and difficult country,' said Davis, 'and in the heat of the Palestine summer.'

Three Troop went first. Their ordeal forewarned the remaining two troops of what lay in store.

'Scarcely more than eight men succeeded in completing the course out of a total of sixty,' recalled Davis. 'They had been marching in the heat of the day and, under the glare of that summer sun were fainting and passing out like flies.'

One Troop, the golden boys of the squadron, went next. Most of the men 'stayed the course', remembered Davis, 'but through an error in map reading they marched off course ... and took nearly 48 hours to reach the camp'.

Last up was Two Troop. They were driven from the camp to Lake Tiberias, a journey during which, said Davis, they were 'tolerably comfortable ... the breeze of the our motion served to keep us cool'. When they assembled on the start line shortly after 1100 hours it was 'blazing hot, without a cloud in the sky and the sun throwing up a brilliant glare from the chalky, white road'.

The men set off in their sections.

'The word was,' says Payne, 'that if we didn't complete it in the allotted time we'd be sacked.' Payne had only recently got back his favourite pair of boots from the cobblers. 'They were perfect,' he recalls. 'Well broken in and really comfortable.'

Harry Poat and Sid Blanche, a former Guardsman who was in Lowson's section, were experimenting with rope-soled boots.

'We marched for about 50 minutes,' says McDougall, 'then had a 10-minute break. At the second break I caught a good look at Poat's boots and saw they had little spikes on the soles for scaling.'

By 1400 hours six of Harrison's section had collapsed from heat exhaustion. Harrison ordered his men to find what shade they could and lie up for the rest of the day. At dusk they continued marching. By the 20-mile mark Payne 'had a heat rash between the cheeks of my backside and every blooming step was agony'.

Poat was in trouble after eight hours. 'We had another short break,' says McDougall, 'and when he took his boots off you've never seen anything like it; from the heel to the instep was just one big blister. A couple of hours later it looked like raw liver.'

Lowson's section had to carry their corporal for much of the way. 'Bill Mitchell was a great lad and a regular soldier,' says Lowson, 'but he just couldn't march.'

Sid Blanche hobbled the last few miles. 'By the end of the march,' says Lowson, 'these rope boots were practically nailed to Sid's feet. The nail heads had been driven up into the soles of his feet from the constant marching.'

At dawn Harrison led his section to the top of the ridge that overlooked the camp. They plunged down the valley into the early morning mist, finding themselves at the edge of a fast-flowing stream that ran down the valley into the sea.

'It was beautiful,' says Payne, 'like a swimming pool. I dropped my rifle and went straight in.' Harrison's section crossed the finish line at 1030 hours, half an hour within the time limit. Davis checked in three hours later, Poat just after.

'As we came down from the ridge,' says McDougall, 'Harry Poat said, "march to attention, lads". How the hell he did it I don't know because a few miles before that he'd hardly been able to stand.'

THE PHYSICAL TRAINING was complemented by myriad other disciplines as spring turned to early summer: bayonet practice, wire cutting, foreign weapons training, cliff-scaling in Syria. The men were sent in packs to Jerusalem to attend a revolver course.

'It was run by a bloke called Grant Taylor,' says Lowson, 'who was an expert in instinctive shooting with a revolver.' In Jerusalem Lowson took time to visit the Church of the Holy Sepulchre. 'I'd never even seen the pyramids when I was in Egypt so I was determined to see some sights in Jerusalem.'

Bill Deakins found himself on leave with O'Dowd. Now a sergeant, O'Dowd didn't let his stripes fetter his exuberance. They ended up in a strip bar, the like of which left even a connoisseur like O'Dowd speechless. Along the walls were photographs of various obscenities including, says Deakins, 'a girl taking a donkey'. As the pair drank a beer a girl writhed on stage demonstrating 'how she could pick up large coins in her vagina'. The audience was impressed, and mischievous. Egged on by his pals, a soldier at the front of the stage tossed a coin on to the stage and invited the stripper to scoop it up.

'Unbeknown to her,' says Deakins, 'he'd heated the coin with lit matches.' The shrieks of distress that followed convinced them it was time to leave.

Alex Griffiths spent his free time in more cerebral pursuits. In a letter he wrote to his aunt and uncle he described conditions in Palestine. 'Plenty of swimming and sport, the weather is very nice these days ... I'm swotting up for a job after the war now! An office job would crease me, and I mean to be ready for a good thing when it comes along.'

Sid Payne and others spent their time trying to avoid their commanding officer. 'There were six of us in the tent trying to stay cool when someone came rushing through, saying, "Out, quick, Paddy's looking for someone to booze with!" We all shot out of the tent. He was like that, looking for someone to drink with.'

If it wasn't too hot the footballers in the squadron played games of five-a-side on a strip of wasteland that had been transformed by Deakins and Bill Cumper into a half-sized pitch. Goalposts were fashioned from scaffolding poles and corner flags from surplus timber. The local Arabs provided the spectators. All that was missing was good football. There were several talented footballers in the squadron: Sam Smith, Dougie Eccles, Chalky White, Ginger Jones and Johnny Rose. But there were several not so talented players. This, says Deakins, led sometimes to 'almost a free-for-all scramble ... the unseen shirt pull and gentle trip all part of the fun'.

All the squadron was back from leave by 2 May, for the unofficial Middle East Sports Day. There were six competing units: the SRS, the SBS, the New Zealand Railway Construction Company, their South African counterparts, HQ Raiding Forces and Middle East OCTU.

The day began with field events. Alexander 'Lofty' Baker, a former Grenadier Guardsman, romped to victory in the high jump.

'He was so tall,' says Youngman, 'that with his long legs it was easy.'

In the track events after lunch Tim Ransome left the opposition floundering in his wake in the 100 yards. The football team performed creditably, but didn't win the tournament. The last event, just before 1900 hours, was the final of the seven-a-side rugby.

'We were up against OCTU,' recalls Lowson, 'and they fancied their chances because they were all county players.'

The SRS, however, were quietly confident. Mayne was a former international, Wiseman was a whippet-like scrum-half, then there was the dependable Poat in the centre and John Hodgkinson in the scrum.

'Hodgkinson was a former rugby league forward,' remembers Lowson, 'and the equal of Paddy as a player in my opinion. A very tough tackler.' As events had overrun it was agreed the final should be first score wins.

'They kicked off,' says Lowson, 'and the ball went straight into touch. Paddy won the line-out and set off down the pitch. He threw a long pass to me at fly-half and my marker showed me the outside so I just ran straight past him and scored under the posts. After the game this officer came up to me and in this plummy voice said, "I didn't think you'd try that, old boy."'

The Sports Day signalled the end of the frivolity for the SRS. The rest of May was spent training for the impending invasion of Sicily. They were shown 'accurate sketch maps of our future objective', recalled Davis, 'so for the first time we were able to acquaint ourselves with the details of the terrain on which we were to operate ... even though all place names were still omitted and we were ignorant of even the country which we were going to invade'.

Wherever it would be, the men memorized their role in the operation. One and Two Troops would land by assault craft on the south coast of a small foot-shaped peninsula about 300 yards from where three heavy guns overlooked the sea. Two Troop would head for the guns from the northern, inland side, while One Troop launched a frontal assault on a cluster of buildings slightly to their west. Three Troop, meanwhile, would move inland and seize a strategically situated farm, and cut the only road that led to the guns.

To each troop was assigned a Mortar section, an Engineers' section and a Signallers' section. Bill Deakins, now a sergeant, was one of five Engineers under the command of Bill Cumper. In charge of the Mortar section was Captain Alec Muirhead. He was another from the stable of young, handsome, public-school-educated officers, though he was less idealistic than Marsh and Davis. He had put his medical studies on hold at Cambridge to enlist in the Royal Worcesters. Two months before he sailed for the Middle East in 1942 he'd been married in Norwich Cathedral. 'Said goodbye to June,' he wrote in his diary. 'She was very brave but very cut up.'

There was something endearingly amateurish and terribly British about the formation of the Mortar section. A message had been sent to Base Depot in Geneifa asking for forty trained mortar men to be posted. When they arrived only a handful had ever handled a mortar. The rest had understood they were going to learn how to fire a 3-inch mortar. When they discovered the reality they gamely volunteered to remain with the squadron. When the novices looked to Muirhead for guidance they realized their officer was as nonplussed as them.

'Alec had never handled a mortar before,' recalled Davis. 'But this ignorance on his part was put to good effect, for by training his section entirely along his own ideas – and in complete defiance of the training manual – he was able as a result of this conscientious experimenting to mount the mortar and fire the first round accurately within 20 seconds.'

Muirhead had an analytical mind. He loved to pore over his calculations, working out the trajectory and the range. In those early days he occasionally miscalculated.

'He inadvertently directed five bombs rapid fire straight down on to his own Observation Post,' recalled Davis, 'which was about 500 yards in front of the actual mortar position. As soon as he heard the sound of the first approaching bomb, he realized what he had done.'

Muirhead emerged from the debris of his OP grinning sheepishly with nothing worse than a slight cut on the back of his head.

In charge of the signallers was Lieutenant Harding. Most of his wireless operators were attached to the squadron, one of the few exceptions being David Danger. He had learned his signalling skills in Egypt.

'I was put on a truck sending messages and most of the signallers there were pre-war. These chaps were fast. It took me all my time to read Morse and often I would be told to get off [the radio] because I was too slow. You just had to accept it and learn to be quicker.'

Alf and Bill Dignum were two brothers from the East End of London who responded to a notice from the SAS asking for wireless operators. Alf, the elder by four years, had been wounded in the legs by a mortar bomb during El Alamein.

'We both came from the Buffs [Royal East Kents] and in my mind we were just cannon fodder as infantrymen. The SAS was the lesser of two evils.' Neither had experience as signallers but, says Bill, 'they were so desperate for wireless operators they took us. I got quite good in the end, I could do 35 words a minute.' After a six-week course Bill was posted to the SBS, and Alf went to the SRS.

On 6 June the squadron left Palestine for Suez. There they boarded the *Ulster Monarch*, a former passenger ferry between Belfast and Liverpool. The skipper conformed to the naval stereotype with a big black bushy beard. As the men boarded his ship, recalls Deakins, he vowed to 'give the squadron a dry landing in any operation'. The next three weeks were spent in the Gulf of Akaba, practising landings and familiarising themselves with the LCAs [Landing Craft Assault were 40ft vessels that could carry up to thirty-five men].

They were back in Suez at the end of June. On the 28th of that month General Montgomery addressed the squadron on board the *Ulster Monarch*. He congratulated the men on what they had achieved in the desert, then complimented them on their high levels of fitness and skill. Different thoughts were in different men's heads as they listened. 'I thought Monty was good,' says Payne. Lowson considered him 'an arrogant blighter'. To Youngman he was 'full of bull'.

'When he addressed us on the ship he told us we were the advance

110

guard of the operation and he wanted the guns knocked out. He gave us the challenger password [to use during the assault]. "The challenge is 'Desert Rats'," he said, "and the password is 'Kill the Italians', and that's exactly what I want you to do."'

It had been decided beforehand that the squadron would not give Montgomery the customary cheer until he had entered his launch prior to visiting the next ship. Davis remembered that the general 'took his leave in some confusion, not quite sure whether he should depart until we had given him the cheer which was his due'. Montgomery slowly backed up the companion way, muttering to himself 'wonderful discipline, wonderful discipline! Very smart. I like their hats'.

THERE WAS A LOT of nervous chatter on the afternoon of 9 July. The sudden change in weather only added to the men's sense of foreboding. In the five days since the SRS had sailed west across the Mediterranean the weather had been idyllic. Clear blue skies and warm sunshine all the way. Now, as they approached the Sicilian coast, the *Ulster Monarch* pitched and rolled in bad-tempered seas. Men prepared themselves in different ways. Some read and re-read the small blue booklet, *A Soldier's Guide to Italy*, with which they'd been issued on 4 July, the day they sailed; Sid Dignum remembers seeing Mount Etna off the port bow.

Arthur Thomson yearned for an end to the waiting. 'We wanted to get cracking, out of boredom, not bravado. We were fed up with cruising the Med.'

While Derrick Harrison and several others groaned and retched from the effects of seasickness, Cleverley, the squadron's Cornish cook, did his best to make light of the situation.

'One officer suggested putting French Letters over the barrels of our weapons to stop them getting wet during the landing,' recalls Thomson. 'Cleverley stuck his hand up: "What are we going to do with these Italians, sir," he asked, "fight 'em or fuck 'em?"'

The Italians were the unknown factor for the SRS. The information they'd been given indicated the gun battery on Cape Murro di Porco

(Cape of the Pig's Snout) was well defended by Italian soldiers; a 'veritable fortress' said Peter Davis.

'Unless we achieved complete surprise, which seemed unlikely, we knew that the task ahead would be a grim and bloody ordeal.'

The task was imperative to the success of the Allied invasion. Coming in a few hours behind the SRS would be the main British invasion fleet. If the coastal guns weren't destroyed they would inflict severe damage on the fleet.

Darkness brought no change in the sea conditions. Bacon and eggs were served in the ward room but few men had the stomach for them. Above deck, men strained their eyes to catch a glimpse of the RAF bombers they could hear overhead. Ahead of them, they could see the bombs bursting on the island and the hypnotic streak of red tracers from the anti-aircraft batteries. A searchlight from the shore suddenly swept out to sea, its beam dancing momentarily on top of the white-crested waves, before it rose to the heavens.

Just after 0100 hours on 10 July the order came over the loud hailer, 'SRS standby'. The men assembled on the troop deck, at times grabbing hold of one another for balance as the *Ulster Monarch* lurched over another wave. In the eerie red light of the invasion lamps they could hear the landing craft banging against the hull of the ship. The soldiers nearest to the open oiling doors, through which they would embark on to the LCAs, were soaked by gurgling torrents of sea water that crashed over them.

'SRS embark.'

Embarkation in such mountainous seas required skill and nerve and judgement. As the landing craft swung backwards and forwards a matelot crew man readied the men: 'wait for it, wait for it, wait for it, go'. The men, laden down with their kit, leapt from the oiling doors and into the craft. One, Frank Josling got his timing wrong. He plunged into the sea, disappearing into its angry white foam. Suddenly he popped up, minus his webbing, and was heaved on board just as the landing craft crashed back against the *Monarch's* hull. Within a few minutes he was safely ensconced in a landing craft, fully kitted-up and the butt of endless jokes.

112

When the men were in the landing craft they were lowered into the sea.

'We were inundated and drenched by great sheets of water and spray which came flying over us,' said Davis.

Inside the LCAs the men crouched and huddled in three columns, two against the sides of the craft and one down the middle. The cardboard buckets in each craft were soon brimful with vomit. Youngman recalls that there was no noise, no chatter, as they headed for the shore.

'You're scared, of course you are, because you are helpless, unable to hit back. We just wanted to get to the beach because then you've got a chance.'

As the flotilla approached the shore, searchlights skimmed the sea. Most of the men were beyond caring if they were caught in its beam, so strong, says Davis, was 'the longing to have our feet again on firm land'. Harry Poat was one of the few exceptions.

'He was standing in the stern,' recalled Davis. 'Immobile and unperturbed as ever.' As they came within lee of the land the sea grew calmer. Now they estimated the beach was less than 1,000 yards away. Then they heard voices drifting across the waves. Deakins scanned the darkness.

'You could see these gliders with their whole bodies below the sea surface, and their wings being lapped by the sea.'* The survivors, clinging desperately to the flimsy aircraft, pleaded for their lives. Johnny Wiseman ordered the pilot of his LCA to pick up a group of men huddled on top of the wing of one glider.

'It turned out one of them was the commander of the airborne force [Brigadier Hicks],' says Wiseman. 'I said to him, "Look, old boy, I can take you into the beach but you'll have to keep out of my line because I've got a job to do".'

Most of the LCAs left the men to the mercy of the sea.

'They were shouting, "Help, save me",' says Youngman. 'We just had to carry on. It was terrible. Terrible.'

---

* The British Airborne's objective was the Ponte Grande bridge, south of Syracuse. But a combination of strong winds and inexperienced US pilots who released the gliders too early resulted in forty-seven of the 137 gliders falling into the sea. Only twelve landed in the designated area.

113

Duncan Ridler's landing craft ploughed on, too. 'The poor devils were shouting for help but we didn't stop. That's war, I suppose.' The howling of the doomed glider troops ratcheted up the tension in the LCAs. 'We couldn't understand how all the noise raised by the glider men had failed to arouse any answering comment from the shore,' said Davis.

They hit the shore with a 'slight bump' at 0315 hours. There was no incoming fire. Nor was there any great cliff-scaling to do. Youngman and Griffiths, both in Three Troop, remember it was 'easy' to scale the cliffs. Bob McDougall, in Harrison's section, followed his mate Eric Musk.

'Eric walked along the beach and said, "Here we are, let's go this way" and walked up a path that led from the beach to the top.'

Peter Davis led his section to the top 'without exertion'. While he made contact with Poat, his men lay on the ground in defensive positions and listened to the sharp crump of exploding mortar bombs, followed by a ground-shaking explosion. Muirhead had got his calculations spot on, sending a bomb into the battery's cordite dump.

'Muirhead and his mortar team were splendid,' says Lowson. 'Before then I thought they couldn't fight their way out of a paper bag – most of them had come from some buckshee infantry regiment – but they were good.'

After the operation Muirhead was approached by Mayne. '"Well done," he said. "Do you want a medal or a promotion?" I hesitated for a moment,' recounted Muirhead, 'then with recent events in mind, I said, "I'll take the promotion, sir, my widow could do with some extra money."'

Davis realized they had landed half a mile further east than planned, 'with the result that we must now be immediately below the battery, right in the middle of what we had tacitly agreed beforehand would be the most dangerous area. And yet we seemed to be meeting with a complete absence of opposition. Somewhere to our left, the comfortable slow tat-tat-tat of a Bren rang out.'

The Brens belonged to One Troop. Davis remembered the playful goading of Bill Fraser – commander of One Troop – on board the *Monarch*, that 'he would certainly not be content with his troop merely capturing

114

the camp buildings and then sitting back, leaving the guns for Two Troop. "Oh no!" Bill had declared tauntingly. "One Troop will wipe out the gun battery before Two Troop even find out where it is!"'

Wiseman, one of One Troop's section commanders, had led his men effortlessly up the cliffs. His subsequent actions won him a Military Cross, the citation of which described his actions: 'While the battery was under fire from our mortars, by clever use of ground, he led his section to the outskirts of the position without being detected and made his way through the wire. Immediately the mortar fire finished he went straight in, achieving complete surprise, killing, capturing and wounding forty of the enemy ... although the darkness of the night made control difficult, he maintained complete command, and the information which he sent back was invaluable to the proper conduct of the operation.'

The initial information Wiseman gave Mayne was poorly received. He could barely make out a word Wiseman was saying. Mayne told him to get his section off the battery as the engineers were coming forward to blow the guns. Wiseman mumbled something in reply. Mayne told him to speak up.

'I managed to tell him I'd lost my false teeth,' says Wiseman. 'I'd been hit in the mouth playing cricket when I was up at Cambridge and I'd had these false teeth ever since. I had been shouting orders when suddenly out they flew. I fumbled about in the grass for them and luckily I found them.' Even Wiseman, equipped with his ribald rugby player's humour, failed to see the funny side. 'It was amusing afterwards, but at the time it wasn't.'

John Noble was awarded a Military Medal for his part in securing the battery, for what he calls in soldiers' vernacular 'shooting up people ... I had the Bren gun and just shot my way through. The Italians were giving up right, left and centre'.

The first Davis knew of the Italians' reluctance to fight was of a 'most pitiful wailing – a sound akin to the cry of a small child for its mother. It was some member of the Italian garrison, suddenly struck by the horrible realization that there were enemy within 100 yards of him'.

The greatest danger to the SRS in the first jumbled minutes was from friendly fire. Because they had been landed in the wrong places the meticulously rehearsed assault plans were useless. Davis, unable to find the rest of Two Troop, temporized. 'Because we had landed so far from our intended position ... I decided to take my section straight in across the stretch of open ground separating us from the battery which could now be clearly seen standing out against the flames [from the cordite dump].'

As Davis's section crossed the open ground they came under fire from their troops. Davis shouted the password 'Desert Rats'. Back came the response, 'Kill the Italians' from the unmistakeable voice of Chalky White.

Harrison's section, meanwhile, having grasped that the original plan had gone awry, was encountering similar problems. He demurred from improvising, partly because that wasn't his way but also because his job was to escort the engineers to the guns.

'There was only one thing to be done,' he wrote later. 'Retrace our steps and carry on with the original plan.'

Harrison led his men round behind the back of the battery. A machine gun began firing at them from their right flank. Sid Payne moved towards it; as he did so the two-man crew 'stood up with their arms up'. The nest was sandbagged with a coil of barbed wire round it.

'There was nothing I could do about it except shoot the one behind the gun,' says Payne.

As they closed in on the battery a streamer of red tracer glided towards them. They knew the Italians' tracer was green. Red was their own. Harrison dived into some nettles behind a wall. Payne saw a figure on the other side of the wall.

'I recognised the blue shirt but before I could say "Desert Rats" he opened fire with a Bren gun.'

The man firing the gun was John Hodgkinson but even he, a brawny rugby league player with powerful forearms, was susceptible to the Bren's one flaw: weighing 23 lbs, it had a tendency to shoot high and to the right when it was fired from the hip.

'The only reason I wasn't killed,' says Payne, 'is that I was a lot smaller than him and the gun climbed as he fired.'

116

Harrison's troop reached the battery at dawn. Deakins and his Engineer section inspected the guns.

'I'd been given a photo of the guns before the operation,' says Deakins, 'but they were nothing like the actual ones. These were British, manufactured at the end of the First World War.' As Deakins set about his work, scores of Italians milled around the battery. A couple approached Deakins. 'They wanted to help me with my pack but I just booted them out the way.'

Deakins and his two men, Chappel and Bowman, worked quickly.

'We opened the breech and put a charge across the hinges. It was a five-second charge which gave us just enough time to sprint for cover.' There was a deafening explosion, then bits of falling twisted metal rained down. 'I went up to Paddy, saluted and said "Guns out of action, sir."' At 0520 hours Mayne fired the Very light, the signal to the invasion fleet that the guns had been blown. Deakins felt unadulterated satisfaction as he watched them steam towards the shore.

His reverie was shattered by the roar of a heavy gun further inland. The men fell to the ground and braced themselves for the explosion. Nothing. Again they heard the roar. Nothing. Davis looked out towards the fleet and saw a 'fountain of water rise gracefully into the air'. Mayne acted with cool swiftness. One and Two Troops marched their prisoners towards the farm seized by Three Troop and here he established his HQ, devising the plan to capture the second battery. The farm quickly became a holding centre for captured Italian soldiers, local civilians and the remnants of the British glider troops. The hullabaloo was made worse by the dying shrieks of an Italian civilian.

'He'd been shot when we'd taken the farmhouse,' says Griffiths. 'All his family were around him and it took him a long time to die. The women were making a hell of a noise but they didn't bear us any malice. They blamed the Germans.'

Most of the captured Italians were viewed with contempt.

'Fawning, friendly, smiling little creatures,' remembered Davis, 'who came up to us asking for a cigarette.' Initially they were regarded with a mixture of hilarity and condescension. Attitudes changed as more glider troops were brought in with wicked tales. 'Wounded men had been stripped of their clothes and coverings,' said Davis, 'and left to die from exposure, while other prisoners had been beaten up and robbed of all their personal possessions.'

Soon the SRS witnessed for themselves the malignant spirit of the Italians. Youngman and some other men from Three Troop heard the sound of gunfire shortly after daybreak.

'There were about six Italians taking pot shots at the glider boys as if it were a shooting gallery,' he says. 'Needless to say they didn't see their families again.'

As the squadron moved inland towards the second battery across the parched pasture land some of the Italians added treachery to their brutality. Harrison's section was confronted with seven unarmed Italians coming towards them. When they were within 30 yards they dived to the ground and inaccurate machine-gun fire raked the ground just in front of the advancing British. A section of One Troop, led by Reg Seekings, fell victim to a similar ruse. Geoff Caton, a 22-year-old from Wigan who had been in the Scottish Commando with Mayne, was hit in the top of the thigh. An incensed Seekings stormed the machine-gun post killing everyone he found.

Other Italians fought more courageously, but the British blood was up. Seekings destroyed a pill box, an action that won him a Military Medal to go with the DCM he'd been awarded in the desert. The citation described how Seekings 'rushed the pill box and with grenades and finally with his revolver killed the occupants'. John Noble also did sterling work with his Bren, scanning the trees for Italian marksmen who were firing from specially constructed platforms.

'There were a couple of snipers that I hunted down and shot.'

Likewise, Alex Skinner, though suffering from shrapnel wounds to his leg and hip sustained during the earlier storming of the battery, stalked and killed three snipers holed up in a remote farmhouse.

The second battery was taken easily. The defenders' will had been broken by the mortar team, who once again landed a bomb in the cordite dump. Muirhead carried with him a pocket-sized notebook in which he kept a record of his mortar's team activities. After the landings at Murro di Porco, he wrote that at a range of 750–800 yards he had sent down sixty high explosive (HE) bombs and twelve smoke bombs. The results produced were 'hits on buildings or gun area by HE causing casualties and confusion. Smoker caught two cordite dumps'. Under the heading 'Remarks' he jotted 'Smoke invaluable as incendiaries ... HE on hitting the roof penetrates before exploding'.

With the second battery out of action (Deakins didn't have enough explosives to demolish it so he damaged its traversing and elevating gear to render it inoperable) the demoralized Italians threw themselves at the British. Alex Griffiths and Tim Ransome came across a brood of Italians 'waiting with their little cases to be taken prisoner'. Another demonstrated to Davis the 'Italian art of surrendering ... two hands waving frantically over a wall ... we watched fascinated as the hands developed into two arms and finally, cautiously, a very frightened head peered over the wall at us, on which was stamped a look of childish indescribable relief ... we were laughing so much that we could hardly tell him to come over to us.'

Deakins went over to Caton, lying in the shadow of a hedge receiving treatment. 'What the bloody hell have you been up to?' he asked.

Caton laughed: 'I've gone and got myself shot.' Deakins patted him on the back and told him he'd pay him a visit in hospital.

'He died about half an hour after I had spoken to him,' recalls Deakins, 'from loss of blood.'

Caton was the only fatality of what had been a remarkably successful operation. The batteries had been destroyed, allowing the safe passage of the main invasion fleet; approximately 150 of the enemy had been killed and over 500 prisoners – including the Italian commandant – taken. For the next few hours the squadron relaxed. Davis sent some prisoners 'to scour the neighbouring countryside for nuts and tomatoes'. Lowson and Tobin brewed up a cup of tea and sat back in the sunshine watching the landings at Avola. Later they billeted in a grandiose farmhouse that had belonged to a prominent fascist. They handed over the

119

prisoners to the Fifth Division and in their stead obtained some poultry.

'There we remained,' said Davis, 'delightfully inactive for 48 hours.' For a few hours Phil Gunn, the squadron's medical officer and a children's doctor before the war, organized a forage.

'He was so distressed by the sight of the local kids,' says Lowson, 'that we gathered together all the food we could find and gave it to these children.'

On the morning of 12 July the squadron moved down into Syracuse harbour. A minesweeper ferried them out to the *Ulster Monarch* where the ship's crew gave them an enthusiastic welcome.

'It was good to get back on the boat,' says Wiseman, 'and enjoy a bit of a rest.'

ON BOARD THE *Monarch* the men began to clean their equipment and sort out their kit. A queue had already formed for the showers. Few talked about war.

'I never swapped stories with men from other troops,' says Lowson. 'You tended just to stick with your mates.'

Muirhead, however, was gleefully recounting to Davis and Harrison an anecdote involving a mortar bomb and three petrified Italians when they were asked to attend Poat's cabin. They found him standing over a map of the eastern coast of Sicily.

'With a deliberate forefinger,' recalled Davis, 'Harry pointed to a strangely shaped little peninsula on the map ... "You see that town there; well, that is Augusta, an important naval port which must be captured without delay. It seems from reliable reports that a white flag has been observed flying above the citadel, which rather suggests that the town has been evacuated. It's therefore important for our troops to occupy this important base without delay, so it's been planned for the *Monarch* to sail straight into the harbour and land our unit in the town by means of landing craft."'

The officers took a closer look at the objective. Augusta, 11 miles north of Syracuse, was built on a spit of land attached to the mainland by a bridge. It was imperative it was captured so the Eighth Army could use it as a platform from which to continue their drive north. What the SRS hadn't been told, however, was that while the town had been evacuated, the high ground that overlooked Augusta was still occupied by the Schmatz Battle Group of the Hermann Goering Division. At 0430 hours on the morning of 12 July the destroyer *Eskimo* had sailed into the harbour and been badly damaged by shellfire. Other ships had followed but were driven away by heavy fire from the shore.

The assault would be in two waves. One and Three Troop in first, then the LCAs would return for Two Troop and the mortar section. In the meantime Three Troop were to push straight through the town, cross the bridge and capture the railway station. From there they would continue to a crossroads a mile or so outside Augusta and hold it until the advance elements of 17 Brigade reached them. Speed was of the essence, so the landings would begin at 1930 hours, against the backdrop of the setting sun.

Sid Payne was asleep when a pal woke him to tell him the news.

'There was no grouching or grumbling among the men,' he recalls. 'The one thing that did bother us was that it meant we were going to miss the meal that the sailors had prepared for us. It was all laid out for us: eggs, sausages and bacon.'

THE *MONARCH* WAS escorted towards Augusta by the cruiser HMS *Norfolk*, a destroyer HMS *Tetcott* and two MGBs. The sight that met their eyes was one of a tranquil Mediterranean coastal resort. Gleaming white cottages lined the harbour. Boats bobbed gently up and down on the slight swell. The reflection of the deep orange sun on the sea forced the men to squint as they looked at the shore. There was no white flag, but neither did the town look a hive of enemy activity.

One and Three Troops embarked in the LCAs and sped towards the shore. Griffiths remembers 'we were singing and shouting as we came in and the padre [Ronnie Lunt] was with us. He told us to shut up but we were all happy-go-lucky and thought "these Italians are going to be easy".'

121

Noble, in One Troop, recalls that the 'crews of the *Monarch* and the destroyer lined up and cheered us as we went in towards Augusta'.

Up on the peninsula the German gunners followed the progress of the landing craft from ship to shore. When they were about 300 yards from the town they began firing.

'They opened up with everything as we went in,' says Albert Youngman. 'We could hear rounds thudding into the landing craft and the whoosh of shells exploding into the water all around.'

David Danger's thoughts were focused on the landing. 'All I thought about was the ramp going down and running ashore. I had the radio on my back and I was hoping I wouldn't run out and find myself in deep water.'

The *Monarch* opened up with her 12-pounder and 20mm cannons, and the destroyer, said Davis, who was watching from the decks of the *Monarch* began 'systematically engaging any spot where she imagined trouble might be concealed and the frequent accurate salvos were punctuated by the occasional roar of the heavy guns of the cruiser'. The men of Two Troop looked on open-mouthed as the gargantuan navigator of the *Monarch* began dancing a jig.

'That's the way, lads,' he bawled, 'that's the sort of medicine they need! My house in London was bombed flat, so don't mind what you do!'

One shell scored a direct hit on an enemy pill box. A second was targeted by one of the MGBs that dashed inshore and destroyed it with cannon fire.

The first LCAs reached the shore and the ramps clattered down. The men in Three Troop remember it as a comparatively dry landing, hopping across boulders and into the town. Johnny Wiseman and Alf Dignum, short men at the best of times, found themselves floundering in several feet of water.

'We couldn't get in because it was too rocky,' recalls Dignum, 'so the navy chap says "sorry, you'll have to swim for it". I had the radio on my back and I didn't want to get that wet. That was one moment I wished I wasn't half the size of the others.'

Wiseman waded ashore 'holding my rifle over my head'.

As the men clambered ashore they came under heavy small-arms fire. Dignum saw George Shaw, one of the stretcher bearers, tending to a wounded man.

'He lived in the next street to me in London,' he says, 'and we were good friends. He was bending over a colleague when all of a sudden he collapsed to the ground. I just got out of the way quick and hoped I wasn't next. Having a wireless strapped to your back doesn't exactly help matters.'

Three Troop, already racing ahead through the town, had suffered some early casualties. Arthur Thomson, in One Troop, came across his friend Dougie Eccles. 'He'd been shot in the leg. Blood everywhere. You didn't want to leave your mates, but it was instilled into you: keep going and finish the job no matter what. So I told him help was coming and pressed on.'

Two Troop had now embarked in the LCAs. Davis and his section hugged the bottom of the craft and tried to 'distinguish the vicious whistle of small-arms bullets flying overhead'.

Sid Payne, meanwhile, had been determined not to let the navy's food go to waste. 'As we were making our way to the LCAs I grabbed a handful of sausages and ate them as we made our way in.'

They landed with a gentle bump and Davis leapt out into two feet of water.

'As we stumbled over slippery rocks,' he said, 'bullets chipped into the ground around us and someone from the previous wave yelled at us to get into single file and out of the beach area which was under heavy fire.'

Payne ran down the ramp on a full stomach alongside 'one of the medical orderlies [Corporal Bentley] who was practically alongside me ... he gave a grunt and fell down. I dragged him behind a rock but you know a person is dead by the way he goes down'.

Davis's section made it into the cover of the streets without incident. Payne and Duncan Ridler, in Harrison's section, scurried towards the town stooped low like old men.

'One shell landed right in front of us,' says Payne, 'and threw a bloke through a shop window.'

Ridler and Charlie Belsham ran from one doorway to the next, in classic street fighting drill. 'Then Belsham suddenly let off his weapon at a large mirror in one of the houses. "I've always wanted to bust one of those," he said.'

Bill Deakins who, along with his Engineer section, had come ashore as ordinary troopers with no explosives, saw Mayne sauntering down the main street without a care in the world.

'He had one hand in his pocket, his cuffs – as was his habit – turned back and behind him trotted his signaller, David Danger. It was never done out of bravado but simply to give the men confidence.'

Two Troop established its base in a pretty public garden, 'where in better days,' said Davis, 'the more fashionable elements of the community would doubtless have disported themselves'. Davis's section and Harrison's section took up positions in the gardens, awaiting further orders. Payne was with Taffy Pitman behind a Bren gun.

'All of a sudden there was a ping and a round hit the wall above my head; then another ping and a bullet hit the barrel of the gun. We didn't wait for the next one. We rolled out of the way and found some better cover. I think the only reason we survived was because it was getting dark.' Davis remembered well the silent wait as the 'depressing twilight deepens ... if only we knew how the battle was going we would be more able to withstand this strange, dull, clawing sensation in our stomachs ... and these fears that the sounds and indistinct shadows might at any moment develop into a powerful counter-attack'.

Up ahead Three Troop were probing the enemy's strength, though their sergeant, Andy Frame, had joined the casualty list when he was shot through the neck. But still they pushed on, crossing the bridge and securing the railway station. One section then advanced up the railway line on the left, a second one on the right and a third section was pressing forward along the road. Youngman's section, led by Lepine, moved up alongside a dry-stone wall on the other side of which was an olive grove.

'Out of the darkness on the other side of the wall came a patrol of Germans,' says Youngman. 'We filed past each other. We weren't sure

124

who they were and neither were they. They got about 20 yards past us before "Snowy" Kirk let go with the Bren gun and got them. I walked over to make sure they were dead and picked up a Schmeisser [machine pistol] and a Luger. Snowy and I then had an argument because he said they were his. "I got the buggers," he said. But I kept them and used the Schmeisser for the rest of Italy.'

Griffiths, in John Tonkin's section, remembers crossing the bridge without any problem and then 'continuing down the road to see what was beyond it'. Before they reached the crossroads they ran into heavy German mortar and machine-gun fire. Muirhead's mortar team were called up over the radio and he directed three HE and three smoke bombs at the German positions. His notebook recorded the results. 'Nil. Out of range.' Faced with superior firepower, Three Troop took up defensive positions and waited. A runner was sent back into the town.

'The story we heard only served to increase our apprehension,' said Davis. 'It was feared casualties had been heavy. David Barnby and Ted Lepine were thought to have been killed and the majority of their sections lost ... we could expect a counter-attack at any moment.'

Three Troop came under heavy fire from the German forces grouped at the crossroads. A tank came down the road but an anti-tank missile that bounced off its hull spurred them into a rapid retreat.

'They were good troops those Germans,' reflects Youngman. 'During the night my section heard the sound of approaching feet along the road. I called out "Desert Rats" and in a second they had hit the deck and opened fire. A lot different from Murro di Porco.'

At the railway station the telephone started to ring. One of Three Troop picked it up. Three minutes later shells began to crash in and around the station. The squadron's signallers tried to contact the British warships in the harbour but the radios had been damaged by sea water during the landings. Mayne mulled over the situation. With no radio contact, no sign of 17 Brigade and only half their normal complement of ammunition [the operation had been foisted upon them so unexpectedly they hadn't the time to replenish their supplies], he decided to withdraw Three

Troop to behind the bridge. The Germans sent them on their way with a barrage of 4-inch mortar bombs. Muirhead and his mortars, by now up from the town, replied with twelve HE bombs. The enemy mortars went quiet and Three Troop moved back without further casualties.

The squadron, said Davis, 'settled down to watch through the slowly moving hours of darkness, fearing every second to perceive some sign that the expected attack was indeed materializing'. Then, at 0400 hours, they heard the sound of tracked vehicles on the move. Men peered even more intently into the lightening gloom. Wheeled transport could also be heard. '[But] the noises came no nearer,' said Davis. 'And eventually all was silence once more.' At dawn advance elements of 17 Brigade came down the crossroads, past the deserted German positions, and made contact with Three Troop.

The squadron withdrew into the town. Then the partying began. 'Paddy was very good at judging if the time was right to let our hair down,' says Ridler.

'Like any band of guerrilla raiders,' recollected Davis, 'we spent the remainder of that day until late in the afternoon wandering around the town, entering any building we chose, and making deep inroads into the town's alcoholic stocks.'

In a previous life Augusta had served as a quarters for Italian naval officers. The number of brothels discovered by the squadron indicated their needs had been well catered for. The more wine that was consumed the more frolicsome the squadron became. Deakins remembers fancy dress parades with men 'very much in the satire of the original owners, with the wearing of bras, French knickers, petticoats, suspenders, stockings and high-heeled shoes'. The bolder of the soldiers donned lipstick and rouge and pranced around to the amusement of their pals.

Payne was hailed by an officer propped up against a bar.

'There were champagne bottles everywhere and he had one in his hand. "Come and have a drop," he said. He knocked the top of the bottle on a table and we had a drink.'

From a café Bob McDougall heard the keys of a piano being sweetly caressed. 'I went inside and there was Bill Mitchell at the piano playing a piece of classical music. Eric Musk was with me and I turned to him and said, "I didn't know Mitch could play the piano so well." Then he reached up, grabbed a glass from the top of the piano and with the other hand poured himself a drink from a bottle of champagne. The keys were still going but his legs were pedalling away like mad. It was a pianola!'

'They carried the pianola outside,' says Ridler, 'and we had a wild time. Ginger Hines got hold of a cymbal and someone else had a tambourine.'

The men gathered round and began to sing songs, says Deakins, 'many of them sung blasphemously to popular hymn tunes'. The padre, Ronnie Lunt, appeared unfazed by the heresy. He was busily stockpiling bottles of wine presumably, as one wag, commented 'for communion'.

The question of how much looting actually occurred remains a contentious issue. Some men averred there was little if any looting, others readily admit they filled their boots. Griffiths remembers one soldier wheeling a pram down the road packed to the gunnels with booze and other assorted goodies. Wiseman got himself a typewriter, Youngman 'scrounged a lot of wine, some flags and a sword ... we were collecting them for the navy boys because they had no chance to collect them'.

Payne went into a stationery shop and grabbed a handful of fountain pens. 'By this time an infantry regiment was in the town digging in and I started handing out the pens to them, saying, "There you go, write home to mother." Their officers weren't too happy.'

Mayne was after a greater booty than mere fountain pens.

'I was sitting back in the sun enjoying the carnival atmosphere,' recalls Deakins, 'when Tommy Corps [Mayne's batman] came to the square and told me I was wanted by the CO.' Mayne was waiting for Deakins in a bank in the main square of Augusta. At his feet was a safe that Mayne had unsuccessfully tried to open with a pick.

'Sergeant,' said Mayne, 'I want you to open this safe.'

Deakins, however, had a problem. 'Before the operation Paddy had told me there would be no engineer work so I didn't have any explosives, but it was no use telling Paddy you couldn't do it.'

Deakins asked Corps to collect some grenades, some envelopes and a long piece of string. Off went Corps, returning a few minutes later with all the items on Deakins's list.

'I emptied the powdered explosives from the grenades on to an envelope by unscrewing the filler caps. Then I made some sausage-shaped charges using the envelopes and string and fastened them around the inner steel of the safe.'

To fire the charge, Deakins wedged another grenade against the charges and attached a string to its safety pin that he trailed out of the room and down the staircase.

'I thought it would blow,' says Deakins, 'and it did, at the second attempt.' Deakins and Mayne re-entered the room, choking on the clouds of acrid dust. Inside the safe were some documents, a cameo brooch, a gold ring and six silver spoons tied in a small bundle. Mayne placed the haul on the counter.

'Sergeant, these are for you.'

THE REST OF JULY was spent in camp at Augusta. The days were for the most part blissful, remembered Davis, either 'sleeping under the olive trees or swimming in the warm sea of the Mediterranean'. David Danger was having a dip one day when he 'saw several white sea snakes swimming past me ... fortunately they disappeared'. On land, Danger was confronted by equally terrifying spectres.

'We had a very good football team organized by Chalky White but Paddy got us playing some rugby. I hadn't played before. Never again. I got the ball on the wing and ran for my dear life. Suddenly I was faced by Mayne. He didn't bother tackling me, he just swatted me aside with one hand.'

After Augusta Duncan Ridler had been transferred to the incipient intelligence section of the SRS, which at the time consisted of Captain Bob Melot. He was an intriguing character, a cultured yet formidably courageous 48-year-old Belgian who had served in the trenches in the First World War before joining the Belgian air force.

'At the outbreak of the Second World War he was an agent in Cairo for Belgian Steel,' says Ridler. He had joined the British General Staff in the Middle East and then used his vast knowledge of the desert – he was fluent in Arabic – to guide the LRDG and SAS to various objectives. 'Even though he was married with two young daughters,' recalls Ridler, 'he was very keen on tackling the Germans. In the Benghazi raid [September 1942] he had been shot in the stomach, and didn't join us again until after Augusta.'

Davis remembered Melot as 'quietly spoken, well mannered, deeply interested in people ... with a delightfully wry sense of humour'. All in all, Davis concluded, for a foreigner he possessed 'all the qualities of that legendary English gentleman'.

In Sicily Ridler recalls that Melot 'introduced me to lots of European habits that I didn't know anything about ... he came up the road one day holding his beret which was full of little red mullet he'd caught in the sea. We had them for supper and they were very tasty'.

If the days were carefree, the nights were horrendous. From the 17–27 July they were subjected to enemy air attacks.

'We had actually been confined to the Monarch at first,' says Danger, 'but when the ship next door was hit by a bomb we came ashore.' But still the Luftwaffe came. Poat, as usual, took it all in his stride.

'In the middle of a conversation,' said Davis, 'a sudden vicious whistle in the air overhead would send us all flat on our faces ... all of us, that's to say, with the exception of Harry who would remain standing there and carrying on the conversation as though nothing had happened.'

If it was culture Ridler wanted, he'd spend time with Melot. If it was riotous behaviour, McDiarmid was the man. The two Sicilian operations had done nothing to tame his wild ways. There were some graves near their camp, Ridler remembers, 'into which McDiarmid went down to see if there was anything worth acquiring'. Payne says all he came back with was 'a skull that we promptly named Bony'. That night the guard was mounted, with each man doing a one-hour stag.

'I was on the 3 to 4 a.m. shift,' says Payne. 'I woke up at 3 but couldn't see anyone on duty. The chappie who should have been was fast asleep.

When I roused him and asked why he wasn't on guard, he pointed to the skull and said "Bony's on duty". Then he turned over and went back to sleep! So I went back to sleep and left Bony on guard.'

In August the squadron moved to a new camp in Cannizzaro, where the HQ was established in a house that had belonged to a fascist doctor. On 17 August General Alexander, the Allied Deputy Commander-in-Chief, cabled Winston Churchill proudly informing him that 'the last German soldier was flung out of Sicily'. In fact, over 40,000 Germans had been 'flung' safely out of the island across the Messina Straits to Italy, where they now regrouped and prepared for the invasion of the mainland.

Mayne increased the squadron's training regime as a prelude to operations in mainland Italy. The three Troops marched independently to the lip of Mount Etna and back again.

'It wasn't too bad,' remembers Lowson. 'Quite a walk towards the top but not a particularly long way. We all had a good look into the volcano and it was bubbling away nicely with molten lava.'

The average time taken to complete the exercise was $2\frac{1}{2}$ hours, the war diary noted. Mayne was up and down in two.

The squadron moved to Catania on 1 September. Something was in the offing. Bill Deakins waved them off. He wouldn't be going with them. In 1941 he had been crushed by a lorry that left him with multiple injuries, serious enough to prevent him doing his parachute training at Kabrit. Such was his value as an explosives expert, however, that David Stirling had turned a blind eye.

'I would get recurrences of the pain from time to time,' recalls Deakins. 'The pain would spread across my pelvis, then work its way down either my left or right leg.'

Sometimes, if the pain got too bad, he was confined to bed where he could only turn himself over by grabbing hold of the headboard and twisting his body. Shortly before he said a temporary farewell to the squadron, Deakins had a chat with Peter Davis. He was his normal ebullient self.

'He'd had it quite easy in Sicily and was saying that war was quite easy.' Deakins, who had been on the beaches at Dunkirk, cautioned Davis.

'"It's not always easy," I told him.'

HARRY POAT WAS furious.

'Tell your section to expect to be landed within the next few minutes,' he snarled at Davis. 'And almost certainly in completely the wrong place … God knows what this clueless crew think they are up to.'

It was the early hours of 4 September and the SRS's operation against the German-held coastal town of Bagnara in southern Italy had got off to a hapless start. Of the two LCIs [Landing Craft Infantry were 169 feet long and could carry nearly two hundred men], one had been delayed at the port of Riposto after the propeller had become jammed by the retaining cable. The other had run aground at Allessio and the half the squadron had been transferred into five LCAs. But they were now $2^1/_2$ hours behind schedule. Dawn was less than an hour away. Poat imagined what the Germans in Bagnara, 11 miles to the north of the main British landings at Reggio, would do if the assault force was spotted so early in the operation.

The assault craft ran ashore with a jolt. The ramps of the LCI thundered down on to the beach, unleashing a torrent of muttered profanities from the SRS.

'No one knew if the beach was mined or not,' says Alf Dignum. 'Paddy Mayne was first up the beach, walking all the way, and by the time we'd followed him up there was still only one set of footprints. And it was bloody hard for me, being so short, keeping up with his footsteps!'

Up and down the beach officers took their bearings. Davis calculated he was 'two miles out of position'. Poat, his equanimity restored, gathered Two Troop together after a snatched consultation with Mayne.

'Look here, chaps,' he told Davis, Harrison and Marsh, 'Paddy has decided to alter the whole plan because we've been landed so late and so far out of position … we [Two Troop] will push straight through, and hold the bridge which crosses a deep wadi bed at the foot of the main road running up the mountain to the north of the town.'

131

As Poat briefed his section commanders One Troop were moving through Bagnara to seal off the northern approaches to the town. Three Troop were ordered to secure the roads and railways south of the town.

Davis led his troop along the beach and then into the town. The first strands of daylight guided them through the deserted streets. Suddenly there was a loud cry. The two sub-sections on either side of the road dived into doorways.

'Inglesi! Inglesi! Buon, molto buon!'

'An elderly gentleman,' recalled Davis, 'clad in a long flannel night-shirt [was] standing on the balcony above us and clapping his hands for all he was worth.'

By the time they reached the main coastal road, which ran parallel to the sea 300 yards inland, it was pale sunshine. Davis took his men down the road. Then they turned, heading for the bridge.

Davis's section crossed the bridge, exchanging pleasantries with Marsh and his men who were taking up positions. Harrison's section brought up the rear. As the road began to climb, Johnny Hair, Davis's runner, glanced over his shoulder. Marching up through the town in single file behind Harrison's section – though out of sight of each other – was a detachment of men.

'Is that Three Troop on the road behind us?' he asked Davis.

'"I expect so," I replied, "they should be somewhere around here." But to be on the safe side I took the precaution of glancing in their direction through my binoculars.'

Davis looked through his glasses.

'"Yes, they're ours all right." I was on the point of lowering the glasses when I noticed something unusual about the headgear ... where had I seen those caps before? Sergeant Cattell had one, I remembered; but his was a German hat.'

Payne was the penultimate man in Harrison's section. 'The chappie behind me tapped me on the shoulder,' he recounts, 'and pointed to his ear, then down the road. I could hear marching feet.'

The Germans belonged to a sapper unit who had come to blow the bridge.

'Round the bend came the first ones,' says Payne, 'carrying their rifles at ease. They got quite a surprise.'

The ones who weren't killed in the initial ambush scattered back down the road. The firing had alerted the Germans on the high ground overlooking Bagnara. They had been caught unawares by the silent approach of the SRS who, unbeknown to them, had had a stroke of luck in landing on the northern beach. The southern beach, the stretch of sand most conducive to a seaborne invasion, had been heavily mined by the Germans.

There was a battery on a plateau directly above the town, and along a ridge to the north-west were several 4-inch mortars, an 88mm anti-aircraft gun and some Spandau machine guns. One Troop had set up its HQ on the road up the hillside and John Noble was blasting away with his Bren gun. As Davis moved up he ran into Fraser.

'"There doesn't seem to be much on," he informed me, "so I might as well have my breakfast while I have the chance."'

A few minutes after Davis had taken men further up the hill, a cluster of mortar bombs landed in Fraser's HQ. Two signalmen, Charlie Richards and Bill Howell, were killed.

Further down the road a tracer bullet passed through Harry Poat's left thigh pocket as he issued orders to his men. Thomas Parris coming up behind was killed by the bullet. The maps in Poat's pocket caught fire but he continued to pass on instructions as he patted out the flames.

Wiseman's section was told to reinforce Marsh at the bridge.

'We came under a murderous machine-gun fire as we moved down towards the bridge,' he remembers. A German machine gunner spotted Alf Dignum withdrawing down the road. 'I was walking in front of a wall and these bullets tore into the stone just above my head. A couple of inches lower and ...'

McDiarmid was shot in the ankle as he led his sub-section up a road heading east. He told his men to take cover, providing them with protecting fire as they scrambled to safety. Once McDiarmid had wrapped a field dressing round the wound he took his men up another route. (He was later awarded the MM for his leadership.)

133

THREE TROOP WAS having a quieter time of it on the southern side of the town. The railway tunnels they had found to be occupied only by frightened Italian civilians.

'We had to go in there searching for Germans,' remembers Youngman, 'but we didn't find any. They were just chock-a-block with locals.'

Davis, acting on Poat's orders, took his section further up the road, round another of the hairpin bends that cut a tortuous route up the hillside where they encountered Harrison's section taking cover.

'Don't stand there, you fool,' Harrison barked at Davis. 'Don't you realise they're sniping this road like fury?'

Davis recalled that he glared 'scornfully' at Harrison.

'I have explicit orders from Harry to take up a position on the bend above you … and I can't very well disobey those orders unless I'm actually forced to by opposition. And I can't see much sign of that.'

Davis pressed on. Lowson, Tobin and the rest of the section hugged the rocky hillside into which the road was cut, while to their left they scanned the vine-covered terraces that rose like a giant staircase up the hillside.

'Davis dropped my section off at a cutting by the side of the road,' says Lowson. 'He left Bill Mitchell in charge while he took another sub-section on up the road.'

Having split the section into two, Davis rounded the next bend and to his dismay saw that the road ran dead straight for 300 yards before curving to the right.

'Where could we go to?' Davis recalled asking himself. 'That was indeed the question.'

As they doubled along the road a machine gun opened up. They sprinted forward, frantically searching for some cover. Davis heard the bullets smack into the road's asphalt all around them. They reached the bend and there, round the corner, was a small peasant's cottage. In ones and twos they piled into the tiny house. McNinch and Johnny Hair. Sandy Davidson. Andy Storey. Charlie Tobin. The last pair to leap through the door were Johnstone and John Tunstall, a 'big raw-boned Scottish miner'.

Davis peered through a window. He saw that the Germans were positioned less than 200 yards ahead, at a point where the road crossed a deep gully and doubled back to the left at an acute angle which gave them a perfect vantage spot overlooking the town and the road that led up the hillside. It was an unhealthy cottage in which to be trapped. For the next hour they watched as a salvo of mortar bombs rained down on their comrades holding the bridge. At any minute they expected their cottage 'to become the centre of a hail of deadly high explosive bombs'. But the bombs never arrived.

'Perhaps we were out of sight of the mortar OP,' Davis later reflected. 'Or maybe we were too close to permit accurate fire.'

McNinch scanned the gully with his binoculars and counted seven possible machine-gun nests. Tobin asked Davis if he could 'have a bang at them' with his rifle grenade. Davis shook his head.

'The action was not likely to rest unanswered.'

By mid morning there was no sign of Mitchell and his section. Nor had any radio contact been made with the rest of the squadron. But neither had they come under fire from the Germans.

'Worn down by the long hours of waiting', Davis decided to try and crawl back down the road along a culvert that ran under the road. For half an hour he turned the plan over in his head. 'It seemed so easy, so safe,' he recalled, 'and none of us wished to sit idly like cowards.' He asked for two volunteers to accompany him. Storey and Tobin nodded. Davis turned to give final orders to McNinch and as he did so 'the air was torn to shreds by a long, wicked roar from that cursed Spandau'.

Outside the house, Tobin lay dead, his chest riddled with bullets. Storey dashed back inside the cottage, chased all the way by the machine gunner. McNinch and Tunstall fired a long burst on the Bren towards the German positions. The German gunner replied. Then another. And another.

'Soon the bullets were throwing up the parched earth around us, kicking the stones into our faces.'

A bullet went through the material of Davidson's trousers. Tunstall, manoeuvring himself into a better firing position, was hit in the face. As

135

he lay thrashing on the ground, 'emitting a series of terrible moans and gurgles', McNinch dragged him under cover. He did his best to staunch the blood that poured from his mouth. For 30 minutes bullets thudded into the walls of the cottage. Inside dozens of flies buzzed round Tunstall, attracted by his bloody mouth. As the Germans ceased firing, Davis was 'left to wonder what next experience we would have to face'.

Mitchell's sub-section had heard the firing as they waited in the cutting back down the road. Then, recalls Lowson, a message was received over the radio 'telling us to close up to where he [Davis] was'. Davis said later a message had been sent, but it 'must have been misinterpreted for these men to have been sent up that exposed road in that manner'. Davis saw Mitchell and his men as soon as they turned the corner of the road 50 yards from the cottage. So did the Germans.

Davis screamed a warning.

'Look out, Mitchell! Get down!'

Lowson remembers that suddenly 'the earth fell in on us' as mortar bombs exploded all around them. The first salvo dropped just in front of them. Clarke got a bit of shrapnel in the arm. The rest were unhurt.

'We all started to run back down the road,' says Lowson, 'and then their machine guns opened up.'

Davis looked on 'with one's feet rooted to the spot by some unseen force ... we had to watch these friends and comrades of ours experiencing disaster without it being in our power to offer them the least assistance'. Mitchell was shot in the side; Squires through the wrist; Little in the arm; Glacken and Kirk were at the rear of the fleeing band. Davis watched as 'first one and then the other, staggered and fell'. Sanders and Lowson, the latter using the speed that had served him so well on the rugby field, were the only two to get round the corner without being hit.

'Most of the boys could get down the road unaided,' recalls Lowson. 'We went back and dragged Kirk and Glacken to safety.'

Davis was trapped in the house for eight hours, 'our minds filled with a multitude of fears and torments'. At nightfall they crept out of the cottage and back down the road where they met Tony Marsh's section.

They told him none of Mitchell's section was seriously wounded. Neither was Tunstall who, on being examined by 'Doc' Gunn, was informed that he was a very lucky boy. He had been hit by a ricochet that had ripped open his mouth but caused no serious damage.

Davis and Marsh were joined by Poat. 'As we sat around eagerly exchanging our news a runner came up breathlessly from squadron HQ with the welcome news that the army [15 Infantry Brigade] which had been pressing forward to relieve us had reached the town.'

Harrison's section spent the night stranded among some young pine trees, above the terraced vineyards but below the German positions that Davis had seen pummelling the British forces in Bagnara.

'We could hear this German battery chatting to each other,' recalls Payne,' as we lay there through the night.'

The next day, with the advance elements of 15 Brigade well established in Bagnara, a 'British cruiser hove to right in front of us' says Payne. 'The gun swung round and let fly at the battery above us. The shells came whistling over our heads. They made a horrible sound.'

Faced with overwhelming firepower, the Germans withdrew from their hillside positions early on the morning of 5 September. Bob McDougall sat and watched as the British infantry came up the hill.

'"Where the bloody hell have you lot been?" I asked. "We've been sitting here waiting for you." This major came over and said, "That's not very nice language is it?" "No," I said. Then he said, "How are you, Bob?" It was my old boss's son from when I was an apprentice joiner in Liverpool.'

Down in Bagnara, Davis sought out Lowson.

'He asked me if I'd like to accompany him back to the top to bury Charlie Tobin.'

The squadron war diary noted where he was laid to rest. 'Behind a solitary house on the first terrace.'

'When I got back down the lads were all asleep on the railway station,' recalls Lowson. 'In the corner was an Italian local with a little squeeze box playing "Amapola". I could have bloody cried.'

137

THE SQUADRON WAS in billets at Gallico, a few miles down the road from Bagnara, when they heard news of the Italian armistice on 8 September. It was a cause for celebration, but also quiet reflection. Deakins had rejoined the unit and learned of Davis's ordeal.

'He told me that he now understood what war was really like,' remembers Deakins.

Davis himself said that 'no more was I a green and inexperienced young officer, untried in action at whom my battle-hardened men looked askance and with suspicion'.

'We had a lot of respect for Davis by now,' says Billy Stalker. 'He was younger than us, less experienced, but he was a good. He was like a mate and we spoke on first-name terms.'

From Gallico the squadron moved to Scalea in mid September. Mayne was at his roistering best throughout the week-long stay.

'Scarcely a night passed without him engineering a celebration of some sort,' remembered Davis.

The parties followed a similar pattern: drinks all round, then Sergeant Major Rose's rich baritone and a couple of Irish tenors led by Chris O'Dowd. As the booze took effect, McNinch would be called upon to recite one of his comical monologues. Then Bob Bennett, one of the Originals of 'L' Detachment, would croon a couple of romantic numbers. Some of the men became maudlin. Davis remembered McNinch raising a glass to Tobin.

'It's strange how always the best seem to catch it,' mumbled the Scot. 'Charlie Tobin was the best-hearted man in the section ... and here am I, a drunken old reprobate.'

All the while, recounted Davis, 'Paddy would lean back, glass in hand, like some Roman emperor watching his gladiators prove their worth in the arena. At frequent stages in the evening Paddy himself would sing, usually some traditional Irish song, either sentimental or aggressive, depending on his mood at the time'. At other times he would select men to sing.

'You'd start to sing,' says Youngman, 'and he would say, "Not that, an Irish song." Well, few of us knew any Irish songs.'

138

The squadron left Scalea on 22 September. For the next week they cruised the Mediterranean. Sicily. Taranto. Brindisi. Bari. Finally Manfredonia. The men were confined to the craft at one hour's sailing notice. Davis and the other officers watched as General Dempsey, commanding XIII Corps, walked up and down the quay 'in earnest consultation with Paddy'. A short while later Poat was briefing the officers as they sailed north towards the Adriatic port of Termoli, 20 miles above the spur of Italy's boot.

'Insignificant in itself,' said Davis, 'but strategically important by virtue of its position on the eastern end of a busy main road running laterally across Italy.' [The capture of the Termoli to Campobasso road would help the Fifth Army advance towards Naples.]

The SRS's LCI was accompanied by two others, containing 3 Commando and 40 Royal Marine Commando. Together they comprised the Special Service Brigade. 'As we approached our objective,' said Davis, 'we found ourselves wondering if the Germans might not so easily be persuaded to give up their hold of this little town by reason of its assumed importance. It was not a happy prospect as we sailed ... filled with diverse fears and forebodings that this time the enemy might be prepared.' On deck Bob McDougall noticed John Hodginskon was looking pensive. 'What's the matter?' he asked. 'I've got a sneaking feeling I won't be coming back from this one,' replied Hodgkinson.

Lieutenant Commander F. E.W. Lammert, senior naval officer of the Termoli assault force, described the sea conditions before the landings as 'appalling'. Even so, at 0115 hours 3 Commando and HQ of the Special Service Brigade embarked into the LCAs half a mile from shore and headed for Termoli. One and a half hours later they signalled ashore the SRS and 40 RM Commando.

'In perfect silence the files of men moved through each other in the darkness to line themselves in their prearranged order behind the ramps,' recalled Davis. As Syd Davison formed up he knocked over a bucket on deck.

'Blimey, Syd,' joked Sid Payne. 'Don't go kicking the bucket already.'

139

The SRS was going to land in the LCI, but 60 feet from shore it ran into a low sand bank. There were curses and moans of frustration at the niggling delay. Bill Fraser reckoned it was shallow enough to wade ashore and he jumped in. 'Only to disappear beneath the waves,' says Lowson. LCAs were brought forward to take the men the final few yards.

The first minutes of the landings were confused. SRS sections mingled with Commando troops. Officers scurried about rounding up their men. Brian Franks, second in command of 3 Commando, moved past John Tonkin's Three Troop section.

'Jack Hobbs', said Franks, giving the password and waiting for the reply 'Surrey and England'.

Tonkin glanced round at Franks as he gave final instructions to his men. 'Sorry, sir, Hobbs isn't in this section'.

Tonkin led his section towards the Biferno River. His orders were to capture the bridge and hold it until relieved by the British 78th Division. One Troop were heading for another bridge. Two Troop's task was to push 4 miles inland and attack the Germans as they fled Termoli. The Commandos would take care of the town itself.

Major Rau, the battle group commander of the German 1st Parachute Division in Termoli, was stunned to hear the sound of gunfire around his HQ. Within minutes he and his men were in the hands of 40 Commando. He hadn't even had time to destroy sensitive documents. One of these would later reveal that the Germans had expected and prepared for an attack from the south-east.

'The idea of a landing west of Termoli,' said Lammert, 'never entered their calculations.'

Those Germans dug in along the lateral road that faced south-east began to withdraw as they realized what had happened. As they retreated, Tonkin advanced. Just before dawn his section shot up a German vehicle, killing one and capturing three. They pressed on. The quicker they moved forward the deeper they got into the heart of the German withdrawal. The SRS exchanged fire with some Germans on their left flank. At first light Tonkin's section were passing along the floor of a small valley. Alex

Griffiths glanced up at the ridges that flanked the valley and saw scores of figures on top.

'I remember thinking, "Cor, look at all those prisoners our boys have caught", because I could see a lot of them were wearing German helmets.'

Griffiths presumed they had linked up with the British 78th Division.

'Then all of a sudden they opened fire. Tonkin told us it was every man for himself.'

The men scattered in all directions. One small group made a dash for the far end of the valley. There was a volley of gunfire which killed Joe Fassam. Tonkin crawled through some foliage right into the jackboots of a grinning German paratrooper. Griffiths was trapped trying to climb out of the valley.

'There was no chance of escaping from there,' recalls Griffiths, 'because there were lots of them just waiting for us at the top.'

Two men had dived unseen into some shrub and remained there until the Germans continued their withdrawal.

'The rest,' says Griffiths, 'were marched back inland towards a village.'

Another Three Troop section swept into the valley minutes later. This time neither side was taken by surprise. There was a furious exchange of small-arms fire. Staff Sergeant Nobby Clarke got hit in the head by a sliver of shrapnel. Bob Melot was shot in the shoulder.

'He had wanted a 9mm Luger for ages,' says Ridler, 'and that's what he got hit with. It's a wonderful weapon to be shot with because it makes no larger hole on exit than it does on entry.'

'Buttercup' Goldsmith dragged Melot to safety while Eddie Ralphs gave him covering fire with a Bren gun. At the end of the engagement five German paratroopers lay dead and nine had been taken prisoner.

Two Troop had found the going hard as they pressed inland to take up their position.

'The rain had spread a slippery coating over the ground,' remembered Davis, 'on which our smooth rubber soles obtained no grip whatsoever.'

He led his men in a scramble up and over a railway embankment. Further along Harrison's section and Muirhead's mortar team were negotiating the same obstacle. With one eye on the imminent dawn and the other scanning the countryside for the enemy, Davis scampered over 'flat fallow ploughland' for 2 miles. This time, unlike Bagnara, the terrain was on his side. The open country became wooded and undulating.

'We entered this welcome and seemingly heaven-sent cover just as the rim of the sun appeared over the horizon to our left,' he said.

Behind Davis, Harrison had come under fire from a farmhouse. Muirhead sent down four smoke bombs as Harrison and his men worked their way round behind the left flank. A German was ousted from the farmhouse by two of Harrison's men. He wore an armband with the inscription 'Kreta'. The SRS treated their prisoner with a new-found respect.

By now One Troop had realized that they were up against a bloody-minded enemy. Muirhead received a message requesting his presence at a farmhouse where a number of Germans were holed up. When he arrived, he could see Reg Seekings had crawled to within 60 feet of the outhouses.

'I stood up,' said Seekings, 'but I was still under cover of this hedge from the Germans ... over the wireless I said to Alex, "Can you see me?" "Yes," he said. "OK, aim on me, plus a short 25." He put the first shell straight through the bloody roof. He was good. So I said, "Another one". And he did the same. He rained a few bombs down on them.'

Seekings received orders over the radio to withdraw. 'To get out of there we had to dive under pig slime to get through a culvert.' As Seekings made his way back to his section, the farmhouse came under a withering machine-gun fire. The Germans could stand no more.

'The Germans decided to come out,' said Seekings. 'And that's when we first realized who they were because they were wearing the Crete armband.'

The first German to emerge from the shattered farmhouse, recalled Seekings, was a 'big major [who] pointed at another officer being carried on a stretcher. It was his younger brother'. The major pointing at his brother was saying something in German. Chalky White asked for Duncan Ridler, a fluent German speaker.

'Chalky said "he's pleading with me but what is he saying?"' Ridler listened.

'I said, "He's pleading with you to shoot his brother. He's so badly wounded."'

Seekings looked on as 'Chalky took his revolver and shot the Jerry through the head ... it was the right thing to do because he was dying'.

Bill Fraser, meanwhile, was shooting up anything that came down Highway No. 87. Several vehicles were raked by gunfire as they tried to flee to the south. Also attacked was a German 10.5mm gun being towed by a half-track. Two Germans were killed, the rest were captured. Ridler, as intelligence sergeant, was told to take them back to HQ for interrogation. As he escorted them back down the road, there was a burst of gunfire and bullets whined past his head. Ridler raised his Tommy Gun and squeezed the trigger. He had a jam.

'I got down into this ditch that ran alongside the road,' he says, 'then threw my only grenade at them.'

His prisoners had jumped in after him but 'were sufficiently shocked' that they refused to move. Ridler tried a bluff.

'I called on the [five] Germans on the other side of the road to surrender,' he said, saying that more of his comrades were coming up behind him. 'Two Germans emerged with their hands up,' says Ridler, 'but the others didn't. So I stood up, walked towards them and said they were surrounded and all the rest of it. It was nothing terribly brave, just hoping they wouldn't shoot.'*

By midday Termoli was in the possession of the British. The Special Service Brigade had erected a formidable perimeter around the town; the SRS on the left flank, 40 Commando on the right and 3 Commando in control of the centre. They counted over 100 German dead and another 150 in captivity. Apart from the fate of Tonkin's section, and the irritating news that the bridges One and Three Troops had aimed for had already been blown, it had been a good morning's work.

The 11th Infantry Brigade started to move up through the special forces to take up positions further inland. By evening news reached the

---

* Ridler was awarded the Military Medal with the citation commending his courage and his skill in capturing a Schmeisser MP42, the latest German automatic weapon.

Special Service troops that the 36th Infantry Brigade [the 36th and 11th brigades comprised the 78th Division] had now disembarked and would relieve them at 0830 hours on 4 October.

On the evening of the 3rd all the SRS, bar Davis's section that had lost radio contact and was still dug in 3 miles from Termoli, spent a snug night in the town. The men were billeted in a monastery just off the main square. Across the road was a large house in which the officers relaxed. Ridler remembers that evening 'sitting in the square chatting up the local girls'. He was in a 'state of delirium' having just found four bullet holes in his beret. He remembered feeling 'twitches' when he and his prisoners had been fired on in the morning.

'The bullets had gone through the sides of my beret and out the back above my ears. After such an escape I was up for a good time.'

Cleverley, the squadron cook, rustled up a hot meal for the men. Life was good.

Dawn the next day was a beautiful affair. Davis stuck his head out of the barn in which his section had slept to find the 'rising sun [had] revealed to us a welcome sight indeed. The coastal road was covered by a stream of transport pushing beyond us to the north-west. The main forces had linked up with us'. He broke the good news to his men.

'Well, that's about the easiest operation we've ever had,' said one of them.

As Davis led his men back to Termoli, a multitude of British regiments were advancing: the 56th Reconnaissance Regiment, the 8th Battalion Argyle and Sutherland Highlanders, the 6th Battalion Royal West Kents, the 5th Battalion East Kents (the Buffs) and the 2nd Battalion Lancashire Fusiliers.

Davis's section came in for some good-natured ribbing when they got back into the squadron's billets during the morning and heard 'to our chagrin that the rest of the unit had spent the preceding night in considerably greater comfort that was afforded us by our barn'. Davis was shown to the officers' billets and 'settled in a pleasant state of relax-ation'. Half an hour later Mayne appeared. He didn't look unduly concerned, but he casually asked Davis if he knew anything about a

144

German counter-attack. One or two Tiger tanks had been seen on the high ground not far from the barn in which his section had spent the night.

As a precaution 3 Commando and the SRS were placed on 30 minutes' notice. At 1230 hours confirmation came through that the Germans had decided Termoli was worth fighting for. A message was received from 36 Brigade saying that their right flank appeared insecure and 3 Commando were sent out immediately to reinforce the line.

At 1400 hours Brigadier Arbuthnot arrived at SRS HQ and said he 'was not satisfied about his flank'. Harry Poat told Tony Marsh and Derrick Harrison to prepare to move out; he took pity on Davis's recently returned section and instead took Sandy Wilson's section from One Troop. They climbed into two 3-tonners and drove along a dusty track towards the east ridge at Torrente Sinarca. As they moved forward on foot to their positions, they passed a troop of 40 Commando digging in on the ridge. There were nods of acknowledgment but few words. Wilson established himself near the railway line that ran parallel to the beach in the forward position. Slightly behind him were Marsh and Harrison. There was no further activity for the rest of the day. The German attack had petered out. The greatest problem for Harrison was the cold. He shivered the whole night.

PETER DAVIS PASSED a cosier evening in the officers' billet. But at dawn on 5 October he was woken by the 'ear-splitting burst of a German Spandau ... 600 yards away'. The news he heard upon investigation was dire.

The Special Service Brigade report noted that it was at this moment that 11th Brigade 'asked the SS Bde to assume responsibility for the immediate defence of Termoli and reconnoitre positions so that troops could occupy them at short notice in case of need'. Just after dawn six Mark IV tanks appeared in the forward positions of the Royal West Kents (RWK).

According to one Divisional account of the battle, 'considerable confusion followed and the 6 RWK were seen to make a hasty retreat

145

towards the Termoli–Larino road'. The 5 Buffs also withdrew. In fact, this was just a diversionary raid. The main attack was now launched by the 64 Panzer Grenadier Regiment and a battalion of 79 Panzer Grenadiers against the Argyle and Sutherland Highlanders on the high ground that had been occupied by Davis's section two days' earlier. The Scots fell back to the brickworks and a company of Lancashire Fusiliers was moved up to reinforce the area. The 11th Brigade account of the battle said that German tanks were seen on the road having 'infiltrated through 8 A.&S.H.'.

At 0900 hours five Sherman tanks belonging to the County of London Yeomanry were sent to push back the Germans. Four were knocked out. The fifth withdrew to the area of the brickworks. At 1115 hours the anti-tank guns of the Highlanders were overrun. Two hours later the regiment 'evacuated' the brickworks.

The Royal West Kents, said one 78th Divisional report, were by this time 'completely disorganized'. They had withdrawn down from the high ground towards Termoli. The demoralized remnants were 'collected together by their CO' and told to dig defensive positions on the Termoli to Larino road. At 1400 hours a furious Brigadier Howlett visited the British infantry and 'ordered that there was to be no further withdrawal and that the new positions were to be held to the last'.

The SRS's first intimation of the debacle was a salvo of shells that fell behind Poat's force. Then they ducked as some German planes roared overhead and bombed the harbour. Harrison, waiting for his promised 1000 hours relief, began to suspect it wasn't to be. One of his Bren gun teams reported a number of German tanks moving against the left flank. Then Poat came on the radio. The 56th Recce Regiment was buckling under the German onslaught. Harrison was to take his section and go towards the left flank where the counter-attack was at its fiercest. As they moved off it became apparent that the shells had landed in 40 Commando positions.

'There were a lot of Commandos lying dead and wounded,' remembers Payne. As they neared the position of the Recce Regiment, the shelling

146

intensified. Payne recalls that 'the British troops were going, so there was only us left'.

McDougall says that when they arrived at the position they found 'brand spanking new armoured cars abandoned'. There were even some rations lying around. 'There was a big fight to see who got the ciggies and the chocolate.'

With no armoured support, Harrison's men crawled back to the Commando position. Leaving his section spread out at 5yd intervals, Harrison wriggled through some trees to Tony Marsh and his section. They decided to push up in front of the Commandos; not just to give them support but to escape the murderous shellfire to which they were being subjected.

'I can't remember exactly what went on,' says Payne, 'but it was turmoil. Someone had spotted some Germans and we were about to have a go at them when we got hit.' The shell that wounded four of Harrison's troop also left John Hodgkinson, the rugby league fanatic, with a piece of shrapnel embedded in his back. 'He was in agony,' recalls Payne. 'The normal field dressing we carried was no use for him and he kept asking me to shoot him.' Hodgkinson was given a shot of morphine but he died a short time later.

McDougall wrapped Trooper McLachlan in a blanket and with McDiarmid and Ginger Hines carried him back to the casualty clearing station on a barn door. Harrison instructed Payne to report the seriousness of the situation to Mayne.

'I was shot at along the railway,' says Payne, 'but got back OK and told Paddy what was happening. He told me to go and tell the brigadier [of 78th Division]. I went across the road and did so but he didn't believe me. He ordered a RSM to escort me back to the front and find out what was going on. We had gone a little way up the road when a Spandau opened fire and the RSM dashed back to tell the brigadier.'

The approach of the Germans – the 16 Panzer Division sent to retake Termoli on the express orders of Kesselring – emboldened the few Italians in the town who still harboured fascist sympathies. McDougall, McDiarmid

147

and Hines were making their way back to Harrison from the casualty clearing station. 'I'd stopped to light a fag,' says McDougall, 'when this Italian looked out of a window with a rifle and pointed it at the other two. He hadn't seen me so I gave him a burst. He ducked down and McDiarmid went in after him. When he came out he said, "He'll fire that Beretta no more. I wrapped it round his fucking head."'

The Germans continued to push inexorably closer to the British command centre. At 1330 hours a shell landed on the Special Service Brigade HQ, killing Captain Leese, acting staff captain. Mayne was asked by 78th Division to send all his remaining men to the front line. Davis had just 'managed to eat a scraped lunch [when] at about 2.30 the expected orders came through. Every available man was to be rushed out to help stem a fresh and powerful attack'.

Davis led his section outside into a side street alongside a public garden. There were several lorries waiting for them. In the garden Johnny Wiseman was telling his section to jump on board one of the trucks. Reg Seekings got the men to their feet. Chris O'Dowd, Alex Skinner, Syd Davison and the rest of the section started to move out.

As Davis's men trooped out into the street, McNinch leaned out of the cab of the first lorry and waved. He'd been left out of the initial raiding force because of a foot injury but he came ashore with the main landing as a driver.

'When we saw McNinch we all piled into his lorry,' remembers Stalker, 'which was the front one. Then John Wiseman appeared and told us to get out because this was his section's lorry. So out we got and went to another lorry.' Lowson remembers Stalker complaining in colourful language about Wiseman's hair-splitting as they climbed aboard the second lorry.

Wiseman exchanged a few brisk words with Bill Fraser and then hopped in beside McNinch. Seekings saw the last of the men into the back and began to fasten up the tailboard. An Italian family were standing in the doorway of their house watching the scene.

'Then I saw Mayne's messenger coming to speak to me so I got out of the truck,' says Wiseman.

At that moment, recalled Davis, 'the world seemed to fall in pieces'. Five 105mm shells screamed down and exploded 'around us and upon us'. The side street was engulfed in a thick, choking fog of dust and smoke. Men reeled like deranged madmen down the street, numbed by the shock-waves of the explosion.

'A form of blind panic developed,' said Davis, 'with a mad rush for cover.' David Danger 'ended up in the flower bed ... with a piece of shrapnel in my behind'. Bob Lowson dived behind the wall of the garden with 'lots of little bits of shrapnel in my chest and arms'.

Davis stood transfixed to the spot. As the smoke cleared he looked down the street. 'Great lumps of masonry and shattered vehicles littered the roadway.'

Most of the trucks had suffered remarkably little damage. But the front truck had 'virtually disappeared'. 'And around it lay ghastly morsels of burnt and shattered flesh,' he said. A shell had landed right in the middle of the truck. Miraculously, two men had survived with barely a blemish. Seekings had lost a fingernail.

Wiseman 'wasn't even scratched ... I didn't hear it coming, just heard the explosion. The fellow I was talking to ... there were bits of him all around'.

Seekings remembered that he was 'smothered in bits of flesh'. The Italian family's curiosity had proved fatal. The parents had been obliter-ated and their young son, said Seekings, was running around with his stomach 'blown out like a huge balloon'. He shot the boy. 'You couldn't let anyone suffer like that.' There was a body on fire. Seekings doused it in water. He was just able to recognize the charred remains of Alex Skinner, the handsome young soldier from Essex who had won the Military Medal three months earlier.

Lowson was having his flesh wounds dressed by Billy Stalker when 'Andy Storey stuck his head up from the other side of the wall and asked us to come and help'. The scene that greeted Lowson's eyes was 'a mess,

149

absolutely terrible … Spike Kerr was lying on the ground praying to God to help him. Lunt, the padre, came up and slapped him across the face: "You are not going to die," he told him.' A few yards from Kerr, Bill Fraser sat in the middle of the road, his eyes staring vacantly into the distance. Blood spurted from a hole in his shoulder. Graham Gilmour stood quietly with his eyeball hanging out of its socket. David Danger put an arm round his shoulder. 'Am I blind?' Gilmour asked.

'No,' said Danger, 'you'll be OK.'

Davis watched the teenage daughter of the Italian family now strewn across the street as she 'sat calmly amid the rubble of what had once been her home dressing the wounds of those who were not so seriously injured'. Then Davis's attention was caught by 'a lump of flesh that hung from the telegraph wires'. It was the remains of O'Dowd's head. Davis turned his back on the carnage and vomited.

Lowson continued to 'pick up the pieces, arms and legs everywhere'. He saw Phil Gunn, the medical officer, helping Doug Monteith.

'He had a charmed life, that boy,' says Lowson. 'All his clothes had been blown off him but he'd survived.'

Gunn concentrated only on those who had a chance of living. Once he saw a soldier was beyond help he passed on to the next one. He came to Syd Davison, glanced forlornly down at the 20-year-old, and moved on.

Bill McNinch was still sitting in the front of the cab, which was relatively undamaged. From a few yards it looked as if he was asleep. In fact, says Stalker, 'he'd been cut in half' by a piece of shrapnel. Gunn counted fifteen corpses, with another two men close to death. All the while, reflected Davis, Wiseman 'plodded stolidly' among what had been his section, finding out how many men he had left.

'I'd lost my whole troop,' he recalls. 'I had nobody left to command.' He went and reported to Mayne.

'Paddy said "what the devil are you doing here?" I said "I'm sorry, sir, I haven't got anyone to command any more." ' Mayne attached the survivors to HQ squadron and sent them out to buttress the railway line on the right flank.

150

'I'd been with those chaps for three months,' says Wiseman. 'And with one shell I'd lost them. But what could I do? It was the luck of the draw, it was war. You just accepted it.'

Duncan Ridler arrived in the side street with a message for David Barnby, the senior uninjured officer present. 'Major Mayne states that you must hurry forward at once.' Barnby replied that nothing could be done until 'this mess is sorted out'. Ridler was insistent. 'It's most imperative that you should, sir. I believe the situation is critical.'

Barnby acquiesced and directed Davis's section up towards the eastern outskirts of the town.

'A member of Paddy's advance party met us,' said Davis, 'and escorted us to our positions in the garden of a large villa. Here we found Paddy calmly waiting.'

Mayne alone seemed unconcerned by the ferocity of the German counter-attack. He told Davis to place his section behind a stone wall. Beyond the wall was a small hill that ran down to the Termoli–Larino road 300 yards away. On the other side of the road was a valley. On the high ground at the far end of the valley were the Germans.

'We chiselled some holes in the wall,' says Lowson, 'and waited. They soon started shelling the shit out of us.'

The Germans softened them up with their 88mm anti-tank guns. Then came the *Nebelwerfer,* a multi rocket-launcher that was capable of firing sixty bombs simultaneously. The British called them 'moaning minnies' because of the noise they made.

'The "moaning minnies" were truly horrible,' says Lowson. 'Finally one of our section, a regular soldier who'd been in India before the war, broke down. He was just lying there, completely finished.'

Davis remembered that 'like a child he lay there sobbing in the ditch … poor fellow, he could of course not be blamed although his fellows were far from sympathetic'.

Fear in Termoli that day was contagious. The sight of the broken man unsettled the rest of Davis's section but no one else cracked. Elsewhere British infantrymen were running scared. Three Commando were left

151

exposed when regiments of the 78th Division took to their heels, leaving behind one NCO and two privates of the Argyll and Sutherland Highlanders who 'preferred to stay and fight'.

The NCO was Sergeant Macleod Forsyth, a 30-year-old who had first joined the regiment in 1933. A few months earlier he'd won an MM while with the Parachute Regiment in Tunisia; not long after he was RTU'd for accusing an officer of cowardice. His memories of Termoli were of a 'complete shambles'. They had radios, but no batteries so the German tanks advanced without meeting any British artillery fire. Even so, recalled Forsyth, he was dismayed by the mettle of his fellow Highlanders.

'They weren't up to scratch, they weren't of the same discipline [as the Parachute Regiment].'

As his company deserted him, Forsyth moved up to meet the enemy. In a field piled high with 'heaps of manure', he encountered a German in the dark not more than 3 feet away.

'I pulled the trigger and my [Thompson] gun jammed. He pulled his trigger and his gun jammed. I threw my gun at him and he turned and ran.'

The Special Service Brigade Operational Report stated that 'towards evening they were attacked by 11 tanks, followed by about 100 infantry'. They had some 6-pounder guns with them, manned by another unit, but when the Germans stormed forward 'they were abandoned and their breech blocks left behind intact'. The report went on to say that throughout the afternoon 'there were many alarmist reports brought into this HQ by officers and other ranks of various units, other than this brigade'. Holes began to appear in Poat's civility. Seeing an officer of the 78th Division, he pointed to his shoulder flash and enquired of the insignia. The officer told him it was a battleaxe. Poat smiled.

'It should be a knitting needle.'

From his position behind the wall Lowson could see the Reconnaissance Regiment abandoning their guns. Davis remembered how 'many units ... had fled individually or collectively down the coast to safety'. Anchored just outside Termoli was Lieutenant Commander Lammert.

On the afternoon of 5 October he received 'news gleaned from demoralized soldiers of two well-known battalions that the Germans had broken through our lines and Termoli was cut off'. He refused to take any of the soldiers on board but instead began to draw up an evacuation plan using Italian fishing boats.

At dusk 3 Commando, sheltering in an olive grove, had repelled the German onslaught. The Germans surrounded them on three sides, in some places they were 50 yards away, but they had sustained too many casualties during the day, most from three Vickers superbly manned by a detachment of the Kensingtons, to risk an all-out assault. Instead they blazed away at the grove. Captain Arthur Komrower, DSO, the officer in charge, sent a message back saying they were on the brink of being 'annihilated'.*

The Commandos were in the epicentre of the counter-attack. On their left flank were Mayne and Davis. On the right, by the coastal railway line, was 40 Commando and Harry Poat's force. Earlier in the day Poat had been bolstered by the arrival of a detachment of 2SAS under the command of Sandy Scratchley. This combined force, consisting of about a hundred men, was strung out along the lip of a cliff that overlooked the railway goods yard. Beyond the yard the ground sloped gently upwards for 200 yards and then dipped down out of sight. On the left just before the dip was a walled cemetery. Positioned among the tombstones were members of 40 Commando and a section of Three Troop under the command of Ted Lepine. On the right of Poat's force the railway line, which ran parallel to the beach, stretched away into the distance.

At 1715 hours three Germans tanks attacked down the railway line.

'When we saw the Tigers coming we really thought it was it,' says Arthur Thomson. 'It was a shame because we had survived so far but it was now looking like curtains.'

At his disposal Poat had one 6-pounder anti-tank gun and a dozen Bren guns. As the tanks rumbled down the line the Bren gunners opened fire.

* Komrower was awarded a DSO for his actions at Termoli. The citation commended his gallantry 'throughout this very difficult period, with a continuous flow of casualties, when all other units had withdrawn … '. Intriguingly, the last part of the sentence was censored.

'The firepower was awesome,' says Thomson. 'Bob Melot [who had refused to be evacuated] was brave that day. He kept walking up and down saying, "Come on chaps, keep going, change that barrel, more ammunition."'

Several times Thomson went on what he called the 'dummy run', running across a stretch of no man's land to bring up more ammunition from the monastery.

'It was in boxes and bloody heavy,' Thomson remembers. 'The boxes had rope handles and me and Davie Orr could only manage two at a time. So we had the idea of roping five boxes together and dragging them across the ground.' When two more 6-pounders were dragged to the top of the cliff the Tigers backed off. 'I've never known why but if they had known it was just us they would have overrun us,' says Thomson.

When it became obvious the Germans had switched their main focus to the railway line Mayne ordered Davis to lead his section towards Poat. Groping their way through the empty streets the scale of the panic became obvious.

'Here lay a pair of Bren carriers ... likewise a Bofors anti-aircraft gun ... with their drivers and crews presumably among the rabble moving back down the coast.' As they approached the sound of fighting they ran into a section post 'manned by all the odd batmen, cooks, drivers, clerks and mechanics of an artillery battery who had been rushed out as infantry to help ward off this dangerous attack,' said Davis. 'We wondered at this strange battle, in which the trained, fighting troops were running away, leaving the cooks and the clerks behind to hold the line.' Davis sited his section close to Lepine and Muirhead's mortar section.

The Germans tried one more attempt that night to break through the railway yard but the foray was driven back.

'They came along the railway line with some half-tracks,' says Charlie Hackney, who was a 2SAS Bren gunner with Jim Mackie's section. 'We were running low on ammo so we could only fire in intermittent bursts and not all at once. They got to within about 600 yards of our position before withdrawing.'

They returned at first light on 6 October. A couple of German fighters

154

swooped low over their heads but they were soon chased away by a squadron of Spitfires.

Despite the heavy shelling of the SRS positions, morale was high. News had reached them that the 38 Irish Brigade had landed from the sea and were preparing for a major assault.

'It was an Irish brigade,' said Davis, 'so we knew that these men, with their characteristic disregard for danger and their thirst for a fight, were not likely to throw down their weapons in a panic.' The Irish brought with them a plentiful supply of ammunition which was being unloaded. Best of all, Bob Lilley had appeared, 'bringing with him supplies of cigarettes'. They were the dreaded 'Victory V' brand, but for the first and only time in Davis's life he watched as they were distributed without a 'single protest'.

The Germans spent the early part of the morning attacking the cemetery. Youngman had been there for nearly 36 hours, 'under almost constant fire … it's a bloody good place to be though, a cemetery, because the headstones offer great cover'. At 1000 hours the British withdrew 50 yards from the cemetery in the face of heavy mortar fire. Half an hour later Muirhead had mortared the Germans into their own retreat after Lowson had brought up fresh supplies of bombs.

'I didn't know where the shop was,' he recalls, 'but I bumped into the RSM of the West Kents. "Have you got any mortar bombs?" I asked him. "Have you got anyone to fire them?" he replied. I said yes so he let me help myself. I backed the truck up and loaded it up. I did several runs for Muirhead.'

Davis watched as Muirhead began 'firing without a break, until their barrels became too hot to touch and their base plates from the constant recoil had been driven so deep into the ground that the weapons, on several occasions, had to be dug out and reset'.

At midday the first rumours began to circulate that the Germans had started to pull back. One hour later 2SAS and 40 Commando advanced and seized a ridge 500 yards in front of their old position. At 1445 hours the London Irish Rifles launched a big offensive. Lowson was back in the

155

monastery with Sergeant Major Rose, 'enjoying some of Cleverley's grub ... I had a grandstand view of it. They lined up along the cliffs and suddenly they were up and away'.

THE MEN RETURNED to their billets in dribs and drabs. Each man, each section, each troop had a different story to tell. In many cases words weren't needed to express the strain of the past 36 hours. Davis was shocked by the sight of Tony Marsh, whose section had borne the brunt of the German shelling.

'Through the mud and the grime his face looked drawn and haggard, wild-eyed as though he had just awoken from a nightmare.'

Marsh brought with him sad news. Sandy Wilson's position had been heavily mortared during the morning and all but one of his men were casualties. Wilson and Rob Scherzinger had been killed, the rest badly wounded. Duncan McLennon, the only uninjured man, had dragged his comrades one by one to safety and then returned to man his Bren gun position.

The squadron had suffered more than any other British regiment in the defence of Termoli. 40 RM Commando lost 6 men with 30 wounded; 5 soldiers from 3 Commando had been killed and 29 wounded; the SRS, which had landed with a strength of 207 all ranks, had 21 killed, 24 wounded and 23 missing. But the Germans had given up the fight. Lammert's naval evacuation, he wrote in his report, was 'not necessary as the military situation had been restored chiefly by the magnificent behaviour of the Special Service Brigade'.

They buried their dead that evening. Sid Payne and McDiarmid were among the burial party that collected the remains of the men on the lorry.

'With the heat you can quite imagine the smell,' remembers Payne. 'And the sight ... I knew Chris O'Dowd was dead because his scalp was strung across the telephone wires and we had to get a pole to poke it down.'

Padre Lunt wrapped each remains in a blanket while Payne and the others dug a neat row of graves in the public garden.

'Into the gathering dusk,' said Davis, 'the silent crowd of men emerged from their billets, with heads bared and softened tread … in a quiet voice the padre read the service.'

Alex Muirhead thought of the handwritten poem he had found on the body of a dead German.

> *I wonder God if you'll check my hand*
> *Somehow I feel you will understand*
> *Funny I have come to this hellish place*
> *Before I had time to see your face*
> *Well, I guess there isn't much more to say*
> *But I'm sure glad God I met you today.*

The squadron remained in Termoli for a further week.

'It was a gloomy week,' said Davis, 'as the winter rains had set in.' The smell of death seemed to linger over the town. Davis discovered why the German shelling had been so accurate. 'The church tower had been used as an artillery observation post, for it had been fitted with an intricate assortment of signalling apparatus.'

They were visited by General Dempsey, who paid a heartfelt tribute to their courage. 'In my time I have commanded many units. I have never met a unit in which I had such a confidence as yours.'

Montgomery turned up a couple of days later but the men weren't in the mood. 'We were just not interested at that time,' said Davis, 'in "How I am winning the war and how I intend pursuing the Hun without respite".'

On 12 October the squadron embarked for Molfetta. No one was sorry to leave. 'I was fine until Termoli,' says Lowson. 'Nothing about the war bothered me. But after Termoli war didn't have much fascination for me.'

IT WAS ALL VERY relaxed at Kairouan aerodrome, in north Tunisia, on the afternoon of Tuesday 7 September. The only man displaying any outward signs of anxiety was Greville-Bell, hunched over a parachute container that had been converted into a temporary card table. Already £80 down to Bill Stirling, he was wishing he'd never challenged him to a rubber of baccarat. Elsewhere Daniels and Stokes carried out last-minute equipment checks, while Len Curtis asked Pete Tomasso, born in Italy but raised in Scotland, how to chat up a woman in Italian. Not too far away Pat Dudgeon pulled a bottle of whisky out of his kit bag and sat down to have a drink with the five men in his 'stick': 'Tojo' Wedderburn, a young, well-bred Scots officer; Harry Challenor, 'Tanky' to his mates, a man with a wild reputation; Bernie Brunt, 21, the youngest member of the party; Bill Foster, 28, a sergeant from Workington who had joined from the Artillery, and his great pal, Corporal James Shortall, a 24-year-old Londoner and former Fusilier. The thirteen men amounted to GHQ's niggardly concession to what Stirling had initially envisioned: hundreds of small parties dropping into Italy to sever the German supply line south to Salerno. Instead, Stirling had been given permission to drop just half a dozen two-man parties. GHQ's generosity just about stretched to two rickety Albermarle aircraft.

At 1800 hours the sticks boarded the two planes. Stirling saw them off. 'If you don't come back I'll have your sleeping bag,' he beamed at Greville-Bell. The bag, with 'very nice camel hair', was a coveted item in the officers' club. Greville-Bell laughed and disappeared inside the aircraft. Thirty minutes later the Albermarles took off bound for a dropping zone [DZ] north-west of Castiglione, a village in a mountainous area to the north of La Spezia. Challenor recalled that on his aircraft they passed the flight talking about 'wine and women'. Little was said about their mission, which involved splitting into pairs and sabotaging the railway line between Genoa and La Spezia. Destroying the lines would be the easy part, it was the thought of making their way hundreds of miles south through German lines that played on their minds. When they'd been briefed on the operation Greville-Bell had asked how they would extricate themselves from deep inside enemy territory. The intelligence officer shifted uncomfortably. 'That's up to you.'

Greville-Bell was in the other Albermarle, along with Len Curtis, Horace Stokes, Pete Tomasso, Tim Robinson and George Daniels. Philip Pinckney commanded the stick. Calling the operation 'Speedwell' was his idea, combining the essence of the mission with his love for all things flora.

Everybody was looking forward to getting out of the plane. Of all the aircraft foisted on the airborne forces, the Abermarle was the most despised.

'It was a craft that no one wanted,' says Greville-Bell. 'You couldn't get out of it, that was the trouble. It was just a hole in the bottom.'

Pinckney, at 6 feet 3 inches, had more problems than most in exiting the plane, but on this trip he was also nursing a severe back injury he'd picked up during Operation 'Chestnut'. He had kept it hidden from Bill Stirling, persuading the medical officer to give him a 'freezing' treatment while keeping mum.

Shortly after 2300 hours they were told they were nearing the DZ. At 2327 hours Pinckney dropped through the hole, followed by Stokes and Robinson. Daniels was last out behind Greville-Bell. They dropped from 7,000 feet, an unusually high altitude that was necessary to avoid the mountains.

'The RAF's navigation point was a reservoir,' recalls Greville-Bell, 'over which I found myself with 2,000 feet to go. I put into action my drill for falling into water, which was to get out of my harness and hang by my hands. Regrettably a gust of wind brought me back to the hills again and so when I actually landed I was clinging on by my hands to the harness and my 'chute caught in the top of a tree. I swung into the tree, got concussion and broke two ribs.'

Few of the men landed elegantly. Stokes ended up on top of a chimney, Robinson just missed a tree and fell flat on his face. Tomasso landed 'about 75 yards from an isolated farm on the side of a hill'. He had seen Pinckney land 300 yards away behind the hill. As Tomasso buried his 'chute he heard Pinckney call him by name, 'which was unusual as there were two NCOs (Sergeants Stokes and Robinson) between us'. They began 'rolling up the stick', No. 1 picking up No. 2, then No. 3 and so on. Tomasso, the fifth to jump, waited an hour before he was found by Robinson. A few minutes later they were all assembled except Pinckney. They searched for

159

nearly two hours, using the call of the curlew – a pre-arranged signal – but he'd melted into thin air. At 0115 hours they gave up and returned to the DZ.*

By now Greville-Bell's stoicism was being unravelled by the pain. He expressed doubt as to whether he could continue. Daniels and Curtis ignored his protestations and put him on a parachute, dragging him to a suitable lying-up position halfway up a hillside. The next morning Greville-Bell, still in considerable pain, said he was fit to continue unaided. The departure was delayed by the arrival of a truckload of Germans below. The six men, hidden on the hillside, watched as they searched the DZ. When the Germans were gone they reorganized their raiding parties. Instead of operating in pairs they split into two groups, Robinson, Stokes and Curtis to attack the Bologna–Prato line, Greville-Bell, Daniels and Tomasso to wreck the Bologna–Florence stretch. They continued together for the rest of the morning, Greville-Bell doing his best to ignore the 'unpleasant grating noise' his ribs made with every step. Daniels looked on in silent admiration. The ladies' man with the 'off-putting accent' who oozed self-confidence, was tougher than Daniels had first thought.

At noon the two parties shook hands and parted company. Greville-Bell, Daniels and Tomasso laid up for the rest of the day, waiting for nightfall when they would start off.

'We were looking across this valley, which was incredibly beautiful,' says Greville-Bell, 'with three villages on the hilltops and all very peaceful ... we were absolutely stupefied by the beauty of the scene. And Bebe [Daniels] said, "I'll say one thing, sir, if it hadn't been for this bloody war I would never have been able to see a scene like this."'

DUDGEON'S STICK LANDED without problems. Within an hour they had all rallied and were able to grab a few hours' sleep. At dawn they located the

---

* Pinckney's body was discovered in Baigno, in the Emilia Romagna region of northern Italy, after the war; how he died remains a mystery. The most likely explanation is that, dazed and in pain after aggravating his spinal injury on landing, Pinckney wandered off in the wrong direction and was caught by the enemy. Whether he died from his injuries or was shot is unknowable.

containers and checked their position on the map. They laid up for the rest of the day and at nightfall they moved off in their pairs: Challenor and Wedderburn heading for the La Spezia–Bologna line, Foster and Shortall for Genoa–La Spezia and Dudgeon and Brunt for another section of the same line. They would rendezvous in seven days' time by a stream between Pontremili and Villa Franca.

To get to their stretch of railway, Challenor and Wedderburn had some 'hard climbing [and] scrambling along mountain tracks with constant compass checks'. When they reached the tunnel they were to blow, it was unguarded.

'We laid our first charge on the outside line of the down-line to La Spezia,' recalled Challenor. 'We then walked for a considerable distance and planted another charge on the up-line.' As they were strolling back towards the entrance to the tunnel, they heard a train approaching. 'Running and falling we just cleared the tunnel mouth as the train thundered in,' said Challenor. There was a 'boom', then a 'crashing, smashing, banging, screeching sound'. As they climbed the mountainside, they heard the faint sound of a train coming down the up-line. There was a second 'boom', as Challenor and Wedderburn congratulated one another on their good fortune.

They were the first to reach the RV on 15 September. The area was more populated than their map had indicated, the result of Italy's surrender a week earlier that had thrown the country into a state of confusion. The countryside was now teeming with soldiers of differing nationalities and differing aims. Italian soldiers making their way home; former Allied POWS, released from captivity, heading south towards their forces; Germans moving either south to strengthen their troops at Salerno or hunting down everyone not in a field-grey uniform.

Challenor and Wedderburn waited at the RV for three days, the time specified by Dudgeon, then set off. The next day they placed the last of their explosives on a stretch of line between Pontremili and La Spezia.

'The explosion echoed round the hills,' said Challenor. 'We laughed like hell and headed south.'

BILL FOSTER AND James Shortall were captured on or shortly before Tuesday 25 September. On 26 September Gerhard Tochtermann, a 33-year-old sergeant in the German Military Police, was ordered to collect two Englishmen from the Italian Carabinieri station in which they were being held. The pair were wearing military uniform and berets, he remembered, though he couldn't be sure what colour the berets were. He drove them to the HQ of the 65th Infantry Division at Ponzano Magra. Waiting for them were Captain Sommer and Lieutenant Interpreter Emil Grether. Foster and Shortall were interrogated separately for 30 minutes. Grether later said that 'the two Englishmen had not made any statement concerning the unit to which they belonged, their mission or the area in which they were to carry it out'. Tochtermann drove the two back to the Italian police station.

Three days later, on Thursday 30 September, he was ordered to bring Foster and Shortall back to Headquarters. As Tochtermann drove to fetch them, Captain Sommer interrupted the lunch of Lance Sergeant Fritz Bost, of the HQ punishment platoon. He told him to form a detail of ten men. Bost asked why. Sommer said 'to shoot two men ... Englishmen [who] had landed by parachute in civilian clothes'.

When Tochtermann arrived at HQ with Foster and Shortall he saw another car containing Lieutenant Zastrow, Lieutenant Grether, Captain Sommer and two Military Policemen. Sommer told him to follow their car. They drove through the iron gates of a disused pottery factory, across what was once the loading area and parked in front of a rusting trolley track. Beyond the track the ground sloped upwards, to a rise on which was a solitary tree.

Foster and Shortall were escorted up the rise, where they stood and watched as the detail from the punishment platoon marched through the iron gates. Bost lined up his men 10 yards from the tree. He looked at the prisoners and noticed they were wearing 'airman's overalls'. The taller of the two was a sergeant. Grether read from a piece of paper, first in German, then in English. 'According to which,' recalled Tochtermann, 'the two prisoners as members of a sabotage party were to be shot by order of the Führer.'

162

Bost, who spoke no English, remembered that Foster and Shortall said something in response to Grether's statement.

Foster was 'taken to the tree and tied', said Bost. 'They tried to blindfold him. This, however, the prisoner refused. He then went on talking when he was already tied.'

Sommer asked what Foster was saying.

'He is asking for a priest,' replied Grether. Sommer shook his head impatiently. 'We have no time for that.' Then he gave the order to fire.

Bost estimated that Shortall watched the execution of his friend from a distance of '7 to 8 metres'. Two Military Policeman untied Foster's body and dragged it to one side. Emil Grether glanced at Shortall as he was led to his death. Four years later he told a British War Crimes investigator: 'His impassive attitude is pictured in my memory.' The men were buried together in an unmarked grave in the grounds of the pottery factory.

Late on the evening of Saturday 2 October a military vehicle was stopped by a routine roadblock at the summit of the Cisa Pass, about 30 miles west of Parma. There were two men inside the car. One of the sentries approached the driver and asked him for his papers. He was a big man, and he spoke good German.

'I want to fetch my paybook and work ticket from my unit.'

Thinking he was another disorganized Italian, the sentry was about to wave him on when he noticed the driver's beret. He told the pair to get out of the car. Asking another guard to cover them, the German telephoned Lieutenant Viktor Schmitt, a platoon commander in the 3rd Field Replacement Battalion, 146th Infantry Regiment, and voiced his suspicions.

When Schmitt arrived he immediately recognized Dudgeon and Brunt as British soldiers. There was fresh blood on their battledress and in their rucksacks was 40 lbs of explosive. He interrogated them at dawn the next day in the presence of Lieutenant Albert Rasshoffer. The questioning, Rasshoffer said, was 'broken off since it had led to no result'. Shortly afterwards they received an order from General von Ziehlberg, commander

163

of their division, to bind the prisoners. Schmitt did so, apologizing, said Rasshofer, for the imposition.

'The English captain protested against the bonds on account of being in full English uniform and therefore he claimed the right to be treated as a POW.'

The berets that had been noticed by the sentry also struck Rasshoffer as unusual.

'The captain and his companion were wearing coloured berets, on the front of which was a badge with two wings.'

At 0800 hours Ziehlberg arrived from HQ with news that the bodies of two German signallers had been found in a roadside ditch a few miles from the pass. Their vehicle was missing. A swift examination of the car in which Dudgeon and Brunt had been travelling revealed traces of blood. Rasshofer looked on as Ziehlberg, through Schmitt's interpretation, questioned Dudgeon and Blunt.

'At first Ziehlberg asked them how they had come to the area and what their route had been, as well as what their mission was. In reply the captain refused to make a statement. After a few minutes the general broke off the interrogation since there was no hope of achieving a result. "Do you know that you will be shot?" The captain replied that he wanted to be brought before a proper court, while the soldier said nothing.'

A few minutes before midday an order came through from HQ that the two prisoners were to be shot later that day.

In a letter Schmitt wrote to Dudgeon's father in 1945, perhaps with one eye on any future war crimes investigation, he said that he'd 'sat beside your son on the straw and we were speaking together all night long. He told me he knew [a] little of Germany; that he'd spent his holidays in Germany'.

In fact, any time Schmitt spent with Dudgeon would have been short. Once the order had been given to shoot the two men events moved fast. Two posts were hammered into the ground 400 yards from the guard-room. Lieutenant Preissner was put in charge of the firing squad and he thought it 'best to select old, experienced soldiers for the execution squad … lance corporals and corporals'.

Schmitt asked for the address of Dudgeon and Brunt so he could inform their families of their deaths. Rasshofer 'saw how the captain wrote his address for Schmitt. His companion, however, refused to give his home address'. Schmitt and Dudgeon talked for a few more minutes in the guard room. In the letter he sent to Dudgeon's father, the German wrote that:

'The young officer of 23 years old had made such an impression that I couldn't help telling him when we were alone, "Your country may be proud of you. If you were not my enemy I should ask you to be my friend." Captain Dudgeon gave me his hand saying, "Thank you for telling me that."'

Brunt remained in the guard room as Dudgeon was escorted outside by Rasshoffer. He asked if he was going to be 'shot from behind'. Rasshoffer said he 'would be taken to the execution place', which was not visible until they rounded the bend of the road. When he arrived in front of the firing squad, Dudgeon was asked if he had a 'last wish'. He said he would like time to kneel down to pray, 'which he did,' said Rasshofer. 'He then rose and stood at the post.'

In his statement to the war crimes investigation in 1947, Rasshoffer recalled that shortly before he died Dudgeon had asked Schmitt 'whether an English lieutenant colonel had also been taken prisoner, which Schmitt denied. Schmitt, therefore, at the insistence of the battalion commander, asked the English soldier [Brunt] at the place of execution whether and how many other English groups had parachuted or had landed in the area.'

Brunt, 21 years old but bristling with sullen defiance, replied that 'it did not interest him what the captain was said to have stated and he gave no further information in reply to the question'.

When asked if he had a last wish, Brunt 'even refused this'. Schmitt once more asked the Englishman for his home address. 'He answered in the negative … he was then shot.'

TWO DAYS AFTER Dudgeon's and Brunt's execution, on 5 October, Greville-Bell was having a beer in a bar in Florence's Piazza Michelangelo.

'I'd gone there on the advice of some Italian partisans who told me there was a British agent with a radio,' he says. 'There wasn't. Usual partisan bullshit.' But as he was dressed in civilian clothes and fancied a drink, Greville-Bell ordered himself a beer. He savoured it sitting next to a table full of drunken German soldiers. 'It was really very poor beer,' he reflects.

It was twenty-eight days since they had dropped into Italy and things had gone surprisingly well. Greville-Bell's ribs had 'knitted together', helped by the morphine.

'We'd been issued with these tiny toothpaste tubes of morphine with a needle on the end and I had two or three of them. They made me feel very good.'

On the morning of 11 September they had reached the tunnel they were going to blow. They concealed themselves in some woods 300 yards up a hillside overlooking the tunnel and for the next 24 hours observed all movement down below. On the evening of the 12th they crept down the hillside.

'We laid the charges about 150 yards inside the tunnel,' says Daniels, who was a recent convert from gun cotton to plastic explosives. 'Plastic high explosive was a better cutting charge,' he remembers. 'It hadn't been out for long but it was so good because you could mould it to the line. We used 4 lbs of explosives: 1 lb on this piece of track, another 1 lb further up the line and so on. The clip-on detonators were based on a similar idea to the fog signals that are used on lines.'

'At 2205 hours we heard a fairly fast train approaching from the north,' says Greville-Bell. The train disappeared into the tunnel. There was an explosion, too loud to be called muffled even inside the tunnel, followed by a medley of judders, hisses, screeches and groans.

'We watched the breakdown people come down and attempt to move the wrecked train,' says Daniels. 'Then cleared off in the evening and headed down towards the road.'

On 18 September they blew another line with a pull switch. Unfortunately the information fed to them by the partisans was wrong. The train came down on the left line, not the right. The next day they sent twelve goods carriages careering off the track. But by now they were out of food. For the past fortnight the three had subsisted on a daily ration of a handful of raisins and two biscuits for breakfast and a piece of cheese and two biscuits for supper. They knocked on one door for help and bought some bread and a few apples. The occupant warned them to be careful who they approached in the future as the Germans were offering 10,000 lire for information leading to the capture of British parachutists.

On 24 September, on the outskirts of Fiesole, an ancient town to the north of Florence, Greville-Bell heard about an owner of a large villa who had been imprisoned for criticizing Mussolini. Desperately short of food, he decided to seek his help.

'There was no way to creep in,' says Greville-Bell, 'just a big door, so I put the men in the bushes and rang the bell. It was opened and I said in my best Italian,"I would like to see the owner, please." This butler looked at me and said in perfect English, "Yes sir, and who may I say is calling?" Then down the stairs came bouncing this chap about my own age, Count Blaise Foglietti . It turned out that he was married to an Englishwoman I had known as a boy in Devon. In fact I used to go to Pony Club meetings with her and her sisters. I'd fancied one of them, I seem to remember.' When the introductions were over, Greville-Bell went to fetch Tomasso and Daniels. 'They were already in the servants' hall – the cook was also English – having cups of strong tea. We stayed there for about three days.'

In the days after leaving the villa the three derailed a south-bound train near Incisa and linked up with a band of partisans that contained a former Yugoslav naval lieutenant called Ratomir Kalocira, 'fearless in a Slavian way', and the only effective operator of the rabble. Again partisans had supplied Greville-Bell with inaccurate information, this time about the British agent in Florence. When he returned from his excursion he severed links with them. Before they left the partisans warned them that a division of Austrian Mountain troops had been brought in to find and destroy the saboteurs.

At the start of November the condition of the four men (Kalocira was with them) was pitiable. They had been surviving on potatoes, berries and grapes but food was now scarce with the end of the autumn. The onset of winter presented them with additional problems.

'We got lost as we crossed Mount Cagno, which was about 6,000 feet,' says Greville-Bell. 'I knew there was a pass between its twin peaks but we could see nothing because it was snowing so bloody hard. So we missed the pass and, of course, by now, we were bloody cold.' All three had holes in their boots and their Denison smocks were lamentably inadequate against the cold.

'There was talk of bedding down in the snow,' remembers Daniels, 'but we carried on and began to descend the mountain through a forest.' As they came down out of the clouds they could see the village of Rovere in the valley below. It was full of military transport.

'Tomasso was just about dead by now,' says Greville-Bell, 'so I said we'd slog down and see if we could find an isolated building.' The edge of the forest stopped a few hundred yards from the outskirts of the village. From his vantage point Greville-Bell could see the soldiers belonged to the Austrian Mountain Division. 'We waited and eventually they got in their trucks and went out one end of the village and we went in the other.'

They knocked on the door of the first house they came to and an elderly woman the shape of a barrel opened the door. Tomasso told her they were escaped POWs.

'She was a wonderful old woman,' says Greville-Bell. 'She said to me, "I have a son who is away in the army. I don't mind if you're German, Italian or English; if you're cold and hungry you must come in and I'll take care of you."' For Greville-Bell and other SAS men who had fought in the desert, they couldn't help but contrast the bravery and endurance of the Italian women with the generally feeble menfolk in the army. 'The Italian women were wonderful,' remembers Greville-Bell, 'they always looked after us. I don't think we could have made it without their help.'

TOP Sergeants Du Vivier and Archer enjoy a drink and a fag in a Tel-Aviv bar in early 1943

ABOVE Five go mad in Cairo: Charlie Cattell, John Byrne, Arthur Phillips, Jimmy Storie and Arthur Warburton

ABOVE New Year's Eve 1942 in El Agheila and (*left to right*) trooper Jeffs, Charlie Cattell, Bob Lilley, Malcolm Pleydell and Johnny Wiseman are en route to Kabrit

RIGHT Bob Lowson (*foreground*) looks on as Charlie Tobin (*far left*) is taught another lesson in a desert card school

OPPOSITE TOP Johnny Cooper (*second left*) and Reg Seekings (*far right*) help replenish ammunition before a desert raid in 1942

OPPOSITE BELOW Some of the original members of the French SAS enjoy a spot of bear dancing in Damascus in 1941. Of the five soldiers pictured only Roger Boutinot (*second left*) survived the war

ABOVE Enjoying the Palestine sunshine in early 1943 are B.P. Schott (*back to camera*), Alex Muirhead, Sandy Wilson, Ted Lepine, Phil Gunn (*in front passenger seat*), Bill Fraser and Pat Riley. The driver is unknown

OPPOSITE TOP LEFT Chris O'Dowd, pirate of the Great Sand Sea, behind the lines in 1942

OPPOSITE TOP RIGHT Bill Fraser resting shortly before the invasion of Italy in September 1943

OPPOSITE BELOW LEFT Alex Skinner won an MM in Sicily but was killed at Termoli

OPPOSITE BELOW RIGHT Reg Redington, DCM, who lost his cigarettes when he was captured with Stirling

ABOVE (*l-to-r*) Vic Page, Chris O'Dowd, Chalky White, Johnny Rose and Tanky Thorne enjoy the fresh air of Mount Hebron in early 1943

RIGHT Peter Davis rests his weary feet after the 45-mile endurance march in Palestine, April 1943, while Alex Muirhead looks on cheerfully

OPPOSITE TOP Bill Deakins and his Engineers prepare to blow the Italian guns on Cape Murro di Porco, July 1943

OPPOSITE BELOW The Boys of Two Troop, SRS, during operations in Sicily. Front row (*l-to-r*), Charlie Belsham, Duncan Ridler, Bob McDougall, Harry Poat, Derrick Harrison and Trooper Smith. Sid Payne is second left in the back row

RIGHT The SRS concert party entertains the troops after the seizure of Augusta with an impromptu sing-song round the pianola

BELOW Reg Seekings scowls for the camera as the SRS take cover during the Bagnara operation in September 1943

OPPOSITE BELOW Johnny Wiseman (*centre front row*) surrounded by his troop after operations in Sicily

TOP Tommy Corps poses next to two dead crew members of a German 105mm gun and half-track attacked during the battle for Termoli, October 1943

ABOVE The wreck of the truck in which most of Wiseman's troop were killed by a shell during the German attempt to recapture Termoli

ABOVE Tony Greville-Bell (*centre*) and George Daniels (*right*), who spent nearly three months operating behind German lines in Italy in 1943

LEFT George Daniels (*left*) and Tony Greville-Bell paying their respects at the grave of a fallen comrade in France, 2002

RIGHT Andree Lemee cuts a fine figure in his original SAS beret in 2003

OPPOSITE TOP A stick of 4SAS shortly before dropping into France in June 1944. The Le Citol brothers, René and Guy, are back row, third and fifth from left respectively. Henri Filippi (*front, right*) was brutally murdered by the SS

BELOW Peter Weaver (*standing*) and Tomos Stephens (*far right*), just days before their Bulbasket camp was overrun by a large force of Germans in July 1944

"I want to be quite certain in my own mind before I volunteer for this Paratroop business!"

" Viva Churchill—viva Roosevelt—viva 2-Lt. Smith, yes?"

LEFT Two of Ian Fenwick's cartoons from his book, *Enter Trubshaw*, published shortly after his death in 1944. The one of fawning Italian soldiers surrendering would have struck a chord with the SAS

ABOVE June 2003: The roof of the house behind René Brossier, André Bouche-Pillon and René Julian is the one Chalky White crashed through on the night of 21 June 1944

RIGHT Padre Fraser McLuskey standing next to the communion table prior to a service in the woods of the Morvan for members of Operation Houndsworth in July 1944

RIGHT James McDiarmid, Sid Payne, Ken Hart and Taffy Pitman on operations near Auxerre, August 1944

LEFT Bob Lowson (*left*) and Frank Clarke after a successful egg-buying operation in a French village, September 1944

BELOW 'Loopy' Cameron, Cyril Radford (*behind*) and Bill Robinson about to embark on a reconnaissance patrol for the Americans in eastern France, August 1944

ABOVE 2SAS veterans reunited at Chatillon in 1982: Alex Robertson (*left*), Roy Farran (*4th left*), Harry Vickers (*6th left*) and Tanky Challenor (*7th left*)

RIGHT Albert Youngman, right, and a Belgian friend in Antwerp in the autumn of 1944

ABOVE Bob Melot, in the driver's seat, shows off an SAS jeep to his relatives in Brussels just days before he was killed in a car crash, October 1944

LEFT Henry Druce, stalwart of Operation Loyton, receives a Dutch decoration for his intelligence work in the Dutch East Indies in 1947

ABOVE Bob Walker-Brown, far right, and the men of Operation Galia underneath the aircraft that dropped them into Northern Italy on December 27th 1944

BOTTOM The remnants of Operation Cold Comfort wait for orders in Italy, 1945. Cyril Radford (*third from left*) is partly obscured by Bill Rigden

ABOVE Soldiers from Operation Canuck on their way to attack Alba in April 1945. Bill Robinson is third from left and Jack Paley is marked with an 'X'

BELOW Peter Weaver stands in the foreground as inquisitive German civilians gather round his jeep during the drive towards Lubeck, 1945

ABOVE Duncan Ridler (*foreground*) was just one of many SAS soldiers to delight in the hospitality of the Norwegians in the summer of 1945

OPPOSITE TOP A group of 2SAS soldiers in Germany 1945. Jim Mackie is standing far right, while Peter le Power is front row, far left, with 'Doc' Patterson sitting next to him

OPPOSITE BELOW May 1945 and soldiers from 1SAS mock the demise of the Third Reich on hearing news of the German surrender

TOP Guards from Neuengamme concentration camp dig their own graves as soldiers from 2SAS wait to stage a mock execution in May 1945

RIGHT The pit in Belsen as photographed by Peter Weaver

They moved on a day later in brilliant sunshine that reflected off the recently fallen snow. By late afternoon all three were suffering the agonies of snow blindness. When that eased, Greville-Bell noticed that one of his feet was frost-bitten. On 4 November, day 58 of the operation, they crossed the Rome to Pescara road near Castel Di Iere.

'We waited 45 minutes to get across the road,' recalls Greville-Bell, 'because there were so many German vehicles rumbling along it. When there was a break in the traffic we got across the road and into a wood. We got out of the wood and found ourselves in the middle of a German Ack-Ack battery.' Greville-Bell led them impudently past two German sentries who 'simply looked at us and when we were very close one of them caught my eye, then looked away. I'm sure he knew ... but he would have died straight away'.

Their luck appeared to improve when they caught a mountain rabbit. They carried it for a couple of days, then sat down for the long-awaited feast. The next day, 8 November, Daniels was violently ill. Greville-Bell suspected dysentery. They laid up in a cave and Greville-Bell went down into village of Frattura and 'bought an egg for two gold sovereigns'. He poached it and fed it to Daniels in the cave. The next day a villager came with an M&B tablet.

'It was supposed to be a wonderful cure for dysentery,' says Daniels. 'That night I felt awful.'

When there was no improvement a woman took Daniels into her house.

'I was feeling better the next morning,' says Daniels, 'having had a good night's sleep in a proper bed. Suddenly this woman came running into the house shouting "*Tedeschi, Tedeschi.*" I grabbed my blanket and hid among some rocks outside with it over my head. Two Germans rode right past me and then back again a few minutes later with a couple of escaped POWs they'd just caught.'

On the evening of 12 November, they crossed Monte Greco. From the summit they could see the Sangro river. The British frontline was along its southern banks.

'We came down off the mountain,' recalls Greville-Bell, 'and entered a shepherd's hut which was full of escaped POWs who had tried and failed to get across the river.' They shook their heads wisely, declaring the river impassable. 'We said we're going anyway,' says Greville-Bell. 'We went down into the valley, then down a gully in which there was a German strongpoint, and all the time we were having to tread very carefully because there was a chestnut forest in the valley and the leaves made such a noise if you stood on them.'

They reached the northern bank of the Sangro late on 13 November. Their shoulders sagged in despair as they gazed at the water in the stygian gloom.

'The river was about a mile wide,' remembers Greville-Bell. They walked further up the bank. 'Then I realized the river was so wide because it had flooded. In fact it was only a small river and I reckoned it couldn't be that deep.'

They waded into it and a few minutes later hauled themselves out on the southern side. They squelched onwards until, at 0200 hours on 14 November, they were challenged by an English voice. 'We were asked where we'd come from,' says Daniels. 'We said it was quite a few miles from here.'

TWO WEEKS EARLIER Tim Robinson and Len Curtis had run into a Canadian artillery battery in the village of Fro Solone, at the end of a gruesome ordeal. The pair, along with Horace Stokes, had derailed a train on 14 September. Nine days later, acting on information from Italians, they'd planned to ambush a German convoy. But it never showed up. A former Italian soldier, on his way home after the armistice, befriended them and subsequently stole most of their money. Even the children couldn't be trusted. Stokes and Curtis used their last bit of money to buy ten cigarettes from two young boys. Robinson watched as they excitedly lit up.

'One draw and a burst of flame and the cigs had vanished, instant cries of, "I could kill the little bastards." Between bursts of laughter we examined the fags to find that both ends had been neatly filled with

170

tobacco and the rest consisted of dried daisy and dandelion petals. The laugh did us good.'

With no money to buy food they quickly became debilitated. Stokes was so weak he couldn't walk, so on 7 October Robinson and Curtis left him with a friendly farmer and continued. Robinson never forgot the agony of the departure, keeping with him for years the mental picture of 'Stokey down in a small valley watching Len and I climbing up over the hill, stopping every so often to wave at him'.*

For the next three weeks Curtis and Robinson lived on potatoes and fruit until they encountered the Canadians. The sergeant major listened to their story and told one of his gunners 'to get two airmail letters so that we could scribble a few lines home as their mail was going out that night'.

Greville-Bell spent several weeks in hospital having his ribs reset and regaining the three stone he'd lost during the operation. None the less he felt immense satisfaction with their part in Operation Speedwell.

'SAS operations rarely went according to plan,' he says. 'I can't remember one that ever did, but one has to make up ways to get round that. Which we did. General Alexander sent us a note later thanking us and saying we really did help slow down the German reinforcements going south.'

When he was discharged from hospital Greville-Bell returned to 2SAS.

'That left me with a slight feeling of discomfort,' he remembers. 'I found it very hard to be separated from George [Daniels]. He would go off to the sergeants' mess and I went into the officers'. It was very difficult.' Most of 2SAS spent Christmas at their barracks in Noci. The celebrations were lightly manacled by frustration. Two operations to sabotage German rail transport had been postponed on 18 December because of bad weather. It had temporarily halted the regiment's momentum that had been gathering since October. At the end of that month two operations,

---

* Stokes remained another week at the farm before cycling to Rome. There he received medical attention before eventually being betrayed to the Germans. He spent the rest of the war in a POW camp.

171

led respectively by Grant Hibbert and Roy Farran, had blown the railway lines between Ancona and Pescara and mined the coastal road. Six weeks later Sandy Scratchley landed on the coast by boat and carried out similar acts of sabotage in the same area.

The regimental Christmas party was one to remember. One of the officers, Lieutenant Jimmy Hughes, recalled that as well as the traditional food, there was also an abundance of wine and sherry. George Daniels remembered that he and a Scottish sergeant, Jock Hay, a 'placid and entirely dependable' man in the words of Hughes, had a sing-song.

'We ate and drank ourselves into a stupor.'

The non-operational members of 2SAS enjoyed Christmas in Philippeville, where the main training camp still was. With them was the collectively disgruntled Special Raiding Squadron. The past few weeks had been miserable for them, ever since their passage home on 21 November was cancelled on the orders of Whitehall. McDiarmid had spent the preceding days buying sugared almonds for his young daughter. When the news was broken McDiarmid handed the sweets to the men. Lowson and Sid Blanche found solace in alcohol.

'Sid and I got boozed and finished up with hair perms,' says Lowson. 'Reluctantly we got them shaved off straight away because we didn't think it wise to return to camp with perms.'

On 26 November the squadron sailed from Taranto to North Africa.

'It was a horrendous trip,' remembers Lowson who, like most of the men, was violently seasick.

David Danger was one of the few whose stomach coped with the turbulent seas. 'My job was to take the food down to the men from the galley. Bacon and baked beans were never so unpopular!'

Paddy Mayne was in England throughout December trying to get his men home but they were still in Philippeville in the middle of the month, though by now they had been reunited with some old faces. John Tonkin had escaped from captivity, Bill Fraser, Bill Mitchell and John Tunstall had recovered from their wounds and Jeff Du Vivier had at last rejoined the squadron having been 'left in charge of the whole blinking kaboo' at Kabrit.

On 17 December 2SAS paid 18,000 francs for their Christmas dinner. The next day the cow escaped. Freddie Oakes, who had recently joined 2SAS as a signaller, was despatched with the rest of the regiment to track down the beast.

'At about 9 a.m. the camp looked like a cattle market and several irate Arabs were hollering outside the gate – anything that looked like a cow had been brought in.'

Their cow was never identified and another was purchased. The SRS was asked to contribute 20 francs per head which they did begrudgingly. Eventually, on 25 December, they sailed from Algiers to England on the SS *Otranto*. The merchant seamen rubbed their hands in glee as they watched the squadron embark and within a couple of days their card school was teaching the SRS some hard financial lessons.

The two 2SAS operations that had been cancelled in December took place on 14 January, a week before the Allied landings at Anzio for which they were designed. Bill Stirling, who had selected the targets, estimated that if the railway lines in the Rimini and Ancona areas were sabotaged the German supply lines would be seriously disrupted. Operation Thistledown, led by Lieutenant David Worcester, did indeed hinder the Germans. Railway lines were cut, a train was derailed and Worcester's party destroyed twenty-five vehicles in a ten-day period. But the four sticks (seventeen men in total) were all captured. The second operation, Driftwood, commanded by Captain Gunston, reportedly carried out demolition work on the railway line. They were seen launching a 22ft boat into the sea south of Porto San Giorgio but no trace of them was ever found. In all probability they were sunk accidentally by one of the many Allied aircraft that patrolled the Adriatic coast.

The versatility of 2SAS continued in January with Operation Pomegranate. For the first and only time during the regiment's Italian campaign, enemy aircraft were targeted. A six-man party, led by Major Tony Widdrington, MC, dropped by parachute near Perugia. Widdrington and his fellow officer, Lieutenant Hughes, became separated from the other four

173

men (who made it safely back and were all promptly RTU'd for making no attempt to engage the enemy) but reached San Egidio airfield. They placed bombs on the seven aircraft present and withdrew. One of the spare bombs, however, exploded killing Widdrington and wounding Hughes. He was taken prisoner but later escaped.

Bill Stirling saved his most enterprising mission until last. The railway bridge south of Pesaro linked the coastal line between Ancona and Rimini. It was of strategic importance for the German positions on the east coast. On 30 January a detachment of 2SAS under Grant Hibbert sailed from Manfredonia on a destroyer called HMS *Troubridge*.

'We had done a lot of practice runs in Molfetta harbour,' remembers Cyril Wheeler, 'climbing down into the canvas canoes from the stern of the schooner.' Wheeler had no idea where the intended target was for Operation Baobab, just 'that it was a bridge'. His job was to escort Captain Miller, the Royal Engineers' explosive expert, to the target.

The day before Hibbert and his eight-strong raiding party sailed in the *Troubridge*, Lieutenant Laws and Signalman Dowell landed north of the bridge. They hid their canoe, scaled a cliff and spent the night in a cave. At 0800 hours on 30 January, the pair set out to reconnoitre the bridge. In the early afternoon Laws sent a signal that said it was heavily patrolled and no raid should be made before 2300 hours.

His final task was to discover if a house near the bridge served as a barracks for Italian Carabinieri. When it was dark he crept up to the building. To open the door he had to pull it; he peered inside and counted nineteen men, seven in Carabinieri uniform and the rest in shirtsleeves. He shut the door and with the aid of Dowell placed a large rock against it. At 2315 hours Laws signalled in the raiding party. Miller and Wheeler were helped into a motor dory. Then the plastic explosives, 160 lbs divided between four haversacks, were passed down to them. The rest of the men canoed to the landing point. When the dory got to within 200 yards of the shore they cut off the engine and paddled in. One man stayed with the boats while Laws led the rest towards the bridge.

'There wasn't one guard on the bridge,' recalls Wheeler. 'That really surprised us. So Miller placed the charges on the buttresses of the bridge and then we ran like hell.'

The charges had a 10-minute fuse, but as they sprinted back towards their canoes, they heard a commotion from the barracks. Corporal McGuire fired a volley through the door as he ran. As the raiders put to sea, says Wheeler, 'there was a load of shit coming over'. The fire was inaccurate, however, and when they were 400 yards from the shore it died down. On the bridge they could see the flicker of torchlights as the Italians desperately searched for any charges. But 10 minutes after Miller had set the charges there hadn't been an explosion.

'Hibbert looked at his watch,' says Wheeler, 'and said, "It hasn't gone off, we'll have to go back." We all looked at him and thought "you must be joking!". As he ordered us to turn round it went up.'

The operational report eloquently described how after 12 minutes there was an explosion that 'resembled the petals of an orange flower opening, while fragments of incandescent material were thrown through the air'. Wheeler recalls seeing 'bodies going sky high'. It took the Germans a week to repair the damage to the bridge.

The men were pulled on board the *Troubridge* by a jubilant crew. 'It was a great feeling,' remembers Wheeler. 'The navy boys loved it. They gave us all plenty of grog and fags. Then we lay down on the floor for a long kip.'

CHAPTER THREE

FRANCE 1944

There were no cheering crowds or regimental bands to greet 1SAS when they landed in Greenock in January 1944. Rather, says Bob Lowson, 'we were lined up on deck while two custom officers walked up and down asking if we had anything to declare'. In perfect step, as if back on the parade ground, the men shifted nervously from one foot to the other.

'We all had our kit bags stuffed with fags and other stuff,' says Lowson. It was raining when they disembarked.

'That was bloody lovely,' remembers Arthur Thomson. 'After years of roasting sunshine we came back to good old British weather.'

Thomson had married Bridget, best friend of his sister, in June 1940. The last time he had seen his wife had been July of that year. For long periods in the Western Desert they'd been out of touch. 'My wife wrote to the War Office at one stage,' says Thomson, 'asking if they had any news of me because she hadn't heard from me for so long. They wrote back and said they had never heard of me.'

The men travelled by train to a small Scottish village called Mauchline, birthplace of Robbie Burns and the temporary base for the regiment. Johnny Cooper, now a lieutenant, and Mike Sadler were there to greet them.

'Then we got a month's leave, a travel warrant and £100,' remembers Sid Payne. 'We were supposed to go to the village hall, prior to dispersing, but they opened the village pub.' The pub was 'My Spouse Nancy', a character in a Burns song. Lowson remembers that the revelry it witnessed on this particular night was wilder than anything Burns's fertile imagination could have conjured.

'The next morning we were staggering down the street towards the station when a local invited some of us in for breakfast. We told him we'd been in the pub the whole night and he said, "Christ, what were you up to in there? It sounded like you were tearing it to bits."'

Payne went down to Birmingham to blow his £100. Lowson caught the train to Liverpool.

'I arrived in the middle of the night and my dad was waiting for me.' As a veteran of the First World War, Lowson's father knew the mind of a returning soldier. 'He never once asked me what I'd been up to.'

The married men reacquainted themselves with their wives. Thomson went to London, and Alex Muirhead to Norwich and the woman he'd married weeks before he had left for the Middle East. June Muirhead was expecting her husband because of a secret code they had devised. If he was about to depart on or return from active service, Muirhead sent his wife a packet of Sobranie Cocktail cigarettes. He'd posted a packet as soon as he had stepped off the boat in Scotland.

Jeff Du Vivier had only a short distance to travel to see his sweetheart, Rea, in Ayr where they had first met in the spring of 1940. They had kept in contact ever since and now decided to get married.

'We got a lot of advice from people saying don't do it,' says Rea Du Vivier, 'and that it would never last. But we went ahead.' As if to mock the doubters they wed on April Fool's Day 1944. Bob Tait, the 'Original' who had designed the cap badge, was best man. A month later Rea accompanied her husband to Buckingham Palace for the investiture of his Military Medal.

'The whole thing was a bit prefabricated,' Du Vivier recalls. 'I don't think he'd [King George VI] heard of the SAS.'

When Du Vivier and Bob Tait, who had been awarded a bar to his MM at the same ceremony, emerged from the Palace a photographer from one of the newspapers took their picture.

'Then along came a high official,' recalls Du Vivier, 'who confiscated

177

the camera because of the regiment.' This cloak-and-dagger approach to the SAS had its benefits, however, because no one knew who the men in blue shirts and black ties and brown boots were. Du Vivier once pilfered a couple of blank leave passes from the regimental orderly room.

'I filled in the details and when we needed something to stamp it with we used the top of a sherry bottle. It had some crest embossed on it and once you smudged it a bit and authorised it with a John Smith signature it looked real.' Du Vivier used the pass to go on a 'jolly' to London where he was challenged by two MPs.

'I said I was in the SAS, they'd never heard of the SAS ... and they couldn't read the stamp. It was so easy.' *

A short while later Tait was despatched to the USA on a lecture tour. Mike Sadler and RSM Johnny Rose went with him.

'We did a grand tour,' says Sadler, 'and the idea was to tell our colourful tales in the factories and shipyards. It was organized by the American Federation of Labor and I think they were more interested in the union situation [in Britain] than the war. I was hopeless at giving lectures but Rose was very good. He did these fireside chats with the workers, which went down very well. But it we had a jolly time going by train from Pittsburgh to New Orleans up to Montana.'

Their final destination was California and the Hollywood studios. 'We were invited into some of the starlets' caravans,' recalls Sadler. 'I took rather a fancy to a very nice girl called Martha Vickers. She was a minor starlet who was very lovely.'

When the men returned from leave it was to a new and more remote camp in a village called Darvel. A few miles north of Mauchline, the base was surrounded by the Cunninghame Hills, ideal for training exercises.

---

* The SAS went to great lengths to limit public knowledge of their activities during the war. When they returned from operations in France says Vic Long of 1SAS, 'there was a slip of paper in our pay telling us not to divulge any information to journalists whatsoever'. At the beginning of August 1944, however, in a deal probably arranged with the press who were becoming increasingly inquisitive about the SAS, the War Office issued a first and last bellicose press release on the SAS. Overnight the regiment became, according to which paper you read, 'Airdevils', 'Hush-Hush Men', 'Daredevils' or 'Modern Robin Hoods'.

The men's billets were in two disused lace mills. 'Opposite the pub,' remembers Lowson, 'was a road and you walked down that, turned left and there were the two mills.' Lowson, now one of the senior NCOs, had the foreman's office but the rest slept on camp beds where the machinery had once stood.

'It was cold and miserable,' remembers Du Vivier, 'because they shut off all the heating in the mills. They weren't going to let the troops have any heating, that would have been far too expensive!'

Fortunately the men were able to warm themselves in the local pub, the Railway. 'We had some wild nights there,' says Du Vivier. 'We were adopted by the proprietress and she looked after us.'

Lowson remembers the 'boozy' sessions that lasted until the early hours, when he would 'crawl into the foreman's office'. 'A' Squadron threw a party one Thursday in the Railway in Darvel. They concocted a brew that was 50 per cent rum and passed it around in a pint glass.

'It had a kick like a mule,' said one, 'and people passed out right and left.'

'A' Squadron, who still regarded themselves as the elite of the regiment, also had their own song-sheet. It contained some of the old favourites – 'Underneath the Arches', 'Moonlight Becomes You', 'Mary of Argyll', 'Sunday, Monday and Always' – but the *pièce de résistance* was the squadron song, 'Uncle Bill Fraser and All' sung to the tune of 'Widdicombe Fair'. It began:

> *I'll tell you all of a horrible dream*
> *all along down along out along Darvel*
> *the whole of 'A' squadron went out on a scheme*
> > *with Reg Seekings, Johnny Wiseman, Pat Riley, Alex Muirhead,*
> > *Johnny Cooper, Puddle Poole, old Uncle Bill Fraser and all,*
> > *old Uncle Bill Fraser and all.*

From a 'boyish' lieutenant in the desert to an 'uncle' and a major, Fraser's transformation from boy to man was complete. No one, Mayne included, mocked his effeminacy any more, even though his nickname was 'Skin

179

Fraser' because, says one of the men 'he had homosexual instincts'. It was just another nickname, one spoken with respect not sniggered derisively.

'It didn't matter to us whether he was [gay] or not,' says Ridler.

The women of Darvel could hardly believe their luck when over two hundred tanned and fit soldiers landed on their doorstep.

'They put on a ball for us the first night we were there,' says Lowson, 'and we had to take part in a sort of beauty parade. Ken Sturmey won the prize for the best-looking soldier and Alex Muirhead won the officers' prize.' In a letter to his parents on 7 February 1944, Muirhead neglected to tell them about his prize, but he did describe their new camp.

'I can't say where we are though I will say it's a slight improvement as far as civilization goes. The officers live in a large house standing in its own ground about 15 minutes from the men's billets. I have a fair size room ... with army beds, table, two chairs, odd carpets and a fireplace. There is little I can say of my work except that I have four subalterns under my command, three are quite new, so I expect I shall be busy.'

By the end of the following month most of the new officers had arrived at Darvel. A good many arrived from the British Resistance Organization's Auxiliary Units, a force created by Colin Gubbins earlier in the war when invasion seemed imminent. Lieutenant Peter Weaver had joined the Auxiliaries from the Dorsetshire Regiment in 1941. 'The gist of it was that each county along the coast of the UK would have its private army of approximately 500 men who would live in underground hideouts, which would be stored with food, ammunition, etc. ... wait for the invasion to pass over them, then emerge from their Operational Bases causing havoc to the enemy's lines of communication.'

Now that it was the Germans waiting for an invasion, the Auxiliaries were obsolete and in need of redeployment. Ideal fodder for the SAS. Mayne held a recruitment drive in front of five hundred of them at the Curzon Cinema in London's Mayfair in March.

The ordeal of addressing so many men cowed Mayne into speaking in a quieter voice than usual, but what he said impressed Weaver and his colleagues. 'He promised us nothing but hard work and action ... this was the sort of thing I was looking for.' Weaver remembered 'about 30 officers and 100 men' being accepted into 1SAS from the Auxiliaries.

Most of the recruits were in their early twenties and from rural communities where they knew how to live off the land. Weaver was an exception. He was born in the Himalayas in 1911 into a 'upper middle class' family. His father was killed fighting in Mesopotamia in 1914, whereupon Weaver's mother, one of those intrepid and fearless Victorian women, moved to Bournemouth. Weaver had that engaging denseness often associated with England's well bred. He was amiable and popular but not academically gifted. He failed the common entrance to Sherborne and when he did finally leave school he never seemed to hold down a job for long. Instead he divided his time between chasing girls, playing cricket (a few times for Hampshire) and dreaming up another hare-brained entrepreneurial scheme, much to the despair of his mother, who wrote to him saying it was time to stop 'living in a fool's paradise'.

Among the other officers selected by Mayne were Roy Bradford, Dick Bond, Tim Iredale and Ian Fenwick. The quartet were all Bright Young Things. Iredale's family ran a brewery in the north of England; Bond came from a military family and had a wife in Somerset; Bradford was an architect who had been the Auxiliaries' intelligence officer in Devon and Cornwall; and Fenwick was the most remarkable of the lot. Educated at Winchester and Cambridge, he was a brilliant cricketer and a gifted cartoonist whose work appeared in a raft of publications.

'He was a terribly nice chap,' remembers Sadler, 'and very easy to get on with.'

Fenwick and the other Auxiliary officers shared a trait with David Stirling: an innate self-assurance. It was something Sadler quickly noticed.

'There was a social element to some of the officers,' he says. 'Some were well connected and it gave them a lot of self-confidence and authority.'

When new officers arrived at Darvel it was Paddy Mayne who was waiting for them. Roy Close, an astute 24-year-old from Haringey in

London, had come up through the ranks having gone to France in 1940 with the Royal Army Service Corps and been told to shoot down Stukas with a First World War Lewis gun. When he reached Scotland he presented himself to Mayne in the bar all 'blancoed and brassed ... with a quivering salute'.

'"Ah yes, Close," he said to me. "You're one of the Sassenachs, aren't you?" "Yes sir," I replied. "Are you strong ?" he asked. "Not too bad, sir." He got a bottle top and bent it between his thumb and forefinger. "Can you do that?" he said. I got hold of the thing and practically stamped on it in my desperation to bend it. "I hope you can fight better," said Mayne.'

John Randall joined the regiment on the same day as the padre, Fraser McLuskey.

'I don't think he was pleased to have either a padre or a signals officer,' says Randall, who had arrived from the Phantom Regiment. 'Fortunately this was on a Thursday and on the Saturday there was an inter-squadron rugger match. I must have acquitted myself rather well on the wing because from then on I had always had a good relationship with Paddy.'

Even when the new officers at Darvel began to feel they were settling in, they were under constant scrutiny.

'Paddy would wait and bide his time,' says Thomson, now a sergeant. 'These officers would go out on an exercise and after they returned he would seek out the sergeant who was on the same job and ask him what he thought of the officer. Depending on the report the officer might stay or he might not.'

Close agrees that 'there was quite a turnover of young officers at Darvel'. He also recalls the unfailingly respectful if somewhat arch looks he got from the senior NCOs.

'When chaps like Reg Seekings, Johnny Rose and Bob Lilley – with their MMs and DCMs – came up and saluted I thought, "I know just what you're thinking!" But in fact they were very good in accommodating recruits for a different kind of operation because it was a complete change of culture for them, after the desert in particular.'

What astonished the old hands the most was the appearance of the new recruits. 'How the hell are we going to win the war with kids like these?' was what went through Lowson's mind when he first saw them. 'But we had looked as young as that in 1939 when we joined up as 18- or 19-year-olds. But what I did feel for the first time was a responsibility to look after them.'

Albert Youngman says the camaraderie was cultivated on nights out in Glasgow or Kilmarnock. 'We went out for a booze-up and we came to accept them because they were volunteers.'

Doug Cronk, an ice-cream seller in Southend before enlisting in the Beds & Herts regiment, remembers there was nothing like being put on a 'fizzer' [a charge] by the Military Police after a night out in Glasgow for improving your standing within the regiment.

'One night we gave some MPs a bit of lip and they took us to the guardroom and said we would be hearing from them later,' says Cronk. 'But Paddy just tore up the charges.'

While 1SAS continued to absorb new recruits into its ranks, there was wholesale restructuring at the top of the command chain. The SRS had reverted to 1SAS on their return to the UK and in January 1944 the SAS Brigade came into existence as an adjunct to the Army Air Corps. HQ was at Sorn Castle in Ayrshire with Brigadier General Rory McLeod as the CO.

Now 1SAS came under the command of the 21st Army Group there was more bad news. The beige beret was replaced by the red airborne one. Though as Muirhead explained in a letter to his parents, 'off duty, as I am one of the older ones, I can wear either. Which colour do you like best?' Mayne continued to wear the beige beret in defiance of McLeod.

As well as 1SAS the brigade constituted 2SAS, two French regiments, the 3rd and 4th, and a Belgian Independent Company. In April, as the brigade struggled to recruit skilled signallers, 'F' Squadron GHQ Liaison Regiment Phantom was attached to swell its ranks to 2,500.

The rumblings of discontent with the new command structure finally erupted into open confrontation when SHAEF (Supreme Headquarters Allied Expeditionary Force) issued the brigade with its operational instructions for the impending invasion of France. These were dated 29 March and they infuriated Bill Stirling in particular. SHAEF envisaged the SAS dropping into France between the landing beaches and the German reserves. They would then act as a barrier, holding back the German reinforcements from reaching the beachheads. Stirling, still smarting at the misuse of 2SAS in Italy the previous year, was apoplectic. Once again the SAS was not being used strategically or in the manner his brother had imagined.

What Mayne's thoughts were on the matter weren't committed to posterity. In all likelihood he agreed with Stirling. But it was Stirling who acted on behalf of the regiment. 'I loved Paddy,' says Tony Greville-Bell, by now a captain, 'and he was tactically very clever. But he was useless in dealing with senior officers because if they did something to annoy him he threatened to punch their noses.'

Stirling drafted a letter to SHAEF in which he lambasted the plan. He had the backing of 2SAS officers, all of whom, says Greville-Bell, considered it 'ridiculous'.

'We were to be dropped 15 miles from the front,' he says. 'One place you don't want to be.' But the plan was being studied by Lieutenant General 'Boy' Browning, CO of the 1st Airborne Corps. Stirling was dissuaded from sending the letter for the moment. Browning took into account the regiment's grievances and suggested to 21st Army Group that it was impractical. The original plan was amended. Come the invasion, small parties of SAS personnel would have a different role; namely dropping deeper into France and laying waste to the enemy's line of communications while arming and training local Maquis groups.

Nevertheless, despite the amendment, Stirling sent the letter. He felt SHAEF had to be made aware of his disquiet at their perpetual misunderstanding of the SAS's capabilities. Stirling was asked to withdraw the criticism. He refused. Browning intervened personally.

'Browning was a gallant chap,' says Greville-Bell, 'but he was a twit. He came for lunch with the 2SAS officers in May and then sat down for a discussion with Bill afterwards.'

Stirling stuck to his guns, refusing to retract his comments. Shortly afterward Stirling resigned as commanding officer of 2SAS.

184

'We were in absolute agreement with his decision,' says Greville-Bell, 'and in fact the senior officers, of whom I was then one, were inclined to resign as well but Bill told us not to. "I'll never forgive you if you don't back up Brian," he told us.'

'Brian' was Major Brian Franks, Stirling's successor who had been his second in command. He had only recently joined the regiment but had seen them in action at first-hand during the battle of Termoli when he was brigade major of the Special Service Brigade. Franks had just the right mix of courage – he had been awarded an MC in Italy – and unconventionality for the SAS. 'The brigade filing system is here,' he used to say, tapping the pockets of his smock. Before the war he'd worked in London's Dorchester Hotel and among his circle of close friends were Ian Fenwick and a rising film star called David Niven. The trio had grown up together on the Isle of Wight and formed the Bembridge Sailing Dinghy Club in their teens. Niven had been secretary, Franks the captain and at the end of their first year they had made a profit of £2 12s. 6d. Niven recalled in his autobiography, *The Moon's a Balloon*, that the money was 'transferred into liqueur brandy. We were both found next morning, face down in some nettles'.

The first the men knew about the imbroglio was a sudden order to parade. Harry Vickers, a small exact man from Cheshire with steady eyes and a keen sense of fun underneath his sergeant's stripes, had recently joined 2SAS from the bomb disposal section of the Royal Engineers.

'We were all in camp at Monkton [adjacent to Prestwick in Ayrshire] when Colonel Stirling addressed us and explained he had fallen out with the powers-that-be over "supplies". Well, of course, we found out later it wasn't about supplies. But I'll always remember the term he used, he said, "I've been bowler-hatted."'

The announcement hit the men in different ways. George Daniels remembers feeling admiration for Stirling: 'It showed what sort of man he was because it hurt him to leave the regiment.' Bill Robinson says that 'everyone went mad when they heard ... a lot of people wanted to return to their units'. Cyril Radford, a 20-year-old who had arrived at Monkton only a few days earlier, 'didn't have a clue what Stirling was talking about'.

The task facing Franks was immense. Command had been thrust upon him just weeks before the regiment was due to undertake its biggest role to date.

'Brian had a problem when he took over,' agrees Greville-Bell, 'but we all knew what a good chap he was so in the end it wasn't too difficult for him.'

One of the pressing problems facing 2SAS was the dearth of good recruits. They had arrived back from North Africa in March 1944, just after Mayne and 1SAS had cherry-picked the best men from the Auxiliary Units. 2SAS looked for suitable volunteers among the ranks of the idle airborne troops around the country. Radford and Jack Paley were at the Airborne Forces depot in Derbyshire when an SAS recruitment team arrived.

'We'd heard about them out in Africa,' recalls Paley, 'this secret outfit where everyone had a beard.' Paley had worked in an ironmonger's shop in Leeds before joining up as a 19-year-old on his mother's birthday in 1941. He was a quiet, diligent man who had served in the Royal Artillery before volunteering for the Airborne.

Radford had also been a sapper, though he had enlisted as a 16-year-old boy soldier in 1939. 'When war broke out we continued training but I still wasn't allowed to smoke. That was a privilege you received when you turned 17.' Radford was a bright Devonian, self-contained and strong-willed, who found depot life intolerable. 'We were all pissed off waiting around and what they told us sounded glamorous.' Radford and Paley were both accepted. 'The SAS didn't waste any time,' says Radford, 'because two days later I was on my way to Scotland.'

A third man poached from the ranks of the Airborne Forces was 20-year-old Ray Rogers. He didn't think he would be accepted into the SAS 'because I didn't have an education'. Rogers had left school in Mountain Ash, mid-Wales, at 14 'to go underground'. He was the incarnation of the downtrodden miner in the 1930s so joylessly described by George Orwell in *The Road to Wigan Pier*.

'We were poor,' says Rogers, 'because there were eight of us and my father had had his leg off down the mines when he was young so money was tight.'

Rogers spent three weeks as a miner before he could afford to buy a pair of long trousers. In his first year underground he suffered two accidents, one of which crushed his leg. Nevertheless when he volunteered for the SAS in 1944 his rugby and boxing abilities impressed the officer who interviewed him. The diffident Rogers voiced his concerns about his lack of education.

'The officer smiled and said, "Do you want to go back to school?" Then I was asked about my time as a miner. I think that helped me.'

In the recruitment of officers serendipity rode to Franks' rescue. On the train to Manchester to do his parachute training at the Ringway Parachute School, Franks struck up a conversation with a cheery captain called Henry Druce.

'I was off to Ringway to play around with a parachute,' says Druce, 'and Brian was looking for recruits. By the time we arrived he had offered me a job, which was lucky for me because I was out of one at the time.'

Having been commissioned into the Middlesex Regiment in 1939 Druce's talent as a linguist – he was fluent in French, Flemish and Dutch – attracted the attention of MI6, who recruited him in 1943.

'The idea was to fly me in to Holland and pick up agents and so on,' he explains. 'But it never happened. My cover was blown by a Dutch agent working for the Germans and that's why meeting Brian was fortunate.'

In his role as a spy Druce had been helped by his appearance. He had a well-fed face and there was little hard muscularity to his physique.

Lieutenant Bob Walker-Brown joined the regiment on his own initiative. He had been badly wounded serving with the Highland Light Infantry during the Battle of the Cauldron in North Africa in June 1942. He was then shipped to a POW camp in Italy where he remained until he escaped and reached Allied lines. To his immense irritation he was returned to the UK where he discovered that 'the prevailing view was that as an ex-prisoner I must be a psychiatric case and I had to go before a board of trick cyclists'. Walker-Brown, found to be in complete working order, was sent to a infantry training depot in Aberdeen, the city of his birth.

'I happened to be in the Caledonia Hotel in Aberdeen one day when I saw a very glamorous-looking officer covered in wings and pistols and God knows what. I asked him what unit he was in and he said the SAS. "Right," I said. "What's your CO's name and telephone number?" I phoned up Brian Franks and joined the SAS.'

Walker-Brown's granite integrity and iron endurance were as impressive as his moustache, which jumped and twitched like a dog with fleas when something unsettled his scruples.

FIRST UP FOR THE new recruits was parachute training. A fresh and daunting challenge for the preponderance of new recruits and an unwelcome refresher course for the desert veterans. Alex Muirhead told his parents in a letter that 'in spite of the course being very enjoyable we were all glad to finish it as it was rather wearing on our nerves'. What chafed nerves most was jumping from a barrage balloon. Freddie Oakes recalled that the 'toilet door hinges would become red hot with use' before the exercise. The balloons had a large wicker basket suspended beneath them and 'a steel hawser connected them to a winch on the back of a lorry ... we climbed into the basket and up we went'. The winching stopped at around 700 feet.

'Then you just gently swayed,' recalls Charlie Hackney. 'And there was no noise. That was the worst thing. In a plane at least you've got the roar of the engine to drown out your thoughts.'

The soldiers' fears weren't assuaged by the instructors, most of whom thought they were born comedians. As Oakes jumped, the instructor yelled, 'Come back, you silly bastard, you're not hooked up!'

'One fell about 180 feet before the 'chute opened,' said Oakes, 'and in that short time I got through the Lord's Prayer.'

After the balloons the men progressed to jumping from aircraft, usually Stirling bombers or Albermarles. They jumped during the day and at night. Parachuting was now a precise art, much more so than 1941 when Warburton and Duffy had jumped to their deaths at Kabrit. There were no fatalities among the SAS at Ringway, but mishaps were a regular occurrence. Peter Weaver and Walker-Brown were caught by the wind on their descents; Weaver drifted towards a hangar and became snared on the roof, dangling for a few seconds, before dropping on to the tarmac below. Fortunately Walker-Brown managed to 'make a perfectly satisfactory landing on top of a double-decker bus which was full of the most charming Wrens'.

The men unwound during the two-week course by 'chasing the local skirt'. Ringway aerodrome, remembers Lowson, 'was surrounded by factories and all the girls who worked in them were loaded with money. I spent a fortnight there, didn't spend a penny, got free ale and as much crumpet as you could shake a stick at!'

Bob McDougall was in a Manchester pub one night with Johnny Cooper when two attractive parachute packers walked in.

'Johnny said, "Hey, we're all right here" and bought them both a drink. Then he bought them another and we were soon pouring drinks down these girls. All of a sudden they got up and said they had to go. Johnny turns to me and says "She drank six pints and didn't even have a piss!" '

Bill Deakins, exempted from parachute training because of the injuries he suffered in 1941, went to Mallaig in the Scottish Highlands with some officers where they received lectures on 'railway lines, engines and rolling stocks'. He also got the chance of driving an engine up and down a few miles of line. On one occasion an SAS officer collided with the buffers so forcefully that the jolt broke the leg of the train guard.

Deakins incorporated what he had learned in Mallaig into the lectures he now gave to the men at Darvel. The instruction was all practical, either in the camp or at the goods yard at Kilmarnock.

'The best way to blow a line was with a gun cotton charge about the size of a small brick. It had a little egg-shaped hole for the primer which took a detonator and could be fastened to the side of the line. But there were many ways of blowing a line using pressure switches buried under sleepers. In the end you just had to be a bigger bastard than the other bastard, if you understand me.'

As the days lengthened and summer approached the training took on greater urgency. It was time to bring together all aspects of the men's

189

training in mock exercises against the police or Home Guard units. Roy Close led his men in a successful raid against Kilmarnock police station; Bob Lowson accompanied a new officer, Lieutenant Peter 'Monty' Goddard, 'on a map-reading exercise but he couldn't read a map. In the end he got me to go to into a phone box and find out where we were'.

Vic Long, a relaxed 21-year-old from Belfast recently arrived in Darvel, took part in an exercise on the Mull of Kintyre.

'We raided the Home Guard's armoury which caused a bit of a rumpus,' recalls Long, 'then we got back to the mainland and pinched a few vehicles to get home, one of which was an RAF officers' bus loaded with supplies. We nicked the lot.'

Sandy Davidson's section in 'C' Squadron had to penetrate the defences of an Ack-Ack battery crewed by WAAFs. One of them took Davidson's fancy and he asked her out. They were married before the year ended.

Ray Rogers found himself cold and hungry in the middle of the Scottish mountains. 'I went into a remote farmhouse and a little old lady opened the door. When she heard my Welsh accent she thought I was a German. After I'd calmed her down she gave me some tea and cake.'

Harry Vickers was told to raid a local Home Guard depot. 'We'd crawled into some bushes, made a cup of tea and then went to sleep. Around noon I heard some footsteps and then felt a bayonet prodding my backside. "Come oot, come oot, I've found you." It turned out the Home Guard sergeant was a gillie [a hunting guide] who'd tracked us all over the hills. But being captured actually did us a lot of good. Before that we'd all thought we were the tops.'

Albert Youngman and Peter Weaver, both in 'B' Squadron 1SAS under the command of Ted Lepine, took part in an exercise just across the English border.

'We parachuted into Carlisle,' remembers Youngman, 'and then had to get to Dumfries without being caught. I completed that successfully but John Tonkin asked me to go back to Carlisle on a motorbike and collect his .22 rifle that he'd left down there. Coming back I crashed the damned thing and ended up in hospital with a broken ankle.'

Youngman didn't get much sympathy from his mates, Dougie Eccles and Lofty Baker, as the rest of the squadron departed to Devon for their final exercise in what Weaver remembered as a 'splendid week'.

'By day cliff climbing in the Windspit area of the coast. At night we prepared DZ's for the RAF, one of which I remember well at South Farm.' On the last evening of the exercise Weaver and the squadron were invited to return to the farm where they were guests of honour at a 'magnificent barn dance with all the trappings'.

When 'B' Squadron arrived back at Darvel in late May the turnround was almost immediate.

'After hurried farewells the regiment entrained at Kilmarnock,' said Weaver, 'our destination being Fairford. It was a long journey down by train and I remember we stopped somewhere for refreshments. The platform was crowded with SAS in their camouflaged smocks and red berets. Everyone was in great spirits … unashamedly I felt very good to be alive and playing a part in it all. To be in the right place at the right time.'

It wasn't until 1 June that the amended operational instruction was finalized. Bill Stirling's sacrifice had not been in vain. Apart from Operation Titanic, which would involve six men dropping just a few miles south of the landing beaches in the early hours of 6 June to confuse and distract the enemy with dummy parachutes, the brigade's role in France had been radically altered. The focus of 1SAS's initial operations would now be hundreds of miles south of Normandy.

If the head of the German Army was in northern France its oxygen was supplied from the reinforcements deployed throughout the rest of the country; the job of Operations Bulbasket and Houndsworth would be to cause as many blockages as possible. Bulbasket, under the command of John Tonkin and involving 'B' Squadron, would establish its base in the Vienne region, between Poitiers and Chateauroux. Bill Fraser would lead 'A' Squadron in Houndsworth, to be based in the Massif du Morvan, west of Dijon. The task was to cut railway lines between Lyon and Paris and arm and train the local Maquis groups. Once the bases had been

191

established the modus operandi would be left to the discretion of the squadron commanders.

But in Brittany it was the 4th Regiment French SAS (*4ème Bataillon d'Infanterie de l'Air*) who were told to give the Germans a short, sharp headache. In the early morning of 6 June thirty-six men in two sticks would parachute in to arm and train the Maquis. Together they would then prevent the Germans in that area from reinforcing the Normandy battlefields. On 7 June, D-Day plus one, the second stage of the Brittany operation, codename Cooney, would begin with the insertion of eighteen three- and five-man parties whose job would be to destroy as many railway links as possible between Brittany and Normandy.

Fewer than half the original contingent of French SAS troopers who went to the Middle East in 1941 remained; those that had survived the desert constituted the heart of 4SAS and were now commanded by the one-armed Pierre Bourgoin. Their numbers were augmented by men who had been released from captivity following the capitulation of the Vichy forces in North Africa.

When the Americans landed in Algeria in November 1942 Lieutenant Pierre Marienne had been under the sentence of death for refusing to renounce his allegiance to General de Gaulle. He was released and joined Bourgoin. Lieutenant Marc Mora was an officer in a Free French regiment that had fought at Bir Hakeim and El Alamein.

'I had first met Bourgoin in Damascus in 1941 and in 1943 he told me about a parachutist unit called the SAS. My initial application was refused because HQ was run by too many Giraudistes. So I went to see Bourgoin and he personally arranged my transfer.' Mora didn't arrive in England until the start of 1944, by which time 4SAS had its full complement of officers. Instead he joined its sister regiment, 3SAS. 'That was a big blow but I couldn't do anything about it.'

No amount of skilful French diplomacy could bridge the gulf of distrust that existed between the two regiments. This wasn't the sort of innocuous rivalry that existed between the two British SAS regiments; this was poisonous animosity.

192

'The 3SAS weren't Free French like we were,' says Alain Papazow. 'They had come from Algeria and they didn't willingly volunteer.'

The two regiments rarely fraternized. The 4SAS even wore their berets in a different style.

'We wore ours as Gaullistes,' says Papazow, 'with the badge over the eye. They wore theirs like the British.'

The 4SAS was fortified by soldiers whose intrepid character boded well for future operations. They were the young men who had escaped from France in the years following its occupation and made their way to England. André Lemée, a 24-year-old furniture-maker from Montlucon, had crossed into Spain at the third attempt. After several weeks of maltreatment in a Spanish jail, a place Lemée says was 'like something out of the Middle Ages', he was interned with the other French escapees in Miranda.

'When the Americans landed in North Africa,' recalls Lemée, 'the Spanish suddenly became much friendlier.' He enlisted in the Free French in Gibraltar and reached Britain in 1943. 'I loved the fighting spirit of the English people,' he says, 'and I loved the English girls. I couldn't believe how emancipated they were; they were smoking in the streets, they were riding motorbikes; they were working on buses. I had never seen this in France. I was lucky enough to go out with a few.'

Guy Le Citol, a 21-year-old from Lorient on the west coast of Brittany, had spent the first two years as a forced labourer in a German submarine yard. In 1943 he and his brother, René, had fled their home after assaulting a German in the street. They headed north, to Carantec, where they stole a 15ft rowing boat.

'We started off just after midnight,' says Le Citol, 'and rowed as fast as we could during the night and when the sun rose we couldn't see the coast any more.' By the end of the day their hands were 'bloody and blistered'. They had taken with them a First World War compass, but forgotten to bring drinking water. Soon their thirst was unbearable.

'By the next day I wanted to drink the sea water,' recalls Le Citol, 'but my brother stopped me.'

193

Late that afternoon a British fighter appeared and came down for a closer inspection. 'We had with us a French flag that we started waving.' A couple of hours later they were picked up 40 miles off the British coast by a motor torpedo boat.

All the Frenchmen who made it to England and contacted the Free French were subjected to a rigorous vetting procedure to root out any Fifth Columnists. Guy Le Citol was asked to tell his inquisitor all about himself, 'from kindergarten upwards'.

'They asked me what I had done on the Sunday before leaving,' says Le Citol. 'I told them I'd been to the cinema. What had I seen? And it had totally slipped my mind. I couldn't remember the name of it. The man told me to come back in an hour when I remembered. But I couldn't. It was a couple of days later when I heard someone whistling a tune from it that I remembered. It was a German film called *L'étoile de Rio*. I told my interrogator and two days later I was released into the army.'

The spirit of adventure that coursed through the veins of so many new recruits in 4SAS made little impression on Roger Boutinot. The camaraderie of those early desert days was gone. Everything had become regimental.

'We went up to Scotland to train and I became very fed up. With all the new parachutists it was like the regular army. We even paraded every morning. I just stayed in my own little group with my friends from Kabrit and didn't bother with the rest of them.'

Cracks were, however, beginning to appear in Boutinot's carapace. In the four years since he had fled France his every waking moment had been consumed by a desire for revenge. But in early 1944 he began stepping out with a young Englishwoman from Manchester called Cecilia. They had first met at the beginning of the war when Boutinot was temporarily billeted with Cecilia's uncle, who was married to a Frenchwoman. When he returned from the desert they began seeing more of each other.

'We arranged to meet one Saturday afternoon in Manchester during his parachute training,' remembers Cecilia. 'But I was a bit late and when I arrived he wasn't there. I waited and eventually got the bus back to my

194

aunt's. There he was. "You weren't there on time," he said, "so I went".'
Gradually Boutinot began to soften.

THE PARACHUTE JUMPING at Ringway was for the French SAS the culmi-
nation of an intensive training course preceded by route marches and
live fire exercises in the Scottish Highlands. Both regiments were based
in Auchinleck, 12 miles east of Ayr, though Papazow remembers that they
'were in two separate camps divided by a fence'. At the start of 1944 Tony
Greville-Bell spent several weeks in charge of a French training squadron.
'The men were very bright and much better educated than their British
equivalents,' he remembers, 'so they were more easily able to learn things.
But their discipline was savage. The officers struck their men and even
though I don't think they were supposed to they used to sometimes
flog them.'

Papazow remembers that one of the exercises in Scotland involved
'running down a hill wearing our Bergens and at the bottom was a
machine gunner firing above our heads. An officer stood behind and
when he tapped him on the shoulder it was the signal to fire a little bit
lower. We took a few casualties.'

Jan Czarski was a Polish instructor who taught the French SAS rudimentary parachute skills in Scotland before they left for Ringway.

'There was no trace of poor discipline,' he says. 'On the contrary they
were keen and seemed to be enjoying it. They were all very desperate to
make up for the humiliation of 1940. But of course the food wasn't too
bad, plenty of meat and potatoes, and most were screwing local girls.'

Some romances lasted longer than one night. Le Citol recalls one of
his comrades who 'got married in a registry office, then they had a drink
in a pub and he returned to base that night. A few days later we went
south to England and parachuted into France. He never returned to
Scotland but as the marriage wasn't consummated he married a French
woman after the war'.

Boutinot, recalls Cecilia, 'never talked about what he was doing and I
suppose I didn't want to know'. When 4SAS moved to Fairford, Boutinot

195

told his girlfriend nothing. But by now his mind was focused solely on the tantalizing prospect of parachuting into France.

'We had expected the invasion long before June,' he recalls, 'and we began to get impatient. 'What's the delay?' we wanted to know.' On 5 June the waiting came to an end.

IT WAS DURING the charcoal hours of 8 June that Boutinot touched French soil for the first time in four years. 'I stopped for a moment and thought about what it meant,' he says. Then he buried his parachute. In a few minutes he was reunited with the other two members of his stick, Albert Deborre, a newcomer to the regiment, and his officer from the desert, Michel Legrand. They comprised one of the eighteen sabotage parties of Operation Cooney, whose mission was to isolate Brittany from the rest of France by cutting the railway lines within 48 hours. They were supposed to have been dropped to the north-west of Merdrignac but Legrand estimated they were 5 miles shy of the correct DZ.

'We had been told before we left England not to contact any locals if possible,' says Boutinot, 'but after 24 hours of trying to establish where we were Legrand told me to go to a small farm that was 300 metres away and find out our position.' As he neared the farm he could see a man pottering outside. Boutinot explained who he was and what he wanted. Then he asked if he had some food.

'Yes, of course,' replied the elderly farmer, 'come inside but don't stay too long because Germans often come here and buy my eggs.' Boutinot followed the farmer indoors. As the old man prepared a basket of food, a German lorry pulled into the farmyard. Boutinot looked frantically for a way out. There was no back door. It was a multi-purpose room with the farmer's bed in the corner. Boutinot looked under it. There was no space.

'There wasn't even a window I could climb out of without being seen,' he remembers. The Germans who got out of the lorry – Boutinot estimates there were seven or eight of them – weren't all armed. The couple who were had their rifles slung over their shoulders as they ambled towards the kitchen.

'I went to the front door,' says Boutinot, 'opened it and began firing. I was using an Italian Beretta sub-machine gun, a great weapon.' When they were all lying dead or dying he stopped firing. 'Before I dropped into France I knew it would be merciless on both sides,' says Boutinot. 'The Geneva Convention didn't exist for the Germans and it didn't exist for me. It was kill or be killed.'

When he returned to the lying-up position, his two companions had gone. 'They had heard the firing and left,' says Boutinot. Within hours there was a frenzied manhunt underway. Boutinot hid for two days in the pouring rain until, cold and starving, he approached another farm.

'At first the farmer thought I might be a German,' says Boutinot, 'but I told him I was a French paratrooper who had shot some Germans. "That was you?" he asked. "Bloody hell, we need to hide you!" He was a good man. For nearly a week he hid me in the top of his barn while the Germans looked for me.'

When the search was scaled down Boutinot was passed on to the local Maquis. He was given civilian clothes and false identity papers. 'For two weeks I stayed in this café in Merdrignac,' says Boutinot. 'Sometimes during the day I served the Germans who came in for a drink.' At the end of June Boutinot was reunited with Legrand and Deborre, both of whom had been sheltered by the Maquis. 'We still had the material to carry out the sabotage work so we began cutting railway lines, attacking vehicles and shooting Germans drinking in bars.'

THE SECONDARY mission for the men of Operation Cooney once their supplies had been exhausted was to head south and RV with the rest of the regiment at either one of two camps established by extant operations. Dingson and Samwest had been launched in the early hours of 6 June. Samwest, in the north of Brittany near St Brieuc, had been rendered useless after the camp was razed by a strong force of Germans. The survivors escaped south to Dingson's camp, which lay near the village of St Marcel above the coastal port of Vannes.

Within hours of landing in St Marcel Lieutenants Marienne and Henri

197

Deplante had made contact with Colonel Morice, the FFI regional commander. Marienne then signalled Bourgoin: 'Urgent, send all available officers, men and equipment immediately … very impressed by organization and immense capabilities.' Bourgoin parachuted into St Marcel on 9 June, as did Alain Papazow, who 'knelt down and kissed France'. Bourgoin was as impressed as Marienne. All the Maquis from the neighbouring departments had been corralled by Morice; there were over two thousand of them in a 500-hectare camp. Bourgoin contacted Brigade HQ and organized a series of resupplies of men and munitions. On the night of 13 June twenty-five Stirling bombers dropped 700 containers. They also dropped a stick of eight men under the command of Lieutenant Maurice Richard. Guy and René Le Citol were among them.

'We landed 8km out of position at a place called Le Roc-St-André,' says Guy Le Citol. 'Some of our containers landed in the grounds of the local chateau [Château Roc-St-André], which unfortunately was occupied by the Germans.'

The men emptied all the containers they could find and then, with dawn nearly upon them, searched for somewhere to lie up. They knocked on the door of a farm owned by Monsieur and Madame Lalys. He had been deported to Germany but his wife, 28-year-old Jeanne, ushered them inside. She fed the SAS soldiers and guided them to the attic. Not long after daybreak the Germans arrived. 'They asked Jeanne if she had seen some "Tommies",' says Le Citol. 'She said no, she hadn't seen anyone that morning. They went away but not long after spotted some boot prints in the farmyard.' Jeanne Lalys saw the Germans return and fled to a neighbouring village with her young daughter.

The first German who went upstairs was shot dead by Le Citol. His comrades withdrew into the yard only to come under fire from the attic window. Several hand grenades were tossed down on to the heads of the Germans. But one exploded prematurely in the attic. Three men, including René Le Citol, were wounded by shrapnel. The smoke sent them reeling out of the attic, coughing and spluttering.

'I had to get out,' says Guy Le Citol, 'because I couldn't breathe in

198

the attic. I went down on to the first floor and came face to face with a German. My reactions were quicker.' The SAS men now tried to fight their way out of the farmhouse. 'I fired a complete magazine at a German hiding in a shed behind a cart,' says Guy Le Citol. 'He stumbled out with his arm hanging out of its socket by a few threads of skin.' But the weight of the German fire forced the French back into the house. The Germans called up reinforcements, while the trapped men husbanded their ammunition as best they could. When it became futile to continue they surrendered.

'We were lined up in the courtyard with our hands in the air,' says Guy Le Citol. 'A German officer asked me how many men were still inside the house. I said none, but a few seconds later Maurice Billon was discovered hiding in a room. This officer came up to me and pointed his revolver at my head. René stepped in front of me.

'"Please don't kill him," he said, "he's my brother." The German looked at me, and lowered his revolver. Strange. Then he ordered the farm to be burned down.'

THE DISAPPEARANCE of Lieutenant Richard's stick was barely noticed at the St Marcel camp. By the evening of 17 June Bourgoin had under his command sixteen officers and 171 men from his regiment. Boutinot's was one of the few sticks that hadn't been able to make it south from Operation Cooney.*

That night Brigadier General McLeod sent a message to the French telling them to 'avoid a pitched battle at all cost. Continue all-out guerrilla warfare and arming of FFI'. But events conspired against Bourgoin. At 0430 hours on the morning of the 18th two vehicles containing German Feldgendarmerie (Military Police) strayed too close to the camp. An excited FFI machine-gun post opened fire. Seven of the eight Germans were killed or captured. One escaped. At 0815 hours the Germans attacked with five

---

* Cooney severely disrupted the flow of German reinforcements to the beachhead; a battlegroup of the 275th Division left Redon in southern Brittany on 6 June and, after repeated cuts in the railway line, were forced on to the roads finally arriving at the battlefront on the 11th.

199

hundred men. Unfortunately for them their main thrust was against the eastern perimeter of the camp, which was defended predominantly by the SAS. At 1000 hours, having called for reinforcements, they begin a second assault using mortars to support the two companies of troops. As the Germans moved through cornfields towards the Château de Geneviève they ran into a superbly organized SAS defence.

'We massacred them as they came across the fields,' says Papazow. 'We had had so many Bren guns dropped to us that we just cut them to pieces.'

In the afternoon the Germans came again, strengthened by a company of Georgian fascists. They took the Château de Geneviève at 1430 hours. Three hours later the farm of Le Bois-Joly, important strategically, was lost. Despite a brilliant counter-attack in the early evening, led by Lieutenant Marienne, which retook the area around the chateau, Bourgoin decided to withdraw when reports reached him of more German reinforcements.

The French force left during the night by the northern flank, the only section of the camp not covered by the enemy. When the Germans realized their quarry had eluded them, they were enraged. The battle had cost them around three hundred dead. The SAS had lost six soldiers and the Maquis twenty-five. Suddenly the Germans appreciated the extent of the organized resistance they were facing. Barbarous reprisals were carried out against the surrounding villages. Anyone even suspected of having Maquisard tendencies was slaughtered. Then they began to hunt the SAS. A collaborator led them to the hideout of Pierre Marienne one morning. One by one the Germans shot them all. Pierre Marienne and the officer with him, François Martin, who had fought with Jordan in the desert, were taunted for a few minutes, then shot.

When Bourgoin heard of the murders he sent a message to General Koenig, commandant of the FFI, asking him to inform the German High Command that any German soldier who in future fell into the hands of his men would be treated in a similar fashion. The threat was wasted on the Germans. A further sixteen men from 4SAS were executed in the following weeks. Guy Le Citol only learned of his good fortune when he returned to England in August. He and his companions had jumped

200

from a prison train bound for Germany and made their way north-west.

'All the French SAS caught after us were shot,' he says, 'I don't know why they didn't kill us.'

Le Citol was just lucky. He was captured by a Wehrmacht patrol, led by a decent man. Around the time Le Citol was caught two other 4SAS soldiers were taken prisoner during the attack on the Samwest base. Corporal Daniel Taupin and Trooper Marcel Ruelle were doused in petrol and set alight. Before they executed Henri Filippi, a good friend of Le Citol's, the Germans punctured his eyeballs with a bayonet.

REG SEEKINGS AND Johnny Cooper were back together after an 18-month hiatus. Cooper was now a lieutenant with a DCM, Seekings a staff sergeant-major with a DCM and MM. A third 'Original', Major Fraser, commanded their nineteen-strong team that formed the main reconnaissance party of Operation Houndsworth. In the early morning of 11 June they dropped in two sticks into the Morvan. It was a poor drop. The men were scattered across woods and fields. Fraser and Trooper Kennedy landed near a German patrol and laid up in the woods; Lieutenant Terry Moore, the Phantom officer, found himself alone and well to the east of the intended position; Cooper hit a dry-stone wall that 'left me lying unconscious in a ditch with my parachute on top of me'.

By 1100 hours Cooper had gathered up his party, which included Corporal David Danger, now the most experienced signaller in the regiment.

'Johnny asked me to send a message to London telling them we'd arrived but some way off the DZ. We also thought it wise to send a message back with one of our two carrier pigeons. I'd parachuted in with them in a tube that hung round my neck. They seemed reluctant to part from me at first. So I gave them a feed with some corn and then after Johnny had written the coded message we set them off and one of them did reach home.'

By the morning of 12 June, Cooper had pinpointed his location: close to the village of Fetigny, 10 miles south-east of the DZ at Vieux Dun. He was told to sit tight for 24 hours while the local Maquis organized transport

201

to pick them up. When the Maquis arrived on the night of the 13th Cooper couldn't believe his eyes.

'We could hear the engine from miles away,' he said. 'I remember looking at Reg [Seekings] and saying, "What the hell is that?" It didn't sound like any vehicle I'd ever seen before. Then it appeared, this bloody great bus.'

The 45-seater bus was a *gazogène*, typical of the time in France (although it was actually a German invention), in which the petrol tank had been replaced by a metre-high gas cylinder attached to the back of the bus. It ran on wood, which accounted for the noise and the fact that it took about an hour for the stove to heat up before it would start. Its driver was André Bouche-Pillon, a 23-year-old from the small village of Montsauche. Up to 1942 his life had been unremarkable. He had trained as a mechanic and worked in the local garage. Then in 1943 the Vichy Government introduced Service du Travail Obligatoire (STO), a law devised by the Germans with the aim of increasing production in its factories. Young Frenchmen were required to work in German factories to boost their industrial output.

'The first group left the Morvan in October 1942,' says Bouche-Pillon, 'and in return the Germans said they would release a French prisoner of war for every STO. But we soon realized this wasn't happening. So we took to the woods and avoided the Germans.'

Within a few months the woods of the Morvan (a region roughly the same size as the Lake District in England) were swarming with an angry cloud of young Frenchmen. But they had no organization and no weapons. All that changed when Jean Longhi arrived in the region. He was one of the early members of the Resistance, what the French call *Résistants de la première heure*. But in 1941 his name had become known to the Germans and he left Paris for the Morvan, 'a very anti-Boche region' says Longhi.

'I established a link with Paris and they then asked me if I would accept to be in charge of the Maquis in the whole of Nièvre and I became departmental manager for the region [in late1943].'

One of the first people Longhi recruited was Paul Bernard, a childhood friend who was appointed leader of the Maquis group known as Camille. In charge of the Maquis known as Bernard, however, was Louis Aubin, the 48-year-old boss of a local agricultural business.

'The Maquis wasn't easy to create,' says Longhi, 'but we were given a little bit of money from Paris [Resistance network] to buy weapons and food.'

Bouche-Pillon had been one of the first to join the Maquis Bernard. After a while he emerged from the woods and continued to work as the village mechanic. His looks and personality were perfect for this type of subterfuge. His doleful face was inscrutable and he moved languidly, without the impatient vigour of other Maquisards. The Germans never suspected that he moonlighted as Maquis Bernard's driver.

Once Cooper had stopped laughing he ordered his men aboard the bus. The first one shattered the rear window.

'I was furious,' says Bouche-Pillon. 'He'd smashed the glass with his rifle butt to give himself a better firing position. His mates were about to do the same thing to the side windows but I ran down the back of the bus and showed them how to open them.' Danger remembers that they set off 'with our guns sticking out of every window in the bus'.

Lieutenant Ian Wellsted had come on the bus with Bouche-Pillon and now he gave directions to the Frenchman.

'I didn't know what my mission was,' says Bouche-Pillon, 'only that I was to drive the bus where Wellsted told me. He sat next to me saying "left, right, left". We arrived near [the village of] Dun-les-Places and he told me to take a little path. We got stuck, the bus wasn't big enough to go down it, so I said to him: "Look, just tell me where you want to go and I'll get you there." So he told me we were to go to the Maquis Camille camp. If he'd told me that in the first place I could have got them there hours quicker.'

It took another couple of days before the entire party had rallied on the Maquis Camille's forest camp. On the evening of 17 June Bouche-

Pillon drove his bus to Les Vellottes, the chosen DZ for the rest of 'A' Squadron. It was a filthy night, one of many in what Bouche-Pillon remembers as 'the wettest and coldest June we'd had for years'. Fraser, Wellsted and Seekings drove to the DZ in a car lent to them by Maquis Camille and prepared the fires.

The three planes carrying sixty-four men left Fairford at 2200 hours on 17 June. John Noble and Chalky White were in plane 'C', under the command of Captain John Wiseman. Alex Muirhead, whose wife had received a packet of Sobranie Cocktail cigarettes on 6 June, her twenty-fifth birthday, was the officer in charge of plane 'B' and Lieutenant Les Cairns of plane 'A'. Noble described the trip in a diary he kept for the sake of his girlfriend, Ethna, back in Edinburgh: 'I admit here and now I was afraid. My chief fear was getting shot down in the drink. However, we crossed the Channel safely. We then ran into some flak. The pilot took evasive action ... eventually we were told, half an hour to go and for the next 15 minutes chaos reigned supreme. There were blokes in all sort of positions, testing chutes, strapping on leg bags, etc.'

For 20 minutes their plane circled the DZ. Down below the reception committee could hear the sound of engines through the dense mist. Eventually it was agreed with the pilots that the most prudent course of action would be to return home.

'We were crossing back over the Channel at dawn,' wrote Noble, 'It was, I think, the most beautiful I've ever seen.'

Two of the planes touched down at 0700 hours. The third plane, Lieutenant Cairns and his fifteen men, never returned, and no trace of it was ever found.

'I knew most of the lads on that plane,' says Noble, 'Barney Bryson was one of my best pals. It was terrible when something like that happened because in such a small unit you know everyone.'

Four days later they jumped successfully, one party at a DZ near Maquis Camille, another led by Captain Roy Bradford near the Maquis Bernard camp at Montsauche. The second drop was the more painful of the two:

Noble bounced off a roof and winded himself; Chalky White hit the branch of a large tree and was catapulted through a straw roof into the house of a terrified family; Fraser McLuskey was knocked unconscious after crashing through a tree; Jeff Du Vivier had followed the padre out of the aircraft and suffered a similar fate.

'I finished up high in a tree with no idea how far the ground was below me. So I tied my parachute line to my commando knife and lowered it to the floor. Then I reeled it in, measuring each yard like a tailor measuring a suit. It was soon clear I was far too high up to let go of my tree.'

Du Vivier heard movement through the trees but he waited in silence for the recognition signal.

'I could see lights coming towards my tree but as I didn't know who it was I remained silent. Then I heard someone whistling "Sur le pont d'Avignon".'

The tune, a popular song in the 1930s, was the regiment's recognition code both in the field and on the radio throughout operations in France. The Maquis knew the code and the man whistling the tune beneath Du Vivier was Bouche-Pillon.

'When Du Vivier responded we got some lights from the DZ and illuminated his tree,' he says, 'then one of the Maquis climbed up and helped him down. He was very grateful, thanking us all in perfect French when he got back down on the ground. Once they were all assembled on the ground,' recalls Bouche-Pillon, 'the first thing they did was open a container and set up a Bren gun as a precaution. The next thing they did was sit down and have a cup of tea. At 3 o'clock in the morning!'

When all of Bradford's party had rendezvoused at the Maquis Bernard camp the next morning three soldiers were unaccounted for. René Brossier, the 16-year-old wide-eyed cousin of Louis Aubin, was sent out to make enquiries as to their whereabouts.

'I went to farms and isolated cottages on my pushbike looking for the missing men,' he explains. 'A lot of the locals were very scared because they had heard the planes and a lot of unusual noises and didn't know what was going on. In one farm I found a soldier holding

205

the family hostage because he was scared that if he let them go they would tell the Germans.'

Chalky White was found after three days, unable to walk because of his back injury and totally reliant on the family who were sheltering him. He was taken to see Dr Martell, the 30-year-old doctor who treated the sick and wounded of all Maquis groups in the region. Dr Martell's real name was Alec Prochiantz. He'd arrived in the Morvan with his wife, Edmee, a few weeks earlier, getting off the bus from Paris, where he'd worked as a surgeon, to be met by Bouche-Pillon. His first operation, of the ninety-eight he would perform, was carried out that same day on a wounded Maquisard.

'We had no material for anaesthetic,' says Prochiantz, 'so André held the man down while I cleaned the wound.'

Prochiantz, with his wife as his assistant, initially based himself in a remote house in Roches, not far from Montsauche, until one day the local Gendarme visited, as he regularly did to reaffirm his allegiance to the Maquis.

'I don't know why,' says Prochiantz, 'but he didn't seem right on this occasion. As soon as he had left I told everyone to evacuate the building. An hour later the Germans arrived and destroyed everything.'

By the time the SAS appeared the new hospital was in the Château de Vermot.

IN THE DAYS immediately after the arrival of the rest of the squadron, a procession of vehicles chugged to and fro between the camps of Maquis Bernard and Camille as Fraser organized his squadron. By the morning of 24 June rural tranquillity had been restored. Bradford's and Wiseman's sections were with Fraser's HQ in the Vieux Dun camp next to Maquis Camille. Muirhead's Two Troop camped a short distance away from the Maquis Bernard in the Bois de Montsauche. The Germans were oblivious to the frenetic activity of the past few days. In the afternoon of the 24th a detachment of Germans and White Russians (Soviet soldiers who had switched allegiance) practised their ambush techniques around

Montsauche. On their way home they were ambushed by a combined force of Maquisards and SAS.

'I opened fire on the first truck with my Bren,' says Noble. ' My shooting was good that day, I was awake!'

His first burst killed the officer in charge who was sitting in the front cab. The soldiers who jumped from the three other vehicles were cut down by the French hidden at the sides of the road. Muirhead, who directed the ambush, counted thirty-one enemy dead.

The next day, a Sunday, the Germans came to collect their dead. On the way they stopped at the village of Ouroux and killed three civilians leaving Mass. When they approached the scene of the ambush they were once more waylaid by the Maquis. A further fourteen Germans were killed. Now they lusted for revenge.

'They burned Montsauche to the ground,' says Bouche-Pillon, 'but luckily all the villagers had already fled. The only people they killed were an old farmer who returned to free his trapped animals, and a man who was fishing just outside the village.'

The Germans ravaged another village, Planchez, at dusk before returning to their base.

Still incensed by the effrontery of the French, the main German riposte came the next day, 26 June, against the men they thought were responsible, Maquis Camille. At 1800 hours a bullet thudded into the headboard of Chalky White's hospital bed in the chateau. It was the start of a concerted onslaught by a force of 250 Germans to eradicate the 'terrorist' problem. White and the other hospital inmates were helped from the chateau to the woods that concealed Maquis Camille and Bill Fraser's camp. The Germans chased them to the edge of the forest but their advance was checked by a heavy Maquis fire from the trees. Instead the Germans brought up their mortars and began to shell the woods.

At 1900 hours a message was sent to Fraser asking him to take up positions on the only road leading from the forest. The Germans had come up it to launch the attack, so they must come down at some stage. Fraser detailed Wiseman to cover one stretch of road, while he took

207

another. As Fraser moved towards his objective he saw two Germans loitering by the roadside. They watched with cold amusement as the pair were joined by around fifty more. The Germans formed up and began marching up the road towards their comrades. When they were only yards away from the SAS position two Bren guns came to life. Fraser later estimated in his report on the ambush 'that not more than ten men escaped injury from the fracas'.

Wiseman worked his way to within 16 yards of his stretch of the road without seeing a soul. It was a miserable night, wet and murky, and Seekings was in an exceptionally grumpy mood. He had a lot of 'green men' with him who hadn't seen any combat before and he disliked the idea of being their nursemaid. He crawled ahead to check the lie of the land and poked his head up yards from a German machine-gun nest.

'I was stupid,' he admitted. 'I misjudged a bit and came up practically straight in front of this bastard machine gun.'

Seekings just had time to yell 'look, enemy' – a statement of the obvious that tickled Johnny Wiseman who included it in his report on the incident – before he was shot in the neck.

'He nailed me but luckily fired just one round before his gun jammed,' said Seekings. Lance Corporal Gibb provided excellent covering fire as the rest of the SAS patrol withdrew, taking a semi-conscious Seekings with them. 'When I got hit it was as though I was in an underground river with the water going faster and faster,' he reflected years later.

During the night the Maquis and the SAS withdrew to new and separate camps in fear of a fresh German attack in the morning. When Seekings woke the next day he 'was feeling terrible … and Johnny Wiseman, cheeky bugger, said, "Come on, Sergeant Major, where's that grit of yours?" That was so bloody outdated I had to grin. I felt better after that.'

The next morning, 27 June, the Germans reappeared. They found only the abandoned Maquis camp. They got back in their lorries and headed through the smouldering ruins of Vermot towards the village of Dun-les-Places. Vermot had been 'cleansed' the previous evening. Six men were shot and a 14-year-old girl gang-raped. Now it was the turn of

208

Dun-les-Places. The Germans went from house to house seizing the men. Madame Pichot was laying the table for lunch when two Germans barged in. 'You must come with us for an inspection of your papers,' they told her husband. He kissed his two young children on their cheeks and left with the soldiers.

The men were taken to the hotel and interrogated. Meanwhile the village priest, 38-year-old, Curé Roland, was taken from the home he shared with his mother. Later Madame Pichot could never rid her mind of the image of him 'tiny in his great cloak, looking very pale but walking calmly' as he was led by the Germans to the top of his church. A rope was fastened to the belfry and a noose thrown around the priest's neck. He asked what his crime was. He was told he had helped the Maquis. Curé Roland denied the accusation. The Germans threw him from the bell tower.

Later they rounded up nineteen men in front of the church, beneath the dangling body of the priest, and machine gunned them. Madame Pichot listened to her husband's execution from her kitchen. 'I held my children close,' she said, '... they were both petrified with fear.'

As Seekings lay cold, wet and reassuringly truculent in the Morvan, 100 miles to the west Peter Weaver had finally located Bulbasket's base camp. It was 30 June, twenty days since he and his small sabotage party had dropped into France. Tonkin was pleased to see Weaver, though he asked waspishly why it had taken him so long. Weaver reminded his commanding officer that they had trekked nearly 60 miles across German occupied territory with very little food or water. In addition they had been detained for three days under false pretences by a communist Maquis group who had claimed to know nothing about the SAS base camp.

'So I'd told my chaps to get their knapsacks as we were off,' said Weaver. '[Then] the chief said he knew where our squadron was, in a wood called Verrières, some 20km away, and he would take us there.'

Weaver was disturbed by the atmosphere he found in the camp. Tonkin told him the original plan had been scrapped a fortnight earlier; the rest

209

of the squadron had not been dropped because of the heavy German presence in the area. Morale had taken a further and more recent blow when Dougie Eccles and Ken Bateman hadn't returned from a sabotage job the day before.

To Weaver some of the men appeared listless. Tonkin had tended to send the same core of experienced men out on missions, leaving many others with nothing better to do than laze in the sunshine (unlike the Morvan, the summer of 1944 in the Vienne was long and hot) smoking the tobacco they had been given by the Maquis in return for soap. Word of the British presence had got back to some of the young women in Verrières, a little over a mile away, and in a spirit of Entente Cordiale they had come flirting. One or two of the more coltish SAS had even gone into the village with them for a drink. Tonkin, thought Weaver, 'was getting a little out of his depth with his responsibilities'.

The 'forebodings' Weaver had experienced on his arrival, as though wisps of doom were drifting slowly through the trees towards their forest hideout, increased when a shot-down American pilot, Lincoln Bundy, was brought to the camp.

'I thought the camp was becoming far too well known,' he wrote later, 'and suggested to John we should split up and disperse in small parties to another area, but he was against the idea. I think he thought he would lose control.'

Tonkin had in fact moved the base camp several times in the past month. The constraint each time, however, was a decent water supply. Without one they would be unable to function. He had been scouting around for a new camp the moment he realized something had happened to Eccles and Bateman; if as seemed likely they had been captured (the getaway driver of their jeep returned without having seen or heard anything untoward), they would be made to talk eventually.

On 1 July Tonkin looked for a new base. A suitable one was found a few miles south in the Bois des Cartes and they moved that evening. By that time Eccles and Bateman, having revealed nothing to their Wehrmacht captors, had spent 24 hours in the company of the German

Security Police (Sipo-SD) and would have almost certainly succumbed to their more forceful interrogation techniques.

The following day the Germans planned an operation to capture the British soldiers in the Verrières forest involving units from a Reconnaissance Squadron and an SS Panzer Grenadier Division. Tonkin was also drawing up plans having discovered that the well in their new camp had dried up after only a few buckets of water. Reluctantly he moved the men back to Verrières while another location was scouted.

Tonkin went off on a solo recce on the evening of 2 July while the rest of the men remained in the forest. With the American and nine Maquis there were fifty men camped in the forest. Too many for Weaver, but as he climbed into his sleeping bag that night he and Tomos Stephens, a fiery Welsh lieutenant, commented on the weather. Weaver told Stephens 'it was difficult to imagine bad weather in England as we seemed to be in the middle of a heatwave'.

A few hours later Weaver was woken 'by large explosions in the wood close by and for the life of me I couldn't think what all the noise was about in my semi-sleepy state'. Then he realized. 'Christ, we're being-mortared!' The Germans had crept into position during the night, and had waited until first light.

Weaver leapt from his sleeping bag and began putting on his boots. 'Someone ran past shouting that we were surrounded.' Weaver now heard bullets pass close by with the 'crack of a whip'. He saw Tonkin, Stephens and Lieutenant Richard Crisp trying to calm an 'agitated Frenchman' (a Maquisard who had sprung the trap as he returned to the camp from an overnight liaison with a local girl). Weaver ran over and asked what was happening. Tonkin said the wood was surrounded by five hundred Germans.

'Tell the men to disperse,' Weaver remembered him saying. 'It's every man for himself.'

Weaver ran to his section of men, the ones who had been with him for the past three weeks. He repeated what Tonkin had just told him, then gave them a choice: 'Come with me, or stay with the others.' He advised them to scatter but he clearly recalled saying to them: 'I am not ordering you to do anything, it's your choice.' They chose to stay with the main party.

In the few seconds Weaver had spent talking to his men the German noose had tightened further.

'The firing was becoming intense,' he said. 'I shot off into the woods and turned south. Weaver was joined by Stephens, whose anger was visible in his face. He was also complaining of a stomach pain. They weaved their way through the trees trying to outrun the sounds of gunfire. Ahead of them the trees began to thin out and beyond a cornfield was visible.

'Then I saw them,' said Weaver. 'A long line of field grey uniforms advancing slowly and silently through the outer fringes of the wood.' Weaver urged on Stephens with a yell of 'Quick!'. But the Welshman stopped.

'"I must have a crap, I can't wait!" I could hardly believe him ... "For Christ's sake, man, you haven't time, look they are there!" He told me to go on.'

In a crouching run Weaver made it to the cornfield and 'began to scramble on my hands and knees through the tall golden corn, and wondered what I would see on the other side'. After 15 minutes of crawling he reached the far side.

'I peered through the stalks of corn and saw about 200 yards of grassland before it joined the spur of wood ... looking carefully around I saw no one and began walking quickly towards the wood.' Barely had he stood upright before a volley of gunfire ripped the heads of some corn to his left. 'I looked round and there, 50 yards away, were four German SS ... they started to move towards me and I bolted for the trees. I could hear them running behind me and the wood seemed an age in coming.' He hauled himself over a stile, 'I hadn't the strength to jump it', and dived under a thicket. He heard the Germans sprinting past him. They didn't come back. There were still shouts coming from the direction of the camp. The occasional gunshot. Then 'everything became very quiet'.

The next day, 4 July, Weaver reached a farm where he was reunited with the other escapees. All seven of them. Tonkin was there and he told Weaver that Stephens had been shot dead. The rest of the men, Tonkin said to Weaver 'had been rounded up and taken to Poitiers for interrogation'.

A little over 24 hours after the capture of the thirty-one SAS men the Germans had another nine in the bag. A twelve-man stick from 'D' Squadron under the command of Captain Pat Garstin had taken off from Fairford on the evening of 4 July. The DZ was near a little village called La Ferte-Alais, 30 miles south of Paris. Once on the ground they would reinforce Operation Gain, which had started on 13 June.

Led by Ian Fenwick from their base in the Forêt d'Orléans the existing members of Operation Gain had spent much of the past three weeks interfering with the rail network that linked the area south of Paris to Normandy. Vic Long had helped blow a section of the Orléans to Pithiviers track and found the main trouble came from 'dogs, not Germans ... it [the line] was 25 miles away and at night each village we went through had a yapping dog every 100 yards'. Long remembers how Fenwick would 'lie on a sheet in the camp sketching'. His first book of cartoons, *Enter Trubshaw*, was at the printers, the introduction written by his old friend David Niven. Praising Fenwick's style, Niven urged people to 'buy this book instead of just fingering it while the bookstall attendant isn't looking'.

As 1SAS's intelligence officer, Mike Sadler briefed and debriefed every party that operated in France. It was crucial work, but it was non-combatant, and Sadler had days when he 'still liked a little bit of adrenaline'. Sometimes he would fly into France with the men and watch them drop on to the DZ. On the night of 4 July he sat in the bomb-aimer's seat of the Stirling. Of the SAS men aboard he knew very little. 'Ginger' Jones, the miner from Lancashire, was the only one who had served in 'L' Detachment; the rest were new to the regiment and he detected the hand of Paddy Mayne at work. Four of them – Garstin, Billy Young, Joe Walker and Tom Barker – had all come from the Royal Ulster Rifles, Mayne's parent regiment.

As they approached the DZ the pilot remarked on some slight

213

turbulence, says Sadler, 'as though a plane had recently flown over the area'. But the recognition signals were correctly displayed and at 0153 hours the men jumped. Down on the ground the DZ was ringed by thirty German security police and a unit of Milice, French fascist paramilitaries with a reputation for brutality equal to that of the Nazis. They had extracted details of the drop from a captured Maquisard. Sergeant Karl Haug, a 50-year-old father of six who had spent three years as a POW in Britain during the last war, was one of the Germans.

'Late in the night a plane came over and circled round the lights, and then dropped something. We saw at once that there were not only drums hanging from the parachutes, but also men.' Garstin was the first to be caught. 'Bring your men over here,' ordered Obersturmführer Schubert, the officer in charge. Garstin refused. Schubert told his men to kill him. He was hit in the neck and the arm by a burst of gunfire and dropped to the ground seriously wounded.

Up above Sadler could see 'flashes on the ground as they landed'. Then he heard the sound of cannon fire.

'We were attacked by an Me110, probably the one that caused the turbulence as he waited for us.' Sadler braced himself as 'we dived down pretty rapidly into the clouds ... I thought the wings were going to come off.'

They lost the Messerschmitt and Sadler returned to England with an unshakeable faith in the RAF. Of the men on the ground, all but three were captured. Troopers Castelow, Morrison and Norman dropped in some trees just outside the circle of Germans. Trooper Howard Lutton, Lieutenant Johnny Wiehe, Barker and Garstin were taken to hospital to have their wounds treated. Lutton died the following day, Wiehe was paralysed below the waist but the other two were soon sent to join their comrades at Gestapo Headquarters in the Avenue Foch in Paris.

There they were all interrogated. Jones was tied to a chair and every time he declined to answer a question a man standing behind punched him in the face. Serge Vaculik, a goatee-bearded Czech-born Frenchman from 4SAS attached to 'D' Squadron as an interpreter, came in for particular attention. He said he was Jean Dupontel, a Canadian from Quebec.

214

The Germans didn't believe him. He was beaten regularly. Their interrogators referred to them constantly as 'terrorists', not soldiers. They threatened the seven soldiers with execution. The prisoners assumed it was nothing more than a warped form of psychological torture. It wasn't. In October 1942 Hitler had issued his 'Commando Order', demanding of his officers that enemy Commandos 'on their being discovered ... all quarter is to be denied on principle'. Field Marshal Rommel famously ignored the Order, and there were one or two other exceptions of regular German Army commanders eschewing Hitler's directive. But most officers complied, Wehrmacht or otherwise, some more willingly than others. Several 2SAS soldiers had been executed in 1943 but they were still listed as Missing. Not until Lieutenant Jimmy Hughes escaped from captivity in March 1944 and was debriefed by Major Eric Barkworth, the indefatigable intelligence officer of 2SAS, did the Commando Order come to light. Hughes had been warned of his likely fate by a charitable German officer who encouraged him to escape.

Barkworth sent a detailed dossier to HQ 1st Airborne Corps but, as he commented in a war crimes report in 1948, 'Hughes' case was dismissed as mere interrogation technique, and reference to other men of the Regiment who had neither returned, nor had been reported as casualties, was explained away by the fact that the enemy probably wished to keep us in the dark about the success of operations.'

TWO DAYS AFTER Garstin and his men were captured, the Bulbasket prisoners were loaded into lorries and driven from Poitiers to deep within the St-Sauvant forest. Dougie Eccles and Ken Bateman were among the thirty-one men. So was Lincoln Bundy, the American pilot, and Alexander 'Lofty' Baker, one of Stirling's Originals. They were ordered out of the lorries, their hands bound behind their backs, and made to line up in front of three freshly dug pits. It was just before dawn on 7 July. Local villagers reported later that they heard long bursts of machine-gun fire followed by several single gunshots. Three other SAS men from the operation, too wounded to stand in front of an execution squad, were given a lethal injection.

AFTER THREE DAYS of interrogation at Gestapo Headquarters Garstin's men were transferred to a prison in the Place des Etats-Unis. Vaculik could see the Eiffel Tower from his cell window. The questioning was desultory, sometimes nothing for a few days and then a four-hour interrogation. The prisoners spent most nights naked and handcuffed. Jones and Vaculik were thrown into the same pitch black cell for some days after angering their guards. Languishing in the darkness, Vaculik let Jones in on his secret.

'At an early stage I had discovered it was possible to unlock the handcuffs with a spring from my watch.'

They passed the time of the day dreaming up far-fetched plans for escape.

On the evening of 8 August two guards came into their cell with a pile of civilian clothes and some shaving utensils. They were told to smarten themselves up, as they were going to be taken to Switzerland and handed over to the Red Cross. Another guard told them they just wanted to wash their uniforms. Jones was uneasy.

'Their replies didn't ring true.' Vaculik asked one of the guards, a sympathetic Russian, if he could have a few words with Garstin. He was allowed 15 minutes. 'I told him we wanted to escape, but he said, "Don't do that because I think we are going to be exchanged with some Nazis in England."' Everyone had been fed a different line by their captors.

At 0100 hours on 9 August they boarded a lorry and, having been joined by several other vehicles, headed north-east out of Paris. Jones remembered that during the journey the three Irish troopers, Walker, Young and Barker chaffed each other about their civilian attire. Barker made fun of his plus fours; Walker wondered why his strange low-cut shoes had holes in the sides; Young had been given a white cycling jacket that was so tight he had to take it off. Sitting at the rear of the lorry were Karl Haug and a man called Alfred Von Kapri, a Gestapo polyglot who claimed he had learned his English at Oxford University. Neither guard noticed anything unusual about Jones and Vaculik. But not long into the journey both had 'loosened their handcuffs'.

At around 0400 hours Vaculik remembered that 'we arrived in a lonely road and they shut the rear of the lorry. They said it was dusty'. Nearly two hours later they stopped.

'The rear of the lorry opened and we were told to jump down,' recalled Vaculik. 'I asked the guard [Haug] in French "are we going to be shot?" He laughed, "Yes, of course you are."'

They were ushered through some woods into a clearing. Garstin, who 'could hardly stand' because of his injuries, was propped up by Jones as the seven men were lined up 10 yards opposite five armed Germans. On the far right was Jones. Next to him was Garstin, then Vaculik and Varey. The three Irish friends were on the left of the line. Hauptsturmführer Richard Schnurr read from a piece of a paper. Von Kapri translated.

'You are found guilty of working with French terrorists and against the Germans and you are going to be shot.'

Garstin protested that they had received no trial. Vaculik remembered his moaning, 'Oh God, we are going to be shot.' Then mayhem.

Shrieking like a banshee, Vaculik sprinted past a stupefied Haug, running 'slightly towards the firing party but away off to the right', where the open ground sloped gently downwards until it met the forest's edge. By the time Haug had unslung his weapon from his shoulder, Jones and another soldier – probably Varey – had taken off in the same direction. Garstin hobbled pathetically after them. Haug later told his war crimes interrogator that he 'found it impossible to shoot at these men with whom I had formerly been on such friendly terms'. Schnurr also absolved himself of blame, saying he was too busy putting the piece of paper in his pocket to shoot. But someone fired a burst into the back of Garstin. And someone shot dead the three young Irish soldiers.

As the other three ran down the hill they were chased by gunfire. Jones instinctively ducked and 'lost my balance as my hands were tied ... I lay doggo in the short grass.' Vaculik and the other soldier made it to the woods. As Jones pretended to be dead he 'felt a German go over me' in pursuit.

'Searching and swearing now began on a grand scale,' said Haug, 'but in spite of the search the two who had broken away were nowhere to be found.'

217

After half an hour of fruitless hunting they returned to the clearing. To their bewilderment they discovered that 'one of the men we had shot was missing; there were now only four corpses'. Jones had feigned death until he was sure all the Germans were out of sight, then 'I lifted my head and saw a big tree just ahead. As I got up I saw at four bodies lying round me. They were all dead. I bolted over a wire and into a wood. I carried on through the trees and into a cornfield. There I lay down and pulled the corn around me to cover my tracks.'

Haug recalled it was at this moment Schnurr had a 'hysterical crying fit from sheer anger'. He ranted at his men, telling them to find the three men. A few minutes later Otto Ilgenfritz spotted one of the prisoners. As the man 'stood up behind a pile of wood ... I made use of my weapon at a distance of 30–40 metres'. Schnurr enjoined a nearby Luftwaffe unit to hunt for the remaining escapees but of Jones and Vaculik there was no trace.

The pair had been taken in by locals and hidden while the Maquis was contacted. Nine days later, on 18 August Vaculik was taken to see a man who claimed to have escaped from a firing squad. Fernard Bourgoin, a forest warden who had been sheltering Jones, said in a newspaper interview twenty years later that their reunion was 'a moment of emotion I will never forget ... each believing they were in the presence of their comrade's spectre'.

FRENCH CIVILIANS KNEW the inordinate risks they ran in giving succour to Allied soldiers or airmen – in June the 2nd SS Panzer Division, *Das Reich*, had slaughtered the entire population of Oradour-sur-Glane – 642 inhabitants, including 207 children – because one of their officers had been shot in the area – but time and again they offered their help.

On the night of 7 July Lieutenant John Randall dropped into Normandy in a seven-strong stick as part of Operation Haft. Their job was purely reconnaissance, to radio back details of German troop movements ahead of the Allies' breakout from the Cotentin Peninsula in Normandy.

The information was sent to the wireless operators at HQ at Moor

Park. One of them, Harry Wilkins, remembers that 'we would get a message encoded into a series of five letter blocks that didn't make any sense at all to us. We just passed it on to the decoders'. It was tedious work, recalls Wilkins, who often found himself on the emergency network, which transmitted 24 hours a day, in case one of the parties in France needed urgent help.

Thirty miles east of Randall, a three-man party comprising Lieutenant William Anderson and Trooper Billy Hull of 1SAS and André Lemée from 4SAS landed close to the town of Courtomer to train the local Maquis group and liaise with Haft.

'Unfortunately we were separated on landing,' says Lemée. 'Anderson landed in some woods on one side of the main road and me and Billy were on the other.' Two days earlier the Germans had broken up the Maquis network which the SAS had come to assist. Its members held firm under torture until after the drop had been made. 'The morning after we'd landed,' says Lemée, 'there was a real commotion in Courtomer as the Germans began looking for us. Anderson was the only one who knew what the mission was, so Billy and I were not really in a good position.'

For the next eleven days Lemée and Hull were chased around the Normandy countryside, staying in one place just long enough to beg or steal some food and then moving on. Eventually they made contact with a member of the Resistance network who guided them to a flour mill at L'Ormois that made bread for the village. It was run by Raymond Girard and his young wife, Juliette. A few days earlier, remembers Juliette, 'two men had come to the mill, one of whom was French, and he asked me to look after a British paratrooper'. Juliette brought Anderson inside the mill to where her husband was working. She told him they must provide shelter. Anderson was hidden in the space above the water wheel.

'We knew perfectly well what would happen to us if we were denounced,' says Juliette. 'My cousin was a Maquisard who had been betrayed to the Germans by a man he knew well. Of course we were scared but what could we do? The British wouldn't have survived if we'd turned them away.'

The three SAS remained at the mill for three days before they were moved. 'Some people were beginning to ask questions,' says Juliette. '"Who were the strange men helping out wearing the military boots?"' They were taken to the house of Juliette's father, a ramshackle farmhouse near the village of Couillery. 'During the night we slept in one of the outhouses,' says Lemée, 'and in the day we moved to a little wooded hollow behind the farm.'

Anderson had always been seen as something of an oddball by his fellow officers; now in France he behaved with increasing indiscretion.

'The officer [Anderson] began to light fires during the day because he was bored,' recalls Juliette, 'and the smoke could be seen from all around.'

Sometimes he would follow Juliette into the village, with his army boots clearly visible beneath his tatty coat, and engage the locals in conversation. He spoke good French, but not like a native.

'I liked Anderson,' says Lemée, 'but, you know, he was having an affair with this woman who was the Maquis' radio operator. He would often send me and Billy off on some mission at night so he could screw this girl. We'd bring back some information and the girl would radio it back to England.'

On 25 July the American VII Corps launched their third attempt to break out of the Cotentin Peninsula. The offensive, mounted on the back of a massive bombing raid by hundreds of Flying Fortresses, was successful, and by 8 August Le Mans was in Allied hands. As the van of the American Army reached Couillery, Anderson pedalled west to make contact with Operation Haft, who had spent a month radioing back precise details of German troop movements.

'One morning we saw this figure coming towards us on an old bicycle,' says Randall, 'and it turned out to be Anderson, who we'd given up as lost.'

Before leaving, Anderson had told Lemée and Hull to make their way to Rennes aerodrome, 'but we went on a pub crawl and missed the plane'. They ended up in the village of Le Mele, having a drink on the steps of L'hôtel du Boeuf Noir. A German staff car pulled up close to the hotel and

220

out got two SS officers, unaware just how far the Americans had advanced. Lemée and Hull hauled the pair inside the hotel.

'Billy was a fighter,' says Lemée, '... a cunning beast. He wanted to kill them and he would have if he'd carried on beating them. But the owner of the hotel begged us not to kill them in the hotel because they were scared of reprisals.'

The Germans were shoved outside but before they could be beaten to death an American armoured column entered Le Mele. 'They took the Germans away,' recalls Lemée, 'tied to a tank.'

On the afternoon of 7 August Paddy Mayne lent Mike Sadler his staff car. 'I popped home to Gloucestershire and had tea with my parents,' recalls Sadler. Mayne's benevolence wasn't an aberration. In the two months since his regiment had first dropped into France, he had been as much a welfare officer as a commanding officer. To the families of all his officers in the field he wrote personally. On 10 July he told Alex Muirhead's pregnant wife that he was in 'fine form ... although he has no way of writing to you we hear from him regularly. He has now been in France some time and is doing terrific work. We can send your letters in to him and hope it won't be very long before you hear from personally. Very best wishes and try not to worry unduly'.

Rea Du Vivier received the standard reassuring message sent by Sergeant Major Rose to the families of the other ranks. 'He is being well fed and clothed, and medical comforts are in good supply ... we keep him supplied to a certain extent but I am sure he would be grateful if you were to send him a small parcel of comforts. I suggest something like this: cigarettes or tobacco, toothpaste, toothbrush if procurable, reading matter, and any small edibles you know he would like. Please do not make the parcel too large ... he is still unable to write, but you may rest assured that he is receiving your mail quite regularly.'

John Noble told his diary in August 1944: 'You've no idea how much a letter means to us. It bucks the morale up no end.'

Letters gave the men a sense of normality. The more banal they were

221

the better. They didn't want jingoistic, chest-thumping letters, they wanted to hear about the minutiae of everyday life back home. June Muirhead told her husband about a daytrip to Lowestoft in June and about the rain and about how she was trying to be brave. But finally her stoicism crumbled.

'I have that awful desperate and helpless feeling as though my spirit were a caged bird trying to get out to come to you ... all my days are like this. I cling to all and any little thing to keep you nearer. You are never out of my thoughts and I share every tiny thing with you ... keep safe and come soon Dearest. My whole life I'd wait for you and yet each day seems like a year when you're away.'

The second most prized commodity after letters was reading matter. Padre McLuskey wrote in his report on 1SAS Operations that in the supply of books 'we were well looked after ... the men read a great deal and valued books and magazines very highly'. The men's tastes were eclectic and, to the disappointment of the padre, not at all reverential. John Noble recalls hiding in a thicket 24 feet from a railway line he was waiting to sabotage, reading *A Midsummer's Night Dream*. Seekings' favourite author was Leslie Charteris, though he was quite partial to American detective novels. The padre once asked him if he never tired of blood and thunder.

'You don't get it,' replied Seekings. 'However much blood and thunder we've seen, it's always nice to read about how it should be done.'

SADLER RETURNED THE staff car to Mayne late on the afternoon of the 7th and a few hours later the two of them, plus Lieutenant Winterson and Tommy Corps, parachuted into the Morvan. Among the reception committee waiting on the DZ in the Bois de Montsauche was René Brossier.

'My job was gather up their parachutes,' says Brossier, 'and hide them from the Germans. The British shouldn't really have given them to us but everyone was helping themselves.' The SAS turned a blind eye to the Maquis' appropriation of the parachute silk; they knew it was put to good use, as underwear for the local women. They even ignored the pilfering of parachute containers which, cut in two, made ideal drinking troughs for livestock.

222

'The only thing the SAS disliked,' says Bouche-Pillon, 'was when we used plastic explosive to light our forest huts. Without a detonator the plastic produced great candles, but they were furious when they discovered what we were doing.'

Mayne's original intention had been to land east of Orléans, into Gain's operating area, before heading south to Houndsworth. Both these two squadrons were to be involved as reconnaissance troops in a major and imminent Allied operation called Transfigure, the purpose of which would be to crush the German Army west of the Rhine. Mayne, however, never liked to commit his men to a scheme before assessing it at first-hand.*

The day before Mayne's insertion, one of Gain's two operating bases was sacked by a large force of Germans. The SAS worked their way out of the forest without losing a man but Fenwick, Gain's OC, sent a message to Mayne advising him to find a new DZ. He chose the Morvan.

After the capture of the Bulbasket party and the disappearance of Pat Garstin and his men, Mayne was pleased with the way things had gone with Houndsworth. Muirhead updated him on what had happened in the last few weeks. With the arrival of the first jeeps in early July, the squadron had become much more ambitious in its aims; Johnny Wiseman had taken a vehicle and established a base near Dijon; Muirhead had wrecked the synthetic oil factory at Autun; innumerable railway lines had been cut, most notably the Luzy–Nevers line by Noble's section, and the Paris–Nevers by Ken Sturmey; a 6-pound field gun had been dropped and used to great effect against enemy transport; and Reg Seekings was back on his feet and none the worse for wear, even though the bullet was still in his neck.

There had, however, been some setbacks. It had taken less than 24 hours after the arrival of the jeeps before the first accident occurred. Trooper Ancona took a bend too fast and Corporal Eric Adamson was severely crushed as the jeep rolled over him. He was taken to Alec Prochiantz, at this time working deep in the Montsauche woods from an

* Operation Transfigure was never implemented because of the US breakout from the Cotentin Peninsula that began in late July.

223

operating theatre constructed out of parachutes and lit by car headlights.

'I gave him an injection of morphine and began the operation,' says Prochiantz. 'He had a vertical double fracture of the pelvis with urinary complications and severe damage to the urethra. As I didn't have a urinary probe I improvised with the inner tube of a bicycle tyre. I carried out a successful cystotomy and two months later he was transferred to England.'

A fortnight later two more men were brought to Prochiantz, one of whom was John Noble.

'We were driving through the village of Ouroux when a car full of Germans turned into our road and came towards us,' he recalled. 'I was driving and said to the guy on the Vickers, "Shoot! Shoot!" But he was a Maquis and didn't know how to use the guns. That's when the battle started, the first time I'd ever been in hand-to-hand combat.' Noble described the fight in his diary a few days later.

'They opened fire first and I got a little nick on the forehead. I dived from where I was standing to our side of the car. I then nipped round the front. The first one tried to hit me over the head with his gun. I ducked just as another shot me through the shoulder. I closed with the first one, hit him over the head with my Colt, at the same time using my knee.'

A second German came to aid of the man's injured comrade. Noble wrestled him to the ground and the pair rolled into a shallow ditch at the side of the road. Even with his bleeding shoulder, Noble was too strong for the German. Within a few minutes he had throttled his opponent.

'I thought he was finished,' he wrote, 'so I got up. He wasn't finished, so Peter [Middleton] shot him.'

Bob Langridge and the German who Noble had been fighting a few minutes earlier were grappling with each other on the road.

'The German was a sergeant major,' remembers Noble, 'a big bloke and a tough man who wasn't going to surrender. So I said "to hell with it" and shot him.'

A third German had tried to run away when the fighting started but the Maquisard had caught and killed him. A fourth had been shot in the leg and was lying in a ditch paralysed with terror.

224

'We decided to take him with us,' recalls Noble, 'because none of us had the nerve to shoot him in cold blood. As it happened Hans came in very useful around the camp, doing our washing and cooking. We used to have fun at his expense, though, because we got our water from the same spring as the Maquis and sometimes we would take him with us to collect water and then sneak off when he wasn't looking. He would come tearing after us because he knew if the French got him they would slit his throat. We tried to bring him back to England with us as the regimental servant but the MPs got him and we never heard from Hans again.'

The most grievous blow to befall Houndsworth, however, and the only two fatalities of the entire operation, occurred the day before the fight at Ouroux on 20 July. A few days previously it had been decided that Roy Bradford's Three Troop should operate in an area 40 miles north of Fraser's HQ. Seven men under Lieutenant Ball, Du Vivier among them, departed on 18 July to cycle to an RV in the Forêt de Dames. The following day Bradford left to meet Du Vivier in a jeep. Alongside were two 'L' Detachment Originals, the fully mended Chalky White and Maggie McGinn, Trooper William Devine and a French Maquisard. Early on the morning of 20 July they ran into a German convoy. The firefight was brief, and left Devine and Bradford dead. McGinn managed to coax the badly damaged jeep round the next bend, momentarily out of sight of the pursuing Germans. The three survivors jumped from the jeep and escaped on foot across the fields.

Lieutenant Ball's party was unaware of Bradford's death as they pedalled laboriously towards the RV on the collapsible bikes. They covered about 8 miles each night, sweating under the weight of their rucksacks. As they cycled through one village in the dead of night, Du Vivier's eye was caught by a large poster in a shop window.

'It was a photograph of me and a couple of others,' he says. 'In German and French it described us as dangerous terrorists and promised a reward of thousands of francs for information leading to our capture. Captain Bradford had taken the photo a few days before we left base camp for the RV. The Germans found the camera on his body and developed the photos.'

225

Lieutenant Ball led his men to the Forêt de Dames and while he remained, in the forlorn hope that Bradford might appear, Du Vivier took two men to blow the line between Entrains and Cosne.

'We spent a couple of hours to lay the charges,' says Du Vivier. 'We had the right explosives for the job but not the right tools, so we had to dig out the ballast underneath the sleepers with our knives and hands. We laid three charges under the same rail and connected them with cortex. And then I placed the pressure switch on the first charge.' When Du Vivier got back to the base camp Fraser congratulated him; he had derailed a munitions train and wrecked a number of Ack-Ack guns.

Mayne drove north from the Morvan on 9 August. Sadler and Tommy Corps travelled with their CO while Major Bob Melot and Sergeant Duncan Ridler, both of whom had dropped into Montsauche on 28 July, were in a second jeep, along with David Danger. A small knitted Union Flag was pinned to the front of each jeep, a present from a local woman.

Danger had been transferred from Johnny Wiseman's camp a few miles outside Dijon, where for the past month he had been calling in RAF strikes on German lines of communication. Of all the three Houndsworth bases Wiseman's was the most exposed. Over 30,000 Germans were stationed in Dijon and as the air strikes and sabotage continued more and more of them were sent to root out the men responsible. Wiseman had only fourteen men in his troop so guard duty was often undertaken by the local Maquis. One day they caught two Miliciens snooping around the forest.

'They were made to dig their own graves,' says Wiseman, 'and then they were shot through the head. I found it quite revolting ... they had done a lot of damage in the district and no doubt deserved to be shot but I don't like to see a man shot like that.'

For every Milicien caught and executed by the Maquis, there was at least one more willing to take his place. One day in late July Danger was on the radio when he saw a civilian walking towards him.

'It looked a bit strange so I gave a hasty message to say I was closing down and while my companion pulled the aerial down we started to

226

withdraw. I was running with my wireless set on my back, they weren't small things, and I'd just about had it after a few miles. The others got me by the shoulders and carried me until we found somewhere to lie up.'

Seven Miliciens were killed in the abortive assault, and Wiseman lost his trousers as he escaped through some brambles.

A few days later the Milice were back, this time with the Germans in a pincer movement. Both units took casualties as they advanced through the forest towards the SAS. Wiseman, who abandoned the camp days earlier, later sent a report back to Brigade HQ in England describing how 'the Boche attacked from one side whilst the Milice attacked from the other. They must have been enjoying themselves for they didn't stop before they had succeeded in killing twenty-two of their own men!'

MAYNE'S PARTY ARRIVED in Toucy, 10 miles west of Auxerre, on the same day they had left the Morvan. Mayne didn't stay long. 'Paddy spent about five minutes with us,' says Duncan Ridler, 'then he shot off. He wasn't interested in all that ceremonial stuff, shaking hands with the local Maquis chief ... or in organising anything. He was only interested in getting in a scrap himself ... we had no idea where he'd gone and neither had the brigadier [McLeod] who was becoming more and more testy about Paddy refusing to return to England to consult with him about future operations.'

While Melot and Ridler, the regiment's intelligence team, remained in Toucy to reconnoitre for a possible new base, Mayne and Sadler continued north towards Orléans and 'D' Squadron. Operation Gain had lost its commanding officer after Ian Fenwick had been killed during a raid on a German-occupied village. Mayne arrived and consulted with Captain Jock Riding, now in charge of Gain. With so much German activity in the area it was deemed wise to limit the scope of the operation to reconnaissance and information gathering.

'Paddy told me to go and do a listening patrol on the Orléans–Pithivers road,' recalls Vic Long. 'John Ion dropped me and Morton about a mile from the road that evening and he said he'd pick me up at grid reference so-and-so at 7.30 the following morning.'

The next day Long and Morton left the main road and began making their way to the RV. When they were within 500 yards of it they heard a long burst of gunfire.

'We moved up a bit and looked through the binoculars,' recalls Long. 'There was a lot of dust but we could see one of our jeeps in the middle of the road. A short time later there were more shots ... this was about 8 a.m. now. We hung around until 10.30 but we saw no sign of Ion, only about forty Germans standing on the road.'

Long and Morton made it back to base 24 hours later and reported to Mayne, who told them that Ion and Leslie Packman were still missing.

'About two or three days later,' says Long, 'one of the Maquis came to say they had found the bodies with the hands cut off.'

BACK IN FAIRFORD the rest of 1SAS still had no idea what the Germans were doing to those of their number they caught. There were regular intelligence reports pinned to the notice-board of the recreational room but they were cheerfully innocuous. In the week beginning 1 August there was news of Bill Fraser, Johnny Wiseman and the members of Operation Haft watching a 'splendid show' laid on by the RAF on an enemy installation. And Bulbasket warranted a mention.

'Captain Tonkin and his men are on their way back from France. They have actually arrived in this country although not yet back in camp. Welcome home boys, and thanks a lot!'

Peter Weaver stepped off the plane unable to believe he had survived.

'We had been away for three months, but it seemed like a lifetime. In the RAF mess, trying to make myself respectable before going into breakfast, I looked in the mirror and saw a very gaunt and strained-looking face.'

In contrast, Albert Youngman was itching to get out to France. Had it not been for his motorbike accident in May, he would have been in the original Bulbasket party. Since the decision in mid June not to deploy 'B' Squadron in its entirety, he and the remaining half had been kicking their heels at Fairford. The whole of 'C' Squadron reeked of a similar ennui. At first they hadn't minded being left behind.

'We were too busy enjoying the fleshpots of Fairford!' says Lowson.

Most of the socializing was done in the White Hart pub in the small village of Nettlebed where ATS girls liked to go. The landlady was a stout-hearted 49-year-old widower called Mrs Clements, known to the regiment as 'Clemmy'. She had lost both her sons early in the war and the boys of the SAS became her surrogate children. Pub lock-ins, organized by the village policeman, were habitual, as were Sunday morning 'Hair of the Dogs'.

There were longer excursions, to Cheltenham for the races and then an evening of jiving or bugging, or the more genteel atmosphere of Henley's ballroom and its 'palais glide'. James McDiarmid preferred Cheltenham. One night he got into an argument with an American soldier in the town hall ballroom. He was bet that he couldn't jump from the balcony down on to the dance floor. McDiarmid leapt first, executing a perfect parachute roll as he hit the floor. The American followed, and broke his leg. No one liked Americans. They were the competition, says Lowson, 'and we stood no chance with the local women. The Americans had the cigarettes and the money'.

By early August the dance halls of Henley and drinking dens of Nettlebed had lost their lustre.

'We read these daily bulletins,' says Lowson, 'and saw that the Houndsworth boys were doing a lot. We began to feel as though we were second class, as though we weren't as good as 'A' Squadron.'

In the second week of August a role in France was at last found for the remainder of 'B' Squadron. The advance party of Operation Haggard dropped west of the Loire and established a base between the towns of Bourges and Nevers. On 15 August Major Eric Lepine, OC of 'B' Squadron, parachuted in with ten men and introduced himself to the leader of the local FFI. Once they had agreed the most effective use of British forces was to shoot up German vehicles retreating east along the Bourges road, the rest of the squadron was brought in.

'Our orders were to cause mayhem,' says Youngman, by now a lance

229

sergeant, 'and we were told to choose our own targets. The phrase they used was "alarm and despondency", that's what we were to spread among the Germans.'

The officer in command of Youngman's stick was a young Scottish lieutenant called Gordon Davidson. He was in the invidious position of all officers new to 1SAS; keen to impose his own stamp upon his men but wary of being too 'regimental'.

'On the night we were waiting to go,' says Youngman, 'the lads were in their tent playing pontoon with quite a kitty going. Davidson walked in and said to me, "Get the men outside. I want to inspect their kit." I told him that I'd checked the kit and had he seen the size of the kitty? No one was going to leave the tent. He got in quite a huff and said, "I'm in charge here, I want to inspect the men."'

Just after dawn on Monday 21 August, two days after dropping into France, Youngman was taking part in his first ambush. 'Some high-ranking German officers coming back from a weekend's R&R in the brothels of Bourges, all nice and relaxed.' The Maquis later reported that the ambush had left twenty-five Germans dead including the commandant of Bourges airfield. The following night the southern section of Haggard carried out an ambush that killed fifty-five Germans. On 23 August Youngman helped blow the Vierzon to Orléans railway. The next day they called in an air strike on the Bourges–La Charité railway, and killed forty-seven Germans in a series of ambushes.

'Planning an ambush was a bit like having a committee meeting,' says Youngman. 'We'd sit down and discuss what to attack and the best way to go about it.' Youngman's relationship with Davidson had also improved. 'Before the first operation he had said to me, "You're experienced and I'm not; if I do something wrong or don't know what to do, tell me." That took courage.'

The Germans tried to reduce the possibility of being ambushed by cutting back to a depth of 50 yards the foliage on both sides of the Bourges –Nevers road. They also placed machine gunners on the top of the lorries. Neither deterrent worked. On 25 August a snaking column of German

230

infantry with horse-drawn field artillery left Bourges and headed north to engage the advancing Americans. The SAS and Maquis laid a joint ambush along a stretch of road that was being repaired. Charges were hidden among the rubble by the side of the road. When the column was alongside the charges were detonated. An estimated five hundred Germans were killed in the explosion and subsequent firefight. The SAS suffered no casualties.

Two days later the point of attack was switched south, to two bridges on the Bourges–Nevers road guarded by SS troops. A detachment of newly arrived 3SAS French soldiers joined the combined Maquis and Haggard assault. While the French blocked off the road, the British SAS killed the guards and demolished the bridges. But the commotion on the bridge had been heard by other SS soldiers and the SAS had to fight what the operational report described as a 'fairly stiff disengaging action' against 20mm guns mounted on trucks. John Wilkinson was killed and Dave Ewing, one of the SRS veterans, was wounded in the arm. Youngman helped drag Ewing to the Maquis transport and they sped off into the night.

'Having gone only 4 miles,' ran Haggard's operational report, 'the party ran into an oncoming German convoy of some ten trucks. Due to the coolness of Sergeant Youngman who was driving the leading car, the party passed untouched.'

Youngman remembers that he had little choice but to keep driving. 'We were driving merrily away,' he says, 'all laughing and joking because the operation had gone pretty well, when this lorry appeared with no lights. I eased off the road to let it pass, then another one appeared, and another one and another one. I couldn't get away so I just decided to keep going. The last couple of lorries had clearly twigged who we were because they tried to push us off the road and they did manage to knock a car full of Maquis into a ditch. Right at the end of the column was a German motorcycle and sidecar which turned round and started chasing us. In the back of the car was a bloke called Blackwell and he had a Bren gun with him. I was yelling, "Shoot the bastard! Shoot the bastard!" but we'd used all the ammo in the earlier fight. Luckily we got into a town and I cut down a couple of sidestreets, switched off the engine and we heard this motorbike go past.'

WHEN BOURGES WAS finally liberated the men of Haggard were bedecked with garlands of dahlias by joyful French men and women. The SAS was having a *vin d'honneur* with the Maquis 'when the Yanks tore into the town square' says Youngman. 'One of them asked, "Where are the Krauts?" and Bob Bergen said, "About 10 miles down the road by now." "Hey, you speak good English," said the American, and Bergen said, "I should hope so. I've been speaking it all my life."'

After the celebrations came the retribution. Women accused of sleeping with Germans had their hair shaved; men known to have collaborated were often shot out of hand.

'Shaving the heads of women,' says Bouche-Pillon, 'was done by men who joined the Maquis at the end so that they could say they had done something for France.'*

The policy of the British SAS was never to get involved, even though they found the spectacle of head shaving as distasteful as they did the rest of Maquis justice. Peter Weaver witnessed the execution of twelve young French women found guilty of passing on information to the Germans. Before their deaths, recalled Weaver, they were 'used as a brothel for the Maquis ... I felt desperately sorry for them'. When Weaver asked the Maquis to show compassion he was acidly told 'not to try and interfere in their rough justice'. Once the Maquis had tired of the women they shot them.

'One of the girls took off her coat,' said Weaver, 'and calmly handed it to me saying, "Would you look after it, it's a nice coat and it would be a pity for it to be messed up." She then went and stood in line with the others, and kept looking at me with tears in her eyes.'

But for Youngman the Maquis had earned the right to pass judgement on their fellow citizens. 'Who were we to intervene?' he asks. 'The British had no idea how much the French suffered during the Occupation.'

---

* On 31 May 1944 André Bouche-Pillon was one of twenty-five members of Maquis Bernard. Three months later Bernard's number had swollen to 1,200.

It was, says René Brossier, 'a very difficult period' for France. Even after the invasion had begun treachery clung to the rolling hills of the Morvan. A father and his 15-year-old son supplied the Germans with the name and address of a prominent member of the Maquis Bernard. They did it for cigarettes. The pair were brought to the Bois de Montsauche. The father confessed and was executed. No one wanted to shoot the boy, says Brossier, 'but you couldn't release any of the traitors without risking the survival of the whole Maquis'.

'I remember him very clearly,' says Bouche-Pillon, 'because before he was shot he said, "I die because of my fucking stupid father."'

OPERATION HAGGARD WAS wound up in early September when it was overrun by the advance elements of a big new 4SAS operation called Spenser, which had left Vannes in southern Brittany in August and driven east through the Loire Valley to an RV in Briare. From there they fanned out in squadrons across the surrounding countryside, harassing the Germans as they retreated towards the Belfort Gap.

While the SS had plenty of fight left in them, a great many of the conscripted soldiers had had enough. In the small town of St Pierre-le-Moûtier, 12 miles south of Nevers, 12,000 nervous Germans were penned in on all sides by the advancing Allies. Commandant Bourgoin heard about the tremulous state of the Germans and sent Lieutenant Le Bobinecq and Roger Boutinot to see if they might be willing to surrender.

'We were a little bit apprehensive as we drove towards the town in one jeep,' says Boutinot.

They approached slowly as they entered the town, to make sure all the Germans milling by the roadside could clearly see the white flag above the jeep. 'Le Bobinecq went to see the German CO and I was left in the jeep surrounded by Germans,' says Boutinot. 'They were clearly an army who knew the end was coming but there were still thousands of them. They seemed quite impressed with the jeep, though, and spent a lot of time admiring it.'

Le Bobinecq told the German officer that he was a British officer in the vanguard of an Anglo-French armoured division under the command of General de Lattre de Tassigny. Nearly 3,000 Germans surrendered to 4SAS. The rest, who would surrender only to the Americans, were marched to Orléans under the surveillance of One Squadron.

Operation Spenser came to an official end on 14 September, the conclusion of 4SAS's missions in France. They had lost seventy-four men in the three and a half months of fighting. Twenty-five of them had been executed.

Their despised sister regiment, 3SAS, had lost sixty men since its first operation in July. They had been no less effective than 4SAS, and at times their soldiers had fought with an almost superhuman bravery. Parachutist André Schmidt drove into the village of Montravers one August morning and began a gun battle with eight hundred SS troops. He was captured (and executed) only after he'd run out of ammunition. Another 3SAS soldier shot down a Heinkel bomber with a Bren gun. Marc Mora had dropped to the north-east of Limoges and driven the Germans out of the town of Bourganeuf.

Those French soldiers that could used the leave at the end of operations to visit relatives they hadn't seen in years.

'I took a jeep and drove down to the Loire to see my family,' recalls Boutinot. 'My sister opened the door and recognized me straight away even though she hadn't seen me for over four years. She took me to my mother who was working on a nearby farm. We had a big party that night with the whole village invited.'

AFTER MAYNE HAD left them abruptly in Toucy on 9 August, Bob Melot and Duncan Ridler made contact with the local Maquis and indulged in the sort of glad-handing of which Mayne was incapable.

'The Maquis in the Forêt de Merry-Vaux were very co-operative,' recalls Ridler. 'Our first job was to find a suitable DZ for the advance party of Kipling and build up dumps of petrol for the Americans who were expected to come through shortly.' Kipling was the name of the operation on which 'C' Squadron would shortly embark. Once Melot was satisfied with the arrangements he radioed England. The operation now proceeded quickly, almost too quickly for Sid Payne.

'On the Friday I went home on compassionate leave,' he says. 'Got married by special licence on the Saturday and caught the train back to base on the Sunday [13 August]. As I walked in I bumped into Derrick Harrison. "Ah, glad you're back," he said, "we've got a job on tonight. Get down the briefing room"... I went down and they showed me this tiny green spot on a big map of France and said, "You're dropping in there tomorrow morning." Then I went to the armoury and drew ammo and 25 lbs of gelignite and some detonators, said cheerio to all my pals and caught the plane.'

Harrison's six-man advance party landed in the Forêt de Merry-Vaux at 0103 on Monday 14 August. Payne, still in a bit of a daze at the turn of events, dropped into France without his battledress jacket or his beret.

'Then when I landed I put my carbine down as I gathered up my parachute and went off without it.'

Four days later, with the advance party shored up by the arrival of a further thirteen men, Harrison was notified of the cancellation of Operation Transfigure, for which Mayne had originally come to France. He was instructed to carry out reconnaissance patrols in the area and locate a suitable DZ for the insertion of the rest of 'C' Squadron in gliders. That plan also failed to come to fruition, the squadron deciding instead to land in Dakotas at Rennes airport and drive to the Kipling base in jeeps. Harrison's men set to work on roadwatch and reconnaissance patrols.

'The situation had become very fluid,' remembers Ridler. 'We could move about the area and transmit various kinds of information from quite a wide area around the base.' Ridler found life 'safe and pleasant ... with the exception of the risk of running into something unexpected'.

Payne and McDiarmid spent the night of 22 August 'counting the traffic on a roadwatch'. They returned to the camp just after dawn on the 23rd. 'We had a bite to eat and then crept into our sleeping bags,' says Payne. 'A while later Curly Hall woke me up to tell me that he and

235

Harrison were going out with Lieutenant Richardson to get the gun on his jeep repaired. Not long after we heard gunfire.'

The two jeeps, one driven by Hall with Harrison in the front passenger seat, the other containing Stewart Richardson, Trooper Tony Brearton and a French interpreter, left the base in the afternoon to find a garage where Richardson could get his Vickers mounting re-welded. They drove into Les Ormes just as an SS unit was preparing to execute twenty French civilians they had taken hostage. The first two, Georges Gauthier and Louis Maury, had been shot when Harrison's jeep appeared from round the corner. He opened fire with the Vickers, and for a moment, a fleeting moment, the Germans looked surprised. But their reaction was swift and savage. Hall was shot dead in the first salvo of gunfire and Harrison was hit in the hand. As Richardson's jeep joined in the fight, the remaining eighteen hostages broke free and ran for their lives. One, a middle-aged man, sprinted down the road leading west out of the village and banged on the door of the Pinon family. Monsieur Pinon, whose son André was a POW in Germany, bundled the man inside and hid him in a vat of wine in the cellar.

Back in the village square Harrison was in desperate trouble, unable to change magazines because of his wound. Brearton, meanwhile, was coolly performing a three-point turn. As Harrison fumbled with his gun, Richardson screamed at him to jump on board. They hurtled away from Les Ormes leaving behind several dead Germans and the body of Curly Hall. Later in the afternoon the SS conducted a house-to-house search of Les Ormes for the escaped hostages.

'A German officer came down to search the cellar,' says André Pinon, 'and my father was sure he would look in the vat but he didn't. It seems strange to you and me but that was the thing the French learned quickly about the Nazis; they didn't have much imagination.'

That evening McDiarmid and Payne went into Les Ormes.

'We spoke to the villagers and they showed us Curly's body,' says Payne. 'They'd had only one coffin and Curly was in it; the two dead hostages were either side of him.' The villagers said they would bury Hall the next day. 'We drove down and about half a mile from Les Ormes we passed a cottage where a woman was waving like mad. She told us the SS were waiting for us in the village. It was a couple of days before we could get to his funeral.'

THEY WERE THE words Lowson had been wanting to hear for weeks.

'We were going to France. I was told to take four jeeps and some men down to Broadwell.'

After weeks of relative lethargy, Lowson organized the move on 19 August with faultless precision. They arrived at Broadwell aerodrome in plenty of time.

'So I got some bottles of Scotch out of the mess and the lads got some buckets of ale and by the time it came to load up the jeeps I couldn't find any of the drivers. I said "that's no problem, I'll put the jeeps in myself". You had to drive the jeeps up two planks and turn left into the hold. I was so drunk I drove up and went straight through the side of the Dakota. Some wing commander came along and I was saying, "I'm sorry, I'm sorry" but he started being sarcastic. "Well, we can't expect you brown jobs [RAF slang for the army] to understand delicate things like aeroplanes." Then he told me his men had been up all last night getting the plane ready. So I said to him, "Well, I'll tell you what, why don't you and your blokes get in the replacement aeroplane and go to France and my lot will stay behind and mend your bloody aeroplane."'

Once Lowson landed at Rennes the forty-strong party under Major Marsh motored east through Orléans – where they met Paddy Mayne briefly – arriving at the Forêt de Merry-Vaux on the same day as Harrison's fracas in Les Ormes. Four days later, 28 August, the second contingent arrived from England. The following day Marsh left Peter Davis and thirty-four men in Merry-Vaux and took the rest of the squadron south to Houndsworth. On their way the rear jeep broke radio silence to inform Marsh that the column now consisted of fifteen vehicles, not twelve. 'Three German lorries had tagged on to us thinking we were their lot,' says Roy Close, who was further up the convoy. 'Marsh told the men at the

237

back to wave to the Germans, which they did, and when we eventually branched off the Germans drove on waving us goodbye.'

Davis's orders, meanwhile, were to attack enemy traffic on the La Charité–Clamecy road. On 30 August he led an ambush against a German convoy near the village of Nannay. The men from the leading vehicles spilled out into the woods surrounding the road while the rest of the column hurriedly reversed. There then followed what Davis described in his report as 'a lively SA [small arms] and grenade battle'. Doug Cronk spotted one German through the trees just as he threw a grenade.

'It caught me flush on the chin,' says Cronk, 'but it didn't go off because the silly bugger had forgotten to take the pin out. I'll never forget the look on his face as he realized his mistake.' Cronk shot him dead.

Marsh arrived in the Morvan to take over from Fraser's 'A' Squadron, which was returning to England after three months. Their scorecard was impressive: 220 Germans killed or wounded, 6 train derailments and 23 vehicles destroyed. They left on 6 September in a convoy of civilian cars accompanied by a reinforcement troop that had arrived the previous week. Among them was Bob Francis, a 21-year-old Devonian who had been rejected from the Fleet Air Arm because he was 'effectively blind in my left eye'.

'Wellsted just told us to "go and maraud",' says Francis, which they did with considerable success. On or around the first day of September Francis's section, led by Sergeant Major Cyril Feebery, ambushed a company of German cyclists.

'We slaughtered them,' says Francis. 'It was almost like being in a fairground. I'd been lying down with the Bren gun and leapt back into the jeep saying to Feebery, "They didn't fire a shot at us!" "Oh, didn't they?" he replied. "Well, what happened to that fucking flag?" We had a Union Flag on the front of the jeep and it was in tatters but because I was so focused … I wasn't conscious of anyone shooting back.'*

While the changeover was being completed Roy Close and two other officers set off to patrol the area south from Nevers to Autun. All three had rich pickings, with Close ambushing a convoy and finding himself

238

fêted as a conquering hero as he returned through the village of Châtillon-en-Bazois.

'They thought they were being liberated,' explains Close, 'so the flags came out and we were covered in flowers. We told them "to get tidied up because the Germans aren't far behind us".'

Marsh also instructed Monty Goddard to collect a trailer of ammunition and mortar bombs that had been damaged on the drive down from Kipling. Goddard, who had struggled with his map-reading in Darvel, was a pre-war chartered accountant who'd arrived from the pay corps. He was eager and enthusiastic and had somehow landed in 1SAS. Roy Close remembers him as 'the most unlikely looking SAS officer you've ever seen. His hat was never right and he always had a startled look on his face'.

Probably because of Goddard's inexperience Marsh detailed a couple of his most senior soldiers to go with him.

'They picked on me and Bob Lilley,' says Lowson. 'So off we went, along with another lad called "Titch" Howes, to pick up this trailer. On the way we ran into some fellows from the Maquis Loup and Goddard said, "Let's go and have lunch with the Maquis." We were in this café having lunch when we heard one hell of a din nearby.'

Just down the road from the café a German armoured column had began pounding the chateau where the Maquis was based. The next few crazy minutes led to a cover-up by senior officers within 1SAS and the subsequent immortalization of Goddard. The official Kipling report described how he 'destroyed one 36mm mobile quick-firer, and wiped out the crew before being killed himself by a burst of cannon-fire from a second gun which he was about to attack. Throughout the action Lt Goddard showed abnormal courage, knocking out the quick-firer with a Vickers "K" gun fired from the hip'. Lowson remembers it slightly differently.

* Some years after the war Francis took his Mercedes for an overhaul in Frankfurt. The chief mechanic was a one-armed gentleman of about his own age. They fell into conversation and it transpired the German had been in the Morvan in September 1944; he'd also been in a Cyclists Battalion; he'd also been ambushed one day and lost an arm. 'I said I'm afraid I was one of the blokes doing the shooting,' recalls Francis. 'And he said, "Well, yes, but I might have killed you." There was no animosity.'

239

'The plan was that the Maquis would attack the column from the front end, while we went for the back. I was in the lead jeep with Howes and when we came to a right-hand bend we could see this armoured column stretched down the road, but no sign of the Maquis. The rear vehicle was a multi-barrelled anti-aircraft gun on the back of a lorry, and it was leathering shite out of this chateau on the hill. Goddard said, "I'm going to attack it." I said, "Look, sir, why don't we just fuck off quietly because we're not going to do any good here?" But he said, "No, you cover me." He put on a pair of leather gloves and took the single Vickers K from the front of my jeep. Off he went, haring down this ditch, with me on the road covering him with the Bren. He didn't get very far, though. The Germans spotted him and cut him into little bloody pieces. I suppose I should have gone and got myself killed but I didn't want to. I'd given up trying to be heroic by that stage. It was terrible, a waste of a life.'

Perhaps embarrassed by Goddard's brave but foolhardy gesture, Marsh concocted a different version of events for his report. There was, however, no posthumous decoration.

Four days later, on 7 September, Lowson ran into another German column, 'on the Nevers road going north towards Orléans'. The column was composed of several lorries packed with German soldiers and an armoured car escort. The two SAS jeeps opened fire.

'It was all over in five or ten minutes,' says Lowson. 'We did what we could and then buggered off when some more armoured cars came down the side of the road.' Lowson was subsequently awarded a Military Medal. 'The citation said we destroyed three lorry loads of Germans infantry but I think that's stretching it a bit far.'

ON FRIDAY 8 SEPTEMBER Alex Muirhead and 'A' Squadron touched down in England. First he sent a packet of Sobranie Cocktail cigarettes to his wife. Then he fired off a quick letter to his parents: '... as to my adventures, suffice it to say that I can only wish I could write a book though it might almost be like Alice in Wonderland; ambushing German convoys after pay day is a very paying business, hence my trip to the bank!'

Back in France 'C' Squadron enjoyed the spoils of war as Operation Kipling petered out in late September. McDiarmid and Payne were approached by a communist Maquis group in need of a Bren gun.

'We said how much?' recalls Payne. '30,000 francs, I think it was, so we said "yeah, all right" ... we had no scruples at this time. A date was arranged ... we handed over the machine gun and they handed over the 30,000.' Lowson had 'opened a stall' at Cosne selling parachute silks to local women. 'I made a killing.'

In 1944, 2SAS saw and heard little of its sister regiment. Jack Paley remembers a gang of 1SAS NCOs coming to their Monkton camp once 'to give lectures on operating behind enemy lines' but the two regiments neither trained nor socialized together. When 1SAS moved south to Fairford at the end of May, 2SAS remained in Scotland. It was deemed necessary on two counts: to allow time for Brian Franks to find his feet as commanding officer and to train the new recruits – 140 of whom had yet to be tested in battle – in SAS skills and techniques.

Those soldiers who were already battle-hardened lived life at a gentler pace. Bill Robinson says life was such a breeze they rechristened the regiment. 'We called ourselves the "Saturday Afternoon Soldiers".'

On 1 June George Daniels, Charlie Hackney and Tony Greville-Bell were among the guests at the wedding of David Leigh in Prestwick. Five days later, as 4SAS and the advance parties of 1SAS parachuted into France, Daniels wrote a brief entry in his diary: 'Tea at the minister's house, supper at Lady Diana Carnegie's.' Lady Carnegie, recalls Daniels, 'was one of those wonderful upper-class ladies who went around in wellies and a flat cap. We were training near her estate and she used to invite us in for tea and let us use her motorboat on the loch.'

Roy Farran and the strong Irish contingent in 2SAS enjoyed the company of Monsignor the Canon Hayes, Troon's Catholic priest, who had the storyteller's art. On the eve of D-Day, one of 3 Squadron's officers, 'Loopy' Cameron (he'd been shot in the head while serving in the 51st Highland Division and his men were convinced he'd gone a bit loopy) converted to Catholicism. Farran, who accompanied Cameron

241

to the church, said, 'I have never been so moved in all my life. I felt the Holy Spirit everywhere.'

TOWARDS THE END of June 2SAS moved down to a tented camp on Salisbury Plain. The upheaval was overseen by Tom Burt, the regiment's quartermaster who had fought at Gallipoli in the First World War.

'He had a big scar down one side of his face,' says Ray Rogers. 'He told us it was from an enemy sword.' On the day of the move Burt conducted a final kit inspection. Harry Vickers' Nissen hut was at the back of the camp, just inside a dry-stone wall, behind which were dumped piles of kit filched from the stores.

'We saw Tom Burt coming towards us with his retinue,' says Vickers, 'but instead of coming into the hut they climbed over the wall. When they emerged they were carrying piles of spare shirts and equipment. Tom looked at us and shook his head: "I didn't join up yesterday, boys."'

Once ensconced on Salisbury Plain the regiment waited for instructions. 'Loopy' Cameron and the rest of 3 Squadron had been primed to drop into France in mid June on Operation Rupert. Then it was cancelled because of objections from SFHQ (Special Forces Headquarters). It was felt that the operational area, destroying the road and railway communications east of the River Marne near Nancy, contained too many Germans. The SOE operative in the region, Major Boddington (the *Daily Express* correspondent in Paris before the war) signalled in June that it would be 'criminally sadistic to send SAS in this area'.

While they waited to go into France, they trained.

'A forced cross-country march in the day,' says Cyril Radford, 'and about 5 p.m., you'd brew a tea, have a Benzedrine tablet, and then do a night exercise.'

Benzedrine tablets, or 'stay awake pills' had been tried on the SRS during their training in Palestine in 1943. One troop who had popped a Benzedrine pill raced against another troop that hadn't; thereafter, while they formed part of the men's emergency escape kit in France, they were rarely used.

'They kept you awake,' says Radford, 'but you didn't feel a lot else.'

At last 2SAS was given its first mission, Operation Defoe. It was the brainchild of SFHQ, its aim to complement 1SAS's Haft operation. Brian Franks was uneasy about it from the start but as he was impatient to see his regiment in action he kept quiet (until later when he criticized it vehemently). The twenty-two men dropped into southern Normandy on 19 July and pottered around for a few weeks sending reconnaissance reports to disinterested British and American regiments.

Two weeks after the start of Defoe, Captain Tony Greville-Bell landed in Normandy in command of fifty-nine men. The operation was called Dunhill, and it was, remembers Greville-Bell, 'a complete waste of bloody time ... although we did do one useful thing'. Having landed east of Rennes on 3 August, Greville-Bell's men were quickly overrun by units of General Patton's 3rd Army careering towards Paris. In the days that followed there were a few small skirmishes with cornered Germans around Messac before Greville-Bell ended up in a Le Mans café. 'The area was still very mixed up,' he says, 'and about twenty-five of us had just sat down for a drink in this café when a retreating German column drove past. Luckily for us they were all looking straight ahead and didn't see us.'

The next day, 12 August, Greville-Bell was approached by a courteous but persuasive Englishman. He introduced himself as Airey Neave, an intelligence officer with MI9. Greville-Bell found him 'delightful'.

'He told us he had about 150 shot-down airmen in a forest about 50 miles away, the other side of the German lines, and could we help him.'

The airmen had been collected as part of Neave's Operation Sherwood. Since May 1944 downed aircrew had been smuggled to the forest by British agents and they now waited patiently for the arrival of the Allied forces. Neave had arrived in Le Mans on 10 August but had so far been thwarted in his attempts to rescue the airmen by the refusal of the Americans to lend him suitable transport. '

We helped ourselves to some buses [six cars and four buses],' says Greville-Bell, 'and drove through what was left of the German lines. They tactfully either turned their backs on us or ran away. When we reached the forest we found that the RAF men were all under the command of a senior officer and behaving very properly. The American aircrew were all drunk and trying to find girls; we had endless trouble getting them on to the buses. Eventually we managed it and I handed them over to Airey in Le Mans.' Greville-Bell also palmed off on to Neave his SOE contact, a 'very pretty girl who carried a grenade in a beaded evening handbag'.

'It wasn't done in a "white slave" way,' says Greville-Bell. 'He needed another agent and I wanted money to buy presents before we returned home. I think Airey paid 6,000 francs for her.'

GREVILLE-BELL AND the main bulk of Dunhill arrived back in England on 19 August, a few days after the return of one stick from the same operation that had been overrun by US troops eighteen hours after dropping.

'They gave us some wonderful grub,' recalls Ray Rogers, whose first taste of behind-the-lines warfare had been bewilderingly brief. 'Then we sat in their jeeps listening to Bing Crosby singing "Home on the Range".' Rogers' stick arrived back at Tidworth on 17 August.

'We got back from Dunhill and were told we had seven days' leave,' says Arthur Huntbach. 'We said our goodbyes to our pals at 3 p.m. and went to collect our warrant passes. But we were told that leave had been cancelled and we were to draw kit and prepare for another operation. I had hoped to be back at my parents that night; instead I was dropped into France on Trueform.'

Operation Trueform was a shabbily cobbled-together operation, one that reflected the sudden and unpredictable fluidity of the fighting in France. Its objective was promulgated just 24 hours before the first of the five parties dropped into France. Trueform would last for a maximum of three weeks; during this time the 101 men of 2SAS and the Belgian squadron would annihilate German road and rail transport between Rouen and Paris. The Brigade report on the operation was of the opinion that: 'Conditions were unsatisfactory for successful operations owing to the lack of accurate information about the enemy; the confused state of the battle and the need to operate immediately on arrival. The parties operated with moderate success for 4 or 5 days until reached by Allied forces. It is remarkable that only two men were missing from the operation.' [In addition Sapper Bintley was killed in action on 20 August.] One of the men was Trooper Harold Ellis. His manacled body, with a bullet hole in the skull, was pulled from the Seine a few weeks later. The other missing man was Captain Simon Baillie, the officer in charge of Huntbach's and Rogers' stick.

'He was a strange one,' remembers Huntbach. 'He came from the Guards and I remember once on Trueform he asked for my torch so he could see to clean his fingernails.'

Like most of the parties dropped as part of Trueform, Baillie had swiftly realized the situation on the ground was confused and dangerous. Germans were retreating through the area from the Americans like shoals of fish darting before the shadow of a large shark. On the morning of their fifth day behind enemy lines, Baillie's stick was laid up in a farmer's barn. When it became light he told his men to go and wait in a copse about 30 yards away. Baillie, remembers Huntbach, said, 'I'm just going to have a cigarette'. The rest of the men moved in to the trees while Baillie remained behind.

'Suddenly these Germans with horse-drawn carts appeared,' says Huntbach. As some of them began collecting hay for the horses, Rogers crawled back to the barn to get Baillie. 'He told me to get back to the boys and he would follow.' By the time Rogers was back in the copse, one of the Germans was edging ever closer to their hiding place in his search for forage. Huntbach thinks the man saw one of their rucksacks. He froze, and one of the men, a Spaniard called Torrents who had fought against Franco, shot him dead.

'All hell broke loose,' says Rogers, 'and we had to run for it.'

Huntbach recalls 'running towards another wood, past a bunch of Germans collecting hay who didn't have their weapons with them because they'd been expecting a quiet time.' The men kept running until they were sure the Germans had given up the chase. There was no sign of Captain Baillie.

245

'When we eventually stopped for a rest,' says Huntbach, 'Jock Sinclair, a devout Catholic from Glasgow, said that if we ever got back he would be going straight to church to offer thanks to God. I said it wasn't God he wanted to thank, it was Torrents.'

Rogers, however, was enraged with the Spaniard. 'I went berserk,' he says, 'he didn't need to have shot him, he could have knocked him out with a rifle. I was also sure the Germans would now shoot Baillie as we'd killed one of them.'

Two days after Baillie's capture, on 25 August, the rest of the men were overrun by American troops. A captured Polish soldier fighting for the Germans told them that they'd caught a British paratroop officer a couple of days earlier. He had been taken away for questioning.

'I used to dream about Baillie for years after the war,' says Rogers, 'wondering if I'd done the right thing.'

OPERATION RUPERT, postponed from June because of concerns from the SOE about the operational area – concerns that were later ridiculed by 2SAS for being 'totally inaccurate' – finally got underway in late July. The objectives were the same, to sabotage the railway lines between Nancy and Châlons-sur-Marne in eastern France. An eight-strong advance party under Major Felix Symes, and including Len Curtis, one of the survivors from the epic Operation Speedwell in 1943, left Fairford in a Stirling bomber on the night of 23 July. As the plane approached the DZ it smashed into a hillside near the village of Graffigny. All those on board, except Trooper Boreham, were killed.

A replacement advance party was dropped a fortnight later (as the men were dropped 'blind' without lights, they had to wait for the right moon period). Lieutenant Cameron's party, including Cyril Radford and Bill Robinson, was scheduled to arrive on 9 August. That drop was cancelled. So too was another attempt on the 11th.

'The second time we actually flew over the DZ,' remembers Robinson, 'but then we came back. Everyone was beginning to get annoyed by now.'

In a relaxation of the normal tight security surrounding SAS operations in France, senior 2SAS officers recognized the strain on Cameron's men and allowed them to leave the holding area (known as 'The Cage') for a few hours to unwind. Robinson went to visit his wife who was working in Warminster.

'We had a cup of tea and I told her to look out for my plane the next night.'

One of Radford's pals, Bob Loud, lived in Cheltenham so he and a couple of others went back for some food and a pint.

'We were walking along this road past a greenhouse,' recalls Radford, 'and for no reason other than to relieve the tension we started kicking in the glass. This old chap comes out and says, "What do you think you're doing?" We didn't tell him who we were but he could see we were wound up about something. He said to us, "I was in the first war, boys, I know exactly how you feel."'

The next night they tried again.

'There was never any chatter or banter in the plane,' remembers Radford. 'For a start the noise of the engines was such that any conversation entailed a lot of shouting. You just sat there, alone with your thoughts: "Why the bloody hell am I doing this?" I'm sure every man felt some degree of trepidation; you wouldn't be human if you didn't.'

Radford recalls that after they landed they spent the next five days 'marching through the forests, lying up by day and moving at night. We eventually reached this place where a Frenchman took us deep into a forest to a woodman's hut, and this became our base'. From here they set out on two- or three-man parties to sabotage the railway lines. The first to leave were Robinson, Sergeant Bill Rigden and 'Loopy' Cameron.

'We walked for about three days until we found a good stretch of line,' says Robinson. 'We knew that the enemy in this area were mounted Black Cossacks and these boys didn't take prisoners, they just slit your throat. So while Rigden and I went to cut the line, Loopy stayed behind to guard the bergens. I was keeping watch while Rigden laid the charges and I suddenly heard this "clip, clop, clip, clop". We got behind a hedge as this horse came down the line. When it got near the horse smelt us and began snorting. The Cossack had been dozing before that and he sat up for a moment, at which point I got ready to kill him, but then he sat back and carried on down the line.'

By the end of August the full complement of Operation Rupert had arrived safely. There were odd skirmishes with retreating Germans and on 29 August they made contact with advance patrols of the American 7th Armored Division. The Germans were withdrawing east, in the direction of the Vosges mountains, and ahead of them lay the River Meuse.

'When the Americans came through we were still waiting for our jeeps,' says Radford. 'We hoped to move east and link up with those 2SAS boys on Operation Loyton.'

Initially the Americans actively encouraged the SAS to undertake reconnaissance missions on their behalf. Jack Paley, who'd dropped into Rupert on 26 August, was in a stick led by Lieutenant Arnold.

'We hired a jeep from the Americans and went on a patrol. On one of them we were ambushed by Germans and a bloke called Eddie Drew was killed.' When the SAS jeeps arrived Robinson, Radford and Cameron carried out some reconnaissance for the Americans but, says Radford, 'when [General] Patton came along he put a stop to it. He didn't like the British so he gave orders for us to be escorted out of the 3rd Army area by US MPs'.

HARRY VICKERS' TURN to go into action came in the second half of August. The 23-year-old had risen to the rank of sergeant even though he had yet to see any action. But his calm air of authority had impressed Roy Farran, a man who, according to Bob Walker-Brown, could be 'quite ruthless' if a soldier didn't measure up. Farran later sacked one officer for being 'weak, wet and windy'.

Farran led Operation Wallace into France on 19 August. They flew from England to Rennes, in Brittany, sixty men and nineteen jeeps loaded into the cavernous holds of some Dakotas. Farran had with him his nucleus of trusted officers and men, including the recently married Lieutenant David Leigh, Captain Jim Mackie, Sergeant Major Charlie Mitchell

248

and Vickers. The plan was intrepid: to drive east towards an operating base in the Forêt de Châtillon, 40 miles east of Auxerre, which had been established by Captain Grant Hibbert's party two weeks earlier. 'On 21 August,' recalled Signalman Freddie Oakes, 'I was conscious of looking back at the forward American positions so we were now in enemy occupied territory.'

They still had nearly two hundred miles until their destination. They laagered in the Forêt de Dracy that night, behind a cabbage patch, then struck camp early on the morning of 22 August and continued east. Farran split the column into three sections; a French officer, Captain Ramon Lee, was out front with five jeeps; next came Farran with eight jeeps; the rear six vehicles were under the command of Leigh. Farran stipulated that there was to be a half-hour gap between sections. The morning passed without incident. Then in the late afternoon Lee's front section ran into a unit of Germans in the village of Mailly-le-Château. One jeep was knocked out and though its occupants were plucked off the streets by their comrades it meant a frustrating detour for Farran.

They didn't depart the next day, 23 August, until 1700 hours. The order of the sections was the same as before – Lee, Farran and Leigh – although the lead section had been reduced to two jeeps. After they had been travelling for about an hour they approached the outskirts of a village called Villaines-les-Prévôtes. Lee asked a passing civilian if there were Germans ahead. The man shook his head and shuffled on. Lee drove into the village, slap bang into the path of a company of Afrika Korps. They had just returned from Italy, so recently they still wore their tropical battledress of khaki shorts and blue shirts. In a matter of minutes the two SAS jeeps were ablaze, Trooper Len Rudd was dead and Lee was running for his life.

Thirty minutes later Farran's section came into Villaines. Round a corner they drove, almost colliding with a German 75mm gun. The gunner fired but Farran was rammed up so close he couldn't depress the barrel enough. As Farran sprinted back to warn the rest of his section, Clarke covered his withdrawal with a Bren.

'While that had been going on I was at the back of the column with Harry Cockerill and a good lad called Bill Holland,' says Vickers. 'Everything had seemed so peaceful. When we heard the explosion we turned the bend and saw Farran getting everyone organized.'

Farran ordered Vickers to 'get on the flank with a Bren'. Vickers and Holland, along with eight other men and three more Brens, scampered up on the left towards the village in the shadow of a tall, thick hedge. Jim Mackie took a section of men and covered the right of the road. Vickers remembers being puzzled by the number of leaves falling on him from the trees above his head.

'I realized it was German bullets cutting down the leaves.'

The Germans sent over some mortar bombs, then launched a demented frontal attack. Mackie's section cut down dozens of them as they came bounding through a field. On the other side of the hedge just up from Vickers and Holland, a large number of Afrika Korps were massing for an assault. Vickers could hear them giving each other words of encouragement. Then they charged.

'I started to spray the hedge with bullets and as did so I could hear the Germans shouting rude things at us,' says Vickers. '"*Englander Schweinhund*" stuck in my mind because when I'd read these comics as a boy about the First World War that's what all the Germans used to say then. I remember thinking as I fired, "So they do actually say it."'

After an hour Farran ordered his men to pull back. They had enjoyed by far the best part of the hour-long firefight, suffering no fatalities to the dozens of German dead littering the fields and roads. But it was clear there was no chance of penetrating through Villaines and to hang around longer would only invite trouble. They withdrew and headed on a detour south of Semur.

The Germans were still collecting their dead when David Leigh's eight jeeps drove into Villaines.

'We hadn't heard anything,' says Alex Robertson, then a 20-year-old lieutenant about to undergo his baptism of fire. 'I was at the back of the column and the first I knew was turning a corner to see David Leigh lying

250

wounded in his jeep and Ron McEachan [a signaller] dead on the ground.' Robertson was told that another soldier, Griffiths, was in trouble up ahead. 'I must have run about 200 yards down the road,' says Robertson, 'before I found Griffiths by a wrecked German vehicle. Goodness knows what he was doing.'

The pair ran pell-mell back to their comrades, jumping on board one of the five remaining jeeps and accelerating away from Villaines.

'David had been hit in the chest,' recalls Robertson, 'and although he was unconscious he was still alive.' Robertson laid him gently in his jeep and took him to the nearest safe town. 'I drove to Epoisses and knocked on the door of a cheesemaker called Pierre Beilhaut. He helped me carry David upstairs to the bedroom while his wife went to fetch a doctor.' Madame Beilhaut returned with a doctor minutes later, Robertson reckons no more than five or six, but it was too late. 'He died on the bed,' he says.

The skirmish at Villaines had drastically depleted Wallace's numbers. The rest of Leigh's section later encountered Captain Ramon Lee and together they drove west back out through enemy territory. Farran was now down to just seven jeeps and around twenty men. His fighting spirit, however, was unimpaired. In the morning as they waited obediently at a level crossing they saw a German goods train rumbling down the line. They opened fire with their machine guns into its side and the train screeched to a stop. The barrier lifted, under the gaze of a beaming French signalman, and the jeeps continued on their way. Vickers remembers glancing in the direction of the train and seeing 'the train driver standing there shaking his fist at us'.

Farran's column arrived in the Forêt de Châtillon later that day. He was impressed with Hibbert's camp and the supplies of petrol, food and ammunition he had stockpiled. They moved to a new base and on 27 August began offensive patrols. That night two drivers parachuted in to reinforce Wallace. One was well known to Farran from previous operations, a 24-year-old Polish Jew called Joe Kalstein. 'Joe was a happy lad,' says Vickers. 'But when he jumped his 'chute never opened. I heard him go through

251

the trees and he never shouted or made a noise before he hit the ground.'

For three days Wallace buzzed angrily round the Germans. Five vehicles were shot up on the forest roads and Vickers mined the Langres–Dijon road. But on 30 August they unleashed all their might on the small German force in the Château Marmont in Châtillon. The enemy was vulnerable, its numbers unusually small (around 150) as it waited to be relieved by a large force of Panzer Grenadiers from Montbard. Farran learned of the German weakness only on the 29th. By the next day everything was in place. The two roads out of Châtillon, south to Montbard and north to Troyes, were covered by his men, and a Bren-carrying section of SAS men were preparing to attack the chateau from the north. At 0700 hours Lieutenant Dayrell Morris, a 2SAS Original who had joined from the Catering Corps, began mortaring the chateau. For 15 minutes everything ran to plan. Then a large German convoy of thirty trucks was spotted coming north from Montbard, heading straight for Harry Vickers' lonely jeep.

'I was on the abutments of the bridge,' says Vickers. 'It was a masonry bridge with little bays protruding out. But there wasn't really much cover.'

Vickers was sitting behind the gun that bore his name. Next to him in the jeep was his driver, Harry Cockerill, with his carbine. On the other side of the bridge was Bill Holland, crouched behind a telegraph pole with a Bren. Jim Mackie, who was positioned in the town itself not far behind Vickers, had warned his sergeant to expect the arrival of some Maquis who had promised to lend a hand.

'"If the Maquis are late," Jim told me, "then they'll probably come this way."'

When the first lorries appeared through the early morning mist, Vickers held his fire. Were they Maquis or were they Germans?

'I waited until the very end,' says Vickers, 'because there were no markings on the lorries. It was only when I saw the big hats I realized who they were.'

The citation for Vickers' Distinguished Conduct Medal, awarded after the battle of Châtillon, estimated he opened fire from a distance of 20 yards. Many, many Germans were killed in the first blizzard of fire.

252

'It was all a bit bloody, really,' remembers Vickers. 'But we soon started to receive quite a bit of incoming [fire]. Jim Mackie had an ability to shut himself out during a firefight. I saw him so focused that he was unaware of the bullets around him. I could never do that, I heard them whistling past.'

Farran joined the fray and in his book *Winged Dagger* described how 'the first five trucks, two of which were loaded with ammunition, were brewed up and we were treated to a glorious display of fireworks'.

Vickers didn't see Holland get hit. 'I turned to look at him and he'd disappeared.' Holland staggered back down the road, blood seeping from his wounds. A French couple, Monsieur and Madame Bienaimé, helped him inside their house (No.4 Avenue Joffre). As his wife tended to his wounds, Monsieur Bienaimé waved from his doorway to a knot of SAS soldiers advancing up the avenue. One of them was Charlie Hackney.

'I was with Jim Mackie making our way towards Harry Vickers. Bullets were flying all over the place and we shot several Germans in that street alone. We saw this man signalling to us from a house. We went over and found Bill Holland lying on the floor. Jim leant over him but shook his head, there was nothing he could do.'

By 0845 hours, one and a half hours after Vickers had engaged the convoy, the Maquis still hadn't shown.

'Farran was furious with them,' says Hackney, 'he was cursing them upside down. They'd promised 500 men; if we'd had them it would have made a huge difference.'

When the Germans began a cautious advance out of the chateau, Farran prudently withdrew. Bill Holland's life had cost the Germans a hundred of their own dead.

TWO DAYS AFTER Châtillon four more jeeps were dropped to Farran. With them came five men, including medical officer Captain Milne and Walker-Brown. The previous week he'd been admitted to hospital with mumps.

'Then one of my fellow officers visited me and told me we were going

253

to drop the next night. So I discharged myself and jumped the following day. When my canopy straps tightened round my balls I think they could have heard the shriek all over Europe. But the moment I got rid of my parachute the mumps had vanished. I can recommend it as a rapid cure for mumps.' The arrival of Walker-Brown's stick brought Wallace up to seventy-seven men and eighteen officers. Farran now split them into three components. He and Hibbert would lead two parties east, towards the Belfort Gap into which the retreating Germans were being squeezed by the US 3rd Army from the east and the US 7th Army from the south.

A third jeepless party under the whimsical Lieutenant Mike Pinci – the Anglo-French son of a Parisian count – would wreak havoc on the route from Langres south to Dijon. South-west of Épinal, Farran's party made contact with a Maquis in the Forêt de Darney. He decided to send for a supply drop to arm the enthusiastic French. The containers were dropped on the night of 6 September and at sunrise the next day Farran took breakfast on the edge of the DZ. Suddenly they found themselves being encircled by a battalion of Germans.

'I can't remember if I thought "this is it",' says Vickers. 'You tried not to think too much or else you'd frighten yourself. It was one thing at a time.'

With the desperation of a cornered animal, Farran led his men to safety through the only remaining route, 'a spinney of young saplings' in the south-west corner. Once they were free, Vickers remembers, 'Farran told me to "stay here and see if you can hold them up". Then off they went, not that I'm complaining. We soon heard these two fast cars approaching and that was that.' Vickers opened fire on the German cars, killing the battalion commander and his second in command.

On 16 September, Farran made contact with the US 7th Army. Hibbert's men, who had succeeded in blowing up some 100,000 litres of German fuel at a dump near Foulain, did likewise the day after. The third party, under Pinci, had received instructions to return to the UK on 15 September. They did so without Lieutenant Pinci, killed four days earlier. Despite his death they had caused serious inconvenience to the Germans. On 8 September, acting on a tip-off from the local FFI, they had ambushed

254

five petrol bowsers en route to Dijon. Pinci had been on another patrol at the time so Walker-Brown organized the ambush.

'We took the advice of the French and chose a position at a point where the country road crossed the main road. We took up positions on a bank overlooking the road, probably 20 feet above the road. It was a good field of fire.'

They allowed the escort vehicles to run through the killing area, then they opened fire. Charlie Hackney was behind a Bren gun.

'My opening burst hit the driver of the leading vehicle and he slumped over the wheel. Then I got the passenger next to him as he tried to jump clear. I can remember seeing bits of his tunic flying off as he was struck by the bullets.' As the bowsers exploded, Hackney remembers a 'wave of intense heat ... and there was thick black smoke for miles'.

On 13 September Walker-Brown went for a 'mortar shoot' on the German-held town of Langres. They used the cover of the surrounding woods to get to within 800 yards of the outskirts. Then they began firing the 3-inch mortar from the back of a commandeered car.

'It had had a sliding roof in the first place,' says Walker-Brown, 'but we enlarged it, took out the back seat and stuffed the mortar inside on top of a lot of sandbags.' Even with this kind of protection, when a bomb was fired its recoil did little for the car's suspension. 'I suppose it says a lot for the Peugeots of that time that it stood up to it. We fired around ten bombs in total ... a flea bite of an operation really ... but as we were pulling back I heard a lot of firing from a couple of miles to my rear towards Dijon and found it was the advance guard of General Leclerc's Free French coming up. So we introduced ourselves and assisted in the capture of Langres.'

HENRY DRUCE WAS in Scotland when Brian Franks phoned him out of the blue.

'The man supposed to lead Operation Loyton in the initial stages had backed out and told Brian he couldn't do it,' recalls Druce, 'which was a very courageous thing to do. So with the men standing by the aircraft I was

255

telephoned in Scotland and told to rush down to Fairford.' He was granted permission to take with him his sergeant, Jock Hay, 'a very fine man'.

Druce was given the 'griff', the operational instructions, when he arrived at the airfield on 12 August. A few hours later they took off, bound for the Vosges mountains in eastern France. The 'griff' was straightforward: now that the Allies had broken out of the Normandy beachhead, the German retreat had begun. It would be inexorable, said SHAEF. Before long the dispirited German Army would be retreating back into Germany across the natural barrier of the Vosges mountains in eastern France. Operation Loyton's job was to make merry hell for the Germans.

'I had passed through the Vosges before the war,' says Druce, 'so I had a general idea of what the place looked like. I thought what we were being asked to do was possible; but it was made clear to me in the briefing I wasn't to go around blowing things up. My job as the advance party was to reconnoitre the area and establish a good DZ for the main party, to select suitable targets [for later action] and to contact the Maquis.'

The terrain of the Vosges was ideal for clandestine skulduggery. To call them mountains is to mislead; they are hills not mountains, carpeted in dark sinister forests. Deep ravines cut through the trees, their nooks and crannies capable of concealing a small army. Nestled among the hills were the villages. A passing visitor, unacquainted with the region, would look on them as communities bathed in rural tranquillity. In reality they seethed with a venomous distrust. For the past seventy-five years the Vosges had been a spoil of war fought over by Germany and France. In 1871 the Prussians arrogated the territory after defeating Napoleon III. At the end of the First World War France seized it. In 1940 the Germans returned. Most of the Vosges' inhabitants viewed them as invaders; but some, those French whose blood was mottled German, welcomed them as liberators.

Druce knew hardly any of the fourteen men in the advance party. There was a three-man Phantom team, led by Captain John Hislop, and a Jedburgh section, captained by Victor Gough, a former Auxiliary officer, and containing a French captain called Barreaux and a buck-toothed English sergeant named Seymour.

256

'I had a French fellow with me called Goodfellow,' explains Druce, 'but whose real name was de Lesseps; I believe he was a great-grandson of the man who built the Suez Canal. His mother, the Comtesse de Lesseps, was a friend of my mother. Unfortunately de Lesseps was not a man of great courage and he left us as soon as he could.'

They dropped at 0145 hours on 13 August near the village of La Petite Raon, 40 miles west of Strasbourg.

'I had a bad landing,' says Druce, who wrote in the operational report that 'I concussed myself slightly and talked nonsense until about 0430 hours.' There were other casualties, too. Wally Ginger Hall damaged his knee and Seymour sprained his ankle. The Maquis who met them expropriated most of their containers as the 'fee' for letting the SAS land in their field.

'I think straight away we got to realize the Maquis weren't playing the game,' says Druce. 'The arms we had taken were to be used as bribe money but they had disappeared before we even got off the DZ.'

On 15 August the Maquis presented Druce with a gift, a 23-year-old Canadian pilot called Lou Fiddick. The previous month his Lancaster bomber had been shot down over the Vosges on the way to a bombing mission in Germany. He had baled out and landed near a small village called Virey.

'I walked around for a number of days, not exactly sure where I was,' he recalls, 'but I'd hurt my leg when I'd landed so I decided to come back to Virey.' Fiddick was taken in by a local family before being passed on to the Maquis. 'I left the house with this fellow and we began walking down the street. Suddenly round the corner marched a German patrol. I was in civilian clothes but I was limping and thought "this is it, game's up". But they went past without a second look at me.'

Fiddick was 'delighted' with his situation. 'I was finally among people I could understand! I was also impressed by the fact they had dropped in to an area so rife with Germans.'

Druce had also begun to notice that the German activity in the Vosges was far greater than he'd been led to believe in his briefing. Forty-eight hours after their arrival a Maquisard reported that 'between one thousand and five thousand' Germans had been seen moving through a neighbouring valley.

The next day some Maquis ran into a German patrol just outside their camp. There was an exchange of fire and it soon became apparent that the Germans were the arrowhead of a much larger force.

'I decided it would be best to split the party into two groups,' says Druce, 'one under Goodfellow and the other under me.'

Druce took the Phantom and Jed teams, while Goodfellow's party consisted of Fiddick and four SAS men: Hay, Dusty Crossfield, Hall and Sergeant Rob Lodge, a 36-year-old German Jew whose real name was Rudolf Friedlander and who had won a DCM earlier in the war. Half a mile from the camp they were attacked.

'It was an ambush,' says Fiddick, 'and for a while it was quite a fierce fight, though I only had a Colt 45 and we were up against machine guns. But neither side could really see each other because of the undergrowth, so we just fired when we saw movement in the bushes and hoped we hit someone.'

It was a claustrophobic few minutes for both sides. Dusty Crossfield remembered hearing the bushes scream as he raked them with his Bren gun. But then he noticed Ginger Hall lying among the leaves.

'I went to drag him away but he moaned, "Leave me, I've had it." He had been hit twice in the chest.'

'I remember seeing Dusty and someone going over and having a look at him,' says Fiddick, 'but they said he was too far gone.'

Druce escaped the initial sweep and made good progress across the hills in spite of Seymour's lameness. But as they descended a precipitous slope they were spotted by a forty-strong German patrol.

'I was going to attack them,' says Druce, 'but then we came under fire from another lot.' The only means of escape was to leave the mountain path and scramble cross country. 'That's when I had to leave Seymour,' he recalls. 'It wasn't a hard decision for me to make and he appeared to accept it.'

258

By the next day, 18 August, the Vosges echoed to the sound of German jackboots. Druce reported at the time that there were over 5,000 troops combing the area. One of the Phantom team, Sergeant Gerald Davis, who had got separated from Druce's party on the 17th, spent three days hiding in the forest. Then he approached a church and asked the priest, Clement Colin, to help him. The priest said he would contact the Maquis. Instead he led the Germans to his church.

Druce was reunited with Goodfellow's party on 23 August. They had lost another man, Rob Lodge, who had disappeared during the firefight in which Hall had died. There had also been conflicting reports concerning Seymour. That he'd shot himself; that he been shot dead; that he'd been bayoneted to death. None of them was true. Seymour was very much alive when he was handed over to the regional security police (*BDS – Befehlshaber der Sicherheitspolizei*) on the day of his capture. He was interrogated by the unit's second in command, Obersturmbann-führer Wilhelm Schneider, a man described by his boss, Dr Eric Isselhorst, as 'pompous, ineffective and fond of drink'. Schneider soon discovered that Seymour was 'not reluctant to give information'. Schneider told one of his colleagues, Marie Uhring, that 'the captured w/o [wireless operator] had shown how to work the wireless set and the cipher' as well as the 'different combinations and colours of lights used in receiving aircraft'.

'After Seymour was picked up we noticed an increase in German activity,' says Druce, 'but we didn't really put any blame on him because we didn't know what had happened to him.' Druce decided to carry on regardless.

Fiddick remembers that 'nothing seemed to faze Henry. He acted as if he were on a stroll through the countryside'.

On 24 August he located a suitable DZ and signalled SAS HQ. Two days later Major Peter le Power, a tea planter in Ceylon before the war and 1 Squadron's CO, dropped with nine men as a reinforcement stick. His signaller was Edwin Weaver, a 38-year-old Londoner with a coarse vocabulary and bad teeth. He was really too old to be on such an operation, but the shortage of competent wireless-operators in 2SAS led to his being selected. The entire stick was dropped 25 miles out of position, a further setback for an operation that was already creaking.

'Early on we had come to the conclusion that we couldn't entirely trust the Maquis,' says Druce.

Some were reliable, in particular a 17-year-old called Roger Souchal who spoke fluent English and was an aspiring lawyer. But all the time there was the smell of perfidy in the air. On 30 August a Frenchman called Fouch was caught near their camp. He claimed to be 'looking for mushrooms' but the Maquis said he was a known informer. His interrogation was interrupted by a message confirming the arrival of Colonel Franks and the main party that evening.

Franks and his twenty-three-strong party landed on the DZ shortly after 0300 hours. The CO was greeted by Fiddick. '"Who the hell are you?" he barked. 'I told him who I was and he invited me to join his little group.' In the next few minutes, however, the forest clearing seemed to descend into some ghoulish burlesque. First one of the ammunition-laden containers exploded on impact.

'It was like bloody Guy Fawkes night,' said Crossfield.

Amid the pyrotechnics Fouch snatched a Sten gun and ran. He was caught and shot on the orders of Druce.

'When he made a dash for it, obviously to rejoin his German pals, it was time to stop it,' says Druce.

Barely had Fouch been despatched before there was a chilling scream from the edge of a DZ. One of the Maquisards had opened a container and seen what he thought was food.

'He had eaten great chunks of plastic explosive,' says Druce, 'and the explosive had arsenic in it so he died a really quite uncomfortable death.'

'We were all pretty hungry at the time,' says Fiddick, 'but he was hungrier than most.'

AT THE MOMENT Franks arrived in the Vosges the American advance had ground to a halt. They had outrun their supply chain and the battlefield became temporarily static. The Germans used the respite to strengthen their new defensive positions along the bank of the River Moselle, 15 miles west of the Loyton party. When the US 3rd Army continued their push east on 5 September – with Patton having bragged that he would go through the Germans like 'shit through a goose' – the going was much tougher. They liberated the city of Nancy on 15 September but the arrival of the Fifth Panzer Army from Belgium further delayed their advance. Far from chasing a rag-tag army of shattered soldiers back across the German border, the SAS now found they were the ones being chased.

'When Franks joined us,' says Druce, 'we were really boxed in trying to save our own skins. The Germans had sent a division from Strasbourg to find us and we were pretty oppressed.'

The sense that there was a German lurking behind every tree affected some men more than others.

'I don't think the pressure in the Vosges was greater than that which I'd known in MI6,' says Druce. 'I was only 23 and at that age you don't really think too hard about what you are doing. But pressure affects men in different ways. The second in command Denis Reynolds [who parachuted in on 6 September with Anthony Whately-Smith, an old friend of Druce's from Sandhurst], was really supposed to take on my job but he just wasn't at home ... he was unsuited to the environment.'

Fiddick, on the other hand, says Druce, 'turned out to be one of our best soldiers'. The Canadian had an innate advantage over most of the other men: 'Having grown up on Vancouver Island the forest was an environment in which I felt comfortable. I took to the SAS type of warfare quite quickly and it was interesting work. I got on very well with Henry's Sergeant, Jock Hay and I accompanied him on quite a few ops. In fact I think I'd even convinced him to emigrate to British Columbia after the war. He seemed pretty set on the idea.'

ON 19 SEPTEMBER three jeeps were dropped. 'Hay and I were on the DZ waiting for them,' says Fiddick, 'and Brian Franks said to us, "Sergeant Hay you take the first one that lands, David [Dill] you take the second

261

and I'll take the third." Well, the first one landed right on the DZ, the third one landed in some fields and the second one landed in some trees halfway up a hill. We eventually got it down but it was hard work.'

Franks was furious with the state of the jeeps. The brakes on one didn't work properly, two were only a quarter full of oil and no spare fuel had been dropped. They spent most of the next day cleaning the guns and reloading magazines 'which were dirty and defectively loaded'. Even the REME fitters were described as 'incompetent'. On 21 September another three jeeps were inserted, as well as twenty reinforcements. In his post-operational report Franks criticized the quality of these men, saying most were ineffective because they were either too nervous or so over-confident as to be a liability.

'I was aware of a drop in standard [of these men],' says Fiddick. 'When you became acquainted with them it was clear they weren't up to the quality of the guys that had been dropped earlier.'

For six weeks Loyton had been on the run from the Germans, helpless in the face of their overwhelming firepower. Now with the six jeeps they began to fight back. Franks, Power and Dill went on patrol on 20 September 'to get a feel of the country'. In the next few days they plundered the Germans whenever possible; three staff cars and a lorry were destroyed on the Celles–Raon L'Étape road; another staff car was shot up on the road to Senones; Druce's patrol was lying in wait near the village of Moussey, not far from their new base, when he saw a little VW car tear into view.

'Unfortunately it turned out to be our very friendly mayor from Moussey, and I'm damned if I know how he got out of there because there were three jeeps with their nine guns trained on him. He must have baled out on the far side. Later he sent me and Brian two bottles of champagne with a little note attached ['Merci pour le salvo tiré en mon honneur ce matin']'.

One morning Druce ventured into Moussey itself with Sergeant Hay and a German-speaking Russian called Kasperovitch. 'I was driving the second jeep,' says Fiddick. 'The German commander of an SS unit was just assembling his men when we appeared.'

262

Druce remembers that 'I wasn't expecting to see them, but then they didn't expect to see me'. The jeeps accelerated towards the Germans 'and we opened fire with the Vickers from about 40 yards,' says Druce. 'In my jeep we fired off two or three pans of ammunition and took off into the mountains.'

The Germans' response was predictably diabolic. The male inhabitants of Moussey, 210 in all, were forced from their homes and deported to Germany. Only seventy returned.

Unable to extract information from the locals, the Germans turned to the Milice. Two North Africans were brought to Franks claiming to be French agents but one of the Maquisards had seen them in the company of Germans.

'Brian asked me to take them up the hill and dispose of them,' says Druce. They set off, Druce walking a couple of paces behind the pair who thought they were being taken to another camp. 'I raised my Tommy gun and fired and the bloody thing jammed. One of them looked round and they started to run. I ran after them, saying, "Come back, it's perfectly all right, you're our best friends!" They came back and we carried on walking, and the same thing happened. I got a jam. This time they both scooted off into the trees but they were caught by the French and shot.'

At 0300 hours on 29 September Druce and Fiddick left Loyton and headed west on foot towards the American lines, carrying a Panzer Division Order of Battle handed to them by a Maquis commander three days earlier. It was of such importance, considered Franks, that it must be delivered to the US Army as quickly as possible. Druce also had instructions to bring back a new radio. They made good progress during the day and that evening reached the western bank of the River Meurthe.

'There was a bridge there with one guard,' says Druce, 'but he didn't see or hear us so we just walked straight across.' On the afternoon of the 30th they were nearing the German frontline and all around them were occupied slit trenches.

'Suddenly we were challenged by a couple of German sentries,' remembers Fiddick. 'They were armed and we were armed, and so we had

263

this kind of cowboy-style stand-off where we just stared at each other. Then they backed slowly off. The tension levels were pretty high by now.'

The final obstacle in their path was a large and seemingly never-ending trench, like something from 1916. Beyond that was a potato field and no man's land.

'We lay some way off this trench,' says Fiddick, 'timing the sentries as they moved to and fro along this trench. When it was dark we moved forward and got across at the right moment.'

Not long after the pair reached the Allied forward positions. Druce and Fiddick shook hands and parted company. Druce passed on the documents and returned to Moor Park, in Hertfordshire, SAS Tactical HQ. He was handed an official letter for Franks, some personal mail for the rest of the men, a new radio and crystals, and a case of whisky by the SAS quartermaster to distribute among the men. On 3 October he flew back to eastern France and left the whisky with Potter Miller Mundy, the SAS liaison officer attached to the US HQ. Druce later learned that the whisky, intended for men who had spent weeks behind enemy lines, had been guzzled by staff officers. The next day he retraced his steps back to the Vosges, 'moving rather slowly'. He made contact with the Maquis two days later; they told Druce that most of the SAS had already begun to withdraw west but that a rear party left behind at the camp had been attacked and captured.

'I wired a message to Colonel Franks back in England asking him what I was supposed to do next and he said, "You'd better come home."'

Franks, who had been instructed by SAS Brigade to exfiltrate his men because the American advance had been held up west of the River Meurthe, had begun his withdrawal early on 6 October. Six men had remained behind to await the return of an overdue sabotage team; they would then make their own way out. The rear party was handpicked by Franks and comprised his most reliable men: Lieutenant David Dill, who had been a member of Druce's advance party, the unflinching Sergeant Hay, Lance Corporals George Robinson and Fred Austin, and Troopers Jimmy Bennett and Edwin Weaver. A day after Franks's departure a French informer led a large force of SS Panzer troops to the camp. It took the Germans over an hour to overpower the SAS, such was the frenzied resistance from the six soldiers and the 17-year-old Maquisard, Roger Souchal, who pretended he was a French-Canadian. Souchal recalled that after their surrender the SS officer 'shook Lieutenant Dill by the hand and said, "You are my prisoner; you are a soldier and so am I."'

Later that afternoon the seven men were held 'in a room in the factory of Monsieur Gerard', the mayor of Moussey. The next day, Monday 8 October, the unit that had captured the soldiers handed them over to the security police. They were taken to Saales, where they were put in a cell already containing four members of Loyton; three soldiers and Captain Victor Gough, the Jedburgh officer. Two of the British soldiers stood out in Souchal's memory: Jock Hay, as he alone of the prisoners was beaten by a thuggish Prussian guard, and Edwin Weaver, because whenever a German entered their cell he would bellow 'Fucking Germans!'

On the morning of Sunday 15 October, recalled Souchal, 'a small German came in and read out the names of those he wished to take away. They went out saying that they were going to a prisoner of war camp'. All but Souchal, Gough and Dill were led into a waiting lorry. Its driver was Georg Zähringer, a pleasant-faced 34-year-old who had been a printer in Strasbourg before the war. Next to him in the cab was Alfred Schossig, a schoolteacher before he joined the Nazi Party.

'I was ordered to drive along the road leading from Saales to Grand Fosse,' Zähringer recounted later. 'After passing through this group of houses, and after driving for some distance through a wood on both sides of the road, we came to a spot where there was a thick fir wood on the left side. I noticed no one until I saw Oppelt or Dietrich who was standing by the turning of a track to the left at the end of this wood. He waved me to back my truck up this track which I did for a distance of about three truck lengths.' Oppelt told Zähringer 'to open the back of the truck'. One of the SAS men, Reg Church, was told to climb down. He did as he was told, even though the handcuffs made his movements clumsy and slow. Zahringer unlocked his handcuffs.

265

'Schossig, who spoke English, told him to take his clothes off. This the prisoner did. He was then taken, held by the arms by Wottke and Gaede, into the wood.' Zahringer stood by the back of the lorry, watching with the other prisoners as Church was led into the right of the wood. 'Practically immediately I heard a shot,' said Zahringer. 'The remaining English prisoners on the truck did not say anything, but remained silent.'

The two Germans returned and took away Fred Austin. 'This went on from one prisoner to another,' Zahringer said, 'until it was the turn of the last.' Edwin Weaver climbed down silently from the lorry. This time there were no oaths or profanities. The previous contempt he had shown for the Germans had vanished, replaced by a serene self-composure. Weaver turned to Schossig and said something. With no more prisoners to guard Zahringer followed. 'He was made to stand near the edge of the grave which contained the naked bodies of his comrades,' he told his war crimes interrogator in 1947, 'which from his position he was able to see. He was not trembling.' Wottke raised his pistol and shot Weaver in the base of the skull. He pitched forward, dead before he landed on top of Jock Hay. As the execution squad filed back towards the lorry, Zahringer asked Schossig what Weaver had said to him moments before his death. 'He told me that the Englishman had said, "We were good men."'

OF THE THIRTY-ONE SAS soldiers captured during Operation Loyton, all but one were executed. Gough and Dill were murdered on 25 November. Also shot that day were Majors Denis Reynolds, who had been beaten until the whites of his ribs showed, and Anthony Whately-Smith. Sergeant Gerald Davis, the Phantom radio operator denounced by the French priest, was found buried in the hills overlooking the church to which he had gone for sanctuary. At times during the slaughter, the Germans amused themselves with practical jokes. The corpse of one SAS soldier was stuffed in the boot of the CO's car, so it would fall out when the boot was opened. The joke was a great success.

The only man to escape execution was Sergeant Seymour. He returned home at the end of the war and was interviewed by Major Barkworth,

2SAS's intelligence officer. He soon came to the conclusion that 'his value as a witness is doubtful'.

'We wrote Seymour off as a traitor,' says Druce, 'not thinking of the damage to Loyton's plans ... because of my late appointment to lead the advance party of 2SAS I hardly knew or could recognize him. But the Germans could be very persuasive if ever they caught you, although the SAS on operations weren't trained on how to handle heavy questioning by SD or SS measures. However, I have always been led to believe his betrayal was freely given.'

Druce's contribution to Loyton was recognized with a DSO. The citation praised his 'skill, energy, daring and complete disregard for his own safety [which] won the admiration of not only all British troops with whom he came in contact, but also that of the local French people amongst whom his name became a byword for courage'.* Druce was dismayed to learn that despite his best efforts, 'neither David Dill nor Jock Hay were sufficiently rewarded by the award of only a Mention in Despatches, while several of us including Brian Franks, Peter le Power ... and myself received higher decorations. There is no such thing as justice in this world'.

* SAS Brigade estimated that as a whole in operations in France they killed or wounded 7,753 enemy personnel, captured 4,764, destroyed 348 lorries, 141 cars, 7 trains (derailing a further 33), 29 locomotives and one aircraft.

CHAPTER FOUR

THE END IN SIGHT 1945

THE SAS CHRISTMAS card for 1944 brought Ian Fenwick back to life temporarily. Alongside maps of North Africa, France and Italy were two of his cartoons, a jeep standing in the shade of a palm tree and a soldier dangling at the end of the parachute. The greeting inside the card read: 'Changing countries but the same thoughts'. It was an appropriate card at a time when the SAS Brigade was scattered throughout Europe.

The lucky ones, 'A' and 'D' Squadrons 1SAS and all but 3 Squadron of 2SAS, spent Christmas at home.

Alex Muirhead enjoyed his first Christmas with the wife he had married two and a half years earlier. There were three of them now, following the birth of their first child in November 1944. In a letter to his parents on 27 December Muirhead told them his daughter 'can now laugh and make cooing noises ... and seems to love going out in the pram in the garden whenever the weather is fine [but] the weather has been very Christmassy with sharp frosts and thick fog'.

The reason for Muirhead's letter was to inform his parents that he had been recalled from leave on Boxing Day. There was a bit of a scheme in the offing.

'It seems we might have to deal with these Jerry paratroopers and are now at 24 hours' notice.'

268

2SAS were on a similar standby, remembered Freddie Oakes, primed to parachute into the Ardennes to hunt down the 'small German parties, dressed in American uniforms and speaking fluent English with Yankee accents, [who were] creating havoc and confusion amongst the Americans'.

Already in the Ardennes was the Belgian SAS squadron, who had been operating in France and Belgium almost continuously since the end of July. In the first few weeks they had attacked the German 15th Army as it bolted east from the rapid advance of Patton's US 3rd Army. But after the Allied failure to capture the Rhine (Montgomery's Arnhem operation) and the consequential logistic emaciation of Patton's drive through eastern France (which had created such complications for Operation Loyton), static warfare had returned to Belgium for the first time since 1918. The problem for the Allies, in particular the British 21st Army Group under Field Marshal Montgomery, was to clear the Germans from the Scheldt Estuary so that Antwerp, captured on 4 September, could be used to bring in supplies. It took the Allies the best part of six bloody weeks to rid the estuary of Germans; then they had to sweep the river for mines. Not until 28 November did ships begin to enter Antwerp, eighty-five days after its capture.

The hiatus had not only driven Montgomery to distraction, it had convinced Hitler that Germany was far from defeated. He began planning a counter-offensive in the Ardennes, re-equipping and reinforcing his armies, with the ultimate aim of retaking Antwerp. When the offensive was launched on 16 December, the twenty-five German divisions overran the six unsuspecting American divisions. But reaction from the Allies was swift; reinforcements were despatched and on 26 December – the day 1SAS was recalled from leave – the German advance was halted just outside Dinant, a town on the eastern banks of the Meuse.

The Belgians had arrived in the Ardennes a few days before Christmas where they carried out reconnaissance patrols for the 29th Armoured Division. As the Germans began to fall back the Belgians came under the overall command of 6th Airborne Division and were in action around the villages of Bure and Wellin.

On Christmas Eve two hundred soldiers from the French 4SAS arrived in Belgium to protect the left flank of the US VIII Corps. Their American allies were twitchy, suspecting everyone and anyone of being an incognito German. Every French soldier carried with him a slip of headed and stamped VIII Corps paper on which was written: 'This person whose signature appears below is a Frenchman operating under control of this headquarters and in the VIII Corp's sector only.' 4SAS drove north-east through Mortehan and Bertrix towards the German frontline. It seemed to get colder the further north they went.

'At Libin it was about minus 20,' says Guy Le Citol. 'One evening an officer instructed me, André Lemée, Sergeant Judet and another soldier to carry out an ambush at a nearby crossroads. We spent four hours hidden at the side of the road during which time we saw nothing and became frozen. There was a farm about 200 yards from our position so eventually we decided to go there. We climbed into the hay loft, huddled together and covered ourselves in straw to try and keep warm.'

The farmer found them early the next morning. He took the four into his house where, says Le Citol, 'there was a great big stove in which we put our boots to defrost'. The farmer fed them royally, and warned them that the neighbouring village of Poix St Hubert, 2 miles north, was occupied by a company of Germans. They decided to attack, says Lemée, 'out of boredom more than anything else'.

They had with them a 2-inch mortar which began raining down bombs on the village just as dawn broke. Judet, Lemée and Le Citol ran into the village 'whooping like Red Indians to confuse and frighten the Germans as much as possible'. Le Citol threw a grenade at the first house he came to.

'It blew the front door off and I fired a long burst down the hallway without showing myself. The first room I looked in had a Christmas tree lying on the floor; then I found in the cellar a couple and their two young children. I asked them where the Germans were and they told me they had left by the back door.'

Le Citol emerged on to the road behind the house. It was an astonishing sight. Houses were belching dazed Germans on to the streets.

'It was as if we'd kicked over an ants' nest,' remembers Le Citol, 'and the ants were running for cover in panic.' Lemée 'emptied his magazine at the panicking Germans and then ran back into the hills laughing all the way'.

'It was a crazy thing to do,' says Lemée, 'but we were young and I at least was a fatalist. I had told myself I would die in the war and I had come to accept that. "So what", I told myself, "I will be one of millions."'

A few days later the French returned in strength to the village. The Germans had pulled back, glad to distance themselves, the villagers told Le Citol, from the hollering Canadian-Indians who had launched a dawn raid. Le Citol went to see the family whose front door he had blown off.

'I gave them all the chocolate I had on me and apologized for wrecking their Christmas tree.'

Early in the New Year of 1945 Le Citol found himself on mine detection work. 'I was gently prodding the snow with a stick,' he says, 'when I heard a click.' It was the sound of a German tripwire being sprung. 'As I dived forward the mine exploded,' recalls Le Citol. When he regained consciousness he couldn't move. 'My brother, René, put me on his back and carried me to a lorry.' Le Citol spent many weeks in hospital before he rejoined his regiment, free from any lasting injuries.

AFTER THE END of Operation Haggard Albert Youngman had spent a dreamy few weeks motoring up through France, into Paris, and beyond towards Belgium.

'We had a lot of fun and got drunk in more bars than I care to remember,' he says. By the middle of September Youngman's 'B' Squadron and all of 'C' Squadron had assembled in Brussels.

'Mayne was back in England planning and exploring the role that 1SAS could play further north in Europe,' recalls Duncan Ridler. 'Brussels seemed to be a good place for SAS units while this planning was determined.'

The squadrons remained in Brussels throughout October, while to their north the infantry cleared the Scheldt Estuary. The men were billeted in the St Jean barracks, arranged by Bob Melot, who was delighted at taking an enforced break in the city of his birth. He lodged with his mother, as did Duncan Ridler.

'She very proudly showed us around to the family and friends,' Ridler recalls.

On 27 October Melot took the jeep to go to a party in a suburb of Brussels. When he hadn't returned the following day Ridler began to worry but 'his mother said he'd be annoyed if we worried about him and tried to find out what he was doing'. It wasn't until Sunday 29th that a policeman called on Madame Melot.

'Bob ran the jeep off the road and hit his head on the armour plating that had been installed on the front of the jeep,' says Ridler.

Fate had unpicked the stitches of Melot's battle wounds from Libya and Italy, and left him to bleed to death on a Belgian roadside. Even to a regiment inured to death the mundane demise of Melot 'shocked a lot of people', says Ridler. 'He was buried a couple of days later in one of the big Brussels cemeteries.'*

The two squadrons were assigned a cluster of different roles a couple of weeks after Melot's funeral. Peter Davis's troop from 'C' Squadron headed towards the Wessem and Noorer Canals with XII Corps; Derrick Harrison's troop were with VIII Corps when they occupied the town of Meijel; a section of 'B' Squadron under Ted Lepine carried out reconnaissance patrols for XXX Corps in late November between the rivers Wurm and Meuse.

Others worked in smaller roles. Roy Close and a section of men were 'sent to Eindhoven for about 10 days ... they wanted to get the Phillips factory intact, as there were a lot of valuable armaments'; Sid Payne and James McDiarmid were attached to various intelligence sections 'raiding nightclubs and such ... looking for people who had worked for the Germans'; Bob Lowson and an efficient Scottish officer called Tommy Bryce were doing a similar job further south in Geleen, just outside Maastricht. 'We were billeted with a dentist and his wife,' says Lowson, 'and

---

* Captain Phil 'Doc' Gunn, who had won an MC for his work as the SRS's medical officer in Italy, suffered an equally cruel death in December 1944 when he was killed in a car crash in England.

272

we used to play bridge with them in the evenings. We'd bring the whisky, they'd provide the food, and they murdered us! After one thrashing the dentist asked us if we'd keep a look-out for any dental drugs because he was desperately short in his practice. By an incredible stroke of good fortune, the next day we came across an abandoned and well-stocked dental surgery. So we got a lorry and filled it with everything – chairs, lights, instruments and drugs and drove it round to our dentist friend.'

The German counter-offensive in the Ardennes had surprised the SAS as much as it did the Americans. On the day it was launched the regiment's airwaves were humming with festive discontent. Mayne had instructed Tony Marsh to despatch Fraser McLuskey back to England. Marsh expressed his astonishment at the order in a signal he sent to Mayne early on the morning of 16 December: 'Padre in middle of arrangements for the Squadron's Christmas party. Will have to cancel if to proceed to UK.' Mayne's retort was characteristically brusque.

When the extent of the German offensive became known the SAS were quickly redeployed; Harrison's troop were withdrawn and used as 'anti-parachute troops'.

'We were told the balloon had gone up,' says Sid Payne, 'and we were told to get down to a bridge and not let any soldiers wearing American uniform get across because the chances were they were Germans.' 'B' Squadron began reconnaissance patrols ahead of XXX Corps along the western bank of the Meuse between Dinant and Liège, the furthermost German thrust.

'We were instructed to infiltrate and report on German positions,' says Youngman. 'On one patrol, led by Paddy Mayne, we came across a bridge where a bunch of Americans told us that as the Germans "were just down the road" and they were about to blow it. Paddy told them that we were going to cross the bridge. When they insisted that they were going to blow it, Paddy left one jeep with orders that if the American officer tried to blow it before our return they were to shoot him. We went over the bridge, found that the Germans were 3 miles away, and returned to find the bridge intact with our jeep keeping guard.'

273

By the end of December the German offensive had been halted and contained along a line that ran south-west from Monschau to St Hubert. On New Year's Eve the Allies were still preparing their counter-offensive, but the threat of a breakthrough had dissipated. Sid Payne's section had been pulled back to billets in a little village somewhere north of the Ardennes.

'Our HQ was in a school and we had three jeeps in the playground with the Vickers loaded up as anti-aircraft guns.'

Payne had spent the last evening of 1944 with McDiarmid in a village café.

'Everything was quiet when I got back and no one was about so I went on to the first jeep, tripped the safety catches, pressed the triggers and fired streams of tracer up in the air; I went to the next one and did the same and the third one, too. Having let in the New Year, I went to bed. The next morning there was a hell of a row because during the night we'd been strafed by some Messerschmitts. Someone said they had run to the guns but they were empty. Somehow Roy Close found out it was me and he said, "I'll have you court-martialled for this, Payne." But nothing ever happened about it.'

Close recalls that 'he could be forgiving at times'.

The parlous situation in the Ardennes was of no interest to Captain Bob Walker-Brown and the thirty-one men of No. 3 Squadron 2SAS deployed on Operation Galia. They had parachuted into northern Italy on 27 December, to counter more German audacity. This time a division had mounted a reconnaissance-in-strength against the 91st US Negro Division holding the Allied left of the Gothic Line; the Americans had fled, and the British 8th Indian Division was moved from the Eighth Army to bring some semblance of order to the Line in anticipation of a major German offensive.

'It was at once decided to mount a deception operation in order to make the enemy think that the 2nd Parachute Brigade, which had just left Italy for Greece, had returned,' recalls Walker-Brown. 'My troop was ordered to parachute behind the advancing enemy division and attack main supply routes behind the Gothic Line.' The hope was, remembers Walker-Brown, 'that the enemy would be persuaded for a short time that a substantial airborne operation was being mounted in the rear'. In his opinion it was something of a 'naïve' hope.

They landed near the mountain village of Rossano, 14 miles north of La Spezia. The DZ, on the side of a terraced vineyard, was 'grossly unsuitable' says Walker-Brown. 'We were fairly scattered when we landed and had a few minor jump injuries.' When the men collected their containers a sizeable proportion was missing; their disappearance presaged future difficulties with some of the multitude of partisan bands operating in this area.

'The mountains were dominated by two different groups of partisans,' Walker-Brown says. 'One being the so-called Justice and Liberty Brigades, who were anti-fascist and pro-Allies; the other being the communist brigades whose aim was to receive all the weapons dropped for the other partisans and store them for the post-war revolution. They were a tricky lot ... on one occasion I had a run-in with the commies.'

To counter-balance the capriciousness of the Italian partisans, Walker-Brown had the help of an SOE officer called Major Gordon Lett. The two had been in the same POW camp in Italy and shared a love of brevity. The briefing he gave Walker-Brown on landing was concise and 'first-rate': 'the enemy was in the deep valleys some four hours' march away; the mountain passes were covered in thick snow and ice; there were no motor-able roads; some partisans were well disposed, others – the communist Red Brigades – were unreliable'. Finally Lett cautioned Walker-Brown that 'news of our arrival would reach the enemy rapidly via informers'. Within a couple of weeks Walker-Brown learned that he was known to the Germans as 'Captain What-What'.

'I had a habit of saying to my men, "Shall we do so and so, what-what?", which certainly showed how many informers were around us.'

Fully briefed by Lett, Walker-Brown split his troop into three sticks. These sticks would be further sub-divided into patrols of five men. They were to fan out around the countryside and 'by descending into the valleys

275

to attack enemy transport ... to use limited explosives as opportunities allowed ... to attack by fire isolated posts ... and above all to maintain a high level of activity'.

Lett had warned the SAS about the treacherous ice-covered mountain paths. What he didn't tell them, because he didn't know himself, was that the winter of 1944/45 in northern Italy was one of the coldest in living memory. Peasants, partisans and soldiers all suffered.

'When we landed,' recalls Walker-Brown, 'all we were wearing was a silk vest, battledress and a camouflage jumping smock. We had no snow clothes, although I did send a signal asking for some snow cladding. I received a drop of khaki drill tops.'

The greatest problem, however, was boots. The army issue boot was useless because it wore out in no time. In the end Walker-Brown used operational money to have boots made by the local shoemaker.

'But grip was always tricky because to attack the roads we had to drop down from the mountains on goat tracks that were covered in ice and snow.'

Walker-Brown's HQ stick, consisting of himself and six men, carried out its first attack on 30 December. Three German vehicles were destroyed on the road from La Spezia to Genoa. All sticks, reflects Walker-Brown, 'had successful shoots, except one half stick [of six men] which made the classic mistake of moving into an empty building while waiting to ford a river ... it was spotted by Fascisti and surrounded'. Lieutenant Shaugh-nessy and the five men with him were taken prisoner; their Italian guide was shot on the spot.

Walker-Brown greeted the New Year with an early morning attack on the town of Borghetto di Vara, 10 miles north-west of La Spezia, on 1 January. From a distance of a little over 1,000 yards his stick sent down thirty-four mortar bombs on to houses occupied by German and Italian fascist units. Two lorries driving into the town during the mortar shoot were destroyed by Bren-gun fire. That evening the enemy withdrew temporarily from the town.

On 4 January Lieutenant Jim Riccomini mined a road and blew up a

German lorry, leaving twelve dead and eight wounded; two days later another stick shot up a German staff car, killing a high-ranking fascist official and relieving the vehicle of its hoard of Italian lire, estimated to be 125 million; on 11 January Walker-Brown gathered his sticks together and returned to Borghetto di Vara. They ambushed a German column, which included a captured British staff car and trailer, peppering it with thirty-two magazines of Bren-gun fire. They withdrew leaving behind two burning cars and their trailers, a smoking 10-ton lorry and twenty-three dead Germans. When Italian fascists began burning houses the next day in the village of Brugnato as a reprisal, Walker-Brown attacked them with the 3-inch mortar. The enemy brought in reinforcements from Borghetto di Vara but they were attacked by four Thunderbolt fighter planes. The SAS hadn't called them in, they just happened to be overhead. But it reinforced the German view that a large force of British paratroopers had indeed dropped in behind their frontline.

'At one stage we caught two Germans,' recalls Walker-Brown, 'and they told us they were engaged in a search and destroy operation for 400 British parachutists. We were suitably flattered.'

Walker-Brown wasn't one for dishing out facile compliments to his men. That was one of the many things they admired about him; on the rare times he praised a soldier, it was heartfelt. When he'd joined 2SAS in the summer of 1944 the men weren't sure what to make of him; he was like a Highland terrier, a snapping bundle of boundless energy.

'When I first heard him talk,' says Bill Robinson, 'I thought "Christ, what school did he go to!" Then one day on exercise he came and sat down with us and we got to the bottom of him. He was all right.' Jack Paley remembers him as a 'great guy, even though we all used to take the mickey out of his accent'.

Another of Walker-Brown's useful qualities as a troop commander was his humility; success never sneaked far enough past his moustache to swell his head. He always operated with assiduous deliberation. But when Gordon Lett brought him a report in the middle of January that Mussolini was at the town of Pontremoli en route to visit the Monte Rosa Division on the Gothic

277

Line, Walker-Brown decided to mount an attack. From their base in Rossano the troop moved north-east into an abandoned village that overlooked Pontremoli. They carried with them two Vickers machine guns that had been dropped a few days earlier. Walker-Brown climbed to the top of the church tower and selected a suitable ambush position.

'It was on a bend in the road with a fast-flowing river between the road and the ambush position. There was a drop of about 20 feet to the river with a steep bank opposite.'

They spent that night in the abandoned village. At first light the next day, 19 January, they moved into their ambush position. For a while the only sound was the surging river. Then from the direction of Pontremoli came the drone of many motor vehicles. Simultaneously the clatter of horses' hooves reached their ears as a battery of horse-drawn artillery approached the town. They waited for the two columns to converge. When they did, Walker-Brown gave the order to fire.

The two Vickers caused pandemonium among the Germans. Tracer arched across the river ripping into the vehicles and sending their occupants leaping for cover. Those whose initial reaction was to dive down the bank towards the river were picked off by small-arms fire. The damage inflicted by the Vickers on the horses was gruesome; many were eviscerated, their innards cascading across the road. There was no sign of any car pompous enough for Mussolini but that hardly mattered.

'We inflicted substantial casualties,' says Walker-Brown who, in the orgy of destruction, kept his wits about him. Out of the corner of his eye he detected movement on their flank. It was around 1,000 yards away, if that, just out of range of the natural eye. He squinted through his binoculars.

'It turned out to be a company of German ski troops moving towards us on our side of the river. They were wearing snow smocks but luckily for us they were dirty. Had they been clean I wouldn't have seen them until it was too late.'

The SAS were now faced with what Walker-Brown calls an 'extreme emergency'. They withdrew rapidly, reluctantly ascending the mountain track which had been their approach route. As they climbed higher they saw troops climbing upwards about 2,000 yards in front of them. It was a German unit tracking their footprints from the night before back in the direction of the abandoned village.

'Simultaneously a message came from the rear of the troop,' says Walker-Brown, 'that we were being followed by a second column of enemy.'

In danger of being concertinaed, Walker-Brown led his men off the track into virgin snow. In places it was 'waist-deep' but they were now involved in a race to reach the village before the Germans. There they had left mules, ammunition and a radio. They won the race, getting to the village after what Walker-Brown concedes was an 'exhausting climb through deep snow'. They picked up their equipment and pushed on to Coloretta, a 10-mile march that left the men 'extremely tired' when they arrived at 0700 hours on 20 January.

'I told the men to get their heads down,' says Walker-Brown, 'and I took the first watch.' It wasn't a long one, around 15 minutes, long enough for the lavender-grey dawn to blow away the vestigial darkness.

'About 1,000 yards below me were two companies of Germans in extended order advancing towards us.'

Walker-Brown roused his men and told them to split into gangs of four and head for an arranged RV. He smashed the radio and destroyed the code books. As he led his party west towards the village of Rio, they came under fire from the Germans. There was no thought of surrender. News of what the Germans did to captured SAS soldiers had become common knowledge after the return from France. They reached Rio at 1700 hours. At 1730 hours they were fired on by a German artillery battery and headed north towards the daunting sight of Monte Gottero. Walker-Brown's men spent the night of 20 January at the foot of the mountain, conscious that at first light they would have to scale its 5,380ft peak.

'It was necessary to change the leading man every five minutes,' remembers Walker-Brown, 'the snow being waist-deep for much of the way.'

Having surmounted Gottero, they continued on to the village of Montegroppo, reaching the partisan-held town at 2100 hours. The men, shattered after nearly 60 hours' forced march, were asleep within seconds. Two hours later a partisan arrived to warn Walker-Brown that a force of 400 Germans were less than an hour's march away. The SAS struggled to their feet and made north for Boschetto; they grabbed a couple of hours' sleep but left at first light on 22 January. One hour after their departure the village was attacked by 2,000 Germans. The partisan leader and several of his men were caught and summarily executed.

Walker-Brown reached Buzzo at lunchtime, stopping just long enough to pick up most of his other troops who had made for the town. Then they waded once more through the snow, marching for an hour before hiding up in the mountains. The men's exhausted bodies craved sleep and for 12 hours they got it; but the next day, 23 January, Walker-Brown put the men on a state of alarm as the Germans swept into Buzzo. Two days later a detachment of Mongol troops arrived to hunt down the SAS. Walker-Brown moved south-east to the deserted village of Nola and remained there on stand-to until 27 January. Only then did Walker-Brown judge it safe to return to their main base at Rossano.

The men recuperated for several days, and on 2 February, Captain Milne, 2SAS's medical officer, was parachuted in to deal with the increasing number of sick men. Walker-Brown had an endless respect for the pilots who resupplied Operation Galia, whatever the weather. On the day Milne and several containers were dropped, remembers Walker-Brown, the weather was terrible, 'thick fog lying halfway down the mountains'. The American pilot flew round the DZ for 90 minutes before he saw the signals on the ground. When his cargo had been despatched the pilot made a farewell pass over the DZ, 'and in 9/10th cloud flew straight into a mountainside'.

Walker-Brown continued the previous patterns of attacks in early February but the element of surprise was no longer there; nor was the cooperation of the local population whose support for the SAS had been beaten out of them by the ferocity of the German reprisals. Walker-Brown signalled a request to exfiltrate the party in the middle of February and 'I was given a point in the Gothic Line, between two German regiments, for the passage through the enemy positions'.

The operation had achieved much with little cost to the SAS. The six men captured early on by the Italians weren't handed over to the Germans and they served out the war in a POW camp. The rest of Walker-Brown's men returned safely, estimating that during the course of Galia they had killed between 100 and 150 Germans and destroyed twenty-three enemy vehicles. Even during their withdrawal there was time for one last small triumph. Having forded a river at night they came across an isolated cottage in which they found a German captain 'cementing international relations with an Italian girl'. Walker-Brown's scornful gaze fell on the lovers. 'You're coming with us,' he told the German.

WITH GALIA SAFELY through to American lines the operational baton was thrust into the hand of Captain Ross Littlejohn. On 15 February, the same day Walker-Brown led his men home, he and two corporals, Clarke and Crowley, parachuted into northern Italy as the advance party of Operation Cold Comfort.

Littlejohn was new to the regiment, having arrived in the autumn of 1944 from No. 4 Commando. He was a 23-year-old Scot with a bold muscular spirit. Captain Joe Patterson, a medical officer who joined 2SAS at the same time, remembered him as a 'rather serious lad whose quiet modesty and obvious resolution marked him as a most exceptional young officer'. If Littlejohn's modesty precluded him recounting the story of his MC there were others only too happy to do so; both Crowley and Patterson had served with Littlejohn in No. 4 Commando during the invasion of France.

'He had been awarded an MC for his fortitude when severely wounded on patrol,' recalled Patterson. 'He feigned death while German soldiers took his watch and other items and then stabbed him in the face with a bayonet. After dark he made his way back to our positions.'

Littlejohn and Patterson had joined 2SAS in time to take part in a

281

mountain training course in the north of Scotland. The temperatures prepared the men for what awaited them in Italy. Patterson said 'never before or since have I known such cold, even in the Alps. The trestle tables in the baronial hall in which we were lodged were scrubbed each morning before breakfast yet they were a sheet of ice for the meal'.

The hall was palatial compared to what followed when they moved to Loch Rannoch. For a week they lived in huts on the edge of a forest. During the day their Norwegian instructors taught them how to construct shelters from fir branches and how to find dry wood in a damp forest. At night the Norwegians became Germans and the SAS had to raid various targets without being caught.

'One time we had to carry out a raid on a dam on Loch Rannoch,' says Jack Paley. 'We laid up in the mountains waiting for darkness but just as we were about to move down towards the loch I collapsed in agony. Ross Littlejohn looked me over and said, "Paley, I think you've got appendix trouble." The boys were mad with me because they didn't want our position to be given away but fortunately Littlejohn took great care of me and I was carried to the house of a local priest from where an ambulance took me to hospital.'

Drama had followed No. 3 Squadron from Scotland down to Liverpool, where they were billeted prior to sailing to Italy. Their store hut was burned down one night. Gone was a lot of their mountain equipment. Special Branch were called in and an Irish soldier called Lynch was arrested and charged.

'Turned out he had done it on the orders of the IRA,' says Cyril Radford.

Even the boat trip to Italy wasn't without incident. An explosion in the ship's galley left Corporal Dave Crowley with burns on his hands and face.

But once they reached the squadron HQ, a villa in Cecina near Leghorn, things went well. The men trained hard and encouraging reports filtered back from Operation Galia. Then on Valentine's Day they were called to a briefing by Littlejohn. Roy Farran was also present, remembers Radford, but it was the officer who would be leading the operation who did the talking. With his soft Scottish brogue, Littlejohn explained that in a valley between the cities of Bolzano and Trento there was a fissured precipice. Blow it, he said, and the resultant landside would block the road and railway that ran through the valley, disrupting the main supply route to the Gothic Line. A mischievous smile then spread across Littlejohn's face.

'Once we'd carried this out,' recalls Radford, 'he told us we'd snatch Mussolini from his villa on the shores of Lake Garda.'

Littlejohn and his two corporals jumped the following day, 15 February. They were met on the DZ near Pasubio by a band of Italian partisans. Once Littlejohn was satisfied everything was in place to receive the main party he arranged their drop for the night of the 17th. The news was taken to the Germans by one of their partisan informers. The next night a ski patrol attacked the reception committee as they floundered through the snow on foot towards the DZ. Littlejohn and Crowley were captured, so were most of the partisans. Clarke and a couple of Italians bringing up the tail of the column escaped into a forest.

A short while later four B24 Liberator bombers appeared over the DZ. There should have been six but two had become separated in the short flight from Cecina. Waiting to jump from one of the planes was Bill Robinson.

'The door was wide open and it was bloody cold,' he says. 'Our despatcher was called Clarkson, a quartermaster, and he was a sensible sort of bloke. As we circled the area looking for lights he kept saying, "No, no, no." Then we would go round again. Finally he turned to the RAF chap and said, "Tell the pilot to go home; they're not dropping because I can't see any lights down there."' The despatcher on Jack Paley's plane thought he had seen some lights on the ground. They circled the area again but the lights he had seen bore no resemblance to what should have been visible. The pilot scrubbed the drop and with the other three planes returned to base. When they touched down at Cecina there was no sign of the two missing planes.

'We insisted on hanging around until they returned,' says Paley. 'When they did they were empty.'

Two sticks had jumped, one of them Cyril Radford's. He landed in deep snow, 'up to my chest' but away from the rest of his party. As he buried his chute he heard voices coming closer.

'Two men on skis were coming towards me,' he recalls. 'I aimed my carbine at them and they bellowed "amici, amici".' Radford shook the outstretched hands of the two partisans, then produced his map. 'When I asked them to point out our location they looked a bit puzzled.' Relying on a mixture of elementary Italian and vigorous hand gestures, Radford realized he had dropped off the map. 'I was about 40km north-east of the DZ.'

The partisans guided him to their mountain hideout, a two-hour hike through the snow. It was a hut lit by a single kerosene lamp and containing around fifteen other partisans. One of them was a well-built Yugoslav woman who, a few weeks later, presented Radford with a pair of German jackboots.

'When I asked her how she got them she drew her forefinger across her throat. She was a good soldier.'

The partisans belonged to the right-wing Fiammiverdi [Green Flames], led by a man called Furco. They gave Radford a bowl of polenta, the local fare which was to become his staple diet, and the next morning set out to search for the rest of the party. One by one all ten NCOs and troopers were collected. Most had spent the night employing the survival skills they had learned in Scotland.

A few nights later Corporal Clarke was brought to them by another partisan group. His story drew the sting from the men's fury at the Polish pilots who had dropped them so inaccurately.

'We made contact with base explaining the situation and asking for orders,' says Radford. 'We were told to stay put and await instructions for a resupply drop and possible reinforcements.'

OPERATION COLD COMFORT was now moribund. There were half-hearted attempts to resupply the eleven men who had dropped miles from the DZ but the focus of No. 3 Squadron switched elsewhere. Roy Farran was scuttling between Cecina and 15th Army Headquarters in Florence, fine-tuning Operation Tombola, which was scheduled for early March under the command of a Canadian officer Robert 'Buck' MacDonald. MacDonald's name was as Scottish as his birthplace, New Glasgow in Nova Scotia. He was one of those schoolboys who made all sports look easy: captain of his college football, basketball and athletics teams, he had won the 440 yards title in the 1937 Dominion Junior Athletics Championship.

'MacDonald was a good officer,' says Paley. 'We were a bit wary of him at first, not being British, but when we had been on this mountain course in Scotland he and another Canadian officer, Keith McLellan, had mucked in with everybody else. It was unusual to see officers behaving in such a way.'

MacDonald trawled the various infantry holding depots in Italy to find new recruits. The poster 'Volunteers for Paratroops wanted', pinned to notice-boards as David Stirling's had been four years earlier, aroused men's curiosity. Nearly 150 men applied and twenty were picked to attend a selection course at the squadron's Cecina HQ. One of them, a young Scot called Jock Mackinnon-Patterson, remembered standing on the parade ground in front of Walker-Brown, not long back from Galia, as he ran a mordant eye over them.

'What a shower!' he said, before handing them over to Bill Robinson.

'We licked them into shape in about two weeks,' recalls Robinson. 'I had to get them fit first because few of them were fit to do anything. I took them on long runs and route marches with rucksacks, and just got them fit to jump.' Parachuting training consisted of a day's ground training in how to roll. By the time Robinson had finished with them, only twelve of the original twenty remained.

FARRAN HAD ALSO been looking for new recruits, though he was concerned more with officers than other ranks. In early February he visited an Infantry Reinforcement Transit Depot (IRTD) at Incisa near Florence. One of the applicants interviewed was a young lieutenant called Ken Harvey, a 20-year-old possessed, said Farran later, of 'that baby-faced beauty that

285

is so typically English'. Harvey was in fact a Rhodesian, raised into a prosperous middle-class Bulawayan family. He was tall for his age and his time, well over 6 feet, and there was a touching innocence about him that recoiled at some of the sights he had seen while wandering through the more louche districts of Cairo in 1944. Even though Harvey was untested in battle, Farran recognized his potential as an officer and a leader.

'I think Rhodesians tended to produce leaders,' Harvey reflects, 'because we ruled the black population and were used to leading.' His first encounter with British soldiers after sailing from South Africa had left him slightly startled. 'The one thing I noticed quickly was the lack of strength among many British soldiers; in Rhodesia we had the sunshine, the food, the outdoor life – I had been hunting and shooting in the bush since a young age – and I think we were better equipped [for fighting].'

Harvey arrived at squadron HQ on 18 February. After three weeks' training under Bill Robinson, he dropped south of Reggio with the main party of Tombola. The advance stick had parachuted in three days earlier, on 6 March. To the anger of 15th Army Group HQ and the consternation of Walker-Brown, Farran had led them in against the wishes of his commanding officer. He later attempted to exculpate himself, writing in his account of the operation that 'permission to jump into the Reggio Valley had been flatly refused by 15th Army ... which considered my proper place to be beside the controlling wireless set in Florence [but] I knew that Walker-Brown, who deserved a rest, was just as capable as I of organizing our air supply.' Walker-Brown remembers that at the time Farran told him he had 'fallen out of the aeroplane by mistake'.

Walker-Brown had a tremendous regard for Farran, an officer he describes as 'a born soldier [with] drive and initiative', but his occasional bouts of mercurial unorthodoxy offended his own sense of probity.

Two weeks after he had dropped into the Reggio Valley, Farran sent Walker-Brown a signal, 'saying he had located the HQ of the German [51] Corps'. Walker-Brown contacted 15th Army Group in Florence and was soon standing in front of its commander, the American General Mark

Clark, who told Walker-Brown the proposed attack on the HQ must not go ahead until after the Allies had launched their next offensive.

'He then said "I am going to tell you the date on which we cross the front line and if there is any breach of security I will hold you responsible." I said, "General, understood."'

Walker-Brown sent an immediate signal to Farran, saying 'for reasons I am unable to explain do not, repeat not, repeat not, launch proposed operation until word from me'. 'Whereupon,' recalls Walker-Brown, 'Roy switched his radio off and complained about base buggers and that sort of thing.' Farran attempted to dissemble the truth in a carefully crafted contemporary report on the attack, writing that '15th Army Group agreed to an immediate attack but revoked their decision later. Unfortunately I had already left on the long march to the plains when the cancellation was received on my wireless set'.

On 24 March Harvey led one of three columns from their camp in Secchio on what he remembers as a 'long approach march, about 50 miles, over mountainous rugged country to our assembly point via Valestra'. The 100-strong raiding force had all reached the RV, a cow shed at Casa-del-Lupo 3 miles from the HQ, by 0200 hours on Monday 26 March. They lay up that day, checking their weapons and going through the plan of attack over and over again. Harvey prepared to be blooded in battle. In the short time he had been with 2SAS he had gained a measure of respect for his fitness and skill with a rifle.

'Also my parents used to send me Biltong and I would chew it in front of the men. One time I heard one of them say, "God, he must be tough he's chewing tobacco."' Harvey's job was to lead nine SAS soldiers and twenty partisans on an attack against Villa Calvi, one of the two buildings that comprised the German 51 Corps HQ. In it was housed the operational hub of the corps and also, it was hoped, Colonel Lemelson, the chief of staff. Simultaneously, Lieutenant Riccomini would take a similar force and assault Villa Rossi, the soldiers' billets that lay on the opposite side of the road.

Jim Riccomini had been on Operation Galia with Walker-Brown, a 'first-class officer' in his opinion and one for whom he had recommended a Military Cross. The pair had first met in an Italian POW camp in 1943. Riccomini escaped at the same time as Walker-Brown but instead of going south he headed north-east into Yugoslavia where he spent four months fighting alongside the partisans. He and another Galia veteran, Sergeant Sid Guscott, had both volunteered for Tombola, but neither was gung-ho. Riccomini yearned for the war to be over, so he could return to the wife he'd married in September 1939, three weeks after the outbreak of war. Before he went on Tombola he wrote her a letter from Cecina: ' ... the real thing that worries me is that I might never be able to settle down after all this ... however, darling, remember that I do think of you very often, and that one day I will be home again.'

At 2300 hours Farran led his men out of the cow sheds. The 3 miles to the HQ were covered in excruciating slowness. At every step they expected to be challenged by a sentry or see a flare burst over their heads. The ploughed field they had to cross to reach the trees at the foot of Villa Calvi seemed to last for ever. Farran snagged his jumping jacket on a piece of barbed wire and the fence seemed to vibrate with a wicked jangle as he freed himself. At 0200 hours they were all in position. Riccomini led his men off first, his target being further back and to the right of Harvey's. Three minutes later Farran, who would fire a flare after 20 minutes to signal the withdrawal, watched the young Rhodesian scramble up a small path towards the villa's lawn.

'I dropped off my Bren gunners with orders to shoot anyone who appeared at any of the windows or came out of any of the doors except the front door, which we would use.'

Harvey led some of his men to the front door. It was securely bolted. He signalled silently for the bazooka. Once, then twice, there was just a dull click as the weapon malfunctioned. As they tried to fix the bazooka Harvey 'heard the unmistakeable crunching of boots on the gravel road between the two villas, and then deep guttural voices'.

'I got everyone to lie flat in the shadows on the lawn and ran the 10 yards to the gate on the road.' Harvey hid behind a masonry pier, waiting

288

as calmly as he had done hunting game in the Rhodesian bush. 'I could see the sentries now only a few feet away,' he recalls, 'four of them marching up the road.' He stepped into the road and began firing. 'It was essential this was all done at point-blank range to ensure they were killed immediately because the shots would set off the whole area.'

Harvey could see windows being flung open as he raced back across the lawn. His Bren gunners opened up, 'taking a good toll and easing our job'. Harvey shot off the lock on the front door, his men lobbed in a few grenades and then in they charged. Inside they were enveloped in darkness. Harvey heard 'scuffling noises'. Bullets started to fly. Some smacked into walls, others into men. One of the SAS soldiers, Mulvey, was hit in the leg. Ear-piercing shrieks and screams emanated from the darkness. 'The din was deafening,' says Harvey who, disorientated, decided he had to take a big risk. He switched on his torch 'and had a quick look around' holding it out to his side at arm's length. A German fired at the light. Harvey's sergeant shot him dead. They then rushed up the staircase but were repelled by the weight of fire from the balustrade. Harvey heard a series of irregular clunks, something bouncing down the iron staircase. It was a grenade, dropped from above.

'It exploded between my legs,' recalls Harvey. He received a piece of shrapnel in his leg; Corporal Langbourne behind him was peppered with a dozen fragments.

Having realized the futility of trying to reach the first floor, Harvey and his men started a fire in one of the ground-floor rooms.

'We helped it get a good start with some explosives that we'd brought. Added to this was some furniture to keep it going and we made our exit.' The Bren gunners, meanwhile, had killed numerous Germans who had either lingered too long at a window or who had tried to escape out of the back door. For a few minutes all the firepower was concentrated on the upper floor windows. As the flames spread higher, some occupants became more frantic in their search for an escape route. They were the ones who made the easiest targets for Harvey's men.'

It was now 35 minutes since Harvey had killed the four sentries; the raid had already lasted 15 minutes longer than planned. Gathering up their wounded the raiders withdrew back through the wood towards the RV.

'We didn't go straight back into the mountains,' says Harvey, 'because the Germans would expect that. I decided to head in the opposite direction to that which we would ultimately take ... further north towards Reggio and then in a large circle back to Casa-del-Lupo where we all met up.'

There Harvey learned what had happened at Villa Rossi; how Riccomini had shot the sentries through the iron railings and stormed through the unlocked gates into the building; how Captain Mike Lees, a Special Forces liaison officer, had been seriously wounded leading a charge up the staircase; how Guscott had been shot dead in a second attempt; and how Riccomini had been killed by a grenade blast. Subsequent partisan reports confirmed that as many as sixty Germans were killed in the raid, including Colonel Lemelson.

SIX WEEKS AFTER the debacle of Cold Comfort, the men whose pilots had returned to base finally got to jump. On 3 April they dropped west of Genoa, into the mountainous Liguria region, under the command of Buck MacDonald on an operation whose name tipped its hat to the country of his birth, Canuck. Jock Mackinnon-Patterson remembers being greeted on the DZ by a pretty 20-year-old girl brandishing 'a Sten gun and wearing leather bootees, bobby socks, a print dress and a leather waistcoast'. The girl had a sister, equally cute, according to Paley. The drawback was they were the daughters of the local partisan leader, a particularly fierce character, and he 'warned us not to mess with them'. Robinson recalls that one of the girls was also exceptionally brave.

'One time she put a homemade bomb in a sack of potatoes and walked up to a German picket. The guards asked for her papers and she replied that she'd forgotten them at home.' The girl said she'd nip back and get them, but could she leave the potatoes at the picket? 'She got a few hundred yards up the road and the bomb went off destroying the picket.'

MacDonald's brief before jumping was to bring the local partisan bands together, give them some rudimentary arms training, and then lead them in an assault against Alba, a strategically important town for the Germans and Italian fascists. At 0500 hours on 15 April the SAS were in position overlooking the town. On the edge of Alba a considerable force of partisans had assembled on the far bank of the River Tanaro. The idea was they would swim the river and then launch an infantry-style attack while the British provided supporting fire with two 3-inch mortars, a Browning heavy machine gun and small-arms fire. MacDonald gave a loud blast on his whistle to signal the start of the assault. Robinson was on a mortar, taking orders from Lieutenant Philip Fell, who directed fire through his binoculars.

'We had a lot of bombs,' recalls Robinson, 'and there was one bloke sitting on a large heap of them giving us whatever we wanted, smoke or ordinary bombs, cap on or cap off ... if you left the metal cap on the bomb, it didn't explode straight away, it went through two or three floors and then exploded. It wasn't long before the barrels were red hot.'

Paley was firing the Browning with its 'lovely big rounds, 50 calibre, with tracer every fifth round'. The assault on Alba was Paley's first time in action, an experience he found 'exhilarating', even when the well-armed defenders began returning fire.

'They began lobbing mortar bombs back at us,' says Paley. 'You could hear their whizz as they went over but they never really got our range.'

The partisans' attempt to ford the river was repulsed and the attack degenerated into a stand-off between two unevenly matched sides. After eleven hours MacDonald ordered a withdrawal.

'The partisans had taken off,' says Paley, 'and the fascists were beginning to work their way up the hillside towards our positions.'

The town was finally taken two weeks later in another combined attack. 'We only fired about ten rounds and the white flags came out,' says Robinson. 'The fascists had cleared off leaving just the local police.'

The SAS stood by and let the partisans enter the town as its liberators. When they got into the town later that day 'blood was running down the streets,' remembers Paley.

'The partisans were taking revenge on some of their own people, shaving the heads of women ... shooting men and women in the streets.'

The SAS left them to it. 'You didn't get mixed up with the local people,' says Robinson, 'because they'd soon turn on you.' Instead they booked themselves into the best hotel in Alba, ordered some wine and enjoyed a good night's sleep in a proper bed.

A MONTH AFTER parachuting into Italy 40km wide of the mark the remnants of Operation Cold Comfort were no clearer as to their role. To attempt the original mission was impossible. They had few weapons, fewer explosives and only a third of the original unit. Efforts had been made to resupply the eleven soldiers – once with an officer – stranded on the Asiago Plateau but bad weather had beaten back the aircraft each time.

'We never did get a resupply drop,' remembers Radford, 'and rightly or wrongly we got the feeling base had lost interest in us.'

This wasn't just the irrational fretting of leaderless soldiers. A request for new boots was met with the reply: 'Partisans can operate without boots, so can you.'

When the snow began to thaw in April the men split into two sticks and tried to cut the railway lines. 'This was a bit difficult,' says Radford, 'because by now the area was inundated with German troops making a defence line.' Then one day Radford and Clarke were in Asiago, having a trim in a barber's.

'An Italian came in and told us there was an ambush up the road – by this time we knew quite a bit of Italian – so I picked up my Bren and Clarke, halfway through a shave, got his weapon and off we went.'

The pair arrived just after the partisans had sprung the ambush on a mountain road. The leading bus in a convoy of three packed with Germans had run over a mine, blocking the path of the other two. The partisans opened fire from their vantage points overlooking the road, their bullets inviting the Germans to jump from the bus on to the downside of the road. For 30 minutes there was sporadic firing. Every now and again

292

Radford fired a salvo from the Bren 'just into the bushes because I couldn't see anyone as they were all under cover'. Then a white flag appeared. A German climbed up the hillside and there was a brief parley. Radford and Clarke told him they were British soldiers and they would be treated as prisoners of war. A few minutes later the Germans surrendered en masse.

'They were all veteran paratroopers,' says Radford, and most of them wore these wounded badges [a German helmet on top of two crossed swords sewn on to the left breast pocket]. There was also a number of uniformed female auxiliaries – some were big and butch but there was one lovely little thing – and the paras told us that if they hadn't been with them they wouldn't have surrendered.'

Farran returned to Britain at the beginning of May, having escaped punishment for his earlier indiscretions. He credited Colonel Riepe, the officer in charge of special operations at 15th Army Group, with smoothing ruffled feathers, but Walker-Brown had spent 'most of my time trying to stop Farran being court-martialled'. After the HQ attack Tombola's energies had been channelled in to shooting up traffic travelling down Highway 12, a main supply route for the Germans facing the offensive launched by the US IV Corps. Harvey had distinguished himself once more, ambushing a column of Germans so ferociously that 'the following day my twenty-strong unit found itself with 600 surrendering to us. They had thought we were a much larger force'.

He was subsequently awarded a DSO for his part in Tombola. The citation concluded by saying: 'The damage he did to the whole German Army from Bologna to Massa was grievous. His behaviour inspired his men to follow anywhere an officer they love and trust.'

The rest of Farran's No. 3 Squadron followed him back to England by boat later in the month. Operations Galia and Tombola had achieved significant successes, while Canuck had helped to embolden and discipline the hitherto ragged partisan groups. Only Cold Comfort had failed. Even when they captured Asiago airfield at the end of April, says Radford, they were 'told by base to leave it alone as they did not want to hinder the German retreat to the north'. Of Littlejohn or Crowley there had been no news since their capture. Then on 25 April a radio signal flashed between Major Barkworth and Christopher Sykes, 2SAS's intelligence officers responsible for tracking missing personnel: 'Littlejohn and Crowley of COLD COMFORT officially reported PW.'

But Barkworth had been misinformed. Whoever fed him the information had either made a genuine mistake or was trying to camouflage the truth, because by 25 April Littlejohn and Crowley had been dead for five weeks. By early July the two men responsible for their deaths were sitting opposite Barkworth in an interrogation centre. He had grown wearily accustomed to German atrocities in his role as 2SAS's intelligence officer but even Barkworth blanched at what he heard from Heinz Andergassen and Albert Storz.

For days the Germans had been unable to break either Littlejohn or Crowley. So they were handed over to Sturmbannführer Schiffer, Josef Placke and a female doctor called Marianne Schifferegger. Littlejohn was given what Storz described as a 'thorough interrogation'. Still he said nothing. Then, said Andergassen, he was subjected to a 'stricter interrogation'. The prosaic euphemisms with which the Germans couched their methods were in fiendish contrast to the ingenious creativity they used in their torture.

'The "stricter interrogation" system,' Andergassen told Barkworth, 'was not sufficient to make him [Littlejohn] talk, [he] was then tied and an iron bar passed through his elbow junctures and his knee junctures and then suspended to a stepladder.' This, Barkworth learned, was known as the 'Schaukel' [swing] position. Andergassen couldn't remember if it was at this point that he and Storz had 'whipped ten times Littlejohn'. After several minutes hanging from the stepladder, Littlejohn signalled he was ready to make a statement.

'Sergeant [sic] Crowley was brought from his cell into the machinery room,' recounted Storz, 'where Littlejohn released him from his oath of secrecy and authorized him to speak out as he was doing. Littlejohn in his conversation, however, signified to Crowley that he should not talk too

294

much. The attending interpreter Josef Placke immediately caught this remark and brought it to Schiffer's attention.'

On the afternoon of 19 March Storz and Andergassen were called into Schiffer's office. He ordered the pair to 'go on the same evening and before dark to the police "Durchgangslager" (transient camp) to pick up three terrorists,' remembered Andergassen, 'and to shoot them while they "would try to escape".' Littlejohn, Crowley and a downed American airman called Charles Parker were collected in a six-seater car. They were driven towards an isolated and pre-arranged place of execution but, said Andergassen, 'while riding on the highway that leads to the Merano Road from the camp, just before a secondary road that turns to the right, we really had a flat tyre on the left back tyre.' Storz, who was driving, 'bade the three of them get out of the car'. They did so, although Littlejohn and Crowley were 'acting curiously, wanting to make sure that we had a flat tyre'. The sight of the genuine puncture dispelled any fears they harboured and they began walking down the street in front of Andergassen and Storz.

'After about fifty steps Andergassen asked me whether I was ready to fire, which I acknowledged, whereupon he gave the order "ready".' The two men levelled their Italian machine-pistols at the backs of Littlejohn, Crowley and Parker, and fired. Later that evening Andergassen made a verbal report to Schiffer. 'Good,' he was told by his CO, 'you did the job bravely and you did it for Germany.'

WHEN THEY RETURNED to England from the Ardennes in February 1945 the French SAS, 3rd and 4th regiments, were billeted at a camp in Suffolk. Roger Boutinot was now one of only twenty-seven surviving men from the original batch of fifty-two who'd sailed to the Middle East under Georges Bergé's command four years earlier. Then he had been a plump 19-year-old, a former patisserie assistant who had gorged on too many cakes. Now he had the body of a blacksmith, one that had been tempered in battle. When he had visited his mother in France in the autumn of 1944 he'd worried beforehand that she wouldn't recognize him after four years.

At the camp in Suffolk, Boutinot remained among his chosen clique. He had little to do with the men who had enlisted in the regiment since the liberation of France. He looked on them as disdainfully as he had the men who'd joined 3SAS in 1943. But the new recruits to the French SAS in late 1944 were as impossible to stereotype as had been the men from North Africa. Some had been imprisoned by the Germans, others had worked for resistance networks, one or two had sat idly by as the Germans occupied France; others, like Mike Alexandre, had been too young to fight.

When he joined 4SAS in the autumn of 1944 Alexandre resembled a 'stringbean', like most 16-year-olds. His chin was speckled with pimples and when he took his English girlfriend out on a date they went 'to the cinema and held hands'. What marked out Alexandre in 4SAS wasn't his youth – he recalls that there was one soldier younger than he – it was his nationality: he was an American. He'd been born in Le Havre in 1928 to American parents. His father was a successful businessman and for the first five years of his life he was brought up by an elderly French nurse.

'She was part of the generation who remembered the Franco-German war of 1870,' says Alexandre, 'and I was raised as very patriotic and I was made to listen – against my father's will – to American marching songs.'

His father had been one of America's Doughboys in the First World War and he despised the military and the way it fooled young men with its meretricious finery. When he heard his son had enlisted in the French Army after the liberation he told him he never wanted to see him again.

Once in England Alexandre's personality had been subsumed into 4SAS. 'Boots were shined to a mirror polish, our webbing was khaki green, our brass was brassed to a fine polish; pleats in the back of the blouses, creases in the trousers, soap inside the creases. We were trying to look like soldiers ... personally I was trying to prove I was old enough to be a soldier.' Only on one small point did Alexandre stage a teenage rebellion. 'I tried to find a US shoulder title indicating my nationality.'

On 3 April the two regiments of the French SAS moved south to Mushroom Farm transit camp in Essex. Two days later Brigadier Mike

Calvert arrived at the camp. The previous month he had replaced McLeod as commander of the SAS Brigade when the latter took up an appointment as Director of Military Operations in India. Calvert had won his reputation as a soldier fighting the Japanese, but the French knew nothing of that. They listened as he told them they were going to be dropped en masse into north-east Holland, 'the Groningen–Coevorden–Zwolle triangle', in advance of the First Canadian Army. They were then to seize and hold key road and rail bridges [eighteen in total] and three airfields until the Canadians arrived.

'This is going to be a different mission from those that some of you have participated in before,' Calvert said, 'because you are landing in an area that the Canadian Army hopes to reach 48 hours after your arrival.' He finished with a joke. 'I know that the French are good marksmen, well, this is a country with some good game. So, gentlemen, I wish you happy hunting.'

The speech, delivered in French, went down well. The new recruits believed implicitly in Calvert's words; some of the more experienced men scrutinized its small print. What if the Canadians didn't reach them within 48 hours? What then, stranded in German-held territory? Similar thoughts had troubled Calvert. Thus, on 3 April he had instructed the Belgian squadron to move east from their barracks in Tervueren towards the Dutch town of Coevorden where, under the command of II Canadian Corps, they were to support the French should the Canadians be unable to relieve them within the allotted time.

The Belgians were an unknown quantity to Calvert, his knowledge of their fighting prowess was second-hand, passed on to him by his predecessor, Brigadier McLeod, in whose opinion, voiced after the war, they were 'well-disciplined, well-trained and ... much the easiest of my five very different [SAS] units to command'.

THE BELGIAN SQUADRON in 1945 numbered around 300, a homogeneous force with a convoluted history. Some had fled their homeland in 1940 and arrived in Britain as refugees where they were dispersed throughout

London: 18-year-old Jean Switters was billeted with a family in Southgate, on the northern edge of the capital; Yvan Brasseur was taken in by a couple of ageing spinsters in Streatham who lived in a house without electricity. The two young men soon enlisted in the Belgian Forces and were sent to a training camp in Great Malvern.

In early 1942 a large detachment of Belgian volunteers arrived from North America. Among them was 19-year-old Jean-Claude Heilporn who had fled Brussels with his father, an eminent lawyer, in May 1940. They'd headed south-west, over the French border, down to Bordeaux and then into Spain and Portugal, where his uncle was waiting to escort him on a boat to the Belgian Congo. In early 1941 Heilporn sailed alone to New York, to continue his university studies so his parents thought. Instead he went to the Belgian Consul and joined up.

In July 1942 the Belgian Independent Parachute Company came into being. It was a verbose title for a force of callow volunteers who had fervour but little in the way of soldiering experience. Their commanding officer, 36-year-old Eddy Blondeel, was a trained dentist. He possessed leadership skills and resourcefulness, qualities he had honed as the chief scoutmaster in Flanders during the 1930s, but he was relieved when in the late summer of 1942 a small band of seasoned Belgian soldiers arrived in Great Malvern.

Their leader was Jacques Goffinet, 19 years old and young enough to be Blondeel's son. He had been born in Sedan, in the north-east of France, to Belgian parents. The scars of war pockmarked the region; his great-grandfather had fought in the Franco-Prussian War of 1870, his father and uncles in the Great War.

'Fighting was in my blood,' says Goffinet.

Despite the family's martial lineage, his family had wanted him to become a good European. His father had sent him to school in Germany in 1937 and England the following year, where he was when war broke out.

'I joined the Free French in London and got my parachute wings on 10 March 1941,' Goffinet recalls. 'Next day I turned 18.'

In July he sailed to the Middle East with Georges Bergé's French paratroopers. He was friends with Roger Boutinot, a man he still remembers as 'the baker from St Malo'. But he was unhappy in the Free French. 'They were too nationalistic,' he remembers. 'Everything was done the French way.' At the end of November 1941 he transferred to the Foreign Legion and became an instructor. 'It was there I met a party of Belgian Legionnaires who wanted to desert, so I deserted with them.' They worked their way back to England and enlisted in the Belgian Independent Parachute Company. The day after they arrived, Blondeel called them into his office. '"You are all professional soldiers," he told us. "Therefore you must set an example to the others. You must bring them up to your standards."'

Goffinet was what the Belgians called a *'bon enfant'*, a man whose spirit of fun padded alongside him wherever he went. His mantra when he took weapons drill was to 'squeeze the trigger gently, like one would squeeze a woman's breast'. He had a strong handsome face, a cliché of every comic-book war hero: lantern jaw, steely gaze, a shock of dark hair swept dashingly to one side. But his exploits came to lampoon such fictitious drivel. In September 1944 he had singlehandedly destroyed a Mark IV tank during an operation in the French Ardennes.

'I chucked a gammon bomb that exploded against it and then the commander stuck his head out of the turret, which wasn't very sensible.'

Then he had led his section on a string of ambushes, attacking any vehicles branded with a swastika, regardless of whether it was soft-skinned or armoured. In November 1944 his was the task to train the 200 new recruits to the squadron who had been harvested after the liberation of Belgium. Like the rest of the squadron they were a mixture of Walloons and Flemings. To sidestep potential rancour, says Goffinet, Blondeel 'would always address the men in English, French and Flemish ... but there was never any problem between the Walloons and the Flemish. We all considered ourselves Belgians'.

ON THE NIGHT of 7 April the 684 French parachutists climbed in an armada of forty-seven Stirlings. In each plane was a stick composed of approximately fifteen men. Boutinot was reunited with Michel Legrand; Papazow

299

was with Captain Antonin Betbeze, Alexandre was with Lieutenant Lasserre. One of the sticks in 3SAS was led by Lieutenant Maurice Duno. He waited at the door of the aeroplane as the pilot searched for the DZ.

'My feet were wedged either side of the door and for seven or eight minutes I just stared at the red light,' he recalls. When it turned green he leapt. Duno's stick landed just 1 mile south-west of their DZ, a good result when a quarter of the pilots dropped their loads 5 miles or more off target.

Duno's objective was the Appelscha bridge; by 0600 hours on 8 April it was in his possession. For the rest of the day he and his men scoured the surrounding woods for stray paratroopers. All they found were three German soldiers. The next day they attacked a German staff car as it approached the bridge.

'We dragged out an SS officer from the car,' says Duno, 'who was on his way to Groningen. When we searched him we found an execution order for forty-five Dutch Resistance fighters who were being held in Groningen. He was handed over to the Dutch and I imagine they shot him.' The other Germans caught by Duno were more fortunate. 'After a couple of days we had about forty prisoners,' he says, 'so I asked a nearby farmer if he had any space. As the Germans had recently taken the last of his pigs he was only too happy to offer us his empty pig pens.'

Boutinot's stick had landed east of Assen, near a village called Gasselte. 'Four sticks had all landed in that area,' he says, 'so we all formed one big unit.' On the morning of 9 April Boutinot sprang an ambush on the road between Rolde and Gieten, shooting up a German Red Cross lorry.

'We didn't know it was Red Cross,' says Boutinot, 'until after we'd opened fire.'

They pulled a doctor alive from the wreckage, and took him into their forest hideout. 'He spoke good French and said he knew the war was over so he wouldn't try and escape.'

Later that day fifty soldiers mounted an attack against Gasselte, headquarters of the NSKK, the Dutch fascists. 'As we entered the village,' recalls Boutinot, 'some Dutch civilians at a window were gesturing towards a

300

house opposite. I banged on the door and it was opened by a pregnant woman.' Boutinot looked at the Dutch woman. 'Are there any Germans in here? "No, no," she said, "none", but I could hear movement upstairs. In one of the rooms upstairs I found a man in civilian clothes.' Boutinot asked to see his papers.

'"No papers," he said. So I asked him to remove his jacket.' The man hesitated, then slowly took off his jacket. Boutinot's gaze fell on the SS number tattooed on the man's upper arm. 'I shot him.' *

After the SS had wiped the village of Oradour-sur-Glane off the map, says André Lemée, many of the French SAS tore up the Geneva Convention. 'Some horrible things were done to the SS,' he recalls. One German might have his throat slit, another might be tied by his ankles to the back of a jeep and taken for a ride.

Based in and around Groningen was the Dutch SS Brigade. To the north of them was the North Sea, to the south the advancing Allies. So they stood and fought, the way cornered animals fight.

'They were full of piss and vinegar, contrary to what we were told,' says Alexandre, 'and believe me they knew how to fight.'

His stick had been dropped just south of Zuidlharen and on the evening of 8 April they lay up in an old hangar. A couple of sentries were posted but shortly before dawn there was a volley of gunfire from outside. One of the sentries, Paul Duquesne, lay dead in front of a large force of Germans. There was a brief exchange of gunfire. Lasserre, the officer in charge, and a couple of others managed to escape. Alexandre was shot, 'by a 7.9mm bullet ... which hit me in the upper leg, right under the backside'.

Alexandre's captors were *Kriegsmarine,* German marines. He and the others were taken to their HQ in Zuidlharen, where he was relieved of several boxes of cigarettes he had bought in England.

'I told the captain that I'd paid for the cigarettes out of my own money

---

* A captured Luftwaffe lieutenant colonel told the British that apart from tattoos, the SS could often be identified by their names: Thor, Alaric, Wotan, Attile and Hagen being particular favourites. If a soldier's religion in his papers was marked 'Gott-Glaubig' [believer in God] and not Protestant or Catholic, he would probably belong to the SS.

301

and it wasn't fair.' The captain piled the cigarettes on the table in front of Alexandre. 'He looked at them, looked at me, took out one packet and gave it to me. Then he pushed the others aside and said "war booty". I can't complain because not so far from us six [French SAS] fellows were burned alive.'

From Zuidlharen they were taken to Groningen, 'to a school where we met a lot of other prisoners of different nationalities'. After two days there were sent to Oldenburg in Germany by train. 'That night the RAF came and bombed the pants out of us.' The next day the Allied prisoners set out east to march 20 miles to Bremen. They crossed the Weser by ferry and continued into the suburbs of Bremen.

'It was in ruins when we got there,' remembers Alexandre, who by now had grown accustomed to the agony that every step brought. The German in charge of the prisoners allowed them to rest for a few minutes. Alexandre lay down on the road and stretched out his legs across the pavement, whereupon a German civilian walking along took exception to the obstruction and trampled on his legs. A French soldier leapt to his feet, there was a scuffle and the pair had to be pulled apart by guards. The German officer listened to the two versions of events and, recalls Alexandre, 'put this civilian at attention, had him about turn and kicked him in the arse'.

The whole scene had been watched by a group of local women, queuing disconsolately outside a bakers for their meagre bread ration. One of them crossed the road and, pointing at Alexandre, said something to the officer. The two of them walked over. 'This woman would like you to have her bread,' said the officer. She smiled and handed over her small loaf.

THE BELGIANS REACHED Coevorden on Saturday 7 April, 36 hours after it had been liberated by the Canadian 2 Corps. For 24 hours they were attached to the Canadian 4th Armoured Division but that changed when their tanks were ordered east, across the German border and into Meppen. On 8 April the Belgians were seconded to the 1st Polish Armoured

Division to act as their ears and eyes. The next day they pushed north, towards Groningen and the Dollard Sea, the objective being to reach the coast and cut off the SS soldiers retreating from the advancing French SAS.

For three days they made solid progress using a tactical structure unique to the Belgian squadron. Their experiences during the winter offensive in the Ardennes had revealed the weakness of the jeep; it gave them great mobility and speed but once the enemy lured them out of their jeeps they were exposed by their lack of firepower. To counter this Blondeel had assigned four assault troops to each of 'A' and 'B' Company. These troops, each one composed of approximately ten men, travelled alongside the jeeps in 15cwt lorries and acted as infantry. The system got them to the southern side of the Mussel Canal shortly before lunch on 12 April without losing a man. But the task now was to cross the canal at Veele. Beyond it lay the coast, a mere 20 tantalizing miles north. Even closer that that, however, the Belgians had been told by the Dutch Resistance was a large force of *Kriegsmarines* dug in around the village of Veele on the canal's northern banks.

The assault troops of both companies began moving on foot towards the southern banks of the canal. Those of 'B' Company headed 300 yards west of the blown road bridge; 'A' Company's assault troop were further east making for a sluice gate directly in front of a row of houses. The sergeant in charge of one of 'A' Company's assault troops, Sergeant Rolin, was shot dead by a sniper as he neared the canal. Two of his men who went to help him were killed by the same marksman.

'B' Company's assault troops had reached the southern bank of the canal and were now trying to figure out a way to get across. Moored on the northern side was a barge. Two soldiers, Jean Bastin and Andy Segelaar, dived into the water and started dragging the vessel to the southern side. As they did so their comrades in the jeeps lay down a covering fire.

'We opened fire with everything we had,' says Jean Switters. 'The noise was deafening, amazing … it felt mad.' Then the Germans retaliated. 'When they started firing back it was incredible,' he says. 'There were

303

mortar rounds coming down and I remember some trees behind us that were shot to bits.'

The two sides traded fire for several furious minutes. One of the Germans captured in Veele was a veteran, recalls Brasseur, 'who had been fighting since 1940 and he told us that never before had he experienced such terrifying firepower'. When Switters woke the next morning his comrades looked at him strangely. 'My blond hair had turned grey overnight,' he says.

A few hundred yards east of Switters, Lieutenant Jean-Claude Heilporn and Sergeant Jacques Goffinet were weighing up their options; their jeep section was lined up on the banks raking the houses opposite with fire, but there were no barges in which they could get across. Goffinet turned to Heilporn.

'Jacques said to me, "I'm going to try and run across the lock."' Heilporn screamed at the jeeps to stop firing.

'As soon as they stopped,' recalls Goffinet, 'I ran forward towards the lock leading my men.' The lock gates were narrow, just wide enough for one man, and as they crossed Goffinet 'could hear the bullets whipping past. I was sure one was going to hit me'. None did. All his troop got safely across, inspiring the others to follow. 'A' and 'B' Assault Troops linked arms on the northern side of the canal and started clearing the Germans from Veele. Goffinet, his blood up, encountered a flock of Dutch civilians on the road leading north.

'I asked them if there were any Germans up ahead and they said no.' A few yards further on Goffinet was confronted by several *Kriegsmarines*. 'When I'd dealt with them I turned back to the Dutch civilians and told them to get back to their village. To help them on their way I fired a few bursts at their feet.'

The depth of Goffinet's *noblesse largesse* hinged on the nature of the enemy and the circumstances. 'This whole question of taking prisoners,' he muses, 'when you're fighting a battle it's not easy because of all that is happening around you. If the occasion arose when we could take them safely we would. I respected the Wehrmacht. But the SS, they were evil

304

and I knew what they had done. I had no pity for them.' Expediency was also a factor for the Belgians in determining the fate of captured Germans.

'If you're behind enemy lines,' says Switters, 'and you capture a prisoner you need one of your own men to look after them. If you take several you need more men, so our orders were to kill.' Initially, Switters says, he didn't look forward to the prospect, 'but you got used to it'. When his section captured two Dutch SS troops they had them dig a hole in the ground 'and then "Bang, Bang" ... it's brutal but it's war'.

By 13 April a bridge had been constructed over the Mussel Canal and the Sherman tanks of the 1st Polish Armoured Division galloped across, following the Belgians who had already darted further north into Wedde.

On the 15th they were in Winschoten, the last major town before the Dollard Sea. They could smell the sea on the breeze that blew south. Lieutenant d'Outremont and a Polish liaison officer decided to lead a patrol north in a bid to become the first Allied troops to reach the Dollard coastline.

'We set off in two jeeps and a Polish scout car,' recalls Brasseur. 'We went through a tunnel under two dykes and when we came to the third the sea was just beyond it. I remained with the vehicles while the rest of them went on foot to the sea. I was a bit uneasy during this time because not too far away was a very heavily armed German coastal fort so I did my best to keep a low profile. When they returned d'Outremont showed me his water bottle full of sea water.'

Those Germans still in Groningen were now stranded. On the way back, however, the patrol came under fire from the coastal fort.

'I could hear the thump of the guns and then I saw the plumes of water as the shells landed in the canal,' says Brasseur. As they entered the village of Beerta, a shell landed feet away from his jeep. 'Dubois, sitting next to me in the front passenger seat, was hit in the chest by a shell fragment but he was wearing one of the flak jackets we'd been issued with and was fine.'

The patrol arrived back at Winschoten to find the Belgians embroiled in an argument with the CO of the Polish Armoured Division.

'He wanted me to attack this fort,' says Heilporn. 'I asked him how he proposed to do it and he said in daylight with my assault troops attacking across the open ground. I said that if he could get me a plan of the fort then we were prepared to go at night. Otherwise, no.'

Goffinet, listening in on the argument, was staggered by the Pole's intent. 'It was crazy. There was no cover at all, not a tree, not a trench, just open ground that gave the Germans a great field of fire.'

Blondeel came up to confront the irate Pole.

'He listened to what he had to say,' says Heilporn, 'and calmly replied that he was quite prepared to authorize a daylight attack so long as he and his men join us.' The Poles declined.

MRS HANBURY, OWNER of Hylands House, Essex, was there to meet 'B' and 'C' Squadrons of 1SAS when they returned to the regiment's billets in early March. She liked to portray herself as a virago, but she had taken the regiment to her bosom and treated them as an extended family. She lived in a separate part of the 200-year-old house, situated near Chelmsford in Essex, but was frequently seen by the officers with whom she shared Hylands. The men were billeted in Nissen huts dotted around the house's 500 acres of wooded gardens. 'A' and 'D' Squadrons had given the place a homely feel since they'd moved there in November 1944; a German prisoner of war, smuggled out of France as a regimental servant, had decorated the sergeants' mess with cartoons, 'one of which,' says Vic Long, 'was a very impressive work with charcoal called "Parachute Drop by Night". Above the entrance to the bar hung a sign: 'Open Dawn to Dusk'. The officers worshipped Bacchus with equal devotion. Paddy Mayne presided over the evenings with a shillelagh that he banged to make a point of order.

David Danger remembers hearing about an incident involving Harry Poat and Captain McEwan, the motor transport officer, after a few drinks.

'They rang up the Prime Minister and made some rude remark and the next day there was an awful hoo-ha.'

Peter Weaver recalled that 'most evenings we drank late into the night, singing our favourite songs with our padre at the piano. "Lilli Marlene", "My Brother Sylveste" and our parachute songs being the most popular. Sometimes we would be interrupted by the sound of an approaching V bomb and we would dash up to the roof and have a grandstand view as it roared its way to London'. One Saturday night, recalls the recently commissioned Bill Deakins, when the officers' mess was in full swing, 'there was this tremendous explosion; the whole building shook, the plate glass in the large, lounge windows smashed'. The officers ran outside, fearful at what they would discover, but to their relief the rocket had landed a couple of hundred yards from the nearest hut. The crater it left, says Deakins, 'was in the region of 50 feet across and 30 feet deep'.

The men of 'B' and 'C' Squadrons snorted with derision when they heard such tales. Their experience of the V2 rockets was infinitely more harrowing. Once the Ardennes flap had calmed down in January they were pulled back to Antwerp.

'We were getting three or four V2s hitting us each day,' says Youngman. The damaged they inflicted, mainly on the Belgian civilians, horrified the SAS who had never seen destruction on such a scale.

'It beats me how there was anything left of the city,' says Doug Cronk. 'From our billets we used to watch them drop on the city centre. Unless you were there you just can't picture the carnage.'

For Lieutenant Ronnie Grierson, they were 'some of the nastiest memories of the war ... digging out dead civilians from cinemas and restaurants'.

As 'B' and 'C' Squadrons went off on leave, the rest of 1SAS prepared to leave for Ostend for a joint operation with 2SAS called Archway. McEwan arrived with a new version of the jeep.

'It had two circular armour plated glass windscreens,' said Weaver, '2 inches thick, protecting the driver and front gunner. Armour was also protecting the front of the jeep.' They still had the twin and single Vickers, but now every third jeep was mounted with a .5 Browning. 'A dozen spare drums [of ammunition] were studded to the bonnet and sides of the jeep,' Weaver noted. 'Also carried in the rear was a bazooka and a Bren gun ... a smoke screen device was also fitted to the rear.' Arthur Thomson, whose job it was to make sure all the jeeps were in working order, recalls that 'there was a searchlight on the .5 Browning so where you pointed the gun the light went'. Later in Germany, says Thomson, 'we did away with the half moon windshield because we realized that the reflection of the sun could be seen for miles away by the Germans'. Another item that most of the men discarded after a few days in Germany were the flak jackets they had been issued with.

'Few people bothered to wear them because they were so uncomfortable,' says Duncan Ridler.

Following the death of Bob Melot, Ridler had become the regiment's sole intelligence source in the field. 'But the intelligence was a farce,' he remembers. 'There was no real intelligence training [as] so many people like Paddy wanted to get on with the killing.' One thing the regiment's intelligence unit had discovered, however, was the fate that awaited them if caught by the Germans. 'So everything had been changed to make us look like Tank Corps,' says Vic Long. 'We wore their black berets, their insignia, we even had our pay books changed to Tank Corps. But I don't think it would have taken even a half-clever German long to work out who we were from the jeeps we were using.' They were also told, recalls Lieutenant Denis Wainman, a new officer to 'A' Squadron, to refer to ourselves over the radio as "the little ones".'

Wainman had volunteered for the regiment at the end of 1944 having spent months wasting away at the Commando training centre in Wrexham. He was interviewed by Paddy Mayne rather than Bill Fraser who excused himself, saying that his hangover was too severe.

'I marched in to see Paddy carrying my swagger stick,' he remembers. 'He looked at it and said "why are you carrying one of those?" "Regimental Order, sir," I replied. Mayne shook his head, "Oh, well."'

They left Hylands on Sunday 18 March, escorted by the Metropolitan Police along the A12 through Romford to Tilbury. Several of the jeeps' number plates had already been personalized. Jeff Du Vivier's was 'Just Married', in honour of his gunner, Sam 'Digger' Weller; Wellsted's was

308

'Rhino'; Johnny Cooper's was 'Connie' after his girlfriend, and Sergeant Geordie Cunningham had christened his 'The Grimble Pig', the nickname of Pringle Gibb, his gunner. The jocular nature of the number plates was mirrored in the men themselves. They were in good spirits as they disembarked at Ostend and began the drive towards the assembly point on the western banks of the Rhine.

Wainman noticed the 'free and easy' atmosphere among the men, brought about in part by the welcome return of some old faces to 'A' Squadron. Jim Blakeney, the Grimsby trawlerman who had been captured on that disastrous first raid of Stirling's in 1941, had rejoined the unit after escaping from his POW camp; he was Wainman's rear gunner, 'a terribly nice fellow', he remembered. Roy Davies, Jock Lewes's batman in the Welsh Guards, was another of Stirling's 'Originals' who had been captured only to escape when Italy changed sides. There was also a trio of former SBS soldiers in the squadron, men who had joined the SAS in late 1942 and then been transferred to the SBS. Troopers Bill Brown, Neil McMillan and John Murray had been part of the raiding force that had landed in Sardinia and been captured by the Italians in 1943. Reg Seekings grabbed McMillan, a Canadian, as his rear gunner: 'I guess it was a compliment for Reg to do that,' remembered McMillan. 'And it was great to discover that he hadn't changed in the three years since we'd last met; Reg was still "Reg".' All the additions confused Captain Wellsted, their troop commander who had joined the squadron only the previous year. He was still calling them by the wrong names even as they neared the Rhine.

One man who was missing from 'A' Squadron was Johnny Wiseman. Early on in his military career Wiseman had double-bolted his mind against thoughts of survival.

'I adopted this couldn't care less attitude,' he recalls. 'I never thought I would survive the war. Even after my escape at Termoli I was convinced I would get it eventually because I'd seen so many killed.'

But after Wiseman's return from France, where for three months he'd operated under the noses of 30,000 Germans in Dijon, the bolts to his mind began to loosen. One day Paddy Mayne called him into his office.

'He said to me, "Look, Johnny, you're no bloody good to us any more." He was right, I think. I'd reached the end of my tether.'

Wiseman was left behind at Hylands, in charge of HQ. Others reckoned Bill Fraser was in desperate need of a rest. With each passing operation his eyes had become more lifeless. It seemed only alcohol could resuscitate them. Alec Prochiantz, the Maquis doctor in the Morvan, admired Fraser enormously, even though he had glimpsed his frailties. On one occasion Prochiantz arrived at the SAS camp with some news only to find Fraser asleep 'on a very special mattress entirely made out of empty bottles of Bourgogne'. David Danger recalls that Fraser 'was a bit of a drunkard. He was very brave but he deteriorated'. One of the officers who knew him in 1945 remembers that he was 'hitting the bottle by the end ... you could see when we were getting ready for the operation he began to tank up'. The war had always been a struggle for Fraser, a man who appeared to be fighting on two fronts: against the Germans and against himself. By 1945 what Mike Sadler called Fraser's 'internal demons' could be kept at bay only by alcohol.

THE COMMANDOS OF 21 Army Group began crossing the Rhine on the evening of 23 March. Just before 1000 hours the next morning the last great airborne operation of the war, codenamed Varsity, got underway as 1,590 troop-carrying aircraft dropped the British 6th Airborne Division in Hamminkeln and the US 17th Airborne just a few miles east of the Rhine. Richard C. Hottelet, an American reporter travelling as an observer, wrote that 'here in the centre of green and fertile land was a clearly marked area of death'. Some 440 aircraft were destroyed or badly damaged in the operation.

'We felt rather glad that this was not a parachute operation for us,' said Joe Patterson, 2SAS's medical officer watching from the west banks of the Rhine. At 1130 hours on 25 March Frankforce* began crossing the 500ft wide river in a fleet of 'Buffaloes' – amphibious landing craft that

---

* Rather confusingly, the operation was codenamed Archway but the men of 1 and 2SAS involved were referred to as 'Frankforce'.

took two jeeps at a time. Du Vivier watched as 'the Germans sent floating mines down the river with our blokes shooting at them'. In a week it would be his first wedding anniversary. His wife was carrying their first child and she was never far from his thoughts.

'I was never one for bravado,' he says. 'You took risks the whole time of course but not unnecessary ones. I valued life too much and I'd begun to be a little nervous that perhaps my lucky star might desert me.'

They landed at Bislich, says Ridler, 'and had the most wonderful breakfast from the Americans. They had a mobile breakfast system with cornflakes and milk and bacon; we had never seen anything like this.' A bit further on they came across boxes of American 'K' rations strewn across the ground. 'Their soldiers had taken out the cigarettes and dumped the rest,' Ridler says. 'They were far superior to our rations so we grabbed handfuls of dried fruit and gum and biscuits that didn't break your teeth.'

A bit further on they came across more American detritus.

'We drove through this wood and there were dead Americans every-where,' says Charlie Hackney, 'hanging from the trees, lying on the ground on top of their parachutes. One of them had obviously been bayoneted as he tried to get out of his harness. He'd managed to shoot the German and the two of them were locked in a horrible embrace.'

The day after crossing the Rhine, 26 March, Frankforce split. 1SAS began reconnaissance patrols for the 6th Airborne north-east from Ham-minkeln and 2SAS were attached to the 6th Independent Guards Armoured Brigade. Led by Lieutenant Colonel Franks, the 129-strong detachment from 2SAS headed in a more easterly direction towards Munster.

1SAS had their first contact with the Germans on the morning of 27 March, after a battalion of Canadian paratroopers had lost eight men to accurate Spandau fire from a wood up ahead. They requested assistance and Fraser led his jeep section across some dead ground on the Germans' left flank. They emerged into view 30 yards from the Germans. The Spandau sent a shower of bullets into Fraser's jeep, hitting him in the hand. With the position of the German machine-gun nest revealed, Alex

311

Muirhead's troop drove round their right flank and removed the threat.

Wainman saw Fraser a short while later as he was being evacuated to a field hospital. 'He didn't seem to be relieved,' remembers Wainman. 'I think he wanted to see it through to the end.' As Wainman watched Fraser depart he recalled Reg Seekings' words. 'Reg had said that he'd used to keep an eye on Fraser because he was sure he was frightened before an operation but that he'd stopped [doing that] a long time ago. Now he rated him as one of the finest operators he'd ever known, someone who was very conscientious and planned things down to the last detail.'

On the morning of the 28th 1SAS were resting at a farmhouse near Schermbeck. Harry Poat told Ian Wellsted he was to take over the command of Fraser's troop and support the 6th Airborne Division as they advanced the 7 miles from Erle through Ostrich and on to Rhade. Two Dingo armoured cars led the column of twelve jeeps east. In the wireless jeep Reg Seekings was grumbling away to himself. Poat had asked Seekings if he would have any objections if John Tonkin's wireless operator was transferred to his jeep in exchange for Neil McMillan. Seekings asked why.

'"Well this w/o has physically threatened him." I said to Poat, "Why the hell has he got a crown on his shoulder for? You mean to tell me a major can't handle a bloody signalman? It's a bloody disgrace, you call your-selves bloody officers?"' The swap was made, but Seekings bearded Poat, 'If I smack him you don't bloody charge me.' Poat agreed. The signaller, a man called Perkins, climbed into Seekings' jeep. 'I said to him, "One squeak out of you and I will flatten you for bloody good."'

They passed through the village of Ostrich along a quiet country road. Most eyes were on the trees that lay ahead on either side. A large barn was on the edge of the wood. No one saw the young German leap up from the ditch and send a rocket from his *Panzerfaust* into the leading Dingo. Suddenly the trees unleashed a squall of gunfire. Vince Andrews was mortally wounded in the throat; Grundy, his rear gunner, was shot in the stomach. Bullets ripped through Maggie McGinn's jeep as he tried to reverse down the road. As rounds pierced the jeep he dived into the verge.

Dixie Deane accelerated forward, between the burning tank and the hedgerow, raking the barn with Vickers fire. Seekings followed him towards the woods through a spray of machine-gun fire. Further down at the back of the column Jeff Du Vivier and 'Digger' Weller began mortaring the woods. Wellsted and Jack Terry led a foot party round the side of the barn and pounced on some Germans in a slit trench.

Seekings started to tend the wounds of Mackenzie, his front gunner, who had been hit as they tried to burst through the blanket of fire.

'I looked Mackenzie over and couldn't find anything wrong with him,' said Seekings. '"Are you sure you're bloody hit?" "Of course I'm bloody sure," he said. "Can't you see I'm bleeding like hell?" and there was this pool of blood ... it was his armpit. A bullet had exploded into his armpit and ripped a bloody big hole.'

Seekings stuffed two dressings into the hole and told Mackenzie to clamp his arm down. From behind him he heard Perkins grunt in pain. 'He must have had seven or eight bullets all down his arm, smashed it in several places.'

Seekings helped the pair back on to the jeep. Perkins, his arm saturated in blood, sat in the back, with Mackenzie in the front, the two field dressings pressed tight under his arm. 'What can you do to man the guns?' Seekings asked, before they 'bolted through with Mac firing the Vickers with one hand and the wireless operator [Perkins] firing the other with his one hand. I put my ruddy foot down and broke through and then about 500 yards up the road we ran into the first of the Airborne troops'. After the British paratroopers had cleared the woods of the last few Germans, the SAS counted eighty German dead and seventy captured.

They pushed on towards Rhade, their progress momentarily halted by fire from a 'red house at a bend in the road' which was soon silenced by Johnny Cooper's jeep. In Rhade Wellsted circled the jeeps in the town square and reported to the Parachute Battalion commander. He asked the SAS to hold the town while his men consolidated their positions on the railway line leading east from the town.

In the town square the men milled around. Wainman recalls that three

313

or four soldiers from his section told him they had found a safe in the town hall.

'I said, "All right, let's go and have a look at it." I stayed downstairs and suddenly a sergeant major came in from the Paras and then the brigadier with his entourage. "Ah, you're one of those SAS chaps aren't you?" I said, "Yes, sir, and my men are just upstairs clearing out." The whole time I was keeping my fingers crossed and thinking, "Please don't blow the safe, boys." The brigadier then said, "Well, you've done a marvellous job taking this place two days ahead of the armour." I thanked him and then I saw my men come down the stairs. "Everything all right?" I said. "Yes, sir, everything cleared upstairs," and off we went. They hadn't managed to open it.'

Late in the afternoon of 28 March Wellsted received orders from Poat to pull back to Raesfeld while the armour advanced to Rhade. They spent the night in some farm buildings with John Tonkin's section.

'We went into the farmhouse and indicated that we wanted some meat,' says Du Vivier, 'and they brought out a whole cow.' Wainman, who says that Du Vivier was the self-appointed squadron cook 'because he'd been a chef before the war', remembers coming across Jeff struggling with this cow in the farmyard as he tried to kill it. "Jeff, what are you doing?" I asked. He said, "No bloody German cow is going to get the better of me!"'

The SAS approach to the German population was one of civilized firmness. 'If we came into villages or farms we spelt out that we wanted to take over a place,' says Wainman, 'and that was that.'

Joe Patterson said that none of 2SAS took 'any notice of the rather ridiculous order that we must not stay in the same houses as the Germans, but turn them out. It is much more comfortable to have them cook and wait on us'. Patterson's own experiences with the conquered Germans varied. The most recalcitrant were the young and the old. On one occasion he told a bunch of inquisitive children to scram from his aid post and 'the smallest, a nipper of 3, turned round and gave me the Nazi salute'.

The most fearful Germans were women and parents. Joseph Goebbels had spent months terrifying the population with stories of what would

314

happen to their womenfolk once the British arrived. Patterson sat down to supper in one farmhouse with the farmer and his wife.

'They were rather frightened at first. However, they soon settled down when they found that there wasn't any roughness, and produced their two daughters, explaining that they had been told on their wireless that the English would carry away their women to slavery in England.' Another woman Patterson encountered had been learning English because German radio had told her she was 'going to be deported to work in England'.

Even so, Peter Weaver found that many Germans 'accepted us with a surly forbearance, knowing that they had no option, [and] only thankful that we did not molest them or loot their property'. The Germans' surliness often increased when the SAS disabused them of the fantastic hopes they held. Granville Burne, a 19-year-old who had joined 2SAS in late 1944, remembers in one village in which they were billeted 'talking to two girls, university students, and we had a big argument because they thought it wouldn't be long before the British and the Germans would start fighting the Russians'. Weaver noticed that 'the further east we drove the more the German civilians seemed relieved that it was the British ... who had overrun them'. The spectre of the Russians haunted the Germans. They had heard how their soldiers treated women.

'We drove into one village,' recalls Ray Rogers, 'and there was this girl in the street, 15 or 16, absolutely hysterical with fear because she thought we were Russians. I calmed her down and explained that we were British and that she was safe.'

2SAS JOINED THE 6th Independent Guards Armoured Brigade near Schermbeck, 13 miles west of the Rhine. On 29 March they were approaching the town of Dulmen, protecting the armour's left flank as they advanced towards Münster. Harry Vickers was in one of three jeeps under the command of Lieutenant Lord John Manners, whose mother was the Dowager Duchess of Rutland. Lieutenant Alex Robertson was in the third.

'These side roads we were going up [to the left of the Guards Brigade],' says Vickers, 'were nothing more than muddy lanes and one of the jeeps became bogged down.' It was Manners in trouble, so while he and Robertson tried to free the jeep Vickers was sent back to report to Jim Mackie that there were 'Germans wandering about a couple of fields away in gun positions'. As Vickers drove back down the track he met Mackie coming up. 'He asked me what I was doing,' recalls Vickers. 'I said there were Jerries up at the top of the field and I'll always remember his reply, "So why aren't you fighting them?" He took a dim view of things like that. I went back with him and he sent me and my two men round to a flank to attack them while he went at them frontally.' As Vickers crossed an open field he became aware that the Germans had started to 'blaze away' at them. 'I got a rifle round in the left arm, and that was it for me.'

Robertson drove Vickers to Patterson's aid post and he immediately arranged for him to be taken to an American Casualty Clearing Station.

'The bullet had shattered my bone,' says Vickers, 'and taken about a 2-inch chunk out of my arm.' The American medical orderly at the clearing station shot Vickers a baleful look when he was brought in. 'He said, "We'll see what this goddamn Kraut wants." "I'm not a Kraut," I said, "I'm an Englishman!" To punish him for his insolence Vickers presented the orderly with two hand grenades and asked him to look after them. He was taken east to a little camp on the Rhine and operated on that night. When he woke on the morning of 30 March 'a young lad brought me a pint of tea and a cold enamel plate with a slice of bacon congealed in its own fat. I drank the tea and left the rest'.

On 1 April, Easter Sunday, Münster was occupied by the Allies. 2SAS spent the day 15 miles north-west in Osterwick attached to VIII Corps Reserve. On the same day Padre McLuskey held Easter Communion for 1SAS in Elte, about 25 miles north-east of their sister regiment. Du Vivier, who had attended McLuskey's services in the Morvan during Houndsworth, was in the congregation. Like most of the men in the regiment he was ambivalent about religion. 'I suppose it did give you a bit of security and comfort, but it was also something to do.'

SIX DAYS LATER, in the early evening of Saturday 7 April, 1SAS were at Petershagen waiting to ford the Weser river. The Commandos had crossed earlier in the day at Stolzenau about 10 miles upstream. On the other side they'd clashed heavily with the Waffen SS. The SAS, who were accompanied by the Inns of Court, the reconnaissance regiment of the 11th Armoured Division, waited nervously for their turn to cross the narrow pontoon bridge. One of the jeeps in 'D' Squadron, recalls Vic Long, had sprung a puncture so he and Joe Costello started to change the wheel, ignoring the sporadic German shelling.

'Costello bent down to put the wheel on when there was a "phut". He looked up at me and said stop being a so-and-so. "I didn't do anything," I said. 'You thumped me in the back,' he said. "No I didn't." He stood up and said, "Well I felt something on my back." I had a look and a small piece of shrapnel had ripped through his smock from right to left. If he hadn't bent down it would've gone through his head. "When this bloody war is over," Costello said, "I'm never going to do a day's work for anybody ever again. I'll do what I want to do."'

They crossed the river without casualties and spent the night in the village of Windheim. On the morning of 8 April Tonkin's 'D' Squadron struck off north-east towards Neustadt as the advance guard of the Inns of Court Squadron. Muirhead's troop from 'A' Squadron acted as their protector on the left flank. Wellsted's troop was brought out of reserve and instructed to support an Inns of Court unit on the Nienburg–Neustadt road, north-east of Muirhead, who that morning had overpowered a small but determined bunch of SS troops.

Wellsted led his nine jeeps towards the village of Scheernen, a motley convoy. There was a bridal veil and a baby's dummy hanging from Du Vivier's jeep, symbols of 'Digger' Weller's recent marriage and Du Vivier's imminent baby. To another jeep was fastened a policeman's helmet, which had been picked up in Weseke. The men's attire was similarly irreverent. Wainman remembers looking down the line of jeeps and thinking 'what bloody army do we belong to! ... some of them wore German flying jackets or camouflage jackets ... I had a German flying helmet and goggles'.

317

After Scheernen the column emerged from a track through some woods on to the Nienburg–Neustadt road. A Dingo scout car was waiting for them at the crossroads. They turned left towards Nienburg, some way behind an armoured car and two other Dingos of the Inns of Court. Then the trouble began.

'One of these youngsters hiding in a hedgerow,' says Wainman, 'fired his *Panzerfaust* at the Dingo. Those boys were nothing more than suicide troops.' Over his radio, Wellsted heard the radio operator in the Dingo gasping that he could see Germans in the woods to his left. Wellsted and the soldiers in the leading jeeps dismounted and charged into the woods. Further down the column the SAS were steadily taking casualties. Corporal Jack Corbett's jeep had been knocked out by a *Panzerfaust* at point-blank range. John Glyde, the Welsh gunner famous for his catchphrase 'Another Redskin bites the dust!', had practically been decapitated in the blast. Another rocket from a *Panzerfaust* had blown Tom Rennie, Charlie Backhouse and Roy Davies out of their jeep. Rennie had a slight wound to his hip and Backhouse to his ankle. Roy Davies had escaped without a scratch. Du Vivier's jeep was sixth in line, unmistakable with the veil and the dummy. A young soldier wielding a *Panzerfaust* sprung up metres from him, crouching on one knee ready to fire. Du Vivier swung round his Vickers and fired just as the rocket was launched. The German, remembered Wellsted, 'was blown to bits'. Johnny Cooper raced to the head of the column and told Wellsted they were in danger of being encircled.

The armoured car led the way as the jeeps withdrew towards the crossroads. Du Vivier, meanwhile, had caught two more of the teenagers before they'd had the chance to fire their *Panzerfaust*.

'They were very arrogant,' he remembers, 'so we made them sit on the bonnet of the jeep so the Germans wouldn't fire on us as we moved to a safer location.'

The column made it back to the crossroads with the loss of only Corbett's jeep. They were joined by Harry Poat's jeep and another driven by Lieutenant McNaught. As Wellsted briefed his CO, Seekings gave a shout. There were Germans less than 100 yards away coming up through the woods from the east. 'Swag' Jemson set up his 2-inch mortar and sent over half a dozen rounds. Then to his relief Wellsted heard the sound of armoured vehicles coming up the track from Scheernen, the route they'd used half an hour earlier. Wellsted assumed it was '6th Airborne catching up with us'. The two jeeps furthest down the track were Wainman's and Du Vivier's. Wainman stared long and hard at the three armoured vehicles coming towards him.

'I sent my corporal, Alec Hay, off to tell Wellsted they were Germans,' says Wainman, 'but he wasn't having it. He insisted that intelligence had reported there were no German troops in that area.'

One of the two German prisoners on Du Vivier's jeep jumped off and 'the wee fellow tried to escape into the woods but Weller put paid to that'. Wellsted had just reported to Poat that three British armoured cars [the third vehicle was in fact a troop carrier] were approaching when he heard the sound of cannon fire. He looked in its direction and saw the 'British' cars 'coming up the sandy track towards Denis's jeep. They appeared to be firing at it. Denis and the two nearest jeeps, Du Vivier's and Rennie's were gallantly firing back'.

'I was hammering away at this armoured car,' says Du Vivier, 'and the whole time it was bearing down on me. I could see the fire coming from it [its 20mm cannon] and then I felt a pain in my leg.'

Alongside Du Vivier's jeep was Wainman's, and on board was another of the SAS Originals, Jim Blakeney, who had been hit in the arm. 'I told Jim to get back up the track towards the crossroads,' remembers Wainman. 'Then there was a bang. The whole bloody jeep had gone up.'

Somehow Wainman and his crew staggered unscathed from the wreckage as Alec Hay screamed, 'Out, get out, through the woods!' Digger Weller told Wainman later he watched as they fled with 'bullets coming up around our legs'. Wainman and Hay escaped unhurt. Blakeney didn't. He was shot dead by one of the armoured cars.

Wainman and Hay sprinted through the woods and back up towards the crossroads where the rest of the column was fighting off German attacks from the direction of the initial attack and from the east.

319

'WE WERE PRACTICALLY surrounded by now,' says McMillan, who was back in Reg Seekings' jeep. 'At the crossroads we formed into a defensive position – circled our wagons, so to speak – and so we had a pretty destructive field of fire. But I remember Reg saying something like "Blimey, there's a lot of the buggers, aren't there?" I was glad I was with Reg at a time like that, he was never one for looking concerned.' When Wainman got back to the jeeps, 'I reported to Harry Poat that I thought Blakeney was dead and my jeep was down on the track. "Well, go back and get it," he said. "I can't, there's a German armoured car next to it." Harry walked over to the armoured car and directed fire on to the Germans. It was all very Harry, quietly and calmly.'

The British armoured car scored direct hits on its two German counterparts. Heartened by such accuracy, Wellsted ran down the track. Wainman's jeep was a smouldering wreck and the other two were badly damaged. From under Rennie's vehicle he heard groaning. It was Roy Davies. Wellsted gave him a shot of morphine, saying 'Don't worry, Backhouse, we'll soon have you out of here'. Davies managed a weak smile.

'Even at a moment like this, you can't get my name right, can you?'

A trail of bloody footprints plotted Du Vivier's agonizing route back to the crossroads.

Wellsted had expected to find shaken crews from the two burning armoured cars, but at Du Vivier's jeep he saw 'Germans forcing their way through the thick shrub with their rifles held at the high port'. They were armoured infantry from the third vehicle, a troop carrier, coming forward to attack. The crossroads was 100 yards up the track. Wellsted started to run back past the abandoned jeeps. The first round caught him in the left leg. He got up and limped a further 20 yards before he was hit in the other leg. Dixie Deane sprinted down the track and carried Wellsted to safety while Tony Trower gave covering fire. As Wellsted's wounds were dressed he told Poat that Davies was alive but badly wounded. Dougie Ferguson, Poat's batman and a little Glaswegian all 'skin and bone' who had been with the regiment since the desert, volunteered to go and bring in Davies. He disappeared down the track and didn't return.

Wellsted's report of dozens of infantry rampaging through the woods inveigled Poat into shooting their way to freedom down the Neustadt road.

'I sent Johnny Cooper off first with the wounded at top speed,' Poat wrote to Johnny Wiseman five days later, 'then made a dash with the rest later. The Jerry was about 30 yards away when we left, and believe me, I never thought the old jeeps were so slow; 50mph seemed a snail's pace. The first vehicle we met at our lines was the ambulance and so we got the wounded straight aboard. I then went and asked for tanks to clear the woods in an attempt to reach Ferguson.'

By late afternoon the SAS had recovered the bodies of Blakeney and Glyde. There was no sign of Davies or Ferguson, although a prisoner reported seeing two wounded British soldiers in the hands of the SS at the crossroads shortly after the SAS had pulled back. That evening Duncan Ridler and Poat's adjutant, David Barnby, went in search of Ferguson.

'We wanted to see if we could find a hospital to see if the SS had dropped him there,' says Ridler. 'We got to one hospital and its director showed us where some Allied soldiers had been buried in the grounds but they weren't there.' Davies's body was recovered a couple of days later when 2SAS entered Nienburg on 10 April. He was in the hospital morgue.

Ferguson was reported by a doctor to have been brought in wounded, but that was as much as Ridler knew. His body was later retrieved but no one was able to establish whether he was killed in action or executed.

AFTER NIENBURG 2SAS continued east, reaching Esperke on 11 April 1945. They rested there while the armour roared on towards the town of Celle. The weather had been fine for the last few days and Joe Patterson spent a soothing afternoon relaxing in a pinewood forest. They entered Celle at 0500 hours the next morning. Patterson visited the town's hospital where a local civilian told him there were 'some bad casualties in a concentration camp in the town without any medical attention. The words "Konzentration Lager" didn't have any particular significance to me then'.

321

Celle was an annexe of Belsen Concentration Camp, a few miles to the north. When Patterson and a bunch of SAS arrived at the outside of the camp he couldn't see inside. The wire fence had a high screen of matting to deter the inquisitive. He ordered the sentry to open up. Once inside he gagged. The first figures he saw reminded him of 'filthy animated skeletons'. They could barely speak but Patterson gleaned they were French Maquisards. Patterson asked to see inside a big long stable.

'Some straw had been spread over the thick manure and there half buried in the manure were ten creatures with life in them, not much, but a little ... the horrible stench from the rotting wounds in the manure and the staring eyes gleaming out of the slaty skeleton faces in the filth made an impression it is impossible to describe.'

Next Patterson entered one of the shacks.

'There we found about a hundred creatures who once were human. They were utterly filthy, starved to a degree hardly credible ... and all wounds were vilely infected. The stink was choking.'

Some of the SAS men were unable to keep themselves in check.

'I can always remember one chappie, a corporal going in,' says Cyril Wheeler, 'and he gave this skeleton he found the gun to shoot a guard but he couldn't hold the gun so the corporal took it and shot him.'

Patterson was beside himself. He took two of the inmates in an ambulance and drove to Celle hospital.

'I brought out the first doctors I could find to the ambulance, more or less by brute force, and stormed and raged at them in French, German and English ... the two women doctors were reduced to tears by my eloquence.'

Later in the day the population of Celle were brought up by the SAS and given a guided tour.

'We took a selected party of Germans round the wards to show them what these prisoners were like,' said Patterson. 'We deliberately chose the more decent and cultured people, which included the people with whom we were billeted, the Countess Von Molkte and her daughter ... these gentry were pretty shaken by the sight and smell of the prisoners. One stood staring at a battered living skeleton who was a Russian and turned to me: "I don't think we should treat anyone like that, even though he is a Russian."'

That evening 2SAS sent a signal to Brigade HQ. 'Tell England that Nazi Concentration camp has to be seen to be believed.'

THREE DAYS LATER, 15 April, a patrol from 1SAS was driving along a sandy track through a thick pine forest. Up ahead they saw some figures dressed, so Duncan Ridler recalls, 'in strange orange-brown uniforms'. They were lined up on either side of the road as far as the eye could see. Ridler asked who they were and what they were doing. They were Hungarians, docile and eager to answer any British questions.

'They told us there had been an outbreak of typhus or typhoid in a camp,' says Ridler, 'and their job was to prevent anyone leaving.'

The SAS drove on past the Hungarian cordon until they came to a road junction in the forest. Ridler was impressed by the 'spotless gravelled concrete kerbs and military signposts'. But there was something else, a stench that was almost overpowering in its awfulness.

They took the road towards the camp in the hope of liberating some British prisoners of war. What they found was Belsen Concentration Camp.

'It was all quiet,' says Ridler, 'with shuttered huts, no sound from the watchtowers.'

There were some German guards milling round but they appeared unconcerned by the British jeeps which drove through the gates of the barbed wire perimeter fence. The next few minutes were a compendium of depravity.

Ridler remembers seeing a pile of rotten potato peelings, about 6 feet in height, with what looked like 'scarecrows' feasting on the putrid mound. A German leant out of the cookhouse window and shot one of the scarecrows.

John Randall remembers 'emaciated figures throwing themselves at my jeep pleading for food'. 'Tommo' Thomson remembers kneeling down beside a young woman with a baby clutched to her bosom and giving

323

her a bar of chocolate. When a starving mob surged forward, desperate for a share of the chocolate, Tommo drew his pistol and snarled 'anyone comes near her and I'll shoot them'.

And then they saw the vast pit.

'I don't know how deep it was,' says Vic Long, 'but the bodies were piled high to nearly the rim.'

The men stood and stared, numb with incomprehension at the ocean of corpses. Then Peter Weaver began taking photos so others would know what crimes had been committed among the pine trees. Reg Seekings grabbed the nearest guard and beat him to a pulp in a blind fury. John Randall stumbled away from the pit, taking with him images that remain.

'It was the most horrifying and gruesome nightmare,' he says. 'The smells and the awful sight of these dead bodies haunted me.'

The SAS didn't stay long in the camp. 'We had no transport and a lot of the prisoners couldn't walk so we had to explain help was coming up quickly and could they be patient a little bit longer,' recalls Randall.

Vic Long remembers that before they could push on 'a message came through telling us not to leave the camp before we were fumigated and a relieving force arrived. At around 4 p.m. a fumigation lorry arrived and we were all sprayed'. Some of the SAS were already infested with lice.

While the rest of the squadron pushed on, Ridler remained in the camp as interpreter for Lieutenant Colonel Taylor, the officer in command of the 63rd Anti-Tank Regiment, Royal Artillery, who had arrived as the 'official takeover party'.

'I stood for a few minutes interpreting what each other was saying,' says Ridler. 'I can't remember now what he was saying ... but Josef Kramer [Belsen's commandant] claimed he had surrendered because he couldn't control the inmates with typhoid.' Ridler later rejoined the squadron and left others to reveal to the world the horrors of Belsen.

That night Randall was billeted on a trout-breeding farm, 'owned by a very sophisticated German lady and her two daughters, both of whom had been educated in Britain, so their English was perfect'. Randall struggled to describe to his hosts what lay a few miles up the road.

'They did not believe it at first,' he says, 'they couldn't believe their countrymen were capable of such things.' The next morning they were treated to a detailed inspection of Belsen.

AFTER CELLE, 2SAS progressed rapidly towards the River Elbe in tandem with a reconnaissance unit from the 15th Division. On 19 April 1945 they reached Neetze, 5 miles west of the Elbe and just 65 miles from Berlin itself. They were ordered to halt. 1SAS entered Lüneburg on the same day behind the armour, crushing some perfunctory resistance on the heath just outside the town.

'One burst from our guns and they came tumbling out of their trenches as fast as they could with their hands up,' said Peter Weaver.

'They were a mixture of Home Guard and Hitler Youth. Some were mere boys, no older than 15 ... how terrible to be asked, or rather ordered, to stop tanks with rifles and the odd *Panzerfaust*. When I looked at them, these young boys and old men, it would have been murder to have killed them.'

These were the last of the so-called 'Werewolves', the paramilitary unit with which Martin Bormann, the Nazi Party chairman, had taunted the enemy.

'Every Bolshevik, Briton and American on German soil is outlawed and the prey of the organization ... wherever the opportunity offers to kill them we shall take it with the greatest enjoyment.' That had been his boast a few weeks earlier. 2SAS had rounded up a large force of them near Uelzen the previous day. In his diary Joe Patterson wrote: 'Forlorn groups of German soldiers are wending their way back along the roads ... I can't imagine anything less like Werewolves.'

A week later both regiments were still waiting west of the Elbe while Montgomery planned 21 Army Group's crossing of the river. Once across Eisenhower had instructed Montgomery to 'advance to the Baltic and thus cut off Schleswig–Holstein and Denmark and proceed to seize the Kiel Canal'. The British commander was preparing with his customary thoroughness.

'The Elbe operation demanded very considerable tonnages of bridging,' he wrote in his memoirs, 'in addition to the normal administrative build-up.' Montgomery added that while the German Army was 'fast approaching disintegration … it was estimated that there were some eight or nine battalions facing 2nd Army on the east bank of the Elbe'.

The hiatus allowed the remainder of 2SAS, under Hibbert, to drive up through Germany and rejoin their comrades after the end of the ill-conceived Operation Keystone in Holland.

'A complete waste of time,' is how Henry Druce remembers it. The intention had been to parachute the men into Holland on 7 April, the same night the French SAS began Operation Amherst, and capture seven road bridges over the Apeldoorn Canal ahead of the 1st Canadian Army. But a week later the operation was scrubbed after several attempts to insert the men had failed because of bad weather. Major Druce, however, was still instructed by Brigadier Calvert to lead a column of ten jeeps north from Arnhem to penetrate the German lines.

'He outlined what we were supposed to do,' recalls Druce, 'then turned to me and said, "What do you think?" I said, "I think it's the silliest thing I've ever heard. Here we are about a week away from the end of the war and you want me to penetrate the German lines, which are pretty strong." He said, "Druce, are you a regular officer?" "Yes, sir." "Well, I think you should be shot." We didn't leave on the best of terms.'

Druce's column drove north on 14 April. Granville Burne remembers that as they drove through Holland they would stop occasionally while 'Druce visited his friends he had known during his spying days'. They lost a man, Martin Tyson, in a brief contact with the Germans on the 16th, but the following day Druce led them on an ambush.

'We heard the sound of marching troops,' says Burne, 'so we got ourselves into the wood and Druce said "when I fire, you fire" and he went up front; he was the sort of officer who was always at the front. The Germans came down this road and we just mowed them down.' They killed twenty of the enemy and took sixteen prisoner. On the 18th they drove to Nijmegen, picked up Hibbert and his men, and motored east to the banks of the Elbe where the rest of 'Frankforce' was camped waiting for the order to cross the river.

326

BOB LOWSON HAD spent most of his leave in a Liverpool nightspot called Reeces' Restaurant.

'It was a lovely little place,' he remembers. 'It had a great band with a pocket dance floor.' Lowson's regular dancing partner was a woman he'd first met in 1937, 'at the local school of dancing'. One Saturday afternoon in March 1945 the two of them were walking to the pictures when they passed a jewellers. 'She looked in the window and said, "Oh, isn't that a lovely engagement ring?" I said, "Yeah, would you like it?"' They carried on to the cinema and later that night threw an impromptu engagement party.

Albert Youngman also became engaged during his leave, to the childhood sweetheart he'd first met at school in Norfolk. Sid Payne, on the other hand, married the previous August, two days before he'd dropped into France, finally got to see his wife again.

'It was wonderful,' he remembers, 'but I'd only been back a matter of days before I got a telegram recalling me to Chelmsford.'

Not all the men were disappointed to have their leave curtailed. David Danger says he 'was pretty keen to get back to the regiment because I felt a fish out of water ... yes, you wanted a rest but you also wanted to get back to the boys'. Danger had been recommended for a commission and was supposed to be off to OCTU. 'But I didn't really want to go because I knew I would end up as an instructor so Paddy said, "Right, you can come with me, then, and look after my wireless." He always carried a gramophone with him in the jeep and the idea he had was to call on the German forces to surrender through the loudspeaker. In fact we ended up playing his Irish records on it as we drove into Germany.'

On 6 April the two squadrons followed the same route taken by 'A' and 'D' Squadrons nearly three weeks earlier.

'In the morning,' remembers Lowson, 'we all lined up outside Hylands and helped ourselves to this big breakfast all laid out on tables.'

The men tucked into the bacon and eggs and chuckled at the thought of Sergeant McDiarmid missing out on a good feed.

'The regiment hadn't been able to get hold of him.' says Payne, 'because he had no fixed address. He caught us up a couple of days later.' One welcome addition to the force was Dougie Arnold, last seen by Paddy Mayne on the November raid in 1941 when he had left Arnold and Bill Kendall in the desert. Arnold had spent two years in a POW camp before escaping and spending twelve months fighting with a band of Italian partisans near Ascoli Piceno. On his return to England in 1945, Arnold's mum 'had written to Paddy telling him I was home and asking if I could rejoin the unit'.

They looked identical to their 'Frankforce' comrades as they drove to Tilbury docks; with the same Tank Corps berets and insignia and the same modified jeeps. But there was one difference; there wasn't the same light-hearted bantering as there had been with their predecessors. They were tired, jaded, in need of a long rest. All they'd had were a few days, not time enough to banish morbid thoughts from some minds. The end of the war in Europe was teasingly close, but they had seen in France and Belgium how fanatically some of the Germans fought. How desperately would they defend their homeland?

Sandy Davidson, who'd joined the SAS at the same time as Lowson, had only recently married the WAAF he'd met on exercise in Scotland in 1944. He was even more morose than usual when he returned from leave.

'I don't want to do this one,' he said to his friends, 'I don't fancy it at all.' Roy Close remembers as they set out his sergeant, Dick Higham (who had won an MM at Bagnara) saying, 'We've got to get through this one, sir, we've got to get through this one'.

'You always had a brief thought about death before setting out on an operation,' says Youngman, 'but then once you got into it you were too bloody busy to think about stuff like that.' No one was too busy, however, to ponder their likely fate if caught during the imminent operation. Not only had Ginger Jones rejoined the regiment but he'd led Mike Sadler's investigation team to the execution spot.

'Digging up Pat Garstin and his men wasn't particularly pleasant,' remembers Sadler. John Tonkin had had to endure a similar harrowing ordeal when, shortly before Christmas, a Frenchman out hunting wild boar had unearthed the thirty-one corpses of the Bulbasket massacre.

The discoveries came just a few weeks after a German officer had been caught with an Order of Führer HQ dated 18 October 1944. The order reiterated the infamous Kommando Order of two years previously, demanding a 'written account, starting today, of the number of saboteurs liquidated'. At the beginning of 1945 Brigadier McLeod had written to Mayne, Brian Franks and Major Eddy Blondeel about the Kommando Order, saying that 'during the past few months evidence has been accumulating that the majority of SAS personnel taken prisoner by the Germans have been shot'. He concluded by giving the three commanding officers two alternatives. Either they could 'put all facts in front of the men at once and ... release those who are not prepared to remain in the SAS under these conditions, [or] in view of the possibility of a German collapse in the near future to make no general announcement on the subject since it may be a pity to draw attention to danger which may no longer exist'.

Blondeel said he thought it best if they kept the matter quiet because 'the spreading of rumours would raise alarm in some families the timorous elements of which would tend to have a constant restraining influence on some men'.

Franks, however, followed the first course of action with 2SAS. 'Colonel Franks got us all together,' remembers Harry Vickers, 'and told us that a lot of our lads had been tortured. We were given the opportunity to leave the regiment, no ill feelings or recriminations, we were all perfectly free to leave. Nobody left.'

Mayne appears not to have done anything, preferring instead to let his Furies off their leash when he reached Germany.

ON THE EVENING of 9 April, Mayne addressed his men just south of Meppen. Their mission, he told them, codenamed Operation Howard, was to act as reconnaissance patrols for the 4th Canadian Armoured Division, one of the divisions that had originally been intended to strike into the north-east of Holland behind the French SAS. They had been

329

redeployed. Now the SAS was to punch into the north of Germany, towards the city of Oldenburg. The news did little to dispel the feeling that the 2nd Army didn't really know what to do with them: 'We weren't properly equipped for what they wanted us to do,' says Lowson, 'and we were going across terrain that was easy to defend because it was heavily wooded and full of hedgerows running alongside the road.'

They set off early the next morning, two squadrons travelling in two parallel columns only a few miles apart. Tony Marsh led 'C' Squadron, while in charge of 'B' was Major Dick Bond, one of the 1944 recruits from the Auxiliary Unit. He had been promoted to command 'B' Squadron because the first choice, Tommy Langton, had been stood down on medical grounds.

They crossed the River Hase and headed north towards the village of Borger. Danger, travelling in Mayne's jeep with 'C' Squadron, received an anxious message over the radio saying 'that Bond had run into ambush, one officer was killed, and the rest were pinned down. Paddy asked what was happening and when I told him he threw me off the jeep and set off down the road'.

The dead officer was Bond, shot through the head just yards from where Albert Youngman and his section now lay trapped in a ditch.

'We had been patrolling up a road,' says Youngman, 'when we came under heavy gunfire from a house. We baled out into a ditch to make our way back to the column but as we crawled along the ditch we found we were trapped by a drainage pipe.' Youngman, Lieutenant Phillip Schlee, 'Jig' Eden and a couple of others decided to remain under cover at the bottom of the ditch. Bond was killed by a sniper as he crawled along the same deep ditch towards his men. His driver, a Czech Jew called Mikheil Levinsohn, had tried to reach Bond but the marksman shot him dead. The trapped men now began to come under fire from *Panzerfausts*.

'We hugged the bottom of the ditch and kept our heads down,' recalls Youngman. 'There was absolutely no way we were going to show ourselves.'

Mayne arrived and told Scott to get in the back of the jeep and fire the Browning as he drove down the road towards the stranded men.

330

Youngman remembers lying in the ditch as Mayne accelerated down the road. He slowed down momentarily as he neared his men 'and leant over to us and yelled, "I'll pick you up on the way back." Mayne raced to the end of the road, instructing Scott to fire at the woods where most of the Germans were hidden, and then turned round. When he got to the drainage pipe he leapt from the jeep and pulled his men on board.*

The reconnaissance continued the next day, on 11 April. Despite the loss of Bond, the SAS had made good progress on the first day of Operation Howard. They had passed the village of Esterwegen but ahead of them lay an area of flooded woodland.

'The main opposition was from these young lads lying in ditches with *Panzerfausts*,' says Lowson. 'But a lot of them were just kids.'

Bob McDougall recalls that 'if you shot one little bastard the others would start crying'. As they bore deeper into Germany's core the fighting became meaner.

'We stopped in a village,' says Billy Stalker, 'and Peter Davis, who spoke German after a fashion, tried to get some information from a couple of women in the street. Next thing there was a bang and he'd been shot in the shoulder by a sniper.'

'Things were getting a bit messy,' agrees Payne. After another bulwark of resilience had been overrun a wounded SS officer was dragged from the undergrowth.

'He looked as though he'd just stepped out of the office,' recalls one veteran. 'He was immaculate, a real Nazi with his blond hair and black uniform. I brought him out on to the road and Ginger said, "I want him, sir." Mayne passed the German to Jones. 'I won't tell you what Ginger did to him,' says the veteran, 'but it wasn't very pleasant.'

In the desert Mayne had grudgingly observed the niceties of war, although Malcolm Pleydell recalled that he considered 'the days of noblesse oblige and the Knights of King Arthur stuff had drawn to a close'. Three years later, having leafed through the files relating to Bulbasket and Pat Garstin, Mayne had dispensed with etiquette. One veteran says

* Mayne was later awarded a third bar to his DSO, one for every campaign in which he'd fought.

331

that 'if Mayne picked up a German in a ditch and he wouldn't give him any more than his name and number, then he'd disappear into a house with them and bang!, that would be the end of them'.

James McDiarmid was capable of similar callousness when his blood was up. There had been stories about him from France; of how he was supposed to have 'lined up a bunch of prisoners against a wall and turned the Vickers on them'. In Germany the rumours became reality. Doug Cronk remembers McDiarmid questioning a teenage German soldier.

'He said "OK, clear off" and the German began to walk away and McDiarmid shot him.'

There were other witnesses. 'McDiarmid was closer to death then than he'd ever been,' says one veteran. 'Half of our fellows were ready to shoot him for what he'd done and there was a Canadian tank crew who'd witnessed the killing. The machine gun in their turret swivelled round and I really thought they were going to shoot him.'

Yet in a contest of savagery, the SAS fell way short of the standard set by the Germans. Even in 1945 when they knew the enemy had been ordered to 'liquidate' them, the SAS nearly all showed remarkable restraint in abiding by the rules of the Geneva Convention.

'I think it was important not to descend to their level,' says David Danger, 'if you wished to retain some semblance of civilization.'

For Bob Lowson, as for most of the men, the question of shooting prisoners was one of morality, and easy to answer. 'It was just plain wrong,' he says. 'Not my cup of tea at all.'

In the afternoon of 11 April the two squadrons reached the outskirts of Friesoythe, 35 miles west of Bremen. 'B' Squadron approached the town along the main road, while on their left Harrison's troop advanced down a narrow track bordered on each side by a ditch and a hedgerow.

'About 100 yards in front of us,' says Sid Payne, 'was a German truck. For some reason we'd lost radio contact so Harrison went back to speak to Tony Marsh to find out what was happening.'

Payne was the lead jeep and the more he looked at the truck the more convinced he was that it was a trap.

332

'I turned to Pitman, my front gunner, and said, "Open up on it, Taffy." Pitman fired a short burst at the truck and immediately all these mortar bombs start coming over. I swung the jeep round and put my foot down.' Bob McDougall was in the next jeep back from Payne's. 'We suddenly saw Sid come hurtling down the track,' he remembers. McDougall began to turn round. As did so, he heard a sound. 'It was a sort of "plop". I screamed "jump!" and leapt from the jeep.'

Payne, coming up behind McDougall, instinctively ducked as he saw the jeep 'go up in a great big flash'. As Payne drew alongside the burning vehicle he saw that the front of it had vanished. He glanced into the ditch where McDougall was 'covered from head to toe in filthy water'.

'As Sid belted past,' remembers McDougall, 'he yelled "grab" and stuck out his hand. I caught it and with my other hand grabbed one of the rails on the side of the jeep and rolled into the back.'

'How Bob survived that I will never know,' says Payne, 'I can only guess that the mortar landed just in front of the engine and that took most of the blast.'

As McDougall collected his senses he stared back glumly at the wreckage of his jeep. 'The worst thing was that at the front of the jeep we had a cage where we kept our kit; I'd liberated a great set of tools from a Yank depot and it was terrible to see it go up in flames.'

The Germans ranged mortar bombs all along the track, prompting several soldiers to leap into the ditch and crawl back towards safety. Peter Davis, his shoulder wound strapped, brought his section up to give covering fire.

'I began laying down fire with the Browning,' says Lowson, 'and as I did so I could see all these soaking wet figures emerging from the ditch. Tony Marsh being one of them.'

The mortar bombs had alerted 'B' Squadron to the danger ahead. Ted Lepine decided all roads into Friesoythe were too risky. Youngman recalls that he told them, 'There's another section pinned down over there, about half a mile away, leave the jeeps and go and see what you can do'. They set off across a field towards Payne and McDougall.

333

'We had quite a bit of trouble,' says Youngman, 'as we crossed the field, mainly from snipers and small-arms fire from the village.'

Gordon Davidson, the officer in charge of the patrol, decided to make for the shelter of a wood. 'Then we saw a convoy coming down the road with the white star of the American Army,' says Youngman, 'so we stood up and started waving. As soon as they got out of the lorries we saw they were Germans.'

The soldier who pointed his Schmeisser at Youngman was a German-born Canadian in the Afrika Korps. 'When he asked me my unit I told him Eighth Army. He laughed and said, "Ah, so you chased us out of Africa, chased us out of Sicily, chased us out of Italy, chased us out of France, but now we've got you."'

Youngman and the rest of the patrol were made to sit on top of the lorries and driven back towards the village.

'The idea was to deter our own troops from attacking the convoy,' he says, 'but as we drove along I saw a jeep come out of a wood, turn and I thought, "That's Paddy and we're in the shit." Before I could roll off he was having a go with the Browning.' For the second time in 24 hours Youngman ducked as bullets whistled past his head.

The SAS pulled back. They had lost six jeeps, four captured intact by the Germans along with Youngman and nine other men.

'The problem,' says Roy Close, 'was that we were working to a schedule; we had to reach certain points at certain times. We were on schedule but the Canadian armour wasn't.'

That evening, 11 April, they laagered in a gloomy forest of conifer saplings and waited for the 4th Armoured Division to catch up. Next morning the Canadian armour came crashing through the forest, scattering a company of Germans who had moved up during the night and begun to snipe at the SAS. Mayne's men withdrew south past the Canadian tank line until they found a quiet village in which to have breakfast. As the men brewed up it was noticed they were a man short. Bob Lilley yelled 'Sergeant Lowson!'

'By now I was a senior NCO in "C" Squadron,' Lowson says, 'and that's a very bad situation to get into because you begin to loathe your own name.'

Lilley told Lowson to go and search for the missing soldier. He set off in a jeep with Andy Coutts driving. A couple of miles down the road they passed through a hamlet and saw Nobby Clarke, 'B' Squadron's sergeant major, and his driver, Sam Cooper. 'Clarke got his map out and said, "We can go down this road, it's a short cut." We motored along past a sea of white flags and through the Canadian tank line,' recalls Lowson.

Clarke's jeep led them into the forest along a track. Up ahead on the left were hundreds of densely packed conifers. To their right the ground fell away sharply to a boggy glade. Lowson had the radio tuned to 'Dufflebag', an American GI music request show 'better than anything on the BBC'. As they penetrated deeper into the forest he sat back in the passenger seat, tapping his foot to the music. Over the music came the crack of a rifle bullet. Cooper slammed on the brakes of the lead vehicle. Lowson's jeep 'rammed them straight up the arse and we both became trapped in a ditch'.

There was a second crack and Cooper slumped forward, shot through the head. As Clarke tried to take cover he was hit in the lower leg. In the second jeep Coutts ducked down out of sight as Lowson scrambled towards the protection of the embankment. He felt a blow to his thigh.

'I slid down this bank and pulled my trousers down,' he remembers. 'There was this bloody great hole in my leg and another one on the other side where the bullet had exited.'

He plugged the hole with his field dressing, then asked Coutts for his. 'The way the blood was pouring out one was clearly not going to be enough.' Coutts threw it down and asked Lowson if he was OK.

'Not too bad,' he replied. Coutts then disappeared back down the track offering himself as a crutch for Clarke. Lowson crawled into the glade and hunkered down in a furrow half full of water out of the sniper's sights. 'I wasn't thinking about dying,' he says. 'By that stage of the war I'd begun to think I was immortal. But I knew what the Germans did to captured SAS men and I didn't fancy that much.'

No German came to finish him off but neither did any of his squadron

335

come to his aid. Word had reached Tony Marsh that 'Lowson had had it', and he jibbed at the prospect of losing any more men just to retrieve a corpse. They would return to the glade at nightfall. But Billy Stalker and Dougie Arnold refused to believe Lowson was dead.

'Let us have a go,' they said to Marsh. Two hours after being shot Lowson remembers 'seeing these two figures legging it across the marshy ground'.

Stalker jammed a cigarette in his pal's mouth and Arnold, grinning from ear to ear, asked him 'Are you ready?'

'Ready for what?'

'I'm going to carry you back.' Lowson laughed. He still laughs at the thought of it. 'He wasn't a big fellow, Dougie, and I told him I didn't think he'd be able to. "Yes, I bloody well will," he replied.'

Arnold hoisted Lowson over his shoulders and the three made it safely across the glade.

Lowson was handed over to a Canadian field hospital. 'At this stage I still couldn't feel much pain.' A medical officer examined his thigh and asked how he felt. 'Thirsty' was the laconic response. 'So he gave me a tin pint pot full of rum and a cigarette. Then I was carted off in an ambulance and that's when the pain started. I lost count of the number of pot holes we went over.'

ALBERT YOUNGMAN WAS handed over to the SS hours after his capture. He and his men were interrogated in a farmhouse.

'They gave us the full SS treatment and as a sergeant I got special attention. It wasn't very nice.' Their chief tormentor resembled a 'mini Himmler'. Youngman remembers that 'it didn't take him long to get angry'.

'I gave them the usual name, rank and number and this SS bloke says "OK, take him out." As I was being dragged out of the door he called me back and said, "Oh, by the way, you'll be shot in the morning."' Youngman was thrown into a pigsty with the rest of his section.

'Being told you're going to be shot doesn't sink in immediately,' says

336

Youngman. 'But gradually I started to think, "Hell's Bells, this is the end of the road for me."'

Throughout that night the sounds of battle continued to their west. In the morning the ten prisoners were mustered by a unit of elderly German soldiers who told them the SS had moved up to the frontline to counter the Allied advance. 'So these blokes started marching us deeper into Germany while they cycled alongside us on their bicycles,' recalls Youngman. 'Every village we went through we were kicked and punched, sometimes they threw stones at us, and these guards just laughed.'

For seven days the SAS were marched east, on a diet of dry bread and brackish water. On 16 April they arrived at Stalag Xb in Sandbostel. Most of the inmates were French; there were a few Eastern Europeans and an assortment of downed aircrew, but mostly Frenchmen captured in 1940.

'After a couple of days the Gestapo turned up,' says Youngman. 'They were threatening us again so me and Davidson decided if we're going to be killed we might as well be killed trying to escape. The rest of the boys said they didn't want to come, and that they would take their chances in the camp.'

The pair turned to the French for help. 'As they were long-term POWS they had a certain amount of latitude,' says Youngman. 'One of the privileges they'd been given was an Arbeitskommando permit, which allowed them to go outside the camp once a week. They gave us a couple of passes and two big greatcoats.'

The next working day, Sunday 22 April, they donned their coats and, recounted Davidson, 'strolled past the guards at the camp entrance and made for the west along the autobahn'. They quickly branched off the road into a country lane where they reckoned there would be less chance of recapture.

'We had gone a couple of hundred yards,' said Davidson, 'when two German tanks approached with their guns trained on us. "Where are you going?" demanded the commander. Youngman thrust his permit in the direction of the tank and said in German, "Arbeitskommando, we are visiting friends in so and so."'

337

'I pointed vaguely in some direction,' says Youngman, 'to which the German said, "Well, you're heading the wrong way, you want to go that way." I thanked him and off we went.'

Just after dawn on 25 April they were walking down a twisty forest road when Youngman 'heard the Home Service on the radio. Round the next corner was the Guards Armoured Brigade having breakfast'.

Having walked over 30 miles through enemy-held territory, the pair were flown for a debriefing by General Dempsey. 'He asked us about German movements and everything we had seen going in and out of the camp,' says Youngman. 'Then he said to me, "I suppose you think you've got some repatriation leave coming your way?" I said yes. "Well," he said, "as you now know all about German troop concentrations I want you to go back in the SAS and use that knowledge." What could I say? I got some transportation back to the regiment and Paddy met me with a large gin in his hand. "Welcome back," he said. "How did you find my shooting?" "A bit too high, sir."' *

THE FURTHER NORTH the SAS pushed the fouler the going became . On 13 April Mayne sent a signal describing the terrain as 'absolutely bloody to work in. The battle is turning into a slogging match and ourselves into mine detectors'.

On 14 April Roy Close's section was patrolling not far from Cloppen-burg. Bob Francis's jeep had been the lead vehicle for 40 minutes when Close called a halt.

'We all pulled into the side of the road to have a cup of tea,' says Francis. 'The next stint at point was going to be done by Sandy Davidson.'

Close sat in his jeep next to his driver, Chris Tilling, as Davidson drove past to the front of the column. 'Suddenly Tilling pointed to something up ahead, "Look, in front of them, in front of them!" There was a small mound in the middle of the road. We stood up and yelled "Stop!"' The mine detonated under Davidson's jeep. Francis remembers seeing Caldwell 'sitting in the back wearing this motorcyclist's jacket he'd acquired from somewhere'.

* Mayne awarded Youngman with an MM for his conduct throughout Operation Howard.

338

Davidson was killed, troopers Berrie and Caldwell were pulled alive but badly wounded from the wreckage. 'What saved Caldwell from being seriously burned,' says Francis, 'was he had the collars of his jacket pulled up high around his face.'

As the countryside degenerated into a never-ending bog the men discarded the jeeps and travelled as tank-borne infantry, a transition by no means seamless. 'We came across McDiarmid,' remembers Close, 'with blood pouring out of a head wound. There was a lot of swearing before he told us he'd been walking alongside a tank when an empty ammo box had come flying out of the turret and landed on his head.'

The fighting for Mayne's men was all but over by the end of April. Only those determined to die for Germany remained. 'I was walking from my section towards a Canadian tank,' remembers Payne, 'when I heard a bang behind me. I turned round and there was a German lying dead. He'd actually been hiding in a little hole in the ground and I'd walked right over the top of his shelter. When he heard me go over the top he'd come up out of his hidey hole to shoot me but Taffy Pitman was walking behind me and got him first.'

On Sunday 29 April Tom Kent stood on a mine near Westerscheps. It took him several hours to die. Mayne sent a signal to Harry Poat as his force prepared to cross the Elbe further south. 'Squadron now plodding along through bog and rain on their feet. Tpr Kent killed by mine. Nobody very happy.'

THE CROSSING OF the Elbe began on the same day. Grant Hibbert led his 2SAS squadron across at 1500 hours. Montgomery wrote in his memoirs, 'opposition was generally light and over 1,300 prisoners were captured. The main trouble was caused by the shelling of the selected bridging sites, and some activity on the part of the German Air Force'. The Luftwaffe attacked in Me 262s, their new jet fighters that could reach speeds of over 500mph.

'Just after crossing the Elbe,' remembers Granville Burne, 'we had our maps laid out on the ground examining them. Suddenly, whoosh!, these

339

jets roared over sending our maps flying. We just looked at each other, we didn't have a clue what they were.'

Captain Dayrell Morris led his troop north towards Leutow. 'He was in the first jeep,' says Renee Roberts, 'I was in the second and Robbie Boxhall in the third.' Arthur Huntbach was with Roberts, 'with my headphones on trying to tune in … when we came under fire from some airburst shells'. One exploded yards behind Roberts's jeep, killing Boxhall. They pushed on, the whole time watching the sides of the road.

'That was the problem,' says Roberts. 'If you were fired on from the side you had no means of defending yourself. I always had my Colt .45 tucked into my smock, cocked but with the safety catch on.'

On the outskirts of Leutow they were halted by a wayward volley of small-arms fire. The SAS returned fire with the Vickers, prompting several petrified Hitler Youth to come tumbling out of the ditch their hands thrust towards the heavens.

'Morris got out of the jeep as they began surrendering,' recalls Roberts. 'But for some reason he didn't have a side arm with him. As he went forward one of them picked up a Schmeisser and shot him dead.'

Druce guided his troop towards the town of Schwarzenback the next day. They overtook and shot up a small convoy of SS troops fleeing north towards Denmark. One of the few survivors was a staff officer from their GHQ at the hospital in Wangelau. He told Druce that the SS battalion was looking to surrender.

'I thought I would go and have a chat with these Germans so I went off with this officer and Jock Hanna, my corporal.' Major Barkworth, the intelligence officer, came too. The SS commander invited them to join him for a Schnapps.

'He was a very impressive man who had lost a leg on the Russian front,' recalls Druce. 'Then I think the conversation went something like, "For God's sake, quit now while you are ahead and save everyone's life." "I can't do that, Major, I'm SS and that's a crime worse than any other. And I'm afraid we will have to shoot you." To which I replied, "I wouldn't do that if I were you, why not go home to your families?"'

The tone of the conversation, says Druce, was courteous throughout. 'It wasn't nasty or menacing. They were very nice Germans, very clean. I wasn't overly concerned because I knew, or I thought I knew, they would back down in the end.'

As the conversation reached its impasse, Druce heard the sound of artillery and small-arms fire outside. 'One of our Commando units had started attacking.' The commotion brought the SS commander to his senses. The 2SAS signal to Brigade HQ that night trumpeted: 'Battle Gp HQ and 50 survivors in Wangelau handed over to Commandos ... Druce and Barkworth OK. Watch press for further details of story.'

On 3 May, 1SAS reached the port of Lübeck and were ordered to accompany 11th Armoured Division on to Kiel. Behind them 2SAS skirted east of Hamburg, still encountering the odd hostile German. 'Renee Roberts and I were driving along a track,' says Huntbach, 'when a burst of fire slammed into the jeep. Renee was driving and you never saw anyone reverse so quickly, a great piece of driving.'

The fight had gone out of most Germans, however, even the SS. When it hadn't the SAS quashed it through terror. Patterson recalled that not long after Huntbach and Roberts had been assailed they caught a couple of SS troops and 'two or three scoundrels who had revealed that they had been guards from Neuengamme, which I had heard of from my starved prisoners at Celle as being a particularly evil concentration camp'.

The men were set to work, said Patterson, 'digging their graves on a village green, which kept them warm and scared while we had our breakfast'.

Freddie Oakes was unaware of what was going on until a local woman ran into the house in a panic. 'I went out to check and found three SS men busy digging a hole with another three standing beside it with their hands in the air. A jeep had been placed a few yards in front of them covering the group with its twin Vickers.'

Granville Burne remembers that as the Germans dug this 'little chap was crying his eyes out saying, "I'm not SS, I was just cleaning the toilets." What the Germans didn't know was that Henry Druce, standing on the edge of the green, had "forbidden the execution to go ahead".'

'We knew it was just going to be a mock execution,' says Cyril Wheeler, 'but we wanted to see their reactions.' When the pits had been dug the Germans were made to stand in front of them. 'We then fired a few bursts over their heads with the Vickers,' recounted Patterson, 'which I must say they stood very bravely, only one flinching.' Oakes agreed. 'Clearly brave men but in the wrong outfit.'

'FRANKFORCE' BEGAN withdrawing on 7 May, through Hamburg and Bremen and Osnabrück towards the RV in Poperinghe, Belgium. 'It has been wonderful weather these two days,' wrote Patterson in his diary, 'and certainly Germany is a lovely country. The blossom is all out and the farms are so trim and pretty.'

As they drove west they 'saw long columns of German troops marching westwards to be put in the bag'.

'Nothing is more depressing than a defeated army,' thought Peter Weaver. Denis Wainman 'sat and watched a never-ending column of Germans pass'. He cast his mind back a dozen years 'to when I was about 10 and my parents took me to Cologne. We watched this Nazi Party march, twelve abreast with all the flags and banners. And now, well, they weren't even marching, they were trudging in silence, a shattered army on its knees'.

'Frankforce' arrived at Poperinghe on 9 May, where they were greeted by Ian Wellsted and Bill Fraser. They had celebrated VE Day by driving round the town square firing Very lights over the heads of the revellers. Now they wanted one last celebration before departing the following morning.

'Bill and other members of "A" Squadron gathered outside a little café on the edge of the square and started to sing,' recalled Wellsted. 'Belgians drifted up and grouped themselves around us. Soon they began to sing and we sang back, singing together the old songs of the last Great War.'

For those of 1SAS on Operation Howard the fighting went right down to the wire. At 0600 hours on 5 May – two hours before the ceasefire came into effect – Roy Close set out on 'C' Squadron's last patrol of the European war. 'I was never better than I was during those final two hours,' he recalls. 'We were all good, all our training went into that patrol.'

Close returned to base at 0800 hours. 'It was a very strange emotion when it was all over. I don't know what I felt. I was with Pat Riley and I remember him saying, "I wonder what we'll do now?" Then one of the men came rushing by, yelling, "For Christ sake's, somebody fire a shot, I can't stand the quiet."'

2SAS disembarked at Tilbury having, said Patterson, 'surmounted the chief obstacle, the MPs, without too much difficulty'. Druce led his men through Customs wearing a fur coat he'd taken from a German naval officer in Bremen and ringing a ship's bell he'd acquired somewhere else. 'Customs tried to stop us,' says Granville Burne. 'But Druce wasn't having any of that. He drove through with his bell.'

When the Customs did manage to detain a SAS jeep, they found nothing untoward. Their booty had been too well concealed. Freddie Oakes had eviscerated his radio set, 'the innards had been removed to make way for some loot picked up by one of my friends'.

Cyril Wheeler concealed his spoils of war from prying eyes by 'letting down the air on a couple of tyres, taking out the inner tube, packing in the loot and putting the valve back'.

When 2SAS arrived at Wivenhoe, their base in Colchester, Jimmy Hughes looked on goggle-eyed as out of nowhere the men conjured up 'cine cameras, still cameras, projectors … wine and food and all sorts of long-missed good things'.

Hughes paid Grant Hibbert '£35 for two Robot cameras'. Patterson went off to type up his diary on the typewriter he'd smuggled back. He didn't have long, however, before he was on the move again. This time to Norway, on a 'Goodtime Charley', he typed, 'to take the surrender of the 300,000 German troops there'.

THE BELGIAN SAS were given a more hazardous task. On 10 May 'B' Squadron became the first Allied troops to enter the German town of Flensburg, just south of the border with Denmark. 'We were there to stop the Germans crossing the border,' says Robert Piron, 'and to help in the arrest of Nazis.' Their first target was an old castle on the outskirts of Flensburg. 'We drove up in twelve jeeps just after dawn one morning,' recalls Piron, 'and smashed our way through the gates past the two guards who gave us no trouble. Once we were inside we swept through the floors dragging out all these officers.'

Sixty officers were arrested, twenty of whom were SS. The same day the 500 men billeted in the grounds of the castle meekly handed over their weapons. The border, however, attracted the abject from the north as well as the south. Hundreds of Germans stationed in Denmark began streaming back into their country. Jean Switters had a ragged column under surveillance when his eye was drawn to one soldier in particular.

'Something wasn't quite right about the way he was marching,' he says. 'So I went over for a closer look.' The soldier kept his head down, his face hidden by his peaked cap. Switters stopped him. 'He was a she, so we took her out for questioning.'

He had apprehended one of Denmark's most notorious collaborators.

To the south of Flensburg 'A' Squadron was engaged on a similar operation in Hamburg, 'a horrible place flattened by bombs', says Yvan Brasseur, 'that smelt of dead bodies'. In their search for suspected war criminals the Belgian SAS were reminded with prissy regularity that fraternization with locals was forbidden.

'There were big notices everywhere telling us not to mix with them,' says Brasseur. 'Sometimes on our days off we'd sit in a park next to a big lake and give the girls the eye but we were all too scared to do anything.'

Jacques Goffinet, however, confesses that occasionally 'as we had the power to stop and question anybody suspicious we would stop and question the prettiest girls we saw'. There was more work, however, than play. By the beginning of June the Belgians has arrested dozens of Nazis, including General Fust, the chief of the security police in Hamburg,

General von Schaumburg, a former high-ranking Gestapo officer in Paris and the nucleus of Neuengamme Concentration Camp's administration.

At 0800 hours on 15 June Goffinet arrived at their office from his billet at Fust's former villa. Waiting outside were two German civilians. They said they knew where Joachim Von Ribbentrop was staying.

'I didn't believe them,' says Goffinet. 'We got a lot of people turning up with information that turned out to be false.' The pair hadn't been motivated by any sense of moral decency; Von Ribbentrop was a former business associate who had swindled them out of some money in a wine deal. Revenge was a dish best served cold early one morning.

'I handcuffed them to a radiator and told them I would go and investigate,' Goffinet explains. 'I said if they were right, I would free them and if they were wrong I would kill them.'

Goffinet drove to the address given by the two men. It was on the fourth floor of a boarding house under the name of Von Riese. On his way the three British officers briefed him on Von Ribbentrop's background; a First World War veteran who had joined the Nazi Party in 1932; ambassador to Britain from 1936 to 1938, and an avowed Anglophobe as a consequence; the negotiator of the non-aggression pact with Russia in 1939; and one of Hitler's most obsequious and unpopular acolytes.

'We pulled up outside this boarding house and I banged on the door,' says Goffinet. 'After I had banged a second time there was still no answer so I knelt down and began to pick the lock.'

Suddenly the door swung open and Goffinet was 'looking up at this smashing-looking blonde who was wearing very little'. They bounded up the stairs to the fourth floor and entered the room of 'Von Riese'.

'He was fast asleep when we came in so I woke him up quite firmly,' remembers Goffinet. 'I spoke to him in French and he asked who we were. I said, "I'm asking the questions, not you." At first I wasn't sure if it was him but when we got him out of bed in his silk pyjamas it was definitely him, even though he had grown some whiskers. I looked him in the face and said, "Who are you?" "You know perfectly who I am" was all he said.'

With Von Ribbentrop's false teeth lying by his bed, Goffinet ran his

345

fingers round the inside of his mouth searching for any cyanide capsule. He found nothing, 'but later on a capsule was found somewhere rather unpleasant' [Von Ribbentrop's rectum]. A further search of the room unearthed '200,000 brand new marks in a suitcase and a big package for Churchill and Montgomery, which the British officers took away'.

Von Ribbentrop was arrested and told to dress. 'He asked for a shave,' Goffinet says, 'which we agreed to. But then he produced a cut-throat razor and I seized it from him. He protested and the British officers told me to let him shave. I thought that was a crazy decision so I stood right beside him to make sure he didn't do anything silly.'

1SAS AND 2SAS LANDED at Stavanger on 12 May. They drove first to Kristansand in the south, then up to Bergen on the west coast. The Germans were made to clear minefields and dismantle coastal defences. The rest of the time they were confined to barracks, from where they never caused any trouble. On one occasion Peter Weaver and some fellow officers entertained some German officers from one of the POW camps.

'It was fascinating listening to their stories,' he recollected, 'I was especially taken by their description of the horror of having to fight in a Russian winter campaign in their summer clothes.'

The SAS had been fêted on their arrival in Bergen. The city's newspaper, *Bergen Tidende*, carried a front-page photo of some grinning soldiers and a report of a ball at a local school. 'The atmosphere was at its best,' the paper trilled. 'The idea is to arrange such a ball once a week as long as the "Red Devils" are in town. This should contribute to strengthen the friendship between the young people of Bergen and their Allied friends.'

It did, at least between the local women and the SAS who were all, said Weaver, 'impressed by the attractiveness of the girls', just as the British women had been bowled over by the American GIs. Weaver squired two in one night, the memory still fresh years later as he recalled how 'we undressed, it was a bit of a squash, but I was not one to complain as I squeezed in between those two beautiful naked girls'.

Some of the girls who now bestowed their charms on the SAS had been just as amorous with the Germans, earning the contempt of their fellow citizens who called them 'Tysketose' [German Whore]. 'Our troops could not have cared less about the previous behaviour of the Norwegian girls,' said Patterson. 'They were good-looking blonde girls.'

Ray Rogers asked his girlfriend if she had gone with a German. 'She said no but it wouldn't have bothered me anyway,' he says.

Matters came to a head, however, remembered Patterson, when 'it was decided to hold a grand dance in the city hall and notices were posted up accordingly. In the barracks the posters carried the legend "Bring Your Own Collaborator. No Vetting."'

The Norwegians politely asked the SAS to remove the posters, pointing out that until a few weeks ago the city hall had been home to the Gestapo where, said Patterson, 'many of their friends and relations had been tortured and murdered and it would not be seemly to celebrate there ... with the inevitability of numbers of "Tysketose" emerging from a prudent obscurity and being escorted to a fiesta in a place with such sinister associations'.

If the SAS showered the Norwegian women with affection they largely ignored the men, most of whom strutted around the streets claiming to have fought a dogged resistance campaign against the Germans.

'We called these jokers the "Grey Shadows",' says Charlie Hackney, 'because most of them had spent the war in Sweden wearing their fancy grey uniforms but not actually doing very much.'

There had been a few minor spats between the two factions, but nothing that amounted to more than a bit of handbag throwing. Then one day in Bergen, Ray Rogers was out walking with his girlfriend. 'One of the boys who worked in the cookhouse came up to me and said, "Taff, there are Norwegians downstairs pushing us around." I thought I should go down and have a look. I walked in and there was a load of "Grey Shadows". One of them pushed me so I said "Fair fight?" He said "Yes".'

It didn't take Rogers long – a former miner and rugby prop forward – to get the better of the Norwegian. 'But then their sergeant started hitting me across the legs with a stick, so I took off my belt and caught him one. I thought the best thing to do now was a runner, which I did back to the boys.'

Rogers arrived bleeding and minus his beret. He explained what had happened and 'it was agreed something had to be done, so we all went down and there was quite some scrap'. The scrap became known as the 'Battle of Bergen'. Freddie Oakes estimated it involved 'most of the SAS Brigade [who] gathered in the city centre beside a large ornamental lake ... the officers took off their jackets and joined in the fray which lasted for about an hour.'

Charlie Hackney was resting 'in our billets when someone came up telling us get down to Bergen as quick as possible'. He ran down to the centre and began 'bashing them up and throwing them in this bloody big lake with all the coppers rushing around trying to arrest people'.

The Norwegians blamed the SAS with one paper carrying the headline 'Red Devils Go Home'; the SAS blamed the Norwegians; Paddy Mayne carried on drinking, unconcerned. Weaver remembered that for most of his stay in Bergen 'he held court in the mess on the top floor of a large building ... there still seemed to be a plentiful supply of free champagne available'.

Mayne was perhaps beginning to face up to the future, a life without war. By the time they sailed for England in August, Japan had surrendered. There would be no role for the SAS in the Far East, which had been the intention of Mike Calvert and the recently liberated David Stirling. They had lunched with the Prime Minister in May and received the go-ahead to begin planning an operation in China to sever the Japanese supply line to Malaya. When Mayne arrived at Hylands House he sent for Johnny Wiseman, still in charge of 1SAS's HQ.

'I was living outside the camp,' Wiseman remembers, 'as I had got married earlier that year.'

He got a message to report to Hylands as the 'CO had returned unexpectedly and he was in a hell of a mood'. Wiseman presented himself before Mayne.

348

'Where were you?' he demanded.

Wiseman explained.

'That's not good enough,' snapped Mayne, who was furious to discover Wiseman was living with his wife and not his regiment. Wiseman tried to reason with his CO, saying that as the war was over, he was running the camp from an admin point of view, not a training one.

After three faultless years in the SAS, Wiseman was dismissed in a matter of minutes. 'He even tried to get me reduced to rank, which I thought was hard, from Major to Captain, but the War Office wouldn't do it.'

On 21 September the Belgian Independent Squadron was incorporated into their army; the two French regiments left the Brigade on 1 October. One week later the SAS paraded for the final time before Brigadier Calvert. Then they were disbanded.

'No one could tell us why we were being disbanded,' recalled George 'Bebe' Daniels, 'they just told us "thanks very much, on your way".' Men said their goodbyes, swapped addresses, promised to organize reunions. Daniels moved among them with an autograph book collecting signatures. Danny McSweggen from 1SAS wrote: 'Who Dares Wins, Who Cares Who Wins, was nice knowing you, Bebe'; Ginger Jones scribbled: 'Let's hurry up and get outta here, because I'm going to blow the bloody lot, Cheerio, Bebe, and all the best.' Daniels handed the book to a sergeant recently discharged from hospital. 'Here's a time that none surpasses, for honest men and bonnie lasses'. Jeff Du Vivier handed the book back to Daniels, and walked out on to Civvy Street.

EPILOGUE

On Saturday 4 October 2003 a group of elderly men filed into a London church. Passers-by didn't give them a second glance as they hurried past. Inside the church the autumnal air outside was replaced by warmth. The men took their places, some with a briskness that defied their age, others more slowly, easing into pews helped by a son or granddaughter. Nods of acknowledgement and smiles of recognition as they spotted a familiar face. Bob Lowson and Bob McDougall, a couple of Scousers reunited; Jack Paley and Cyril Wheeler and Charlie Hackney, a trio of 2SAS stalwarts; Sid Payne and Roy Close, laughing at some shared memory of 'Mad Mac' McDiarmid; Vic Long and Reg Redington and Arthur Thomson; Albert Youngman, his face no longer 'artless'; and Tony Greville-Bell, grey and lined, yet still with a twinkle in his eye. Johnny Wiseman, 87, and back in the fold.

They had gathered to remember their mates and for a few minutes the years fell away as they panned their memories: Chris O'Dowd singing one of his Irish ballads, looking for all the world like a pirate on the high seas; the joy on David Leigh's face as he stood at the altar on his wedding day; Charlie Tobin's grimace as the cards conspired against him once more; Ross Littlejohn, grinning from ear to ear as he explained how they would capture Mussolini. And they thought of those who had gone before them in the years that followed the peace.

2SAS

Jim Mackie joined the Colonial Service in Nigeria and died of a heart attack during a routine operation in 1967. His old CO, Roy Farran, emigrated to Canada where he became a cabinet minister in Alberta and wrote a best-selling account of his SAS career entitled *Winged Dagger*. Bob 'Buck' MacDonald, returned to his native Canada and the legal profession, serving for ten years as a judge of the Supreme Court in Nova Scotia before his death in 1995. Joe Patterson went back to his medical practice in the Lake District and later became a gynaecologist in Northern Ireland. David Leigh's wife never remarried; she lives in Scotland and remains in contact with many of his former comrades who remember him with great affection. Gordon Davidson entered the business world and died in 1990. Brian Franks resumed his career in the hospitality industry and was general manager of the Hyde Park Hotel from 1959 to 1972, in which several regimental reunions were held. He died in 1982, aged 72. The man he had succeeded, Bill Stirling, held a number of dull administrative jobs following his resignation from the SAS. After the war he made a name for himself in the business world and died in 1983. Freddie Oakes stayed in the army until 1975 and died in 1997. 'Tanky' Challenor joined the Metropolitan Police but suffered from mental health problems and left the force in disgrace in the 1960s having been found guilty of planting evidence on a suspect.

Harry Vickers spent a year in hospital recovering from the wounds to his arm. He received his DCM from King George VI in December 1946 and later settled into a new life as an estate surveyor in the old Ministry of Works. He lives in Cheshire, in the house in which he was born, and remains active despite his failing eyesight. Ray Rogers reluctantly returned to the mines after the war, the only work available in South Wales. He later worked for the council tarmacking roads and resumed his rugby career with Mountain Ash RFC where he still has the occasional pint. Years later he found out that Simon Baillie, his officer in France, had survived captivity and returned to the UK. Cyril Wheeler worked in a Portsmouth bakery for twenty years before becoming a security guard at the Guildhall. One of his granddaughters served in the Royal Navy during the 2003 Gulf War. Keith Kilby went into the family meat business in London and in 1989 was one of several former British POWs who founded the Monte San Martino Trust, an educational charity that awards bursaries to young Italians to study in the UK, in recognition of the 'courage and generosity' of the many Italians who sheltered British POWS. He was awarded an OBE for his work in the 1990s. Sid Downland left the Grenadier Guards in 1958 with the rank of colour sergeant major and found employment in a Hampshire electronics firm; Dick Holmes, who was awarded a Military Medal in the SBS, became a PE teacher, first in London and then in Ontario, Canada, where he and his wife still live. Charlie Hackney worked in the Glasgow shipyards and for Rolls Royce and is now a Chelsea Pensioner. After serving in the Intelligence Corps for a number of years, Arthur Huntbach became a partner in a company of technical translators in the Midlands.

Jack Paley accepted an offer of employment with his old engineering firm in Leeds but was unable to settle down; he emigrated to Canada in the late 1940s, married a girl from Toronto, and worked for De Havilland. 'But even when I was working there,' he reflects, 'I found myself thinking back to the camaraderie of the SAS. All this stuff about fighting for your King and Country, you fought for your mates.' Bill 'Robbo' Robinson and his wife worked as a domestic service team, he as chauffeur and butler, she as cook and housekeeper. Their loyal service was recognized by the family with a house in Surrey as their retirement present. Bob Walker-Brown took a detachment of SAS veterans into the Parachute Regiment and he himself later rejoined the Highland Light Infantry. He became second in command of 21SAS in the 1950s and gave lectures to the regiment right up until the late 1990s.

Cyril Radford went with Walker-Brown into the Parachute Regiment and left the army in 1949 to join the Customs & Excise. He was posted to Cyprus in 1956, where he still lives. In the summer of 2002, on one of his frequent trips to northern France, Radford was reunited with his French girlfriend from Operation Rupert. She still had in her possession a photo of him taken in 1944, and which is reproduced in this book. Ken Harvey became the architect he had always hoped to be, designing many of Rhodesia's finest buildings in Harare and Bulawayo. He revisited the Villa Calvi on more than one occasion after the war, but each time 'the woman who owned it refused to speak to me because she was so upset with the damage I'd inflicted on her home'. She maintained her silence right up to her death but Harvey has since been warmly welcomed by her sons.

George Daniels survived a serious car crash and a long illness with TB to become the manager of an engineering firm. For his 83rd birthday he fulfilled a long-held ambition of flying in a Tiger Moth and looked back fondly on his active service. 'You find out something about yourself when you go through a war. It's only afterwards that you realize what it's done for you and how it's made you a better man.'

Like Daniels, Tony Greville-Bell has nothing but fond memories of his time in the SAS, calling it the 'happiest part of my life, perhaps the fear and danger were part of it … the SAS provided me with a tremendous self-confidence, but then I suppose I have to admit I wasn't short of self-confidence before I joined the SAS! But contrary to what some people might think, being in the army during the war meant that one didn't actually grow up at all; it was like being a school prefect, really, because while you had a lot of responsibility everything outside that was organized.' Greville-Bell remained in the SAS after the war and was due to command them in Korea, but he resigned his commission when his wife was killed in a car crash. 'I had two young daughters to raise and a war theatre isn't the best thing for a family.' He dabbled in the City, tried his hand as a National Hunt jockey, and then 'got into the film business'. For thirty years he worked as a scriptwriter in America, his most notable success being the cult British horror film *A Theatre of Blood*, starring Vincent Price and Diana Rigg. 'I absolutely hated Hollywood,' he says. 'It was the absolute opposite of everything in the SAS – crooked, mean and insincere.' He returned to Britain in the 1990s and has since enjoyed some success as a sculptor but now restricts his artistic activities to playing in an amateur orchestra. Having lost contact in the early 1950s, Greville-Bell and Daniels were reunited in 2000. They met regularly over the next few years right up until Daniels' death in July 2003.

Henry Druce continued working for MI6 after the war, first in Holland 'paying off agents who were working for the British, and in August 1945 the fellow who was running MI6 in Indonesia broke down or something so they rushed me out to take his place'. He left the intelligence services in 1951 and emigrated to Canada where he worked in the shipping industry. In 1979 Druce moved to Victoria, British Columbia, just down the road from Lou Fiddick, the Canadian pilot who had performed such sterling work during Operation Loyton. The pair meet for lunch each month, along with John Noble who represents 1SAS. Druce remains troubled by the murder of Lieutenant David Dill and his sergeant, Jock Hay, at the end of Operation Loyton. 'It's still on my conscience,' he says, 'that I didn't make any effort to save them from German hands ... they were caught by the Germans whilst waiting for me to return from going through the lines with Lou.' But the day of reckoning did at least come to many of the men responsible for the crimes committed during Operation Loyton. 'One should have no sympathy [for the Germans] – the bastards that so many were,' says Druce.

Wilhelm Schneider, the man who delighted in torturing captured SAS soldiers, was hanged in January 1947. His superior, Dr Erich Isselhorst, was executed by the French for the murder of Maquis personnel. The driver of the lorry that took Jock Hay and his seven compatriots to their death, Georg Zähringer, was given two years. His accomplices received sentences ranging from four to ten years. The British media was incensed. 'It is difficult to understand the comparatively small sentences,' said the *Observer*. 'A lenient attitude to such abomination is surely as unwise as the ill-treatment of ordinary prisoners is unworthy.'

Heinz Andergassen and Albert Storz, the murderers of Littlejohn and Crowley, were hanged in 1946; General Gallenkamp, ultimately responsible for the Bulbasket massacre, was sentenced to death, later commuted to life imprisonment. He was released in 1952. Karl Haug and Richard Schnurr were sentenced to hang for the murders of Pat Garstin and his

354

four men. The Archbishop of Cologne begged for clemency, saying, 'In the words of Christ on the cross, "Father, forgive them, for they know not what they do."' They went to the gallows regardless. Otto Ilgenfritz, who tracked down and killed Tom Varey, was given fifteen years. Alfred Von Kapri was killed fighting in 1945. Von Ribbentrop was tried at Nuremburg and hanged in 1946.

French Maquis

Alec Prochiantz's wife died of a brain tumour not long after the war. He remarried and for many years worked as the chief surgeon in the children's unit of the American Hospital in Paris. In 1988 he received a letter from Eric Adamson, the man whose life he had saved over forty years earlier.

'My health is good and I'm fit,' he wrote. 'When I watch the rugby on television I am always pleased to see France win.'

As soon as René Brossier was old enough he joined the French parachute regiment and served with distinction in several theatres of war. He now lives back in Montsauche in the house that was the first Maquis hospital. André Bouche-Pillon emerged from the Bois de Montsauche and resumed his career as a mechanic and the owner of Montsauche's garage, which is now run by his son. Juliette Girard, now a widow, lives in her father's farmhouse in Normandy in which for eleven days she hid three SAS soldiers. She cherishes the letter she received from the regiment at the end of war, which praised the 'selfless devotion and memorable courage with which you aided them in the accomplishment of their tasks ... we are full of admiration for the disregard of danger and the generosity of spirit with which that help was given'.

Belgian and French SAS

Eddy Blondeel, CO of the Belgian SAS, died in 2000, aged 94. A veterans' lunch, dedicated to his memory, is held annually in Brussels. Jean-Claude Heilporn and Yvan Brasseur spent most of their post-war careers working in the Belgian Congo; Jean Switters and Jacques Goffinet married English girls they had met during the war. Switters remained in England, while

Goffinet carved out a business career in Paris. He lives in Alsace-Lorraine and like all the rest attends the Blondeel Lunch each year.

Of the French SAS veterans Mike Alexandre enjoyed a successful business career in America and France, and now lives in Paris. Marc Mora worked in the French Colonial Office and later the National Scientific Research. Guy Le Citol resumed his career in the marine industry and still lives in Lorient. His brother, René, died in the 1990s; Alain Papazow set up a parachute training school in Nantes and subsequently became the technical director for the French national team. He is in regular contact with Augustin Jordan, addressing him still as 'mon captaine'. Jordan, who like Stirling was imprisoned in Colditz, became a respected diplomat and was France's ambassador to Austria. Now aged 93 he divides his time between Paris and his summer residence near Dijon. André Lemée remained in the French Army and became a respected instructor in the paratroopers during the Indo-China War of the 1950s. He later returned to his pre-war career as a cabinet-maker. He declined the award of the Légion d'honneur after the war, 'because it was given to too many people who did nothing for France', a feeling not uncommon among French SAS veterans.

Roger Boutinot married Cecilia, his English girlfriend. 'I was offered the chance to become an officer at the end of the war,' he says, 'if I would stay in the army.' But Michel Legrand, his officer in 4SAS, advised him to leave the army. 'He was staying in because it was his life,' Boutinot remembers. He took the advice and opened a French restaurant in Manchester. In 1953 he heard that Legrand had been killed fighting in Indo-China.

The Manchester restaurant gained a very good reputation 'and Roger was in the kitchen himself for most of the time,' says Cecilia, 'but I've always shared our marriage with his army memories'. In the 1980s they retired to Spain where Roger continues to rustle up succulent dishes. Yet he admits that 'even now not a week goes by when I don't dream of the SAS boys I knew'.

'L' Detachment, 1SAS and SRS

Of the 'L' Detachment Originals, those sixty-six men recruited by David Stirling in the summer of 1941, only three remained at the start of 2004: Jeff Du Vivier lives on the west coast of Scotland having spent nearly thirty years in the hospitality business; Jim Almonds continued in the SAS until 1954 and now lives in eastern England. Jimmy Storie lives in northern Scotland with his wife, Morag, whom he met early on in the war. After his capture in 1942 Storie spent the rest of the war in the notorious Stalag VIIIB and survived a 500-mile 'Death March' in April 1945 to Zeigenheim. He took a long time to recover from his experiences as a POW. 'For many years I used to get up in the middle of the night and walk for miles just to clear my head,' he reflects. After the war Storie returned to the tiling business.

Bob Lilley and Pat Riley re-enlisted in the SAS in the 1950s and served in Malaya. Riley then spent three years as a publican before finishing his working life in the security business. He died in 1999, aged 83; Lilley later ran a pub in Folkestone. Reg Seekings emigrated with his wife to Rhodesia and farmed for thirty years, while also working in a police anti-terrorist unit. He returned to his native Fens in the 1980s. Bob Francis remembers that age hadn't much mellowed him when he appeared at reunions. 'Often he just grunted, except one time in 1997 during a trip to Northern Ireland to inaugurate Paddy Mayne's statue. He was in great form and you couldn't stop him talking for the three days.' Seekings died in 1999 and great pal, Johnny Cooper, mourned his passing. 'He always remained cool and instilled into my very young boy attitude, confidence and warmth of being together.' Cooper remained in the SAS after the war and was awarded the MBE for his work in the jungles of Malaya. After serving with the regiment in Oman in 1959, Cooper led a multi-national force of British and French troops against Egyptian troops in the Yemen during the 1960s. He finally retired from soldiering in 1966 and moved with his wife to Portugal. He died in 2002, a month after his 80th birthday.

Fred 'Chalky' White was a scout for Manchester City for a number of years and a keen amateur football referee. He paid frequent trips to France, along with several other members of Operation Houndsworth, and after his death in 1995 White's family planted a tree in the Maquis cemetery deep in the Bois de Montsauche; Dougie Arnold worked as a warden in Snowdonia National Park and became a campaigner for CND. 'I think one can be anti-war and pacifist without denigrating the achievements of other soldiers,' he said, shortly before he died in 1997. In bringing up their two sons Dougie and his wife, Myfanwy, forbade them from playing with guns. 'We tried to avoid the glorification of war.' Even in his seventies, Arnold was a regular at SAS reunions, travelling down to London from Wales on his bicycle and sleeping rough along the way.

David Stirling settled in Rhodesia after the war and founded the Capricorn African Society, hoping to establish a community free from political and racial barriers. It wasn't a success and he returned to the UK in 1961 where he became involved in providing security services to foreign heads of state. He was knighted in 1989 and died the following year, aged 74.

Paddy Mayne joined an Antarctic expedition but was invalided home in 1946 with a back injury. He returned to Ulster, was appointed Secretary of the Law Society of Northern Ireland, and bought himself a flashy red sports car. In civilian life his behaviour remained as volatile as it had been during the war; his pleasure came from watching rugby, gardening, poultry farming and drinking binges that often ended in violence. He was killed at the wheel of his cherished sports car in December 1955, aged 40, just a few miles from the Newtownards home he shared with his mother.

Alex Muirhead spent four years in Cape Town as a GP immediately after the war. Upon his return to Britain he became the BBC's chief medical officer for eighteen years. He died in 1999, just a few weeks after his beloved wife and they are buried together in Suffolk. Shortly before his death, Muirhead reflected on the role of Paddy Mayne. 'I know that Paddy was not everyone's cup of tea ... I had several verbal disagreements with him during my years of service but I always found him ready to accept a reasoned argument even in the heat of battle. There's no doubt in my mind that Paddy was a great leader.'

As for Bill Fraser, no one knows for sure. There were shabby stories that told of his disintegration; his dishonourable discharge from the army; his brief career as a miner; his addiction to alcohol; his destitution.

'I heard that one of the boys came across him living rough in some park in London,' says Sid Payne. 'They took him in, fed him, gave him new shoes and then one day he just disappeared.' Denis Wainman thought he saw Fraser one day in a busy London street many years after the war. 'He was on the other side of the road but when I managed to get across he'd gone, vanished into the crowd.' Fraser's medals, including his MC and bar, were sold in the 1970s but no more is known.

After his transfer from the SAS in 1943 Malcolm Pleydell worked in a hospital in Malta for several months; the desert caught up with him, however, and he was invalided back to Britain with a gastric ulcer. At the war's conclusion he wrote a superb account of his SAS experiences, *Born of the Desert*, under the name of Malcolm James, and subsequently devoted his medical career to the public health service. He died in 2001 in Oxford. Bill Cumper remained in the army and died of illness in Africa a few years after the end of the war. Bill Deakins, who remembers Cumper as the 'best commanding officer I ever had', took over his father's Torquay building firm and continued its success. He lives in Torquay and still suffers from the pelvic injuries sustained in 1941. Harry Poat returned to Guernsey and his tomato-growing business. He died in 1982, aged 67. John Tonkin went on the same survey expedition to the Antarctic in 1945/6 as Paddy Mayne and found himself once more in a tight spot. After falling down a crevasse, Tonkin spent several hours dangling help-lessly on the end of a rope before being rescued; he later entered the more sedate world of business and emigrated to Australia, where he died in 1995.

Herbert Buck, the officer in charge of the SIG, the unit of Palestine Jews betrayed in the desert in 1942, died six months after the end of the war, aged 28. Tony Marsh was working as trade commissioner to Bermuda when he suffered a fatal heart attack sometime in the 1960s; he was in his forties. Peter Davis emigrated to South Africa where he became a successful businessman and rode his horses well into his seventies. In 1994 he was shot dead during a bungled robbery at his Durban home; the thieves escaped with £6. Derrick Harrison became a journalist and wrote an account of his SAS in the 1950s called *These Men Are Dangerous*. He died in 2003. Sandy Scratchley became a respected breeder of race-horses and died in 1973, aged 67.

Nobby Redington was sent to Stalag VIIIB in Upper Silesia, the same grim POW camp as Jimmy Storie. 'We were that bloody hungry we ate the prison cat!' remembers Redington, who was repatriated on medical grounds at the end of 1944. Not long after, he met the girl he would later marry and with whom he still lives in the Midlands. His civilian life has included spells as a postman, long-distance lorry driver and a railway-man before he joined Rolls Royce. From time to time small bits of shrapnel from the tank battle in which he won his DCM seep out of his arms. The medal itself lives in a plastic bag at the back of a drawer.

Albert Youngman found the immediate post-war years a struggle. 'I'd had so much excitement in the war,' he says, 'that I couldn't settle down for a quite a while. Perhaps I should've stayed in the army.' He didn't, though, and instead worked in Nigeria for a pharmaceuticals firm. He later set up an import/export business in Hong Kong and only returned to Britain in the late 1990s. 'I went to the first SAS reunion in 1946,' he says, 'and waited until 2001 for my next one.'

Doug Cronk has never been to a reunion. 'When I got demobbed I didn't want to know anything about it [the SAS]. My view was "it's over with now, forget about it".' He moved to Dorset with his young family and became a bus driver. 'I've never had any dreams about the war; I've never really given it any second thoughts.'

Arthur 'Tommo' Thomson didn't find the transition from soldier to civilian so easy. 'It took me the best part of two years to get back my sanity,' he reflects. 'I used to wake up in the morning screaming ... I was a madman.' With his wife's help, Tommo built a successful second-hand car business in south London, so successful that the Richardson brothers asked him to be their driver in the 1960s, an invitation he politely declined. He later moved to Berkshire and became involved in local politics. 'They were hard times,' he says of the war years, 'but they were good times. Sometimes I still sit here and cry into my whisky thinking of Lofty Baker and Dougie Eccles and the rest of my pals.'

Mike Sadler sailed a boat from the UK to the West Indies in the late 1940s, married his shipmate and the pair enjoyed the leisurely life in the Caribbean for a few months before sailing to Norway. He then worked in the US Embassy in London, running their information film programme, and then 'did some more sailing for a while before I was invited to join the Foreign Service and I spent the rest of my career there'. Roy Close returned to France immediately after the war to 'hand out flags and letter of thanks from the Prime Minister and Monty thanking those French people who had helped the regiment'. He then spent six months in Berlin in the military government before leaving the army. He became an economist and was awarded a CBE for his work on the National Economic Development Council. Duncan Ridler enrolled at the London School of Economics and for a few fun-packed months shared a flat with John Noble. In later years he worked as an economist for the United Nations. Ridler is still in contact with members of Bob Melot's family.

John Noble didn't learn of the regiment's disbandment until after he'd completed a three-month PT course in Aldershot. He was sent to the Airborne Base depot and curtly informed that, as the SAS was no more, his parachute pay had been discontinued for the last few weeks. 'It encouraged me to get out of the forces,' he says. He married Ethna, the Edinburgh girl for whom he'd written the diary in 1944, and joined the Metropolitan Police. He still possesses a photograph of himself standing guard outside 10 Rillington Place, the scene of John Christie's crimes. In the 1950s he emigrated to Canada and spent eighteen years in the Canadian Army. John and Ethna live in Victoria, British Columbia.

Ronnie Grierson was knighted for his services to British industry; Denis Wainman joined the Metropolitan Police after the war but left after a few years to become an art teacher in a secondary school. Now something of a demon bowls player on the Sussex circuit, Wainman says of his SAS days: 'The comradeship was what I cherish most. There was an attitude of depending on one another, regardless of rank.'

Vic Long married his sweetheart from Essex and after a spell working for an insurance company he joined the London Underground in 1948 where he worked as a driver for thirty-eight years. In 1947 Long had provided a written submission to the war crimes team investigating the murder of Leslie Packman and John Ion during Operation Gain. Joe Costello, Long's pal, left the army in the 1950s and true to his word, became a 'hobo', roaming across the north of England wearing a tatty leather jacket embroidered with his SAS wings and pushing a pram containing all his worldly goods. He was knocked down and killed by a car in the 1980s.

After giving evidence at the trial of the men accused of murdering their colleagues, Ginger Jones and Serge Vaculik met just once more, in 1980 at a Maquis reunion in France. They died within 24 hours of each other: Jones on 6 December 1990, Vaculik the following day. James McDiarmid was last heard of in Australia in the late 1960s. Having joined the Australian Army he later became a cadet instructor in a New South Wales public school. Sid Payne lost touch with him in the 1960s. Peter Weaver ran a chicken farm in Essex for many years before retiring to his native Dorset. One of his daughters, Jo, became the first British woman to represent her country in the luge in the 1980 Winter Olympics. He died in 1991, aged 79. Tim Iredale, minus the leg he lost in 1945, took on the family brewing business in Cumbria and he died in the 1980s. Fraser McLuskey was minister of St Columba's, Church of Scotland, in London before he retired. In October 2003 he addressed the congregation gathered at St Columba's for the regiment's Service of Re-dedication via video link from his Scottish home. As ever, his former comrades hung on his every word.

Ian Wellsted stayed in the army and served in Palestine and the Far East before retiring in 1967 with the rank of colonel. He and his wife emigrated to New Zealand and for a time he taught at an Auckland school. Later they ran a holiday camp on the North Island. He died in 2002, at the age of 83.

David Danger went into the printing business after the war but later rejoined the army and retired in the 1970s with the rank of lieutenant colonel. 'Looking back now it was an adventure,' he says of the SAS. 'One looks back at the good times and the funny times but it was also something one had to do.'

John Randall's working life was as a London businessman. 'It was a disappointment to me after the war that I never met such men as those I'd had the good fortune to serve with in the SAS. Some of the managing directors and so forth were absolutely in the shadow of the likes of Harry Poat and Brian Franks.'

When Alex Griffiths was released from his POW camp he remained in the army for three years and subsequently earned a good living painting miniature soldiers, which he sold from a shop in Mayfair. The Dignum brothers, Bill and Alf, worked in the printing industry and live a short distance from each other in Essex.

Sid Payne came back to Birmingham and the engineering firm he'd worked for briefly in 1939. 'Life was boring for a while,' he admits, 'and if I hadn't been married I would've probably stayed in the army.' He took early retirement at the age of 62 and has 'hardly missed a reunion since the war'. He and his wife still holiday regularly with Mr and Mrs Bob McDougall who, after the war, worked as a builder's agent for a Liverpool construction company.

Johnny Wiseman returned to his pre-war career with a firm of spectacle manufacturers and finished up running the company. For forty years he had nothing to do with the SAS. Then, in 1984, he received a letter from Alex Muirhead inviting him to an Operation Houndsworth reunion in the Morvan. Wiseman eagerly accepted and has been attending regimental get-togethers ever since. Reflecting on his three years in 'A' squadron Wiseman says, 'I'm quite proud to have been one of the members, it's about the only thing I've done in my life which one could say was worthwhile'.

Bob Lowson was evacuated to the Manchester Royal Infirmary. Not long after his arrival one of the nurses, a 'gorgeous buxom lass, what a

Welsh nurse ought to look like!' came up to his bed. "Are you Bob Lowson?" she asked me. When I said I was she told me that "I'm Myfanwy, Dougie Arnold's fiancée, and he's sent a message from Norway telling me to look after you." And she was a wonderful mother to me during that time.' Lowson spent two years in hospital undergoing several operations, 'the nerves in my leg had been shattered and my ankle hangs like an anvil at the end of my leg'. Out on Civvy Street he soon discovered what his former comrades already knew, that 'people weren't falling over themselves to find employment for ex-soldiers'. He even had to fight for his disability pension. 'Their attitude was appalling,' he recalls, 'it was a case of "Let's see if we can knock this fellow down and give him as little as we can."' But with the support of his wife, Lowson found a job with Shell and finished working in their refinery at middle management level. Once in a while Lowson drives out to North Wales from his home on Merseyside and takes Myfanwy Arnold out for lunch, a little gesture of appreciation for what she and Dougie did for him fifty-nine years ago.

When Jeff Du Vivier left the regiment in 1945 he was bewildered and a little frightened by what lay ahead. 'Like everyone else coming out of the army, once you were demobbed they were finished with you,' he reflects. 'They gave you a cheque for £30 and told you to live on that for a couple of months. They couldn't care less ... I even had trouble getting my medals.' The birth of Du Vivier's first child in 1945 helped in his rehabilitation and after several failed jobs he was appointed restaurant manager of the Prestwick Airport Hotel, a post he filled with aplomb for nearly thirty years. He and his wife still live in Ayr and from their bedroom window the tops of Craigie Woods are visible. It was there in the early summer of 1940 that several hundred exhausted Commandos bedded down after a week-long march from Ayr. The next morning one of them, a Londoner with a jaunty unthreatening face and warm light blue eyes, went in search of his breakfast.

Bibliography

Almonds Windmill, Lorna, *Gentleman Jim* (Robinson, 2001)

Buckley, Christopher, *1939–1945. The Commandos, Norway–Dieppe* (HMSO, 1951)

Byrne, John, *The General Salutes a Soldier* (Hale, 1986)

Canaud, Jacques, *Les Maquis du Morvan* (Académie du Morvan, 1995)

Carver, Lord, *The War in Italy* (Pan, 2001)

Cooper, Artemis, *Cairo in the War* (Penguin, 1995)

Cooper, Johnny, *One of the Originals* (Pan, 1991)

Corta, Henry, *Qui Ose Gagne 1944–45* (L'armée de Terre, 1997)

Cowles, Virginia, *The Phantom Major* (Collins, 1958)

Deakins, Bill, *The Lame One* (Stockwell, 2001)

Deplante, Henri, *Les Companons du Clair de Lune* (Presses de l'Imprimerie Esmenjaud, 1984)

Ducroc, Pierre, *Maquis Bernard* (Nivernais, 1984)

Farran, Roy, *Operation Tombola* (Arms & Armour, 1960)

Farran, Roy, *Winged Dagger* (Cassell, 1998)

Flamand, Roger, *Amherst* (Atlante 1998)

Forgeat, Raymond, *Remember 1940–43* (L'armée de Terre, 1990)

Harrison, Derrick, *These Men Are Dangerous*, (Cassell, 1957)

Hastings, Stephen, *The Drums of Memory* (Pen & Sword, 1994)

Hoe, Alan, *David Stirling* (Warner Books, 1992)

Hughes, Jimmy, *Who Cares Who Wins* (Charico, 1998)

James, Malcolm [Malcolm Pleydell], *Born of the Desert* (Greenhill, 1945)

Keegan, John, *Six Armies in Normandy* (Pimlico, 1992)

Kemp, Anthony, *The Secret Hunters* (Coronet, 1988)

Kemp, Anthony, *The SAS at War, 1941–1945* (Murray, 1991)

Keyes, Elizabeth, *Geoffrey Keyes of the Rommel Raid* (Newnes, 1956)

Lewes, John, *Jock Lewes, Co-founder of the SAS* (Pen & Sword, 2000)

Lewin, Ronald, *The Life & Death of the Afrika Korps* (Pen & Sword, 2003)

Liddell Hart, Basil, *History of the Second World War* (Cassell, 1970)

Linklater, Eric, *The Italian Campaign* (HMSO, 1951)

Lloyd-Owen, David, *The Long Range Desert Group* (Pen & Sword, 1980)

Maclean, Fitzroy, *Eastern Approaches* (Jonathan Cape, 1949)

McCue, Paul, *Operation Bulbasket* (Pen & Sword, 1996)

McLuskey, Fraser, *Parachute Padre* (Strong Oak Press, 1951)

Montgomery, Field Marshal, *Memoirs* (Collins, 1958)

Montgomery, Field Marshal, *Normandy to the Baltic* (Hutchinson, 1947)

Moorhead, Alan, *Desert War* (Penguin, 1944)

Mortimer, Gavin, *Fields of Glory* (André Deutsch, 2001)

Niven, David, *The Moon's a Balloon* (Penguin, 1994)

North, John, *North West Europe* (HMSO, 1953)

Ousby, Ian, *Occupation: The Ordeal of France* (Pimlico, 1997)

Pack, S. W., *Operation Husky* (David & Charles, 1977)

Prochiantz, Alec, *Promenons-nous dans les bois* (Editions des Ecrivains, 1998)

Wynter, H. W., *Special Forces in the Desert War* (Public Records Office War Histories, 2001)

Routledge, Paul, *Public Servant Secret Agent* (Fourth Estate, 2002)

Russell, Lord, *The Scourge of the Swastika* (Cassell, 1954)

Saunders, Hilary, *The Green Beret: The Story of the Commandos* (Joseph, 1949)

Schmidt, Heinz, *With Rommel in the Desert* (Harrap, 1951)

Stewart, Adrian, *Early Battles of the Eighth Army* (Pen & Sword, 2002)

Strawson, John, *A History of the SAS Regiment* (Guild Publishing, 1985)

Sykes, Christopher, *Four Studies in Loyalty* (Collins, 1947)

Temmerman, Jean, *Acrobates sans importance* (privately published)

Thompson, Julian, *War Behind Enemy Lines* (Macmillan, 1999)

Vickers, Philip, *Das Reich, 2nd SS Panzer Division* (Pen & Sword, 2000)

Warner, Phillip, *The SAS* (Kimber, 1971)

Wellsted, Ian, *SAS with the Maquis* (Greenhill, 1997)

Whiting, Charles, *The West Wall* (Pan, 2002)

Unpublished memoirs

Davis, Peter

Oakes, Freddie

Patterson, Joe

Weaver, Peter

Wellsted, Ian

Newspapers and Journals

Bergen Tidende, June 1945

Daily Express, May 1945

Daily Telegraph, April 1945

Derby Evening Telegraph, April 1972

Evening News, August 1944

L'Oise-Matin, September 1964

Lowestoft Journal, September 1939

Mars & Minerva, the SAS Regimental journal 1946–2003

Mid Ulster Mail, October 1964

SAS Veterans News, the magazine of the Belgian SAS

Stroud Journal & Cirencester Gazette, February 1943

The Observer, August 1944

Public Record Office files

WO106/3959	WO208/4669	WO219/2402B
WO201/721	WO218/96	WO219/2403
WO201/747	WO218/106	WO219/2414
WO201/785	WO218/176	WO219/2674
WO204/6856	WO218/177	WO 219/5092
WO204/10285	WO218/192	WO309/99
WO210/2487	WO218/197	WO309/226
WO204/10285	WO 218/199	WO309/659
WO204/13050	WO218/210	AIR37/820
WO205/92	WO218/220	FO916/895
WO205/93	WO218/222	HW1/1983
WO205/211	WO219/2344	HW1/2085
WO205/3959	WO219/2402A	TS26/418

INDEX

368

259, 266–7
Sfax to Gabes lines of communication operation 79–82
SHAEF (Supreme Headquarters Allied Expeditionary Force) 183–4, 256
Shaughnessy, Lieutenant 276
Shaw, George 123
Shorncliff, Kent 11
Shortall, Corporal James 158, 161, 162, 163
Sicily, Cape Murro di Porco 111–12
Sicily, landings in 96–7, 108–9, 110, 111, 112–27, 130
Sidi Barrani airfield raid 57
Sidi Haneish airfield raid 59, 60–62
Sidi Omar 41–42
Sinclair, Jock 246
Sirte raid 34
Siwa Oasis 29, 50, 54
Skinner, Alex 'Jesus' 101, 118, 148, 149
Slonta airfield raid 47
Smith, Sam 102, 107
Smith, Sir Sidney 12
Soldier's Guide to Italy, A 111
Sommer, Captain 162
sores, desert 75–6
Sorn Castle, Ayrshire 183
Souchal, Roger 260, 264
Special Air Service Brigade
 1st Regiment 183, 228, 241
  D-Day operations 191–2
  Operation Archway 311–12, 316–17, 323, 325
  Operation Howard 341
  in Norway 346
  after the war 357–64
 1st Regiment: 'A' Squadron 238, 240, 268, 306–7, 342
  Operation Houndsworth 191, 201–2, 203–5, 206–8
 1st Regiment: 'B' Squadron 190–91, 209–13, 228, 229–30, 271, 273, 306, 307, 327–8, 330, 332–3
 1st Regiment: 'C' Squadron 228–9, 234–7, 241, 271, 306, 307, 327–8, 330, 343
 1st Regiment: 'D' Squadron 213–14, 268, 306–7, 317
 2nd Regiment 241, 242, 343, 346
  recruiting on return from North Africa 186
  Operation Defoe 243
  Operation Trueform 244–6
  Ardennes operation 269
  No. 3 Squadron 225, 274–81, 282–5, 293
  Operation Archway 311, 314, 315–16, 321, 325, 326
  Operation Howard 341
  after the war 351–5
 3rd and 4th regiments *see* French SAS regiments
 Belgian squadrons *see* Belgian SAS squadrons
 comes into existence 183

disbanded 349
'L' Detachment
 formed 13
 assembles at Kabrit 16
 parachute training 18–19
 first operation 20–28
 insignia 31
 motto 31
 Benghazi raids, Spring 1942: 47, 48
 ordered back from the desert 67
 expanded to full regiment 70
 after the war 357–64
 reunion 350
Special Air Service Regiment
 1st Regiment (1SAS) 96, 100, 176
 2nd Regiment (2SAS)
  regiment raised 76
  officers' club 89
  jeep raids in Algeria and Tunisia 93
  Bill Stirling's plans for 96
  Termoli operation 153, 155
  Salerno supply line operation 158–71
  Ancona to Pescara railway line operation 171–2
  Christmas party 172, 173
  Operation Pomegranate 173
  Rimini and Ancona area railway lines operations 173
  Pesaro railway bridge operation 174
 'A' Squadron 72, 73, 75, 76, 77, 179
 'B' Squadron 75, 76, 77
  regimental party in Bir Zelten 76–7
  doubts about future 98–9
  secrecy regarding regiment 177–8
Special Raiding Squadron (SRS) 96, 100, 102, 107, 172, 173, 183
 One Troop 100, 105
  Sicily landings 108–9, 111, 114–15, 117, 118, 121
  Bagnara operation 133
  Termoli operation 140, 142, 143, 150
 Two Troop 100, 101, 102, 105
  Sicily landings 108–9, 111, 117, 121, 122, 123, 124
  Bagnara operation 131
  Termoli operation 140
 Three Troop 100, 101, 102, 104–5
  Sicily landings 108–9, 111, 121, 122, 123, 124, 125–6
  Bagnara operation 131, 134
  Termoli operation 143, 153
 Sicily landings 108–9, 111, 112–20
 Mortar Sections 109
 Augusta operation 120–27
 intelligence section 128
 Bagnara operation 131–7
 Termoli operation 139–57
 after the war 357–64
Sque, Arthur 70
Squires (Bagnara operation) 136
Stalag 8B 360

Stalag Xb, Sandbostel 337
Stalker, Billy 71, 104, 138, 148, 149, 150, 331, 336
Stephens, Lieutenant Tomos 211, 212, 213
Stirling, Bill 48, 76, 89, 92, 93, 94, 96–7, 157–8, 351
 and Operation Chestnut 98
 and SHAEF's orders for invasion of France 183–4
 resigns as 2SAS CO 184–5, 191
Stirling, David 2–3, 7, 8–9, 20, 34, 70, 75, 76, 78, 94, 358
 and Western Desert situation and Special Forces plan 10, 11
 promoted to captain and ordered to form 'L' Detachment 13, 14, 15, 16
 first operation 21, 28
 future plans after first operation 28–9
 North African airfield raids 30, 49, 53–4, 56–7, 59, 60, 61, 62
 SAS motto 31
 meeting with General Auchinleck 41
 and Reg Redington 41, 42
 and new recruits 43–4, 45
 recruits Bill Cumper 46
 Benghazi harbour raid 47
 and Randolph Churchill 48
 relies on Johnny Cooper for logistics 48–9
 heads to Cairo to seek support 54, 55, 56
 and volunteers with specialist skills 64
 and Benghazi large-scale assault 66, 67, 69, 70
 and Johnny Wiseman 70–71, 72
 receives congratulations from Montgomery 77
 Ghademes operation 78, 79
 Axis lines of communication operation 79–80, 83
 captured 84, 87–8, 98
 liberated 348
Stirling, Hugh 8
Stirling, Peter 8, 29, 70
Stokes, Horace 158, 159, 160, 170–71
Stone, Sergeant Barney 28
Storey, Andy 135, 149
Storie, Jimmy 6, 14, 15, 16–17, 21, 31, 32, 44, 73, 357
 first parachute jump 18, 19
 first operation 22–3, 24, 26
 airfield raids 34–5, 46–7, 52–3, 54, 60, 61
 captured 74–5, 360
Storie, Morag 357
Storz, Albert 294, 295, 354
Stroud Journal & Cirencester Gazette 86–7
Sturmey, Ken 180, 223
Sunday Times 31
Switters, Jean 298, 303–4, 344, 355
Sydney 2